Religious Institutions and the Law in Canada

Second Edition

Religious Institutions and the Law in Canada

Second Edition

160201

M.H. Ogilvie

L.S.M., B.A., LL.B., M.A., D.Phil., D.D., F.R.S.C.,
Of the Bars of Ontario and Nova Scotia
Chancellor's Professor and Professor of Law,
Carleton University

Religious Institutions and the Law in Canada, Second Edition
© Irwin Law Inc., 2003

Published in 2003 by

Irwin Law Inc.
Suite 501
347 Bay Street
Toronto, ON
M5H 2R7
www.irwinlaw.com

ISBN: 1-55221-069-3

National Library of Canada Cataloguing in Publication

Ogilvie, M. H.
    Religious institutions and the law in Canada / M. H.
    Ogilvie. — 2nd ed.

Includes index.
ISBN 1-55221-069-3

        1. Corporations, Religious—Law and legislation—Canada.
        2. Church and state—Canada. I. Title.

KE4502.O34 2002   346.71'064   C2002-904748-X
KF4483.C3O34 2002

The publisher acknowledges the financial support of the Government of Canada through the Book Publishing Industry Development Program (BPIDP) for our publishing activities. The publisher also acknowledges the Government of Ontario through the Ontario Media Development Corporation's Ontario Book Initiative.

Printed and bound in Canada

1 2 3 4 5   07 06 05 04 03

In loving memory of my mother and father

"The glory of children is their parents"
Proverbs 17:6

Summary Table of Contents

Detailed Table of Contents

Chapter 4:
CONSTITUTIONAL FUNDAMENTALS   99

Chapter 5:
CRIMINAL LAW   157

Preface to the Second Edition

Re-reading the preface to the first edition of this book, I find that my remarks there remain apposite for this second edition, notwithstanding the remarkable proliferation of jurisprudence relating to religious institutions and the civil law in Canada in the intervening six years. Media reports on a daily basis record numerous interactions of religion, religious institutions, and the law in relation to almost every conceivable human activity. Indeed, impressions suggest their acceleration in volume, intensity, and significance for the future of civil society and liberal democracy in Canada. Recounting the law may, at least, remind us of where we have been but not necessarily of where, as a society, we may be going.

The law is stated to 31 December 2001, but later amendments have been made where possible.

In addition to reasserting the gratitude expressed in the preface to the first edition to those who assisted in the production of that edition, I want to express my gratitude to those who have assisted in this second edition. I acknowledge the kindness of the following who provided new information for chapter three: the Rev. Debra Dempsey, Pastor, First Baptist Church, Ottawa, and Mr. Fred Neal, the Anglican Diocese of Ottawa Archives.

I wish to thank Carswell, the publisher of the first edition, for its original foresight in publishing a volume on this topic, but especially for its gracious reassignment to me of the copyright to that volume so that it might be published beyond the legal community. I am especially grateful to Jeffrey Miller and Irwin Law for undertaking to ensure that this second edition will be presented to both the legal and larger communities for which it is written.

I record my deep gratitude to the trustees of the William Howland Trust Fund, Toronto, for funding to facilitate research and production of the manuscript. I record my deep gratitude to Cheryl Hunter Letourneau, a graduate in law of Carleton University and a third-year law student at the University of Ottawa, for her fine research assistance.

My greatest debt, however, is owed to Marion Armstrong who undertook the undoubtedly disheartening (at times) task of turning my red-penned scribbles, arrows, and slashes into an impeccable manuscript. I am truly grateful. Thank you also to Barb Higgins for ensuring that the final product was publisher-ready.

As usual, my husband, David Conn, has lived with this project as with all the others with his unfailing cheerful support and companionship.

M.H. Ogilvie
Pentecost, 2002
Ottawa

Preface to the First Edition

I believe this to be the only book of its kind in Canada: the first, comprehensive legal textbook on the law relating to religious institutions. My own awareness of the existence of a substantial body of law relating to religion and to religious institutions dates from 1980 when I wondered what it was I was supposed to do, when I was elected a trustee of the Christian congregation to which I then belonged. A born legal pedant, I turned to the law reports to learn something about how religious institutions in Canada are regulated. A compulsive legal scribbler, I ended by writing a guidebook for the use of future trustees within that congregation.

Since then, interactions between law and religion within Canadian society have accelerated for a variety of reasons, of which the coming into force of the Charter in 1982, and the increasing litigiousness within religious communities, are but two of the more important. A wide variety of both public and private law issues have been re-opened for debate by courts, legislatures and religious institutions, themselves, as a result. These issues go to the fundamental purposes of human life and of life in society, particularly Canadian society, and show no signs of abating in the foreseeable future. When I began in 1989, what I believe, to be the first course in a Canadian university law programme on the subject, I was surprised to find it to be fully subscribed, as it continues to be.

Perhaps foolishly, I have written this book with two potential audiences in mind, lawyers who are asked to act in matters relating to religion, and church administrators who are increasingly bumping into the common law while carrying out their duties. Having been consulted by members of both groups over the past decade or so, I have concluded that a single textbook might serve both, although each requires information in ways unique to their respective perspectives. Many lawyers who have grown up in secular contexts require fundamental information about the doctrine, polity and laws of religious institutions in order competently to serve clients, while many church administrators require fundamental information about how the civil law impacts on their religious community.

Lawyers who consult this text will understand how to use it since it is unashamedly written in the "one damn case after another" manner of legal texts. But church administrators should be warned that this kind of textbook is only the starting point for problem solving. It does not contain everything they need to know to run their organizations. It states what the law is insofar as the law has been stated by the courts and the legislatures. How the principles stated are to be put into practice remains within the domain of the legal practitioner. How the principles stated are to be interpreted in relation to new questions remains within the domain of the courts with lawyers able to provide only provisional advice. Administrators will still have to consult lawyers even after reading this text, but hopefully, they will now have a better idea of when they should do so, and what law is applicable to their problems.

Certain features of this book require elucidation. First, in chapters one to three, an attempt has been made to provide brief introductions to the theological, historical and institutional contexts which the law in Canada has been obliged to address. I am painfully aware of how superficial these chapters are but have provided extensive references in the footnotes to facilitate deeper reading in the subjects for those interested.

Secondly, non-Christian readers may be distressed by the overwhelming predominance of Christian materials in this text. In response, I can only remind them that until the 1980s over 90% of the Canadian population recorded themselves as Christians in the Religion Censuses of Canada, and that the law reflects that, just as any legal system generally reflects its own society. Legal textbooks are also historical textbooks. Should the demographic trends revealed for the first time in the 1991 Religion Census continue, it may be anticipated that succeeding editions of this book will be religiously more pluralistic.

However, it is also important to understand, that many of the legal principles stated in this book are simply specific applications of long-standing general principles of the common law, applicable equally to religious institutions as to other non-religious institutions. There is, therefore, no reason, from a legal perspective, to think them any less applicable to non-Christian religious institutions than they are to Christian religious institutions.

Thirdly, the discussions of most topics in this book assume some familiarity with the general principles of the subject under consideration. The present focus is on those aspects of the subjects in which religion related issues have arisen. Time and space do not permit of general introductions to property law, trust law, taxation and so on. Standard textbooks abound on these, in any case.

Fourthly, while inclusive language has been used for the most part in this text, where the historical or theological contexts require the use of "his", "he", or "him" for factual accuracy, gender language specific to that context has been used.

Fifthly, the law is stated to 31 December 1995.

It remains, then, for me to express my gratitude to those who have assisted in the production of this book. I would like to acknowledge the kind help extended to me by the following who supplied the information which appears in chapter three: The Rev. Dr. Barton Beglo, Pastor, St. Peter's Evangelical Lutheran Church, Ottawa; Pastor Donald Friesen, Ottawa Mennonite Church; The Rev. James McGhee, Area Minister, The Baptist Convention of Ontario and Quebec; The Rev. J.W. David McMaster, Pastor, Fifth Avenue Free Methodist Church, Ottawa; Mr. Fred Neal, Archivist, Anglican Diocese of Ottawa Archives; The Rev. Brent Russet, Pastor, Sunnyside Wesleyan Church, Ottawa; Professor Michel Thériault, Saint Paul University, Ottawa. For better or for worse, I have decided to rely on my own understanding of the presbyterian polities in Canada.

Although The Law Foundation of Ontario did not provide funding for this volume, funding for an earlier project on Law and Religion financed some of the research used in this volume, and I wish to record my gratitude to The Law Foundation for that earlier support.

My greatest debt, however, is owed to my secretary, Barbara Higgins, who has done her usual magnificent job with cheerfulness, intelligence and disregard for the difficult and disheartening circumstances in which the severe cutbacks at universities oblige her to work. I am delighted to have this opportunity to thank her publicly for the fine work she has done for me not only on this book but on many other projects over the years. Barb thank-you!

Finally, I would be remiss if I did not once again express my deepest gratitude to my husband, David Conn, for his loving companionship and support in this project as in all other aspects of our life together.

M.H. Ogilvie
Easter, 1996
Ottawa

A Brief Historical Overview of Theories About the Relationship of Church and State

A. INTRODUCTION

How the law of Canada at the beginning of the twenty-first century has come to understand its relationship with the religious institutions and individuals of faith within the geopolitical entity called Canada has been shaped primarily by two traditions of thought, inherited mainly from England, although influenced also by the United States, Scotland, and France — namely, the common law and Christianity. Christianity itself has historically shaped the common law in England, and in Canada, before and after Confederation in 1867, in ways both patent and latent.

Concern with how societies may be ordered has been a preoccupation of Christian thinkers since the time of Christ, if for no other reason than to ensure that societies create and protect a space within which Christians may live out their beliefs faithfully and in preparation for eternal life. But another reason for this preoccupation has been that most, although not all, Christian traditions have also emphasized shaping this world into conformity with Biblical principles of social and moral conduct, which has resulted in the domination of the territories and states within which Christians have found themselves. This feature of the expression of faith is not peculiar to Christians, rather is characteristic and natural to most faiths. The domination of Western Europe and of North America over the past two millennia simply reflects the success of

Christianity in these regions in contrast to the success of other religions in other regions of the world.

The historical formulation of the relationship between religious institutions and the geopolitical units within which they exist as one of "church and state" reflects a conception of their political relationship characteristic of Western Christendom before and after the Reformation and until recently: *cuius regio eius religio*. Each state should contain only one church, that of its ruler, and every subject within that state should concurrently be a member of that church. Thus, the fundamental legal and constitutional issue resulting from this co-existence was the definition of their respective spheres of operation and influence and the ongoing attempt by each to constrain the other within their respective alleged spheres.

In the course of the twentieth century, the accelerating religious pluralism of Western societies, resulting partly from the fragmentation of Protestantism since the early nineteenth century and partly from the global movement of people of non-Christian faiths to the West, has resulted in the re-formulation of the relationship from one of "church and state" to one of "religion and the law." Although Canadian courts have in the last decade or so been required to come to grips with the implications of these changes, especially in *Charter* litigation, the fundamental assumptions on which the law relating to religious institutions has, for reasons of history, been based, remain Christian understandings of the relationship of civil and spiritual authority. Therefore, it seems suitable in an introductory chapter to provide a brief overview of these as a background to the legal text itself.

In fact, there is a spectrum of Christian theological positions on the proper relationship of church and state and many of these positions have been reflected at one time or another in the religious history of Canada. In contrast to the United States, which since 1789 has been constitutionally located toward one end of the spectrum, Canada has been largely located toward the opposite end. While the U.S. position of strict separation of church and state reflects both Anabaptist seventeenth century Puritan and eighteenth century Enlightenment views, the Canadian tradition of their intermingling reflects the more theocratic positions of both Roman Catholic and Reformed thinkers.

The medieval and early Reformed stress on unity within a state is also reflected in the other Canadian inheritance, the common law, and its concept of a Parliament, sovereign over all individuals and institutions within its territorial jurisdiction. The constitutional nature of the sovereignty of Parliament was, in the late seventeenth century, understood to be log-ically coherent with the traditional Christian conceptions of the unity of church and state, despite the disquieting presence of both Roman Catholics and Protestants who dissented from the state church at the time. Subsequently, once concessions were required to be made, first to religious toleration, and then to religious pluralism, the unified vision of society was gradually shattered, creating the potential for conflict between Parliamentary supremacy in the state on the one hand and Chris-tian conceptions of social and political ordering of the state on the other.

The history of Western Christendom amply demonstrates that the potential for conflict between state and church, society, and faith, has never been far from the surface. This is to be entirely expected since Christian hopes are eschatological rather than earthly. The inherent con-flict between the demands of this world and of the world to come is reflected in the statements of the founder of Christianity on the subject, as well as in the position taken by his first interpreter, Paul.

Notwithstanding the large body of political theory produced by Christianity in the past two millenia, the founder showed little recorded interest in political or constitutional theory; Jesus came to save souls, not create states. His few comments about the Roman authorities in Palestine suggest that he was profoundly indifferent to the state even when appear-ing before Pontius Pilate, the agent of the Roman state, who determined that he be crucified. The New Testament suggests that the earliest Chris-tians had no single attitude to the state; rather, at least three distinctive attitudes are evident: Jesus' own attitude of maintaining a critical dis-tance; Paul's position of accommodation, even subordination, to the state; and outright resistance to the state as evil, presented in Revelation.[1]

In response to the question by the Pharisees, designed to entrap Jesus, of whether or not it was lawful for his followers to pay taxes to the Roman emperor, he replied, "Give to the Emperor the things that are the Emperor's and to God the things that are God's."[2] If he had said that it

---

1   For a comprehensive study of these positions and the texts on which they are based see Walter E. Pilgrim, *Uneasy Neighbours: Church and State in the New Testament* (Minneapolis: Fortress Press, 1999). For a study of the forms of the earliest churches, see Raymond E. Brown, *The Churches the Apostles Left Behind* (New York: Paulist Press, 1984).

2   Matt. 22:15–22; Mark 12:13–17; and Luke 20:19–26 (New Revised Standard Version – N.R.S.V.).

was lawful to pay taxes to Rome only, he would have gotten into trouble with the Jewish leaders who refused to recognize the lawfulness of Roman rule. If he had said that it was not lawful, then he would have been in trouble with the Romans for initiating the withholding of taxes. Jesus' response effectively turned the question back on the Pharisees, leaving them and his followers with the dilemma of determining what is the emperor's and what is God's.

More influential from an historical perspective were the views of Paul:

> Let every person be subject to the governing authorities; for there is no authority except from God, and those authorities that exist have been instituted by God. Therefore whoever resists authority resists what God has appointed, and those who resist will incur judgment. For rulers are not a terror to good conduct, but to bad. Do you wish to have no fear of the authority? Then do what is good, and you will receive its approval; for it is God's servant for your good. But if you do what is wrong, you should be afraid, for the authority does not bear the sword in vain! It is the servant of God to execute wrath on the wrongdoer. Therefore one must be subject, not only because of wrath but also because of conscience. For the same reason you pay taxes, for the authorities are God's servants, busy with this very thing. Pay to all what is due to them — taxes to whom taxes are due, revenue to whom revenue is due, respect to whom respect is due, honor to whom honor is due.[3]

Conceptualizing the state as divinely instituted for the doing of good deeds in the world appeared to be the height of folly when that state was actively persecuting the tiny Christian sect of the first century. Nevertheless, the seriousness with which Paul took the state predicted the more sophisticated theological formulations of the two millennia of Christian thinkers whose views, mediated by the church, were reflected in the socio-politico-constitutional structures of the states of Western Christendom. It is to a brief survey of some of the most important thinkers that this chapter is devoted.[4]

---

3   Rom. 13:1–7 (N.R.S.V.).

4   A number of histories of political theory and of theology provide overviews of the major thinkers. Among the best and most recent are the following, on which this chapter is largely based: Leo Strauss and Joseph Cropsey, eds., *History of Political Philosophy*, 3d ed. (Chicago: University of Chicago Press, 1987); Quentin Skinner, *The Foundations of Modern Political Thought* (Cam-

B. AUGUSTINE (354–430)

Although Augustine was the first major Christian thinker to write comprehensively about the state and civil society, the earliest conflicts between the Christian sect and the Roman state set the terms in which this relationship would come to be debated. The example of the martyrs who chose unto death obedience to God over obedience to the state defined the radical distinction between the two and the hierarchy of choices required of Christians. While early Christian apologists[5] emphasized that civil authority was a divine gift for orderly and just governance, and that Christians could be good citizens of the Empire, the absolute obedience to the Roman state required of all citizens, including the veneration of the emperor as a god, demonstrated the choice that might have to be made and, in the final analysis, the radical disjunction between church and state. Anticipating permanent persecuted minority status and never dreaming that the emperor would become a Christian, these Christians of the early centuries had no reason to nor need to devise elaborate polit-

---

bridge: Cambridge University Press, 1978); J.H. Burns, ed., *The Cambridge History of Medieval Political Thought, c. 350–1450* (Cambridge: Cambridge University Press, 1988) and *The Cambridge History of Political Thought, 1450–1700* (Cambridge: Cambridge University Press, 1991); and J.S. McClelland, *A History of Western Political Thought* (London: Routledge, 1996). The volumes edited by Burns have extensive bibliographies of both primary and secondary literature and should be consulted by readers wishing to explore these themes in further detail. Since the primary texts to which reference will be made in this chapter are widely available in paperback versions as well as in scholarly printed editions, no references will be provided to any one edition. However, a good collection of texts has recently been published in a multi-volumed and as yet incomplete series by Cambridge University Press and these are readily available in student editions: *Cambridge Texts in the History of Political Thought*. A useful one-volume collection is by Charles Villa-Vicencio, *Between Christ and Caesar: Classic and Contemporary Texts on Church and State* (Grand Rapids, MI: Eerdmans, 1986). A comprehensive collection of primary texts is Oliver O'Donovan and Joan Lockwood O'Donovan, eds., *From Irenaeus to Grotius: A Sourcebook in Christian Political Thought* (Grand Rapids, MI: Eerdmans, 1999).

5   See for example *The Epistle Concerning the Martyrdom of Polycarp* (c. A.D. 150); Tertullian, *Apology* (c. A.D. 215); and Eusebius, *In Praise of Constantine* (c. A.D. 335). A recent study of political theology before Augustine is Lester L. Field, Jr., *Liberty, Dominion, and the Two Swords: The Origins of Western Political Theology (180–398)* (Notre Dame, IN: University of Notre Dame Press, 1998).

ical theologies. The likelihood of martyrdom sharpened their perception of the simple but real distinction between the two.

Nevertheless, the unthinkable happened in A.D. 312 when the emperor Constantine (305–337) allowed freedom of worship and actively patronized Christians after a conversion experience, although he was not baptized until a few days before his death in 337. The fateful and often fitful partnership of Christians with the state had begun. It was only a century or so before the fall of Rome, whose sack in 410 by Alaric the Goth prompted Augustine to write the first comprehensive Christian treatment of the subject of civil society and the role of the state. Written between 411 and 426 and from a pastoral perspective to comfort the Christian refugees from Rome who had fled to Augustine's diocese in North Africa, *De Civitate Dei* addresses the question of how Christians should regard and relate to the state, mindful that the Roman Empire had been such a great empire that providential purposes must surely be ascribed to it.[6]

Since Augustine accepted that humans are social animals endowed by God with the powers required to communicate with and associate in political communities with others, he accepted such association as requisite for human fulfilment in this world. Such a society would be harmonious and just but for the disruption caused by sin whereby the human desire to dominate others for selfish purposes results in disharmony and the overheaval of the common good. To constrain this abuse of freedom,

---

6   Other important writings by Augustine on these themes are found in *De doctrina christiana, De libero arbitrio,* and *Epistola* 91 (Nectarius) and 138 (Marcellinus). Contemporary studies of Augustine's social and political views include: J.N Figgis, *The Political Aspects of Augustine's City of God* (London: Longmans, 1921); J.H.S. Burleigh, *The City of God: A Study of Augustine's Philosophy* (London: Nisbet, 1949); J.S. O'Meara, *Charter of Christendom: The Significance of the City of God* (New York: Macmillan, 1961); H.A. Deane, *The Political and Social Ideas of St. Augustine* (New York: Columbia University Press, 1963); Peter Brown, *Augustine of Hippo* (London: Faber, 1965), revised edition (London: Faber, 2000); R.A. Markus, *Saeculum: Religion and Society in the Theology of St. Augustine* (Cambridge: Cambridge University Press, 1970); J. Van Oont, *Jerusalem and Babylon: A Study of Augustine's City of God* (Leiden: Brill, 1991); M.Ruokanen, *Theology and Social Life in Augustine's De Civitate Dei* (Göttingen: Vandenhoeck & Ruprecht, 1993); J.B. Elshtain, *Augustine and the Limits of Politics* (Notre Dame: University of Notre Dame Press, 1997); and Donald X. Burt, *Friendship and Society: An Introduction to Augustine's Practical Philosophy* (Grand Rapids, MI: Eerdmans, 1999).

civil society has become characterized by institutions whose purpose is to coerce and oppress humans into peaceful ways, such as government, slavery, and private property, which partially gratifies human greed. Restoration of fallen humankind to justice comes, according to Augustine, through divine grace granted freely by God and without being merited. Thus, civil society has no role in relation to effecting salvation, rather at best it should create the conditions within which the church may exercise its saving ministry.

The insight that God has turned some people but not others to himself, so that some are lovers of eternal things and others of temporal things, leads Augustine to assert the co-existence of two societies in this world, the community of the true worshippers and lovers of God and the community of those who are consumed by self-love. By analogy, Augustine refers to these two societies as two cities, the city of God and the city of men, or the earthly city. These are not identifiable cities or states, rather they exist side by side in every state, invisible in composition and membership to all but God. The city of God is comprised entirely of godly persons, whose whole lives are devoted to the love of God and the practice of virtue; here only, is true justice found. By contrast, the earthly city is comprised of persons who live according to the flesh and practise vice. Whereas obedience characterizes the heavenly city, disobedience, independence, and self-sufficiency characterize the earthly city.

Augustine does not equate the city of God with the visible church, although he assumes that members of the city of God are more likely to be found there. In the final analysis, it is impossible to know who is a truly virtuous person in this world, although performance of virtuous deeds and living a virtuous life may be good indicators of membership in the heavenly city. Augustine does not equate the city of God with the church, nor does he equate the city of men with the state. Instead he asks what is the purpose of civil society and of civil government in light of the division of the human race into the elect and the reprobate — a division that he regards as Biblical.

He answers that every person is a dual citizen of either the city of God or of men and of a civil state. The civil state retains a purpose in this world of ensuring peace and tranquillity, so that the virtuous might lead a virtuous life and the church carry out its mission of salvation. Augustine did, however, reluctantly identify one specific function for the civil state in relation to the church, insofar as he thought it permissible to appeal to the civil state as a last resort to suppress heretics and schismatics, and he did call upon Rome to do so in relation to the Donatists. Augustine does not think, however, that civil states actually perform this work of creating a space within which the citizens of the heavenly city may live. Rather, because civil states rarely seek to conform human law to divine law and true justice, Augustine characterizes the civil state as a band of brigands that differs from ordinary robber gangs only in the magnitude of its wrongful acts and by the impunity with which they are committed.

The sharply conflicting characteristics of the two cities and of the members of the heavenly city with every earthly city within which they are obliged to live, create the probability of actual conflict between them. Augustine suggests that one way to reduce the incidence of conflict is for Christians to occupy office in the state and to govern in accordance with Christian ideals. However, he is not optimistic that even this resolution would succeed, or not for long. The potential for conflict is a fact of life in this world.

Inherent in Augustine's dichotomy is the possibility that Christians will not always be obedient citizens when their faith and the dictates of the state pull in opposite directions. Indeed, the decline and fall of Rome was already being ascribed in his own day to the spread of Christianity and its divided loyalties. Augustine responded that Christianity does not destroy the obligations of the citizen to the state but rather transforms them into a religious duty. With Paul, he accepts the demands of the civil state as a divine ordinance but further suggests that because Christians are called to a higher degree of morality and virtue than others, they can transform the state so that it more closely conforms to the heavenly city — although he admits such transformation may be rare. Christianity, according to Augustine, shows how human society may be perfected, but he is also certain that such perfection is not attainable in this world because of the fallen nature of humankind.

Augustine wrote at a time when the long-known order of his world was, as it appeared to contemporaries, indeed coming to an end. He wrote *De Civitate Dei*, his last and his best book, as a pastoral work to comfort the perplexed Christian community around him. Thus, his political theology is strongly eschatological in nature and devalues the state as a human institution of little importance to those whose hopes are pinned elsewhere. The task of re-interpretation in a more stable sociopolitical environment awaited the restoration of social stability many centuries later.

C. THOMAS AQUINAS (1225–1274)

The disintegration of the Empire, the collapse of local government, and the social and cultural chaos of the remaining centuries of the first millennium were reflected in the intellectual life of Western Europe, and of the Christian communities that had now sprung up over much of Europe. That is, there was little theological or philosophical speculation at all, and almost none has survived. What has survived — by Erigena, Anselm, Abelard, or from the School of St. Victor — have been works devoted entirely to theological issues, narrowly defined. Speculation about the nature of political life and the role of government revived after civil society was restored, local governments had grown up and sufficient affluence had been achieved for some to enjoy the leisure and the space in the new universities and enriched monastic houses to think and write about political life.

Some religious writers did, in those intervening centuries, consider the relationship of religion and political life, such as Alfarabi (c. 870–950) who attempted to harmonize Islam with Plato, and Moses Maimonides (1135–1204) who attempted a similar Platonic harmonization with Judaism, but until Aquinas turned to those issues in the thirteenth century, there was little Christian speculation that could in retrospect be said to constitute part of the mainstream of the Western intellectual tradition.

Prior to Aquinas, there were some fragmentary attempts to provide a synthetic account of how church and state should relate. Pope Gelasius I (492–496), for example, argued that a Christian society should be governed by two authorities, spiritual and temporal, represented by the church and the state. Both had the same goal: to ensure that earthly life is managed so as to facilitate salvation in the life to come. The state's role was to ensure civil order and peace but because the church's role was to teach true doctrines and prepare for eternal life, the implication that that role was superior meant that the church was greater than the state and should determine boundary disputes. The emperor is, at the end, merely another member of the church.

From the ninth to the thirteenth century, conflicts between kings and church increased as both acquired property and wealth and anticipated the political power inherent in ownership. Armed with a recently articulated doctrine of authority said to be inherited from the apostle Peter, the first bishop of Rome, popes such as Gregory VII (1073–1085) insisted that they were the final arbiters on earth notwithstanding the increasingly greater economic, political, and military power of kings at the turn of the second millennium. Such claims were formalized by John of Salisbury (c. 1120–1180) in his treatise *Policratus* (1159),[7] who envisaged the political community as a commonwealth with a body (the people), a head (the king), and a soul (the church). Authority to rule comes from God whose earthly representative is the church. The king is God's steward and must ensure that affairs of state are organized so as to save souls. When a king does not do so, he no longer rules justly and has become a tyrant who should be reproved by the church and removed if necessary. Although John's treatise is somewhat ambivalent, he appears to suggest the supremacy of the church over the state. The stage is set for Aquinas.

In this as in other theological areas, Aquinas initiated a tradition of thought influential until today, particularly in the Roman Catholic Church. In contrast to Alfarabi and Maimonides, he was more concerned with plumbing Aristotle for insights that could then be Christianized in relation to political life. This may simply have been a matter of available texts; Plato's *Republic* and *Laws* were not available in the West until the fifteenth century and Aristotle's *Politics* and *Ethics* were only available in the West but in incomplete texts until about the same time. Aquinas had access to both of Aristotle's works, translated into Latin in his own lifetime. Aquinas' acceptance of life in society as natural to humans owed much to Aristotle and constituted a different starting point from Augustine.

With Aristotle, Aquinas regards humans as political and social beings for whom civil society is natural and necessary for the perfection of human nature.[8] Humans are born more helpless and destitute than any

---

7   John Dickinson, ed., *The Statesman's Book of John of Salisbury* (New York: Russell & Russell, 1963). See also M. Wilks, ed., *The World of John of Salisbury* (Oxford: Basil Blackwell, 1984).

8   Although scattered throughout his vast corpus, Aquinas' views on political life are chiefly found as follows: *Summa Theologiae*, Ia, q. 92; 96, 103; Ia IIae, q. 21; 72; 90–97; 100; 105; IIa IIae, q. 10–12; 40; 42; 47; 50; 57–60; 66–67; 77–78; 104; 147; *Summa Contra Gentiles*, III. 81; *Commentary on the Ethics*; *Commentary on the Politics*; and *De regimine principum*. Several good recent studies include: Dino Bigongiari, ed., *The Political Ideas of St. Thomas Aquinas* (New York: Hafner, 1955); Etienne Gilson, *The Christian Philosophy of St. Thomas Aquinas* (New York: Scribner, 1956); Thomas Gilby, *Principality and Polity: Aquinas and the Role of State Theory in the West* (London: Longmans, 1958); J.A. Weisheipl, *Friar Thomas d'Aquino: His Life, Thought and Work* (New York: Doubleday, 1974); Brian Davies, *The Thought of Thomas Aquinas* (Oxford:

other animals and require both family and community to live. Thus, Aquinas regards the city as the only truly self-sufficient human association capable of supplying human needs. He describes the city as the most perfect work of practical reason and also as being ordered to a higher end. Its perfection consists in encompassing all other associations humans form, and its higher end in facilitating the civil society within which humans can enjoy the fullness of life not available to the solitary person.

Aquinas' view of society is an organic one in which each part has a role that complements the other parts, and just like the human body, it requires one part to regulate the whole, so as to ensure order in its functioning. Thus it requires a government, which Aquinas compares to the soul. The naturalness of civil society and of government to Aquinas is neatly captured by this analogy with the body and soul respectively. But like the human body, the city is more than just the sum of all its parts. The whole is more important than any individual part, so too the common good of all members of the city is more important than the individual good of any one member; indeed, the common good is the proper good of the city and individuals should subject their private goods to it.

The minimum good for a city to pursue is peace and tranquillity but Aquinas expects more of both civil society and government. Rather, its highest good is the promotion of virtue among all its members who, in turn, should aspire to live virtuous lives. Thus, the most virtuous men should rule over civil society to guide it to its proper goal. Indeed, Aquinas' expressed preference was for kingship, not oligarchy or democracy, which he understood to be the absolute rule of a single wise man for the sake of promoting virtue. He acknowledged, however, that such men were rare and that virtue is not as easily recognizable as birth or wealth, nor as appreciated by others, and that all but unusually virtuous men might easily slip into tyranny when possessed of absolute power. Thus, Aquinas' practical best choice for government was for a mixed regime, blending elements of monarchy, aristocracy, and democracy.

Aquinas then considers how civil society should be conducted to virtuous ends, that is, by what standards. In his view, humans are subject to

---

Clarendon, 1992); Anthony J. Lisska, *Aquinas' Theory of Natural Law* (Oxford: Clarendon, 1996); J.-P. Torrell, *Saint Thomas Aquinas* (Washington, D.C.: Catholic University of America Press, 1996); and John Finnis, *Aquinas: Social, Legal and Political Theory* (Oxford: Oxford University Press, 1997).

three authorities: divine law, reason, and political authority. The most immediate in life in society is political authority; Aquinas states that the stability of civil society requires a rule of law rather than of men. Since truly wise men are rare, he suggests that those who do exist devise good laws that can be applied by other governors in the common good in the multiplicity of transactions and events for which there will always be an insufficient number of wise men to decide case by case. He favours, therefore, comprehensive legislation, which in turn reflects the moral principles of divine law. Thus, Aquinas moves toward the true final goal of his politics, and his theory of law was designed to serve that goal.

Aquinas thought that there are four categories of law: (i) eternal law, known only to God and by which he rules the world; (ii) divine law, which God has revealed in the Old and New Testaments; (iii) natural law, which is that part of eternal law that humanity can grasp through the exercise of reason; and (iv) positive law, or the laws of civil states. The first two are beyond the powers of humanity other than the power to obey but the last two require humanity to discern and then enact their principles in order to regulate how a virtuous life should be lived.

In contrast to Aristotle, Aquinas saw the contemplation of God and eternal salvation as the final goal of a virtuous human life, although only attainable thereafter. Aquinas' natural order does not exist apart from but rather is subject to the divine order, the kingdom of God, which is accessible to humans only by grace. Thus, the virtue of civil society is to be measured in accordance with its conformity to divine standards, which humans can understand because God has endowed them with reason and impelled them toward himself as their final goal. Aquinas asserts that by virtue of possessing a conscience, humans are naturally aware of general principles regulating their conduct that by the exercise of reason can be transformed into specific principles, or natural law, on the basis of which human laws can be devised. Violation of the natural law is disobedience to God.

For Aquinas, the natural law is God's determined order for his creation, and to know it is to have insight into God's purpose, which is the source of human happiness. But how is the government of the city to know what that law is and how it should be reflected in the civil law? How are humans to be guided to their true final end, the contemplation of God, by the civil government? Aquinas answers that only the church can give this guidance to the king. While Aquinas regards civil society and its purposes as natural, he also posits that temporal affairs are distinct and inferior to spiritual matters. The king must be subordinate to the priest to facilitate the supreme end of all humans. Thus, although Aquinas does not regard the raison d'être of the state to be dependent on the church, he does see the state as notionally subordinate to it, when viewed from the perspective of the final end of humankind. Indeed, in the treatise, *De regimine principum*,[9] Aquinas posits that final authority on earth in relation to the kingdom of heaven is delegated to the Roman pontiff by Christ himself.

Writing at a time when the papacy was close to asserting its most inflated claims to governance of the earth, it is not surprising that Aquinas, who was often directly employed on papal business, should suggest such a hierarchical vision of society. Nor is it surprising that he should endow the civil state with a greater role and status in both the world and the order of salvation than did Augustine. Aquinas lived at a time when the pre-modern state was starting to appear in Western Europe, particularly in his native area, present-day Italy, whereas Augustine lived at a time when civil authority was disintegrating and new centres of comfort for Christians were sorely required. Aquinas' novel acceptance of the naturalness of the state would resonate not only within Roman Catholic theology but also within Reformed theology and secular political theories.

D. MARTIN LUTHER (1483–1546)

Aquinas' view that the state was a natural good might readily lead to future speculation that the state could also be an independent good. Aquinas would not have gone this far because his was an organic view of life and of a civil society in which all members and institutions tend toward the same final goal of the contemplation of God. Thus, theoretically, there should be little conflict between church and state provided the state acknowledged the intermediate aim of virtue in civil society and the final end of the contemplation of God in eternal life. The political realities of Aquinas' own day were otherwise; conflict was the normal mode of relationship between the church and the burgeoning city and nation states of high medieval Europe.

---

9   Whether or not Aquinas wrote all or even any of this treatise is widely debated: see Weisheipl, above note 8 at ch. 5.

Moreover, the increasing disenchantment with ecclesiastical, and especially papal, claims to territorial and political hegemony made by an institution increasingly characterized by venality and incompetence led many theologians and secular thinkers in the late Middle Ages to re-evaluate the relationship and respective roles of church and state, and to look for other sources of strength and authority for each, especially for the state. Thus, in *Defensor pacis* (1324), Marsilius of Padua[10] (c. 1275–c. 1342) restricted church and state to spheres that increasingly separated spiritual from secular and asserted a notion of popular sovereignty with the potential to transform both institutions. John Wyclif[11] (c. 1330–1384) and William of Occam[12] (c. 1285–1347) combined notions of popular sovereignty and anti-papalism to undermine the temporal authority asserted by the church and to bestow a new value on individuals and their civil institutions.

In the later Middle Ages, church and state tended, in both political reality and political theology, to be increasingly separated from one another, but thinkers who openly challenged the authority of the papacy or the hierarchy in the church might find themselves stigmatized and

---

10 Several recent studies include: Ephraim Ementon, *The Defensor Pacis of Marsilius of Padua: A Critical Study* (Cambridge, MA: Harvard University Press, 1920); Alan Gewirth, *Marsilius of Padua: The Defender of Peace*, 2 vols. (New York: Columbia University Press, 1951, 1956); Dolf Steinberger, *Die Stadt und das Reich in der Verfassungslehre des Marsilius von Padua* (Wiesbaden: Steiner, 1981); and C.J.Nederman, *Community and Consent: The Secular Political Theory of Marsiglio of Padua's Defensor pacis* (Lanham, MD: Rowman & Littlefield, 1995).

11 See H.B. Workman, *John Wyclif: A Study of the English Medieval Church*, 2 vols. (Oxford: Oxford University Press, 1926); Lowrie J. Daly, *The Political Theory of John Wyclif* (Chicago: Loyola University Press, 1962); and William Farr, *John Wyclif as Legal Reformer* (Leiden: Brill, 1974).

12 See L. Baudry, *Guillaume d'Occam: sa vie, ses oeuvres, ses idéas sociales et politiques* (Paris: Vrin, 1949); A.G. McGrade, *The Political Thought of William of Occam, Personal and Institutional Principles* (Cambridge: Cambridge University Press, 1974); John T. Ryan, *The Nature, Structure and Function of the Church in William of Ockham* (Missoula, MT: Scholars Press, 1979); Marilyn McCord Adams, *William Ockham*, 2 vols. (Notre Dame: Notre Dame University Press, 1987); Lucan Freppert, *The Basis of Morality According to William Occam* (Chicago: Franciscan Herald Press, 1988); and Brian Tierney, *The Idea of Natural Rights* (Atlanta: Scholars Press, 1997).

punished as heretics, as happened to Wyclif and Jan Hus (d. 1415). As long as Rome retained authority and sanctioning power over its theologians, it was foolish to be too critical. Nevertheless, once that hold was broken by Martin Luther, the new theological understandings that predicted and postdated the schism of the Western church necessarily led Reformers to re-address the nature and relationship of church and state, particularly in light of the significant roles that secular rulers played in those city-states and nation-states of Europe that adopted the Reformation for their state church.

Although Luther did not write any works of systematic theology after 1517, it is easy to detect a coherent theology of church and state in the voluminous sermons, pamphlets, tracts, and commentaries that he wrote after the break from Rome.[13] His starting point in this, as in all other matters, was the utter depravity of fallen humans who do only evil, but for the free gift of grace from God to some, which inclines them to believe and to perform good works in response. In contrast to Aquinas who thought human reason to have escaped the effects of the Fall, Luther regarded human reason as depraved and therefore on its own not capable of thinking rightly about things. Instead, for Luther, the criterion by which all should be measured is the Bible, to which humans should, therefore, look to discern the standards by which to act and organize social life. Luther did not look to Aristotle, as did Aquinas.

Once sinful humans have been justified, or made righteous, by the gift of grace, they become members of "two kingdoms," the spiritual kingdom and the temporal kingdom. The former is largely the concern of the church, and the latter of the state. As members of the spiritual

---

13   Two treatises may be consulted to get the flavour of Luther's position: *On Secular Authority* (1521) and *The Freedom of a Christian* (1520). A large selection of Luther's political writings is in J.M. Porter, ed., *Luther: Selected Political Writings* (Philadelphia: Fortress Press, 1974). Some of the more recent literature includes: F.E. Cranz, *An Essay on the Development of Luther's Thought on Justice, Law and Society* (Cambridge, MA: Harvard University Press, 1959); S.S. Wolin, *Politics and Vision* (Boston: Brown, 1960); Heinrich Bornkamm, *Luther's Doctrine of the Two Kingdoms in the Context of His Theology* (Philadelphia: Fortress Press, 1966); W.D.J. Cargill Thompson, *The Political Thought of Martin Luther* (Brighton: Harvester, 1984); Bernhard Lohse, *Martin Luther: An Introduction to His Life and Work* (Philadelphia: Fortress Press, 1986); and John Witte, Jr., *Law and Protestantism: The Legal Teachings of the Lutheran Reformation* (Cambridge: Cambridge University Press, 2002).

kingdom, humans are instructed in piety and divine worship and are free. As members of the temporal kingdom, humans are instructed in their duties as citizens and are in bondage to secular magistrates and laws as well as to bodily needs for food and clothing. The two kingdoms are not, Luther asserts, simply church and state, although overlap is possible. Rather, like Augustine, Luther conceives of his spiritual kingdom as the city of God, of which some are members, while still in the flesh.

Luther thinks that the state belongs wholly to the temporal kingdom. It is a necessary institution, created by God a~ ̄ ̄riving its authority directly from him, and not from the Pope, t' ̄ ̄or the people. The state ̄ ̄ ̄ ̄ ̄ ̄ ̄peace and tranquillity a ̄ ̄ ̄ ̄ ̄r, the state also has dutie ̄ ̄ ̄ ̄y, ensuring that it confo ̄ ̄ ̄ ̄ ̄ ̄ ̄ ̄ ̄ ̄contained in the New Testament. This duty should only arise in rare situations, although Luther did appeal to the rulers of his day to advance the Reformation within their territories. He envisioned that the normal relationship between church and state be one of mutual support as between equals in this world.

Conversely, Luther's view of the church is less clear. While it is possible to identify states and rulers in and with the temporal kingdom, it is less clear that the spiritual kingdom and the church are identical. Luther uses the word to refer both to the visible institution that consists of both elect and reprobate and to the invisible communion of the elect throughout the ages. In contrast to John Calvin,[14] Luther places less emphasis on the visible church as an institution. He even thinks that its polity and property may be controlled by temporal governments; all that matters is right preaching and administration of the sacraments. Luther, the former monk, is more concerned with the contemplative and spiritual aspects of life than with the active and temporal aspects. His willingness to permit the state considerable control over the church seems naive and unrealistic unless one recalls how little all earthly concerns mattered to Luther.

In contrast to medieval theologies of church and state, Luther restricts the role of the church to its spiritual functions; the church should not claim authority over the state as the medieval church had done, nor should it aspire to territorial sovereignty on its own account. By so restricting the church's sphere, Luther enhances the state's role and

---

14   Below section E.

authority over individuals. Nevertheless, it remained the case that Luther entertained an organic view of their relationship as separate but equal in the work of salvation, so that the potential for conflict was minimal.

Luther's understanding of law also minimizes the potential for conflict between the temporal and spiritual kingdoms. With most medieval thinkers, Luther recognized three types of law: divine law revealed by God in the Bible, natural law that can be known by all persons, and positive law enacted by states. In contrast to Aquinas, Luther does not think that natural law can be comprehended by human reason; rather, natural law is identical with divine law in its substantive precepts, but could only be known naturally before the Fall, after which it is known from Scripture. Positive law may differ from divine law since it reflects the needs of the enacting state. While Luther would prefer that it reflect divine law, he acknowledges that it may not, but even if this is the case, it is to be obeyed except in certain situations.

Since the temporal authorities are ordained by God, Luther, with Paul, advocates obedience to them. Indeed, Luther argued that even a tyrant must be obeyed; a nation receives the government it deserves and a tyrant may express the wrath of God with it. Moreover, in his view, since a person's soul is not hurt by suffering wrong, obeying a tyrant is a cross to be borne in this world. But is it permissible violently to resist a tyrant? Luther appears not to think so. He advocates moving to another state, but if this is impossible, then it is necessary to suffer an evil ruler. This was the position he took in relation to the Peasant's Revolt of 1525, when he advocated submission to evil rulers by ill-treated peasants and encouraged those rulers to be harsh in suppressing the disturbances.

Luther's reluctance to interfere with the authority of the state should not disguise the relatively low view that he had of it. For Luther, the state was ordered by God to create a space within which the members of the spiritual kingdom could live out their purpose in this world. It was to regulate the externals, like property and contract, but to leave the church to its saving work. For him, the requirement to suffer tyrants simply confirmed the irrelevance of the state to the spiritual life of the dwellers in the spiritual kingdom.

E. JOHN CALVIN (1509–1564)

John Calvin belonged to the second generation of the Reformation and as such he was able to build upon the views of the first generation, such as Martin Luther, as well as to have the benefit of the experience of how the states of Europe had responded to Reformed ideas.[15]

Moreover, whereas the first generation of Reformers was concerned with the core theological revolt against Rome, matters relating to grace, justification, and salvation, the second generation was faced with solidifying the success of that revolt and focused more on institutional matters; polity, discipline, and relationships with civil society. Calvin was also a lawyer by profession, and obliged to practise law from time to time to maintain himself, but he also drew upon his training to draft legislation and to reflect generally upon how law could be used to advance the religious goals of the Reformation. Calvin was, therefore, less accommodating to the secular world than Luther, and had a greater sense of the prescriptive function of law and of state structures in advancing his goals. Perhaps as a reflection of his legal training but probably also of his precise and lucid intelligence, Calvin wrote systematic theological treatises, of which the most famous is the *Institutes of the Christian Religion*, which proved to be an excellent vehicle for the spread of his ideas beyond the small city-state of Geneva.

Like Luther, Calvin's views on civil society and the relationship of church and state were integrated with his theology, so that his starting point was also the total depravity of fallen human nature and the necessity for God's gratuitous gift of grace for humans to do any good works in this world. The authority for this was, of course, Scripture, to which Calvin, more than Luther, looked to discern rules and models for the

---

15   Although conveniently discussed in the *Institutes of the Christian Religion* (1559), IV. 20, Calvin's views are scattered throughout his vast corpus. Some of the better modern studies of his political thought include: H.R. Pearcy, *The Meaning of the Church in the Thought of John Calvin* (Chicago: University of Chicago Press, 1967); Wolin, above note 13; J. Bohetec, *Calvins Lehre von Staat und Kirche* (Reprinted Aalen: Scientia, 1961); B.C. Milner, Jr., *Calvin's Doctrine of the Church* (Leiden: Brill, 1970); W. Fred Graham, *The Constructive Revolutionary: John Calvin and His Socio-Economic Impact* (Richmond, VA: John Knox Press, 1971); Harro Höpfl, *The Christian Polity of John Calvin* (Cambridge: Cambridge University Press, 1982); William C. Innes, *Social Concern in Calvin's Geneva* (Allison Park, PA: Pickwick, 1983); Ronald S. Wallace, *Calvin, Geneva and the Reformation* (Edinburgh: Scottish Academic Press, 1986); Jeannine E. Olsen, *Calvin and Social Welfare* (Selinsgrove: Susquehanna University Press, 1989); and Ralph C. Hancock, *Calvin and the Foundations of Modern Politics* (Cornell: Cornell University Press, 1989).

conduct of Christian life and society. With Luther, Calvin also thought humans to be subject to two kingdoms, which he similarly defined, both in themselves and in relation to church and state respectively.

However, Calvin was more concerned with the visible church than Luther. In Calvin's view, it is possible to discern from Scripture the positive rules of morality that the church ought to teach, and the organizational form and role of the church in this world. Thus, Calvin works out from the New Testament the four-fold offices characteristic of Reformed churches since — minister, elder, deacon, and teacher — and further ascribes to them disciplinary authority over members who are in breach of Biblical injunctions for moral living. Calvin thinks of the church as having disciplinary authority over outward morality and that this should not be given over to the state, though it may also punish. Indeed, the church, in his view, may also punish secular rulers who transgress divine law.

If secular rulers may be subject to the moral discipline of the church, the actual relationship of church and state in Calvin's thought is clearly more intimate than in Luther's. With Luther, Calvin argued that church and state are separate and distinct but he also posited a close collaboration of the two. Thus, in addition to the functions ordinarily ascribed to a state to maintain law and order and to protect property and contract, Calvin also ascribes to it duties toward the church. The first duty is simply to maintain civil order within which the church may thrive. But Calvin goes further, arguing that the state must also assist the church in its work, including the provision of care for the poor and the establishment of godly schools and universities. Calvin wrote:

> Civil government has as its appointed end, so long as we live among men, to cherish and protect the outward worship of God, to defend ... the position of the church, to adjust our life to the society of men, to form our social behaviour to civil righteousness, to reconcile us with one another, and to promote general peace and tranquillity ... If it is God's will that we go as pilgrims upon the earth while we aspire to the true fatherland, and if the pilgrimage requires such help, those who take these from men deprive him of his very humanity.[16]

While Calvin would deny to the state the power or right to decide sound doctrine, saving for the church the exclusive right to interpret and expound Scripture, he looked to the state to defend sound doctrine and

16   *Institutes*, IV. 20.2.

to support materially the church. Neither Calvin nor other Reformed theologians inspired by his writings, such as John Knox or Andrew Melville,
were shy about rebuking secular princes in the light of their theological
principles, leading one to conclude that while Calvin maintained formally to a doctrine of two kingdoms, practically the boundaries between the
two were fuzzy.

The question of what should be contained in the civil law is, again, as
answered by Calvin, to be determined by resort to Scripture. With Luther,
Calvin recognizes three sources of law: divine, natural, and positive law.
Divine law revealed in Scripture is regarded as an expression of the will of
God for his creation who should conform their lives to it. Natural law is,
again, divine law as it is known by humankind, and the positive laws of
the state should reflect these and, therefore, be obeyed by subjects.

More so than Luther, Calvin was concerned with forms of government, again reflecting his view that Biblical models for civil society can
be discerned in Scripture, as well as his legal temperament. Calvin begins
by recalling both that civil authorities are ordained by God and that they
are fallen and depraved, and then goes on to insist on a form of government that might be said to be subject to "checks and balances" as controls on rulers. Although he regards all forms of government as subject
to both advantages and disadvantages, he regards aristocracy as the least
objectionable, provided some kind of popular franchise exists to curb its
potential excesses. Calvin advocated elections within church government, to the office of elder within a congregation, for example, and ten-
tatively thought to extend the concept within civil society. However, the
suggestion is very tentative and Calvin certainly was no democrat in the
modern sense. In his view, an elected magistrate was first and foremost
called first by God to his office and popular election simply recognized
that divine calling.

The final issue, then, is what is to be done about a tyrannical ruler?
While Luther discounted the possibility of revolt, Calvin, in the *Institutes*, suggested that lesser magistrates were under a duty to overthrow
tyrannical rulers on behalf of the whole society on the assumption that
they were put in their office by God to facilitate the common good, which
might mean overthrowing tyranny. Calvin does not address the issue of
whether or not a popular uprising would be permissible and it is difficult
to discern what he might say about that possibility.

In contrast to Luther, Calvin had a synthetic and integrated political
theology, based on a lively understanding of God's work in this world as

revealed in Scripture. Calvin spoke of a "Christian polity" by which he meant a society well-ordered under Scriptural authority and subject to a two-fold government, or a double "ministry" of pastors and magistrates. Both derived their authority from God and both were charged with responsibility for governing the same body of persons in relation to their spiritual and temporal lives respectively. Both were expected to work together under divine law since both had the common goal of building up God's kingdom in this world. But when conflict inevitably appeared, the theocratic tendencies of Calvin's political theology became apparent since he did not doubt that pastors had the right to scold and discipline magistrates who did not conform their temporal policies to the church's understanding of divine revelation.

F. RADICAL PROTESTANTISM

After Luther's views were condemned at the Diet of Worms in 1521, dashed hopes for evangelical reform were vented throughout the Holy Roman Empire in local demands for reform, spurred on by evangelical preachers who attracted followings both in towns and in the countryside. Such preachers, many of them lay or with little university education, seized hold of some of Luther's doctrinal innovations, such as "by Scripture alone" or "the priesthood of all believers," and added their own notions of what these might mean, particularly in the light of contemporary social and economic concerns.

This popularization of what began as a university-based theological dispute between Professor Luther and his ecclesiastical superiors led to more radical calls for social, economic, and ecclesiastical change than Luther had ever contemplated. It released the anticlericalism that had built up over the preceding centuries and exalted the "common man," a phrase first used at this time. In fact, the "Radical Reformation" moved quickly beyond what came to be known as the "magisterial Reformation" of Luther and, in the next generation, Calvin.

While Luther and Calvin had rejected the hierarchy of the Roman church, they had not rejected civil government; indeed, in their respective ways, both had exalted secular authorities to a degree never acknowledged by the pre-Reformation church and both looked to the civil magistrates of their day to advance the Reformation within their jurisdictions. Moreover, both restricted authority and office within the church to university-educated clergy. By contrast, the Radical Reformation challenged authority of all kinds, whether in church or state, and suffered persecution in virtually all the states of Europe, whether Roman Catholic or Protestant, as a result.

The phrase "Radical Reformation"[17] is applied by historians to an eclectic group of reformers who are neither Lutheran nor Calvinist nor Anglican. Radical reformers on the European continent are usually referred to as "Anabaptist," while in England, they are gathered under the rubric "Puritan." However, it is important to emphasize, for the section which follows, that the Radical Reformation was not a theology nor a party nor even a movement, rather a disparate group of reformers and their supporters who seemed willing to literally turn the world upside down.

Nevertheless, it is possible to suggest that some principles were widely shared to a greater or lesser extent by the Anabaptists on the continent. With Luther and Calvin, radical Reformers looked to Scripture but saw little of either the Roman Catholic Church or of the churches envisioned by the magisterial Reformers. Indeed, in the New Testament, they found that the earliest Christian communities were isolated from the civil societies in which they found themselves. The characteristics of those communities were interpreted as the marks of true Christian communities and they sought to replicate them in the sixteenth century.

---

17 Among the better recent studies of Anabaptism are the following: Guy F. Herschberger, ed., *The Recovery of the Anabaptist Vision* (Scottsdale, PA.: Herald Press, 1957); G.H. Williams, *The Radical Reformation* (Philadelphia: Westminster Press, 1962); P.J. Klassen, *The Economics of Anabaptism* (The Hague: Mouton, 1964); F.H. Littell, *The Origins of Sectarian Protestantism: A Study of the Anabaptist View of the Church* (London: Macmillan, 1964); J.H. Yoder, *The Christian Witness to the State* (Newton, KS: Faith & Life Press, 1964); W.E. Keeney, *The Development of Dutch Anabaptist Thought and Practice from 1539 to 1564* (Nieuwkoop: De Graaf, 1968); Cornelius Kramm, *Dutch Anabaptism: Origin, Speech, Life and Thought 1450–1600* (The Hague: Nijhoff, 1968); James M. Strayer, *Anabaptists and the Sword* (Lawrence, KS: Coronado Press, 1972); Steven E. Ozment, *Mysticism and Dissent: Religious Ideology and Social Protest in the Sixteenth Century* (New Haven: Yale University Press, 1978); and Walter Klassen, *Living at the End of the Ages: Apocalyptic Expectation in the Radical Reformation* (New York: University Press of America, 1992). Anthologies of Anabaptist writings include: G.H. Williams and Angel M. Mergal, eds., *Spiritual and Anabaptist Writings* (Philadelphia: Westminster Press, 1959); W. Klassen, ed., *Anabaptism in Outline: Selected Primary Sources* (Kitchener: Herald Press, 1981); and Michael G. Baylor, ed., *The Radical Reformation* (Cambridge: Cambridge University Press, 1991).

For most Anabaptists, the visible church consisted only of those who had been "gathered" into it by the Holy Spirit and did not consist of both elect and reprobate as the magisterial Reformers would insist. Entry into the visible Christian community is by believer's baptism, and a condition of remaining in that community is obedience to Christ as mediated through the community. Thus, in contrast to the territorial churches in the political theologies of the magisterial Reformers, the radical Reformers posited small gathered communities of the elect only. Their emphasis was on local autonomy, local community control, and on egalitarianism, which was implicit in believer's baptism as the entry requirement.

Once the church is conceived of as an alternative community, self-contained and God-directed, it is clear that involvement with the surrounding civil society and the state is likely to be minimal. Indeed, few radical Reformers even took the trouble to develop a political theology setting out an understanding of the state and its relationship with the church. Rather, their focus was on moral norms for everyday life in the local gathered community, whose life together tended to be socially conservative, rural, and structured to ensure peace and harmony, if sometimes at the expense of the individual. Apocalypticism was also a characteristic of some of these groups, intensifying their introspective nature.

Non-involvement with the state came, in the course of the sixteenth century, to be reflected in pacifism and refusal to subscribe to oaths. In fact, Anabaptist communities took little interest in affairs of state and denied authority to the state. These attitudes brought them into conflict with the territorial powers where they lived, and persecution and migration to the fringes of society became their lot in the sixteenth-century world. It was still unthinkable for a state to contain more than one religion: one state-one church was the norm. The formula *cuius regio eius religio* was a sixteenth-century creation of Luther's close friend and ally, Philip Melanchthon.

Yet, paradoxically, the Anabaptists did not distinguish the spiritual and worldly kingdoms as did the magisterial Reformers. Rather, they denied the authority of the civil authorities over their gathered communities but within those communities practised complete integrity of life. All of life was to be sanctified and lived in the light of Scripture and the working of the Holy Spirit. Their social and political vision was little different from that of Calvin except that it was to be lived at the micro- rather than macro- level and excluded the ungodly.

While some surviving groups of Anabaptists, such as the Mennonites and Hutterites, were able to remain largely true to the original vision of Christian community, although at the cost of constantly moving eastward across Europe until they were driven to the North American frontiers in the ninetenth century, some Reformed Christians adopted those views and attempted to reshape entire societies in accordance with them. The experience of Puritanism in England and then in New England is demonstrative.

Puritanism was a complex historical phenomenon. The term is used to encompass a wide range of theological positions drawn partly from Anabaptism and partly from Calvinism,[18] whose chief shared feature was a desire to purify to a greater or lesser extent Roman Catholic practices and beliefs from the only partially reformed Church of England. The various strains within Puritanism, which was never a coherent party as is often thought, are usually gathered into three groups as determined by their views on the relationship of church and state: (i) those who wished to stay within the established church but to purify its doctrine and worship; (ii) those who wished to separate from the established church, such as the Congregationalists, Baptists, and English Presbyterians, to form a religiously more pluralist, but still Protestant society; and (iii) those who espoused radical social upheaval, such as the Levellers, Diggers, Ranters, and Quakers.

While the first group was typically sixteenth century insofar as it subscribed to a one church-one state vision of society, the second was a forerunner of a more modern, pluralistic vision of Christian society and espoused a political theology that attempted to capture that vision.[19] Most began with the Anabaptist understanding of the church as comprised of a collection of local congregations gathered by the Holy Spirit to live in autonomous local communities. From Calvin, these groups adopted the view that Scripture presented positive norms for social and ecclesiastical life and the idea that these communities should be largely comprised of the elect who live in a covenanted relationship with God. They lived directly under the guidance of God, in a relationship that was not mediated in any way by a state church and its clergy.

---

18 As distinguished from the views of John Calvin himself, whose followers developed his views beyond limits he would not likely have crossed.

19 Men such as Robert Browne or Robert Harrison. See A. Peel and L.H. Carbon, ed., *The Writings of Robert Harrison and Robert Browne* (London: Allen and Unwin, 1953).

Thus, Congregationalists and others in this group regarded the established church as a contradiction to the New Testament pattern for Christian communities and denied that the civil authorities had jurisdiction over their communities. Since the outcome of the English Reformation had been to establish the final authority of the Crown-in-Parliament over the English church, this position placed these groups in direct conflict with the state.[20] While some congregations stayed within the established church, many did not and led their collective lives outside the structures of ecclesiastical discipline despite legislation that fined, imprisoned, or otherwise punished them for doing so. It should be emphasized that Congregationalists saw no incompatibility between their understanding of the nature of the church and loyalty to the Crown. Rather, their vision was of a strict separation of the Christian community from the state, combined with loyalty to the state, except when it attempted to restrict or punish religious belief and practice.

While English Presbyterians shared a common Calvinistic understanding with Congregationalists of human depravity and the primacy of Scripture as a positive norm for life, they interpreted the New Testament differently, seeing in it, with Calvin, an hierarchical polity based on government by presbyters rather than bishops. Thus, rather than adopt a strict separation position on the relationship of church and state, they attempted to reform the hierarchical politico-ecclesiastical structures in England so that the national church would be presbyterian rather than episcopal in polity. With Calvin, they espoused a one church-one state

---

20   The major intellectual defence of the state Anglican church was Richard Hooker's *Of the Laws of Ecclesiastical Polity* (1593–1595). The critical edition is W. Speed Hill et al. ed., *The Works of Richard Hooker: The Folger Library Edition*, 6 vols. (Cambridge, MA: Harvard University Press, 1977). See generally: E.T. Davies, *The Political Ideas of Richard Hooker* (London: SPCK, 1946); F.J. Shirley, *Richard Hooker and Contemporary Political Ideas* (London: SPCK, 1949); John S. Marshall, *Hooker and the Anglican Tradition: An Historical and Theological Study of Hooker's Ecclesiastical Polity* (London: A. & C. Black, 1963); W. Speed Hill, ed., *Studies in Richard Hooker* (Cleveland: Case Western Reserve University Press, 1972); Robert Eccleshill, *Order and Reason in Politics: Theories of Absolute and Limited Monarchy in Early Modern England* (Oxford: Oxford University Press, 1970); Robert K. Faulkner, *Richard Hooker and the Politics of a Christian England* (Berkeley: University of California Press, 1981); and Peter Lake, *Puritan and Anglican? Presbyterianism and English Conformist Thought from Whitgift to Hooker* (London: Unwin, Hyman, 1988).

vision of society, in contrast to the Anabaptist strict separation model. This vision was ultimately actualized in Scotland where the established church became presbyterian in polity and enjoyed a legal monopoly similar to that enjoyed by the Church of England south of the border.[21]

The Radical Reformation in both its continental and English varieties posed a fundamental challenge to both the Reformed and Roman Catholic churches in the sixteenth century. By asserting the primacy of Scripture literally understood, and of spiritual life directly under God, it shattered the compromises that even the magisterial Reformers had made in order to accommodate the civil state in their political theologies. The Radical Reformation pressed Calvin's theology, especially, to its logical conclusions so as to have minimum contact with civil authority in favour of local, autonomous theocracies where the elect could lead a fully integrated life of Christian integrity.

G. POST-REFORMATION DEVELOPMENTS

In political theology, as in theology generally, the end of the sixteenth century marked the end of an era of prolific and original writing on theological issues, which had begun in the early thirteenth century. On questions relating to church and state the main positions on the theological spectrum had been largely staked out, ranging from the profound distrust of the state characteristic of the Radical Reformation through grudging acceptance of it by Augustine and Luther, to optimistic co-operation with it characteristic of Aquinas, and virtual appropriation of it for divine purposes by Calvin and Knox.

By the end of that century as well, the patterns of relationships between church and state in the states of Europe had largely settled into the relationships that would persist until the late eighteenth century. Nation-states and city-states took the religion of their ruler as the state religion. Thus, Europe consisted of monolithic Lutheran, Anglican, Reformed (Calvinist), and Roman Catholic states. The existence of other religious minorities within each was not permitted by law and persecu-

---

21 The principal architect of this was John Knox. See David Laing, ed., *The Works of John Knox*, 6 vols. (Edinburgh: Bannatyne Club, 1846–1864). These are not especially good studies of Knox's thought as opposed to his life, of which there are many. The best of these, which also has extensive bibliographical materials is Richard G. Kyle, *The Mind of John Knox* (Lawrence, KS: Coronado Press, 1984).

tion was normal. Only the radical branches of the Reformation eschewed state religious monopolies, although they too sought to live in monolithic communities in the under-inhabited parts of Europe under no secular domination, or, from the early seventeeth century onward, in the New World. This one church-one state pattern was reproduced in the North American colonies, with twelve of the Thirteen Colonies having a state church, and attempts at establishment became a characteristic feature of the British North American colonies until the fourth decade of the nineteenth century.

Whether it was sheer exhaustion from the religious wars of the sixteenth and early seventeenth centuries or the rise of science, the growth of affluence, the spread of doubt, or any of the other possible factors posited by historians for the decline in religious fervour from the mid seventeenth century onward, original speculation by theologians decreased and the new theories about the nature of civil society and of law were increasingly devised by secular thinkers who proposed secular and human-centred theories of government, law, and civic virtue. Machiavelli (1469–1527) was a forerunner of the new this-worldly orientation in political philosophy, which would become further developed by such thinkers as Hobbes (1588–1679), Locke (1632–1704), Hume (1711–1776), Smith (1723–1790), Burke (1729–1797), J.S. Mill (1806–1873), and their continental counterparts such as Spinoza (1632–1677), Montesquieu (1689–1755), Rousseau (1712–1778), Kant (1724–1804), Hegel (1770–1831), Tocqueville (1805–1859), Marx (1818–1883), and Nietzsche (1844–1900). The earlier secular political theorists of the state favoured a social contract explanation for its authority and justification, while later thinkers suggested that will and power alone explained its authority. All theories were immanent; transcendent origins, justifications, and purposes were dismissed as irrelevant. Religion and the Christian churches were demoted accordingly from any public role and relegated to the realm of the private.

While Christian theology experienced revival and renovation in the course of the nineteenth century, especially in Germany, the renewal of original speculation about the nature of civil society and the role of the churches in it did not occur until the twentieth century, when the challenges to the nominally Christian culture of Western society had escalated over the previous centuries to a point where genuine evils within civil societies required the re-assessment of theological fundamentals. Foremost amongst these influences was the rise of Hitler, which challenged two Protestant theologians, Karl Barth (1886–1968) and Dietrich Bonhoeffer (1906–1945) to rethink the Reformed and Lutheran traditions respectively. Moreover, the rise of pluralism, including secularism, in Western societies, and the desire of non-Western societies, particularly in Latin America and Africa, to be freed of the more imperialistic elements of Christianity, has prompted renewed speculation in both the Roman Catholic and Reformed communities about the relationship of religion to civil government and civil societies, which appears destined to continue at a vigorous level for the foreseeable future.

Although contemporary thinkers in political theology demonstrate considerable loyalty to their respective theological traditions, some common themes and approaches appear to be emerging, such as taking the state seriously and expecting from it a moral response to civil society, and the re-assertion of Scriptural standards and values as appropriate for civil society. These may be seen in a variety of thinkers in this century.

Karl Barth's starting point for both his theology and his political theology was his affirmation of the infinite qualitative distinction between God and humanity, resulting in the exaltation of God above humanity, who might know his will through the revelation of Christ in Scripture.[22] Since God is, according to Barth, the Lord of all creation, his kingdom as witnessed by Scripture is an analogy for this world, both church and state, which should seek to express the characteristics of the heavenly kingdom on earth. Barth thought democratic socialism to be the political system best suited to do so in his own time but regarded such to be provisional and changeable in the future in different conditions.

By emphasizing the primacy of the gospel, Barth concluded that the law, including the laws of nations, should reflect that gospel. Thus, while Barth acknowledged the need for civil governments in this world, he saw no fundamental distinction between the civil state and the church since both are subject to the same divine injunctions. Barth, therefore, entertained a positive view of the state as an institution, along with Calvin, and in opposition to Luther's view of the state merely as a force against

---

22 Karl Barth, *The Church and the Political Problem of Our Day* (New York, 1939); Will Herberg, ed. *Community, State and Church* (Garden City, NY: National Student Christian Federation, 1960); and *Church Dogmatics* (Edinburgh: T. & T. Clark, 1957) II/1. For a selection of his writings on political theology, see G. Hunsinger, ed., *Karl Barth and Radical Politics* (Philadelphia: Westminster Press, 1976).

evil, but he also cautioned against the temptation to which states frequently succumbed to regard themselves as autonomous and thereafter to become forces for evil.

Barth did not, however, advocate a theocratic view of earthly society. While he thought that both church and state should reflect the kingdom of God, he remained convinced that they were two different communities. The role of the church in any society was to hold always before the state the ideal of what the state ought to be. Its role was to criticize the state, and the state was to be obliged to countenance such criticism and to amend its ways. The church owes its allegiance to Christ alone, in his view, and as such may be required to take a courageous stance against the state, as occurred during the Third Reich. Barth sees the true church's role as that of ensuring that there is a true state. His political theology, then, is more an ethical position for Christian political action than it is a theology of the state — an emphasis that undoubtedly reflected his historical circumstances.

Karl Barth's neo-Calvinistic attempts to restore the idea of the direct sovereignty of God over state and church resonates in other political theologies characteristic of the renewal of Reformed/Calvinistic theology in the twentieth century that have denied intermediate institutions, including church and state, the authority to intervene between God and individuals.[23] This development in Christian theology has proven to be compatible with the growing religious and secular pluralism of late twentieth century societies since its focus is on facilitating moral integrity for individuals and communities of interest, free from state intervention, direction, and regulation. This radical denial of authority to earthly institutions contrasts with the renewed Thomism in Roman Catholic political theologies of this century.

Two concepts of importance to Aquinas' understanding of the role of the state in civil society have re-surfaced in Roman Catholic views of church and state in this century: natural law and the common good. Natural law is the medium whereby divine law is reflected in human law and in the reflection of the divine reason in the created world. Human reason can discern this in the world, in particular in social community, and can discern the common good to which all parts of the community should be

---

23   An interesting selection of these writings is found in James W. Skillen and
      Rockne M. McCarthy, eds., *Political Order and the Plural Structure of Society*
      (Atlanta: Scholars Press, 1991).

subject. Communities consist of various parts, ordered hierarchically, and tending toward God. Thus, the emphasis in Aquinas' political theology is on acceptance of social differentiation and social hierarchy, topped by the church, as necessary for the achievement of the common good of society and, *ipso facto*, each individual in that society. The notion that the common good consists of the harmonious relationship of persons and institutions in a hierarchically ordered society was termed the principle of "subsidiarity" by Pope Pius XI in the encyclical *Quadragesimo Anno* in 1931, and since then it has been at the heart of Roman Catholic thinking about civil society, reflected in a series of encyclicals since.

Thus, in *Pacem in Terris*, in 1963, Pope John XXIII stated that because government derives its authority from God, its laws should reflect divine laws, especially in relation to human rights and the redistribution of wealth — themes that were relatively new in Roman Catholic theology. The renewal of focus on the role of the state in relation to addressing socio-economic goals espoused by the Church has been reflected in subsequent encyclicals such as *Popularum Progressio* (1967), *Octagesimo Adveniens* (1971), and *Laborem Exercerns* (1981).[24]

This renewed emphasis on the role of the state in working to achieve the vision of social justice espoused by the Roman Catholic Church is in historical continuity with Aquinas' view of the state's role within the natural order. Indeed, while Reformed theology in the twentieth century retreated somewhat from Calvin's position to one closer to Luther and Augustine by regarding the state as a human institution to be chivvied by the church into doing good, both theological traditions share the view that the state exists to do, in some way, divine work so as to facilitate the human pilgrimage through this world to humanity's final end. Social activism, whether expressed in the social gospel movement within Protestantism earlier in the twentieth century, or in renewed Roman Catholic engagement with social issues at the end of that century, reflects a shared Christian trust in the state.

Christian theologies have yet to address seriously the issue of pluralism, both religious and secular within their historic traditions of politi-

---

24   For current official Roman Catholic teaching on the proper relationship of church and state see especially certain decrees of the Second Vatican Council, 1965: *Dignitatis humanae* (7 December 1965) and *Gaudium et Spes* (7 December 1965); and Austin P. Flannery, *The Documents of Vatican II*, (New York: Costello, 1975).

cal theology. It remains to conclude by observing the close relationship between the respective Christian traditions in their understanding of the interaction of church and state in Canada.

Whether it was New France before 1759, or Upper Canada or Nova Scotia at the beginning of the nineteenth century, the common understanding of colonists coming from Roman Catholic, Anglican, or Reformed states was of religious homogeneity, and the hegemony of one church within a geo-political jurisdiction. Whatever view of the state was entertained, whether as a part of the natural or of a divine order, it was widely assumed that the role of the state was to be taken seriously within a Christian civil society and that that role was to promote the particular Christian order favoured by the established or would be established church in that jurisdiction. This was the European heritage.

Challenges to that view came in both Upper Canada and Nova Scotia from successive waves of immigrants from both the United States and Europe who entertained less exalted views of the state and more practical views about the necessity for a religiously pluralistic society reflecting the fragmentation of Christianity begun by the Reformation. The constitutional and legal institutions and norms of Canadian society have evolved over time in response to these realities, and continue to do so today, in response to the new real world facts of non-Christian religious pluralism and the growth of secularism. Legal textbooks are like archaeological digs, exhibiting layer upon layer of past lives; the layers in this text are those of religious hegemonies of the past, but in contrast to civilizations dead and gone, their religious descendants are thriving all around.

Chapter Two

A Brief History of Law and Religious Institutions in Canada

A. INTRODUCTION

The history of religious institutions and the law in Canada was, until the late twentieth century, the history of Christianity in Canada in its many forms, its relationships with governments (whether foreign, colonial, federal, or provincial) and with the society in which it found itself and whose shape it influenced in fundamental ways. Indeed, the assumption brought to the New World by most of the Christian communities of post-Reformation Europe was that the alliances of church and state enjoyed in the originating states in Europe would be replicated in the New World, as would the societies of Western Europe, newly purged of their undesirable characteristics. While the motives for the establishment of overseas colonies were primarily economic, political, and strategic, it was also widely accepted by contemporaries not only that the familiar patterns of Christendom would be continued in the New World but also that this was necessary to civilize the New World and advance the kingdom of God throughout the whole world.

Once the major states of early modern Europe had laid claim to their overseas colonies, the inevitable inter-colonial rivalries, whether economic, political, or military, grew up, reflecting not only local annoyances but also European-based rivalries, including inter-state religious frictions. In addition, since many overseas colonies comprised settlers of rival religious denominations within Europe, intra-colonial religious disputes and manoeuvring for supremacy also inevitably occurred.

In the New World as in the Old World, the division between Roman Catholic and Protestant remained the major fault-line along which states would be built, outranking in social and political importance the divisions of the Protestant Reformation; Anabaptist, Anglican, and Reformed, whose European rivalries also continued in North America. Indeed, much of Canadian political and social history from the founding of New France to the era of the *Charter* can be written as the history of Christianity in Canada, its religious institutions, and the state, so profound has the role of the Christian churches been directly on national life but also indirectly through the peculiar ways in which social and political issues have been framed for much of the history of both public and private life in Canada. While the sectarian disputes of the nineteenth century were explicitly framed as denominational rivalries, the secular debates of the twentieth century on major social issues retained a theological undercurrent about how best to order a moral society in the northern part of the Western hemisphere.

It is impossible to write a thorough history of religion in Canada in one chapter suitable as an introduction to that subject and as background to a legal text. This chapter will survey superficially the major events insofar as they are related to the legal topics to which this book is primarily devoted.[1]

---

1   This chapter is based on several general histories of religion in Canada and not
     on any original research. General histories of religion in Canada are rare,
     although the recent revival of interest in the subject amongst Canadian histori-
     ans, as evidenced by the large number of special topic books published in the
     past two decades, suggests that this history will become better understood.
     Reference to some of these relevant works will be made in footnotes below as
     appropriate to the text. The general histories in chronological order are as fol-
     lows: H.H. Walsh, *The Christian Church in Canada* (Toronto: Ryerson, 1956);
     H.H. Walsh, *The Church in the French Era* (Toronto: Ryerson, 1966); John S.
     Moir, *The Church in the British Era* (Toronto: Ryerson, 1972); John Webster
     Grant, *The Church in the Canadian Era* (Toronto: Ryerson, 1972); updated and
     expanded edition by John G. Stackhouse (Vancouver: Regent College, 1998);
     Robert T. Handy, *A History of the Churches in the United States and Canada*
     (Oxford: Oxford University Press, 1976); Mark A. Noll, *A History of Christiani-
     ty in the United States and Canada* (Grand Rapids, MI: Eerdmans, 1992); and
     Terrence Murphy and Roberto Perin, eds., *A Concise History of Christianity in*

B. FROM NEW FRANCE TO CONFEDERATION

Permanent settlement on the Gulf of St. Lawrence began in the early seventeenth century, with a royal charter of 1603 granting to a Huguenot merchant the fur trade monopoly in the North American lands claimed by France. In the early years of colonization and until the revocation of the Edict of Nantes (1598) in 1685, both Protestant and Roman Catholic communities grew up in New France, and extended in the mid seventeenth century to Port Royal and Acadia. Officially a royal French colony from 1663, New France was predominantly Roman Catholic. This was particularly due to the efforts of Champlain, who extended the colony, which he envisaged as Roman Catholic and firmly under the dominion of France. As the small communities scattered along the St. Lawrence River extended their trading and missionary work (reserved solely to the Roman Catholic Church) into the Great Lakes and down the Mississippi, struggles with both English and Spanish colonies ensued over local issues or as extensions of European wars between their respective mother countries. By the Treaty of Utrecht in 1713, the French lost Hudson Bay, Newfoundland, and Acadia to the British and retreated to the original lands along the St. Lawrence that constituted New France, as well as to outposts such as Cape Breton.

Such Protestant influence as there was in the French-speaking colonies of the New World declined after the decision to exclude further Protestant colonization in 1627 and had disappeared long before 1685. During the seventeenth century, and particularly after the arrival in 1659 of the vicar-apostolic Laval, who was made first Bishop of Quebec in 1674, and directly subject to Rome, the Roman Catholic influence was strengthened. Life in the colony became thoroughly Catholic through the influence of schools, seminaries, colleges, and charitable institutions run primarily

---

Canada (Toronto: Oxford University Press, 1996). Two recent collections of essays explore specific topics and contain extensive bibliographies: Marguerite Van Die, ed., *Religion and Public Life in Canada: Historical and Comparative Perspectives* (Toronto: University of Toronto Press, 2001); and David Lyon and Marguerite Van Die, eds., *Rethinking Church, State, and Modernity: Canada Between Europe and America* (Toronto: University of Toronto Press, 2001). See also E.R. Norman, *The Conscience of the State in North America* (Cambridge: Cambridge University Press, 1968); and for the basic historical documents, see John S. Moir, ed., *Church and State in Canada 1627–1867* (Toronto: McClelland & Stewart, 1967).

by the numerous orders that flocked into the colony at that time. Since senior clergy were also influential in the governing structures of New France, particularly as members of the Council, and the Church derived income from sources, such as tithes, regulated by the civil law of the colony, it is clear that its position in law was that of an established church.[2]

By the eighteenth century, the ultramontanist claims of a predominantly French clergy found a less receptive hearing from the native-born Canadians who resented the dominance of the clergy in civil government as well as their escalating demands for financial support. However, with the fall of Quebec in 1759 and the capitulation of Montreal in 1760 to the victorious British in the Seven Years War, the Roman Catholic Church as the sole major surviving institution was thrust into the role of preserver of the French-Canadian identity in Quebec.

By the Treaty of Paris in 1763, France ceded to Great Britain virtually all her lands in the New World but it was also provided, as the Treaty of Utrecht had done in 1713, that Roman Catholics could worship "according to the rites of the Romish church as far as the laws of Great Britain permit."[3] Given that the penal laws against Roman Catholics in England continued in force until the *Relief Act, 1778,*[4] and were not completely removed until the *Emancipation Act, 1829,*[5] the ambiguity in this provision was clarified by the Commission[6] of 1763 given to General James Murray, the first British governor of Quebec, to work toward the establishment of the Church of England. Moreover, Murray was also empowered to appoint priests, take an inventory of church property, establish Protestant schools and parishes, and to decline to admit in any way to any ecclesiastical jurisdiction of Rome.

In fact, the Roman Catholic population was permitted freedom of worship and practice and relationships with the British colonial governors became amicable; indeed, it was agreed that a new bishop could be

---

2   M.H. Ogilvie, "What is a Church by Law Established?" (1990) 28 O.H.L.J. 179.

3   The standard collection of historical materials is W.P.M. Kennedy, ed., *Statutes, Treaties and Documents of the Canadian Constitution, 1713–1929* (Toronto: Oxford University Press, 1930). The standard student collection is John S. Moir, ed., *Church and State in Canada 1627–1867* (Toronto: McClelland and Stewart Ltd., 1967). The following references are to Moir's collection: Treaty of Utrecht, Article XIV (Moir 23–24); and Treaty of Paris, Article II (Moir 77).

4   (U.K.) 18 Geo. III, c. 60 (1778).

5   (U.K.) 10 Geo. IV, c. 7 (1829).

6   Moir above note 3 at 78–80.

consecrated in France in 1766 without any British recognition of papal jurisdiction. If native Canadian priests were to be ordained, a bishop was required; otherwise the Roman Catholic population would in time be without priests because it was also forbidden for priests to come from France. The Roman Catholic Church became freer from government interference under the British than had been the case before the Conquest and received an unprecedented degree of freedom for any country at the time by the *Quebec Act, 1774*.[7] In addition to providing for the continuation of the seigneurial system of land tenure and of the civil law (although English criminal law was introduced), the Act also permitted Roman Catholics to enjoy freedom of religion subject only to the royal supremacy and allowed Roman Catholic clergy to receive and enjoy "their accustomed Dues and Rights" from Roman Catholic subjects. Religious orders were, however, deprived of their property. At the same time, the Act further provided for the encouragement of the Protestant religion and for its maintenance and support.

The question of which was the established church in Quebec was clarified the following year in the Instructions[8] to Governor Guy Carleton, which stated that only the free exercise of religion was to be permitted to Roman Catholics and that they were not entitled to any of the rights and privileges of an established church, which were to be reserved for the "Protestant Church of England." The Instructions placed further restrictions on Roman Catholics in relation to the acknowledgement of foreign supremacies in both civil and ecclesiastical matters, appointments to benefices, entitlement to Protestant-owned property, missionary and educational activities and other matters, which clearly restricted the expansion of Roman Catholicism in the colony.

That the Roman Catholic Church in Quebec would not enjoy privileges after it was ceded to Great Britain in 1763, which it had before, had been earlier hinted by the provisions made for Nova Scotia, which had been ceded in 1713. When in 1758 sufficient British colonization had led to the calling of the colony's first Assembly, that first session enacted two statutes, which established the Church of England in Nova Scotia[9] and granted freedom of religion to Protestant Dissenters but restricted Roman

---

7   (U.K.) 14 Geo. III, c. 83 (1774).
8   Moir above note 3 at 99–103.
9   (N.S.) 32 Geo. II, c. 5 (1758).

Catholic rights to that of worship, without the right to own property or make wills.[10]

Nevertheless, the freedoms granted by the *Quebec Act* were unprecedented in either the mother country or even in many of the other American colonies, and contrasted most favourably with the continuous physical persecution of Protestants by the Roman Catholic states of Europe. The generosity of British colonial policy toward Roman Catholics in Quebec and the amicable relationship struck with the hierarchy was repaid by their loyalty to the Crown during the American Revolutionary War, as well as at the time of the French Revolution. The ardent anti-Catholicism more characteristic of Puritanism than of the Anglican establishment on the one hand, and the violence and secularism of the French Revolution on the other hand, were rendered unattractive to all but a handful of French-speaking colonists and ensured the neutrality, if not warm loyalty, of Quebec to the Crown.

The migration of Protestant loyalists from the United States to the western part of Quebec, now Ontario, led to demands for accommodation in relation to law, education, representative government, and religion, since the numerical predominance of French-speaking Roman Catholics resulted in a vastly different political environment from that experienced in the pre-Revolutionary colonies to the south. Again, the experience in the previous quarter century in the Maritime colonies presaged that of Quebec at the end of the eighteenth century.

Although scattered settlements had grown up in Nova Scotia (including New Brunswick and Prince Edward Island at that time) following British military successes against the French in the early eighteenth century, it was not until Governor Lawrence's 1759 invitation to New Englanders to migrate north, promising familiar township and court systems, that substantial immigration occurred. It was largely Congregationalists, Baptists, and Presbyterians, rather than Episcopalians, who responded, and they remained neutral during the Revolutionary War. This partly reflected their recent religious renewal, or "Great Awakening" resulting from the itinerant preaching of Henry Alline,[11] who was strongly apoliti-

---

10   (N.S.) 32 Geo. II, c. 2 (1758).

11   J.M. Bumstead, *Henry Alline, 1748–1784* (Toronto: University of Toronto Press, 1971); George A. Rawlyk, *Ravished by the Spirit: Religious Revivals, Baptists, and Henry Alline* (Kingston: McGill-Queen's University Press, 1983); and George A. Rawlyk, ed., *Henry Alline: Selected Writings* (New York: Paulist, 1987).

cal, but also reflected the accommodations reluctantly instituted in relation to government and religious toleration, when it early became clear that Nova Scotia would not in fact become a strongly Anglican colony, notwithstanding the legal establishment of the Church of England.

Despite the determined efforts of the first Anglican bishop in Canada, Bishop Charles Inglis[12] of Nova Scotia, who was consecrated in 1787 as Bishop of all the Maritimes, Newfoundland, Quebec, and Bermuda, religious diversity quickly required legal recognition of religious pluralism in the colony. In 1783, the prohibition against the ownership of property by Roman Catholics was repealed, as was the ban against priests in the colony;[13] the ban on Roman Catholic school teachers was repealed in 1786;[14] although it was not until 1827 that Roman Catholics enjoyed the full legal privileges that had been granted to Protestant dissenters in 1758 when the colony was founded,[15] and 1830 when they could sit in the Council or House of Assembly or hold civil or military office without swearing an oath of allegiance to the Crown.[16]

When New Brunswick was established as a separate colony in 1784, the first session of the Legislative Assembly, in 1786, enacted legislation establishing the Church of England but also securing freedom of religious practice for Protestant Dissenters.[17] In contrast to the Nova Scotia legislation, the New Brunswick act provided that Dissenting ministers be licensed before performing ministerial functions and also required oaths of fidelity and allegiance to the Crown,[18] provisions which may have been more acceptable than in Nova Scotia because New Brunswick was at the time religiously more homogeneous as an English Anglican stronghold. In 1830, legislation re-enacted the *British Relief Act* to grant full rights of subjects to Roman Catholics and Dissenters,[19] although later legislation continued to refer to the Church of England as the established church,[20] as remained the case in Nova Scotia.

---

12   Judith Fingard, *The Anglican Design in Loyalist Nova Scotia 1783–1816* (London: S.P.C.K., 1972).
13   (N.S.) 23 Geo. III, c. 9 (1783).
14   (N.S.) 26 Geo. III, c. 1 (1786).
15   (N.S.) 7 Geo. IV, c. 18 (1827).
16   (N.S.) 11 Geo. IV, c. 1 (1830).
17   (N.B.) 26 Geo. III, c. 4 (1786).
18   *Ibid.* s. 15.
19   (N.B.) 10 & 11 Geo. IV, c. 33 (1830).
20   (N.B.) 6 Wm. IV, c. 3 (1836).

When Prince Edward Island was established as a separate colony in 1802, the Church of England was also established by legislation identical to that in Nova Scotia, with freedom of religion granted only to Protestant Dissenters.[21] Again, in 1830, legislation similar to the *British Relief Act* was enacted for Roman Catholics,[22] Prince Edward Island, like Nova Scotia, being more religiously pluralistic than New Brunswick.

Since there would appear to be no legislation in these provinces disestablishing the Church of England, in legal theory at least, it is still the established church! However, legislation in each province dating from the late eighteenth century in relation to a variety of matters, from rights to conduct marriage, to vote, to hold property, and to hold military and civil office, among others, have resulted in complete equality before the law for all religious groups. Indeed, this could be said to be the case since the 1850s when the practice of Anglican bishops automatically joining legislative councils came to an end. While government funding for the Anglican establishments had always been shaky, it had also come to an end by this time and the Anglican churches were obliged to become voluntaryist, establishing incorporated "Church Societies" in each diocese to raise and manage funds, thereby joining the Methodists, Baptists, Presbyterians, Roman Catholics, and other religious groups as voluntary in nature.

The religious, cultural, and political diversity introduced into the western part of Quebec by the Loyalists, and by increased immigration from Great Britain, resulted in 1791 in the division of Quebec into Upper and Lower Canada, each with its own colonial government and religious arrangement. The *Constitutional Act, 1791*,[23] was enacted to make provision for the religious settlement, *inter alia*, after the Order in Council of 24 August 1791[24] effected the division. Church and state relations in the two Canadas were dealt with in sections 36–40.

Sections 36 and 37 provided that the Crown would authorize the Governor or Lieutenant Governor of each of the colonies to appropriate one-seventh of the lands to be used "solely to the Maintenance and Support of a Protestant Clergy within the Province in which the same shall

---

21   (P.E.I.) 43 Geo. III, c. 6 (1802).

22   (P.E.I.) 11 Geo. IV, c. 7 (1830).

23   (U.K.) 31 Geo. III, c. 31 (1791).

24   A.G. Doughty and J. McArthur, eds., *Canada, Constitutional Documents, 1791–1818*, (Ottawa: The Queen's Printer, 1914) at 3–5.

be situated." Sections 38, 39, and 40 provided for the erection of parsonages or rectories within every township or parish "according to the Establishment of the Church of England" and their endowment. Moreover, presentation to these rectories was to be made by the Bishop of Nova Scotia "according to the Laws and Canons of the Church of England." While the provisions for the rectors clearly indicated that only the Church of England was to be benefited, the ambiguity in the references to a "Protestant Clergy" led to bitter disputes over the clergy reserves in the next half-century,[25] although the debates in the British Parliament prior to the passage of the Act indicated that the Church of England was meant in the legislation.[26]

In 1791, in Lower Canada it is estimated that there were about 100,000 Roman Catholics spread throughout 118 parishes under the oversight of the Bishop of Quebec. Although their precise numbers are unknown, the numbers of Anglicans and Presbyterians were minuscule in comparison. In 1791, for example, the Anglican Diocese of Quebec contained only three parishes and four missions served by nine clergy, and there were two Church of Scotland congregations; nevertheless, rivalry between Roman Catholics and Anglicans for establishment status in Lower Canada was a dominant political theme for the first half of the nineteenth century.

The central figure in the campaign by the Roman Catholic Church in Lower Canada for complete freedom from colonial supervision and full legal recognition was the Bishop of Quebec, Bishop Plessis, who attained the bishopric in 1806 and died in 1825. Plessis was instrumental in ensuring the loyalty of the French Roman Catholic population of Quebec to the British in the War of 1812, and in exchange was granted a larger government subsidy, a seat on the Legislative Council, and some loosening of government control over Roman Catholicism. In addition, in 1819, after negotiations that included the Vatican, Plessis secured the division of the single Diocese of Quebec into five districts and the appointment of

---

25   J.S. Moir, *Church and State in Canada West: Three Studies in the Relation of Denominationalism and Nationalism, 1841–1867* (Toronto: University of Toronto Press, 1959); Alan Wilson, *The Clergy Reserves of Upper Canada* (Toronto: University of Toronto Press, 1968); and Curtis Fahey, *In His Name: The Anglican Experience in Upper Canada, 1791–1854* (Ottawa: Carleton University Press, 1991).

26   Hansard XXIX, 1098; 8 April 1791 per William Pitt at 429.

four vicars-apostolic for Prince Edward Island and New Brunswick, Montreal, Upper Canada, and the Northwest.

The Anglican Bishop of Quebec, Jacob Mountain (1792–1825) led the unsuccessful resistance to the growing authority of the Roman Catholic Church in Lower Canada, arguing that the Church of England should be formally acknowledged as the church by law established in Lower Canada. While neither the Roman Catholic Church nor the Church of England enjoyed proper legal establishment status after 1763, the Church of England slowly expanded its influence in the colony, although without much government assistance. In 1796, Governor Simcoe decided that tithes would not be collected; and the 675,000 acres of clergy reserves in Lower Canada remained undeveloped and therefore yielded little profit. Moreover, the Church of Scotland claimed an equal share as an established church in the United Kingdom. Only a handful of parish schools were opened, and it was not until the 1820s that significant action was taken to establish rectories.

Meanwhile, throughout the 1820s, 1830s, and 1840s, the Roman Catholic Church in Lower Canada experienced renewal and the re-establishment of links with both the French church and the Vatican, acquiring thereby an increasingly ultramontanist character. The liberal political ideas and the anticlericalism of the leaders of the Rebellion in Lower Canada in 1837 once more had the effect of strengthening the alliance of the Roman Catholic Church with the British colonial governors, resulting in greater prestige and influence for the Church. In 1844, the ecclesiastical province of Canada was created with an archbishop at Quebec and bishops at Montreal, Kingston, and Toronto, and from 1847, at Newfoundland, Ottawa, and the Northwest. Under Archbishop Bourget (1840–1880), ultramontanist influences became expressed in attempts to counter what were perceived as threats to the faith and to the social cohesiveness of the French-speaking inhabitants of Lower Canada, such as American economic individualism, democratic policies, social egalitarianism, urbanization, and intellectual innovations. Importing ideas and personnel from the European church, the Church in Lower Canada sought to control schools and colleges, charitable institutions, and frameworks for intellectual life such as the *Institut Canadien*, founded in 1844, but forbidden to Roman Catholics after 1869 when its activities strayed too far in promoting liberal democracy and individualistic capitalism.

Although more successful initially in its claims to be the established church in Upper Canada, the Church of England also ultimately failed to win that prize as it had done in Lower Canada. When Upper Canada came into existence in 1791, its population consisted of about 6,000 Loyalists thinly scattered down the St. Lawrence River and the shores of Lakes Ontario and Erie. However, as the population grew, it became clear that religious diversity would be characteristic, and render impossible the establishment of the paternalistic, Anglican, and Loyalist replica of England contemplated by Governor Simcoe and other colonial officers in the first two or three generations of its existence.

While Methodists were the dominant religious group before 1812, by which time the population was about 90,000, in that and the next decade extensive immigration from England increased the number of Anglicans, while immigration from Scotland and Ireland increased both Presbyterian and Roman Catholic numbers. Smaller groups of Baptists, Congregationalists, Moravians, Mennonites, and Lutherans were also found in Upper Canada by the early nineteenth century. Ministering to small, scattered settlements, the clergy of these denominations were largely engaged in the first two decades of the nineteenth century in stabilizing the presence of their denominations in Upper Canada and in mission work to secure their growth.

However, as the colony was being surveyed and clergy reserve lots identified, it became increasingly clear that controversy would erupt once revenues from the clergy reserves, which amounted to 2.4 million acres, started to flow to the Church of England alone. By 1819, the claims of exclusive access to the clergy reserves by the Church of England as the established church pursuant to section 36 of the *Constitutional Act* were challenged by Robert Gourlay, who resented the restrictions of land sales thereby entailed, and by the Niagara Church of Scotland congregation. In 1819, that congregation petitioned the Lieutenant Governor, Sir Peregrine Maitland, for £100 to rebuild their church, which was burned down by the Americans during the War of 1812, on the ground that the Church of Scotland was the established church in Scotland. The question was passed on to the Law Officers of the Crown in London, who decided that the clergy reserve funds should be divided between the two established churches. Maitland informed only the Anglican members of the Executive Council of this response, which only became known publicly in Upper Canada in 1839, by which time the issue had moved to one of extreme contention in the colony.

To secure an Anglican monopoly over the clergy reserves, John Strachan, originally a Presbyterian, but by now the minister of an Anglican congregation in York and a member of the Executive Council, obtained a charter in 1819 for a clergy corporation for the purpose of assuming control of and managing the reserves on behalf of the Church of England. This served to inflame the opposition in the colony to an Anglican establishment, led primarily by the Church of Scotland, which at first wished to have a co-equal establishment, but which relinquished this idea once other religious groups in the colony joined forces in opposition to any establishment whatsoever. Particularly eloquent in the fight was Egerton Ryerson, a young Methodist minister who responded most effectively to Archdeacon Strachan's claims in the colonial press, the pulpit, and the lecture hall.

legal concessions were made to Protestant Dissenters and ... tion to freedom of religious ...es,[28] and to be free from pay- ...[29] as well as not to bear arms ...erty.[31] But the Church of Eng- ...until the Rebellion in Upper Canada in 1837, when the clergy reserves proved to be one of the significant issues for which reform was demanded. In 1834, a majority resolution by the Legislative Assembly that the reserve lands be sold and the proceeds devoted to the establishment of a public education system was defeated by the Executive Council. Then, in 1836, in the last hours of his administration, the Lieutenant Governor, Sir John Colborne, erected forty-four Anglican rectories and endowed each with four hundred acres.

In the ensuing Rebellion, in 1837, in which political and economic issues were foremost, the churches largely rallied round the government, although on terms of reform of the government and of equality for all denominations in Upper Canada. In his subsequent report to the British government on the rebellions, Lord Durham was highly critical of the virtual monopoly on the clergy reserves enjoyed by the Church of England, which in 1840 was supported by about twenty percent of the population of Upper Canada. Although no specific recommendation was

---

27   (Can.) 14 & 15 Vict., c. 175 (1851).

28   (U.C.) 38 Geo. III, c. 4 (1798); (U.C.) 1 Wm. IV, c. 1 (1829).

29   (U.C.) 2 Geo. IV, c. 32 (1822).

30   (U.C.) 48 Geo. III, c. 1 (1808); (U.C.) 49 Geo. III, c. 6 (1809).

31   (U.C.) 9 Geo. IV, c. 2 (1828).

made, in 1840 Parliament repealed sections 36 and 37 of the *Constitutional Act, 1791*, and provided for the sale of the reserves.[32] The proceeds of the sale went to the Church of England (forty-two percent), the Church of Scotland (twenty-one percent) with the remainder (thirty-seven percent) to be divided among other denominations, including Roman Catholics, Methodists, and Baptists.

In 1851, the legislature of Canada repealed sections 38, 39, and 40 of the *Constitutional Act, 1791*, in relation to the rectories and guaranteed religious equality to all within the colony.[33] In 1853, Parliament granted the legislature of Canada power to alter the appropriation of the clergy reserve proceeds as long as the three-fold basic division was maintained,[34] and pursuant to this, the legislature enacted the *Clergy Reserves Act*,[35] in 1854, which stated the desirability of removing all connection between church and state, and thereafter providing for the payment of existing annual stipends for life, required that all other sums be paid to the municipalities.

The reunion of the two Canadas in 1841 had little immediate importance for the sectarian rivalries over the clergy reserves; in fact, none of the denominations was particularly happy with the outcome or with the protracted and highly politicized distribution process. Moreover, in the 1830s, as the crisis in relation to the clergy reserves was coming to a head, equally sharp differences of opinion over the embryonic school and university systems in Upper Canada appeared and these erupted into a new bout of sectarianism in the 1840s and 1850s.

Throughout these decades, both Dissenting denominations and Roman Catholics enjoyed strengthening numbers from immigration and were largely able to stabilize into working religious institutions with established congregations and parishes, property, and personnel, sufficient to ensure their futures in the British North American colonies. Some Protestant groups remained divided, such as the Methodists and Presbyterians, each of which were represented by several denominational organizations in Canada West, reflecting parent institutions in either

---

32   (U.K.) 3 & 4 Vict., c. 78 (1840).
33   Above note 27. However, the patents signed by Colborne are still valid: Moir, above note 25 at 190–191.
34   (U.K.) 16 Vict., c. 21 (1853)
35   (Can.) 18 Vict., c. 2 (1854).

Great Britain or the United States. But the Presbyterians finally united into one national denomination in 1875 and the Methodists in 1884. Nevertheless, ensuring the religious education of children and the university education of clergy and of others who could be expected to play leadership roles in Canadian society resulted in a new round of controversy over funding for schools and universities within Canada West.

Although the common school bill presented in the Legislature of Canada in 1841 sought to establish a national, secular, elementary school system for both Canadas, its lack of support from both Anglicans and Roman Catholics, who wanted confessional schools, resulted in an amendment to permit minority confessional schools wherever desired.[36] In 1843, the attempt to provide for a single school system for both Canadas was abandoned with legislation providing a denominational system for Canada East,[37] but permitting dissentient schools, both Roman Catholic and Protestant, for Canada West;[38] although this was ended in 1859 when further legislation provided for a Roman Catholic/public school split.[39] Legislative tinkering with the denominational school system established in the 1840s, continued to the eve of Confederation, and was then entrenched in the *Constitution* of Canada pursuant to section 93 of the *Constitution Act, 1867*.[40] Throughout this period, the Roman Catholic Church was most insistent on retaining a publicly funded sectarian school system, while most Protestants regarded or came to regard a single public school system as more appropriate to a religiously plural society.

Even more controversial in the 1840s was the question of public funding for the newly established denominational universities. Although chartered in 1826, Kings College in Toronto started teaching in 1843 as an Anglican foundation. In the early 1840s, other denominations also started their own universities: Victoria College was founded in 1842 by the Wesleyan Methodists, Queen's University in 1842 by the Church of Scotland, and Knox College in 1844 by the Free Church.[41] Non-Anglicans bitterly resented public funding of Kings College, while their own institutions

---

36 (Can.) 4 & 5 Vict., c. 18 (1841).
37 (Can.) 8 Vict., c. 41 (1845); (Can.) 9 Vict., c. 27 (1846).
38 (Can.) 7 Vict., c. 29 (1843).
39 (Can.) 22 Vict., c. 65 (1859).
40 (Can.) 24 Vict., c. 15 (1861); (Can.) 26 Vict., c. 5 (1863).
41 D.C. Masters, *Protestant Church Colleges in Canada*, (Toronto: University of Toronto Press, 1966).

struggled to survive on a voluntaryist basis. In 1849, after several unsuccessful bills proposing various settlements, the Legislature secularized Kings College into the University of Toronto, which alone received public funding. No religious tests were required of students or faculty, and clergy could not become its president or chancellor. In 1852, Bishop Strachan obtained a royal charter for Trinity College, a new Anglican foundation, with the result that Canada West had four denominational universities and one secular or "godless" one, in the words of Bishop Strachan.

In the 1850s nine more denominational colleges were established in Canada West — five Roman Catholic, and four by the Methodist Episcopalians, Congregationalists, Baptists, and Free Church Presbyterians. Over the course of the second half of the nineteenth century these institutions were granted access to public funds, as they became increasingly secular in nature.

With the exception of public funding for denominational schools in the two Canadas, church and state had become largely separated by 1867. That is not to say that Canada had become a secular society because the religious history of the period would suggest otherwise. Whatever the denominational rivalries might be, all were agreed that Canada should be a Christian society whose civil laws and practices reflected Christian teaching. And the history of the period clearly shows that it was, although cracks and strains in the homogeneity and hegemony of Christianity in Canada were becoming evident as the century progressed.[42]

---

42 Over the past decade a number of outstanding studies of the Christian culture of late nineteenth-century Canada have appeared: John Webster Grant, *A Profession of Spires: Religion in Nineteenth Century Ontario* (Toronto: University of Toronto Press, 1988); Marguerite Van Die, *An Evangelical Mind: Nathaniel Burwash and the Evangelical Tradition in Canada, 1839–1918* (Kingston & Montreal: McGill-Queen's University Press, 1989); William Westfall, *Two Worlds: The Protestant Culture of Nineteenth Century Ontario* (Kingston & Montreal: McGill-Queen's University Press, 1989); George A. Rawlyk, ed., *The Canadian Protestant Experience 1760–1990* (Burlington, ON: Welch, 1990); Michael Gauvreau, *The Evangelical Century: College and Creed in English Canada from the Great Revival to the Great Depression* (Kingston & Montreal: McGill-Queen's University Press, 1991); Phyllis D. Airhart, *Serving the Present Age: Revivalism, Progressivism and the Methodist Tradition in Canada* (Kingston & Montreal: McGill-Queen's University Press, 1992); and David B. Marshall, *Secularizing the Faith: Canadian Protestant Clergy and the Crisis of Belief, 1850–1940* (Toronto: University of Toronto Press, 1992).

Although events in the Maritime colonies in relation to church and state in the decades before Confederation did not present such dramatic confrontations as the Rebellions of 1837, the issues involving religion were similar to those in the two Canadas: halting the establishment claims of the Church of England and ensuring equality before the law for all denominations in relation to education, public aid, and public recognition. The legal establishment of the Church of England was never reflected in public support to any great extent. While Kings College in Windsor, Nova Scotia, was founded in 1802, and funded as an exclusively Anglican institution, all of whose faculty and students were required to subscribe to the Thirty-Nine Articles, suggestion that clergy reserves be established to finance the established churches throughout the region largely failed to bear fruit. By the 1830s, New Brunswick was selling crown lands without making provision for the Church of England; in Prince Edward Island the reserves had been returned to the Crown without any provision whatsoever for the established church; and in Nova Scotia, the small land endowments received were the target of such great jealousy among the other denominations that they were not enlarged upon. As stated earlier, by 1830 the civil disabilities previously imposed on Protestants and Roman Catholics had largely disappeared through legislative action.

In the 1830s and 1840s, Roman Catholics, Presbyterians, and Baptists especially flourished in the Maritime provinces, renewed by waves of immigration, particularly from Scotland, but also by religious revivals, particularly among the Baptists. This was a period of consolidation for these groups, all of whose adherents enjoyed access to a rudimentary public school system. On the other hand, denominational rivalry flared in relation to universities, given the funding of Kings College alone from the public purse.

The second earliest foundation, in 1817, was Pictou Academy, started by Thomas McCulloch to provide both Arts and Theology, primarily for future Presbyterian ministers. There were no religious tests, so that the Academy quickly acquired a non-denominational character. When Dalhousie finally started classes in 1838, although building had been started in 1820, McCulloch became the first principal and the faculty was predominantly Presbyterian. Dalhousie was officially a non-denominational institution from the outset, leaving Presbyterians without a college since Pictou Academy did not long survive McCulloch's departure. Nevertheless, denominationally-funded colleges became the norm in the

Maritimes in the course of the nineteenth century, with the secular University of New Brunswick alone joining Dalhousie in 1860 as a public institution.

As in the two Canadas, the principle of separation of church and state had been largely achieved in practice in the Maritime colonies prior to Confederation: the Church of England was "established" in law only and received no state preference, rather all religious institutions enjoyed the same equality before the law.

The evolution of the denominational school system in Newfoundland contrasts with developments in the other British colonies. Recognized as a colony first in 1824 and granted a legislature in 1832, a stable, year-round population in Newfoundland evolved in the course of the nineteenth century, where before, temporary settlement during the fishing season had been the norm. Numerically, Irish Roman Catholics comprised about one-half of the population of Newfoundland in the first half of the nineteenth century, while the Church of England enjoyed the support of another one-third of the population. The remainder were Methodists, Presbyterians, and Congregationalists, in that order.

When in the 1830s overseas financial support for the Church of England was gradually withdrawn, the colonial government was actively petitioned to substitute funding for Anglican schools. Roman Catholics and Methodists reacted so angrily when it appeared that such funding would be forthcoming, that the Newfoundland legislature decided, in 1852, to grant funding to a number of denominational schools. This remained the case until 1949 when the British colony joined Confederation by the Treaty of Union, which entrenched that right.[43]

Although Roman Catholic missionaries followed the fur traders and trappers into the Canadian West before the conquest of New France, the first permanent settlement was established on the Red River in 1812 — a community predominantly of Presbyterian Scots, established by Lord Selkirk. Lord Selkirk also urged Bishop Plessis to provide missionaries for the Roman Catholics in the Red River valley and subsequently Roman Catholic missionary activity in the West was renewed. While the Hudson's Bay Company officially supported the Church of England in its territories, initially most of the permanent settlers were Presbyterians or Roman Catholics. Anglican missionaries subsequently arrived and the first Anglican bishop of Rupert's Land was consecrated in 1849. All three

---

43 *Newfoundland Act*, (U.K.) 12–13 Geo. VI, c. 22, Term 17 (1949).

denominations ministered not only to the new settlers but also to the Indigenous people in these territories.

The Hudson's Bay Company also supplied its early trading posts in British Columbia with Anglican chaplains from the 1820s onward, although Roman Catholic missionaries were also active on the West Coast from not long after. Other denominations followed their respective adherents, especially after the Gold Rush in the 1850s. The first Anglican Bishop of British Columbia was consecrated in 1859, a year after the colony of British Columbia was created. However, prior to Confederation, church/state issues did not arise in public life. The denominations were largely concerned with missionary work in scattered communities of settlers and the evangelization of the native populations, not political manoeuvring for state support.

By the eve of Confederation, Canada was or was about to become in all its parts a Christian nation. Indeed, in contrast to the United States and to Great Britain, it was a predominantly church-going collection of colonies. In pre-Confederation censuses, about ninety-five percent claimed to be members of a Christian denomination and church attendance studies show that church-going was far more common than in other Western countries. There were far fewer denominations than in the already religiously fragmented United States; the bulk of the population was found in five denominations: Anglican, Baptist, Methodist, Presbyterian, and Roman Catholic. It was entirely natural for the new Confederation to adopt the motto for the country suggested by Leonard Tilley, a devout Methodist, from Psalm 72:8 "He shall have dominion also from sea to sea."

But even in 1867, "His Dominion," as contemporaries often called Canada, had yet to resolve important public issues because of the basic religious duality of French Roman Catholicism and British Protestantism. In contrast to the United States, which had largely coalesced around the national myth of Americans as a chosen people set apart by God for a peculiar providential purpose to be revealed in God's own time, no national religious myth emerged around which to focus the new nation of Canada. The sole provision in the *Constitution* in 1867 in section 93 relating to denominational schools pointed to a future not unlike the past: denominational rivalry for public school funding. In short, religious business as usual.[44]

---

44   Handy, above note 1 at 258–261.

C. FROM CONFEDERATION TO *CHARTER*

The Christian churches in Canada were enthusiastic about Confederation and about the possibilities for national expansion that it presented, although the Roman Catholic Church was somewhat disappointed in not achieving a constitutional guarantee for the informally recognized Roman Catholic schools in the Maritimes. The political unification of the country from the Atlantic to Pacific Oceans over the course of the late nineteenth century prompted church unification along national denominational lines and also raised the ecumenical hope of denominational unification to form a national Protestant church.

The first confessional group to unify into a single national church were the Presbyterians in 1875, overcoming the fragmented Presbyterian inheritance from Scotland which had hitherto been reflected in the colonies. The Methodists followed suit in 1884 uniting both English and American originating denominations into a national church. While the Church of England had largely established a diocesan organization for most of the country by 1867, in 1893 it became an autonomous church no longer subject to the Archbishop of Canterbury, and chose its first Primate in that year. National organizations continued to elude both Baptists and Lutherans, as they still do today; however, some mergers occurred, thereby reducing the competing groups within their respective confessions.

All of the Christian churches, after Confederation, set about extensive missionary activities in Western Canada. In Manitoba, in particular, Protestant/Roman Catholic tensions, which were never far from the surface nationally, erupted around 1870 when Manitoba joined Confederation. From the 1850s onward, hostility between these camps had grown, exacerbated by a number of factors including denominational schools; the increasing confidence of the Roman Catholic hierarchy in Quebec in asserting its claims, backed by the ultramontanist renewal of Roman Catholicism worldwide at the time; Protestant perceptions of "papal aggression"; and the large Irish immigration to Canada bringing a new sectarianism between Fenians and Orangemen.

Against this background, the revolt of the French Metis in Manitoba under Louis Riel in 1869 to protect their territory, and the subsequent murder of a militant Orangeman, Thomas Scott, inflamed religious and ethnic hatreds. The revolt was put down by a Canadian expeditionary force in 1870 and Manitoba joined Confederation by an act that guaranteed the education rights of Roman Catholic and Protestant minorities in the province.[45] The dramatic reappearance of Riel from banishment in the United States to lead the Northwest Rebellion in 1885 to establish an independent Metis nation rekindled French Catholic/British Protestant feelings, particularly after the hanging of Riel when it was over. Sectarian hatred continued to be inflamed by the attempt to create a single English-language school system in Manitoba, finally settled in 1896 by Prime Minister Laurier who procured a compromise whereby Roman Catholic instruction could be given after school hours. The revival of denominational school battles in 1905 when Saskatchewan and Alberta joined Confederation confirmed that Roman Catholic/Protestant rivalries were far from settled.

If denominational school funding was one area where religion and law intersected in the late nineteenth century, the attempts by Protestants to implement the "social gospel" in Canada through legislation proved to be another such intersection.

With the exception of many Anglicans, post-Confederation Protestants were strongly influenced by the Evangelical revival dating from the late eighteenth century in both the United States and Great Britain. Methodists, Free Church Presbyterians, Baptists, and Congregationalists were the primary mediators of evangelization in Canada, which began by emphasizing a personal conversion experience and the sanctification of personal life, and then stretched to the pursuit of the sanctification of the whole of society by all available legal means. Evangelicalism was particularly strong among the professional, business, and political sections of Canadian society, and many religious institutions, schools, colleges, and charitable institutions continue to bear witness today to their personal generosity in promoting the general social good.

The aim of Evangelical Protestants, whose leadership was largely Methodist and Presbyterian, was to enshrine Christian moral principles in Canadian life in all its aspects. Emphasis was placed on moral reform usually in the negative sense, of expelling sinful conduct from the lives of all citizens. The shift in emphasis from private to public and from theology to conduct occurred within the Protestant denominations when Darwinian natural science and Biblical historical criticism caused increasing doubts among the educated classes about Biblical fundamen-

---

45   *Manitoba Act*, (Can.) 1870, 33 Vict. c. 3, s. 22 (1870).

tals as preached from the time of the Reformation.[46] However, the desire to reform society was also a sincere expression of a heartfelt faith, as had already been shown in early nineteenth-century England, where Evangelicals were in the forefront of social reforms, such as the eradication of slavery and the improvement of factory conditions, by the use of legislation in a way unknown to that time in the common law tradition.

So too, in late Victorian Canada, Evangelicals were in the forefront of social reforms to improve the lot of factory workers, children, and the poor, but also in the forefront of moral reform by legislation, since they firmly believed that by creating the right social conditions, individual self-improvement and self-discipline would follow, and in turn reshape society generally. While a number of evils in late nineteenth-century Canada were regarded as ripe for eradication, several causes particularly exercised Evangelicals, such as Sabbath observance,[47] temperance,[48] and a general improvement in sexual morality. These campaigns were largely

---

46   Richard Allen, *The Social Passion: Religion and Social Reform in Canada, 1914–1918* (Toronto: University of Toronto Press, 1973); S.E.D. Shortt, *The Search for an Ideal: Six Canadian Intellectuals and their Convictions in an Age of Transition, 1890–1930* (Toronto: University of Toronto Press, 1976); A.B. McKillop, *A Disciplined Intelligence: Critical Inquiry and Canadian Thought in the Victorian Era* (Kingston & Montreal: McGill-Queen's University Press, 1979); Carl Berger, *Science, God and Nature in Victorian Canada* (Toronto: University of Toronto Press, 1983); Ramsay Cook, *The Regenerators: Social Criticism in Late Victorian English Canada* (Toronto: University of Toronto Press, 1985); Brian Fraser, *The Social Uplifters: Presbyterian Progressives and the Social Gospel in Canada, 1875–1915* (Waterloo: Waterloo-Lutheran Press, 1988); Michael Gauvreau, above note 42; Mariana Valverde, *The Age of Light, Soap and Water: Moral Reform in English Canada, 1885–1925* (Toronto: University of Toronto Press, 1991); David Marshall, above note 42; Jan Noel, *Canada Dry: Temperance Crusades Before Confederation* (Toronto: University of Toronto Press, 1995); Nancy Christie and Michael Gauvreau, *A Full-Orbed Christianity: The Protestant Churches and Social Welfare in Canada, 1900–1940* (Montreal: McGill-Queen's University Press, 1996); and Neil Semple, *The Lord's Dominion: A History of Methodism in Canada* (Montreal: McGill-Queen's University Press, 1996).

47   C. Armstrong and H.V. Nelles, *The Revenge of the Methodist Bicycle Company: Sunday Streetcars and Municipal Reform in Toronto, 1888–1897* (Toronto: University of Toronto Press, 1977).

48   Sharon Anne Cook, *"Through Sunshine and Shadow": The Women's Christian Temperance Union, Evangelicalism and Reform in Ontario, 1874–1930* (Kingston & Montreal: McGill-Queen's University Press, 1995); Jan Noel, above note 46.

successful, and by the end of the century, both provincial and federal leg-islation had been enacted across the country to curb "sinful" excesses by the population at large.

For Protestants, the last decades of the nineteenth century were heady years. Not only had they achieved considerable success, at least on the surface in their social improvement campaigns, but also because these campaigns brought together members of denominations that had been bitter rivals since the Reformation, which raised hopes for ecumeni-cal mergers. Merger talks involving Methodists, Presbyterians, Congrega-tionalists, Lutherans, Baptists, and even Anglicans occurred at one time or another until the time of the Second World War. The creation of the United Church in Canada in 1925 by the Methodists, Congregationalists, and about forty percent of the Presbyterians (as measured in 1941) was the most important merger, numerically and theologically, to result from this era of social co-operation.[49] For others, the social gospel campaigns of the late nineteenth and early twentieth centuries led into socialism, and many early leaders of the C.C.F.-N.D.P. were Protestant clergy, such as J.S. Woodsworth and Tommy Douglas.

If the advance of the social gospel in nineteenth-century Canada pro-duced pan-Protestant action, it also exacerbated Protestant/Roman Catholic rivalries. Strict Sabbath observance had its historical origins in Scottish and English Calvinism in the seventeenth century, and contrast-ed with the more relaxed understanding of the uses to which Christians might put the Sabbath that was characteristic of continental Roman Catholicism. At a time when Protestant/Roman Catholic sympathies were probably at their lowest ebb in Canadian history, Protestant attempts to enact federal legislation to control Sunday activities were regarded as a crass attempt to control Roman Catholics, as many Quebec M.P.s stated in the debates in the House of Commons while the Lord's Day bill was being considered. Together with the heating up of the denominational school issue in the 1890s, the historic division of Chris-tendom within Canada seemed very much in place at the beginning of the twentieth century.

Around the turn of the century, events in Europe played a role in changing the religious complexion of Canada that hitherto had experi-ence of only a handful of religious groups. Persecution in central and

---

49   N. Keith Clifford, *The Resistance to Church Union in Canada, 1904–1939* (Van-couver: U.B.C. Press, 1985).

eastern Europe brought a variety of new Christian groups to Canada, as well as the first large influx of Jews. Mennonites, Hutterites, Doukhobors,[50] Russian, Ukrainian, Greek and other Orthodox, as well as smaller groups of Catholics not in communion with Rome, sought refuge in Canada, settling largely in self-contained communities in the West.

Concurrently, from the United States, came members of the numerous Protestant denominations that had grown up in that country in the course of the late eighteenth and nineteenth centuries, winning converts among Canadian Protestants disenchanted with the historic Protestant churches and resulting in the further fragmentation of Protestantism within Canada. These included the churches of the Holiness Movement; such as the Christian and Missionary Alliance, the Pilgrim Holiness Church, the Church of the Nazarene, the Holiness Methodist Church, and the Standard Church of America. Of the Holiness Movement churches, the Salvation Army and the Pentecostal Church were most successful in ministering to those Canadian Protestants who were not quite socially respectable enough for the Anglican, Presbyterian, or United Churches.[51] Other quasi-Protestant religious groups also entered the country at this time including the Jehovah's Witnesses, the Mormons, and the Seventh Day Adventists.

The immigration of these Christian religious groups to Canada ensured that until the second half of the twentieth century, Canada remained a strongly Christian country. While the intensity with which some aspects of Christian life should be led, might differ from denomination to denomination, there was a widely-held consensus as to how Christian life should be led and that Canada should be a Christian society. Indeed, until the 1960s, Canada was a much more strongly church-going country than the United States, and was so regarded throughout the Western world. It was only in the 1970s that Canadian and American church-going statistics started to reverse, for reasons that are not yet entirely clear to social scientists.[52]

---

50 William Janzen, *Limits on Liberty: The Experience of Mennonite, Hutterite and Doukhobor Communities in Canada* (Toronto: University of Toronto Press, 1990).

51 John G. Stackhouse, Jr., *Canadian Evangelicalism in the Twentieth Century: An Introduction to its Character* (Toronto: University of Toronto Press, 1993); and Lloyd Mackey, *These Evangelical Churches of Ours* (Vancouver: Wood Lake Books, 1995).

52 David A. Martin, *A General Theory of Secularization* (New York: Harper Row, 1978).

Before 1982, when provisions in the *Canadian Charter of Rights and Freedoms* introduced the potential for change in the religious underpinnings of Canadian society, all religious groups enjoyed, in legal and constitutional theory at least, equality before the law. The only exceptions were those denominations that enjoyed a constitutionally entrenched right to denominational school funding. This is not to say that all religious groups enjoyed equal treatment and protection as a result of the application of the law. Many experienced unequal treatment because the law implicitly assumed the theological perspectives of Western European Christianity brought to Canada by the early French, British, and American settlers. Thus, Jews and Seventh Day Adventists experienced discrimination in relation to their religious belief that Saturday rather than Sunday was the Sabbath to which the Fourth Commandment referred; Mennonites and Hutterites experienced difficulties in relation to their religious beliefs in pacifism and oath-taking. And others, such as the Jehovah's Witnesses in Duplessis' Quebec, were quite simply persecuted.[53] The challenge of legal accommodation of religious pluralism within Canada was already as old as the first settlement of New France by Roman Catholics and Protestants, and would become even more daunting in light of the changes that took hold of Canadian society in the last decades of the twentieth century.

D. AFTER THE *CHARTER*

It is at this stage that the advantages of historical perspective fail. The factors influencing Canadian religious life at the end of the twentieth century can be identified, as can their impact on the intersection of law and religion. Their outcome remains for future generations to assess and experience. Urbanization, industrialization and de-industrialization, secularism, socialism, and affluence have all played their roles in the declining influence of the historic Christian churches on both sides of the Reformation divide in Canadian public life, as well as in the weakening of those churches, whether it be through the increasing institutional fragmentation of Protestantism or the indifference of many Christians to the

---

53 William Kaplan, *State and Salvation: The Jehovah's Witnesses and their Fight for Civil Rights* (Toronto: University of Toronto Press, 1989); and Gary Botting, *Fundamental Freedoms and Jehovah's Witnesses* (Calgary: University of Calgary Press, 1993).

teachings of Scripture especially on matters relating to human sexual expression.

In addition, changing global immigration patterns have introduced religious pluralism on a scale hitherto unknown, bringing to Canada members of non-Christian religious traditions, whether Moslem, Sikh, or Buddhist. The result is that since 1982, the religious history of Canada has come to be shaped more by the judiciary than by the religious institutions themselves as adherents of all religions try to make a space for themselves within Canada through the law, as well as the adherents of none.

Moreover, the language in which these accommodations are now sought has changed. A century ago, the language was that of the inherent theological superiority of one Christian denomination over another as measured by conformity to either Scripture and/or tradition. Today, the language is the secular language of equality, whether the issue is access to school funding, employment accommodation, abortion, or homosexual marriage. Whether or not the courts are really the most appropriate forum for resolving matters of fundamental importance for persons of all faiths, and none, remains to be seen.

Chapter Three

Religious Institutions in Canada

A. INTRODUCTION

The 1991 Religion Census of Canada[1] lists some ninety-two different religious groups large enough to be counted as separate religious institutions for census purposes. Six major religious groups are tabulated, all of which, except for Judaism, are comprised of numerous sub-groups, including four Catholic, fifty-six Protestant, nine Eastern Orthodox, eleven Eastern Non-Christian, and eleven para-religious groups. Each of these religious institutions typically has national, regional, and local organizations and structures, regulated partly by the laws and customs of the institution and partly by the laws of Canada, and it may be estimated, therefore, that there are well in excess of 10,000 individual units of these religious institutions operating within the country.

The succeeding chapters of this treatise will discuss the civil law applicable to religious institutions in Canada. This chapter will introduce briefly the various polities, internal organizational structures, and dispute resolution processes for the larger religious institutions, measured by census population membership.[2]

---

1   *Religion in Canada* (Ottawa: Statistics Canada, 1993).

2   The introductory nature of this chapter cannot be overstated. Its purpose is to alert lawyers acting for religious institutions to the necessity for consulting and considering the laws and customs of religious institutions when advising them.

Since the common law regards religious institutions as voluntary organizations, self-governed by contract, the courts defer to the laws and customs of religious institutions, enforcing these except where some internal irregularity has occurred or the rules of natural justice have not been applied.[3] In *Lakeside Colony of Hutterian Brethren* v. *Hofer*,[4] the Supreme Court of Canada looked to the constitution of the Hutterites, the articles of association of the colony, and the oral traditions and customs of the Hutterites, as well as federal incorporating legislation and the common law principles of natural justice in order to determine whether the correct procedure had been followed in expelling a colony member. Moreover, in *Pederson* v. *Fulton*,[5] a lower court declined to hear an appeal of an ecclesiastical dispute because, *inter alia*, it had not fully exhausted the hierarchy of church courts within the Roman Catholic Church, thereby indicating that ecclesiastical disputes should only be appealed into the civil courts after the highest internal tribunal has spoken.[6] Thus, the civil courts both judicially review and defer, if appropriate, to the practices and procedures of religious institutions.[7]

The 1991 census indicated that almost eighty-four percent of Canadians identify, at least for census purposes, with a Christian denomination, therefore it is necessary to describe in this chapter how the various branches of Christianity are organized in relation to ecclesiastical polity, legal structure, and dispute resolution. Then, brief consideration will be given to the legal organization and dispute resolution processes of the

---

3   See generally M.H. Ogilvie, "The Legal Status of Ecclesiastical Corporations" (1989) 15 Can. Bus. L.J. 74; "Church Property Disputes: Some Organizing Principles" (1992) 42 U.T.L.J. 377; "Ecclesiastical Law – Jurisdiction of Civil Courts – Governing Documents of Religions Institutions – Natural Justice: *Lakeside Colony of Hutterian Brethren* v. *Hofer*" (1993) 72 Can. Bar Rev. 238.

4   (1992), 97 D.L.R. (4th) 17 (S.C.C.).

5   (1994), 11 D.L.R. (4th) 367 (Ont. Gen. Div.).

6   *Cf. Davis* v. *United Church of Canada* (1992), 92 D.L.R. (4th) 678 (Ont. Gen. Div.) in which the court heard an appeal that had not yet gone to either the General Council or the Judicial Commission of the church.

7   This may be contrasted with the position in the U.S. where deferral to the highest tribunal in an ecclesiastical hierarchy has created a virtually autonomous sphere for churches by virtue of judicial interpretation of the free exercise clause in the First Amendment: *Watson* v. *Jones* 80 US 679 (1871); and *Jones* v. *Wolf* 413 US 595 (1979).

non-Christian religious groups in Canada, which constitute approximately nine percent of the population, with the remaining approximately seven percent of the population reporting no religious identity at all.[8]

B. CHRISTIAN ECCLESIASTICAL POLITIES

Every Christian denomination is either episcopal, presbyterian, or congregational in polity, that is, in its government, administration, and judicial procedures.[9] This three-fold division dates from the Protestant Reformation of the Western Christian church in the sixteenth century when presbyterian and congregational polities were created in response to the Protestant re-evaluation of the evidence in the New Testament concerning the primitive Christian communities of the first century A.D. In keeping with the doctrine of the exclusive primacy of Scripture (*sola scriptura*) in Protestant theology, both the Calvinist and Anabaptist movements, but not the Anglican or Lutheran movements, within the Reformation, renounced episcopacy as unscriptural and found scriptural authority instead for presbyterian and congregational polities respectively.

The evidence of the New Testament is ambiguous. Since both Jesus and his early disciples, including Paul, whose letters are the primary sources for our knowledge of the primitive Christian churches, were Jews who attended the synagogues,[10] it appears that the organization for the early congregations was modelled on the synagogues, each of which was

---

8   As a predominantly Christian country since its colonial beginnings, virtually all of the common law is about disputes within Christian denominations, therefore the emphasis in this chapter on Christian polities reflects the reality of religious litigation as well as the census statistics. As Canada becomes increasingly multicultural, litigation is likely to reflect that evolution, so that future editions of this book will do so as well.

9   There are a number of dictionaries of Christianity, of which the following are widely regarded as the best: F.L. Cross and E.A. Livingstone, eds., *The Oxford Dictionary of the Christian Church*, 3d ed. (London: Oxford University Press, 1997); Alan Richardson and John Bowden, eds., *A New Dictionary of Christian Theology* (London: S.C.M. Press, 1983); J.D. Douglas, ed., *A New International Dictionary of the Christian Church* (Grand Rapids, MI: Zondervan, 1978); Sinclair B. Ferguson and David F. Wright, eds., *New Dictionary of Theology* (Leicester, England: IV Press, 1988); and Erwin Fahlbusch et al., eds., *The Encyclopedia of Christianity*, multivolume series (Grand Rapids, MI: Eerdmans, 1999–).

10   Luke 4:16; Acts 13:5, 14, 14:1, 17:2 (N.S.R.V.).

administered by a board of elders or presbyters.[11] Paul and Barnabas appointed elders in the congregations they established,[12] but also referred to those elders as bishops or *episcopai*,[13] apparently using the terms "elder" and "bishop" interchangeably to refer to the function of oversight over the congregation.

Probably within two generations of the New Testament church, the term bishop or overseer came to be applied first to the president of the board of presbyters and then to the overseers over a geographical area. Thus, Ignatius of Antioch, who was martyred c. A.D. 107, referred to himself as the "bishop of Syria"[14] and appears to have understood leadership within the church by the early second century A.D. to be divided among bishops, presbyters,[15] and deacons.[16]

Episcopacy, then, as a *system* of church government by bishop, appears to date from the early second century and from after the primitive church of the New Testament. Throughout the medieval period, it evolved into the sophisticated hierarchical system of church government found today in the Roman Catholic, Orthodox, Lutheran, and Anglican communions. By the fourth century A.D. after the conversion of the Emperor Constantine, who ceased to persecute Christians and prepared the way for Theodosius I to declare Christianity as the state religion of the Roman Empire in A.D. 380, the Christian communities in the West had begun to organize on the model of the Roman Empire, where in every metropolis or province, there was a superior magistrate over lesser magistrates — a model followed by the bishops who asserted authority over geographical areas originally co-inhering with Roman civil jurisdictions. By the fifth century A.D., the Bishop of Rome had largely succeeded in asserting the primacy of Rome over the other bishops, assisted by the claims of the bishops of Rome to be in direct succession to the apostle

---

11   Acts 11:30, 14:23, 21:18.
12   Acts 14:23.
13   Acts 20:17, 28; Titus 1:5–9; 1 Peter 5:1–4; Phil. 1:1.
14   Epistle to the Romans 2. The most accessible text in translation from the Greek original is in Maxwell Staniforth, ed., *Early Christian Writings: The Apostolic Fathers* (London: Penguin Books, 1968).
15   The word "presbyter" comes to mean priest in the early Middle Ages.
16   Epistle to the Trallians, 2,3; above note 14. See also The Didache, 15: above note 14.

Peter who had been martyred in Rome and on whom Christ was said to have built his church.[17]

The basis of authority within episcopal churches for bishops is in the tradition that every bishop is in a direct line of succession from the apostles (the "apostolic succession") and as such is a guarantor of the authoritative tradition of the doctrine handed on from Christ to his apostles and then to the church. The imposition of hands at the ordination of a bishop is meant to verify publically that the newly ordained person is a genuine part of the line of transmission, in contrast to those who are not so recognized and who may teach heresy as a result.

The growth in wealth and power, both ecclesiastical and civil, of the episcopal hierarchy of the Western Christian church throughout the Middle Ages and the accompanying corruption and inefficiency in the stewardship of that wealth and power came under attack prior to and at the time of the Reformation by reformers who contrasted the church of the late Middle Ages with the primitive church attested to by the New Testament. While some reformers such as Martin Luther or Thomas Cranmer saw their task as one of purifying and correcting an episcopal hierarchy, which in itself remained an efficient organizational structure whose roots dated to the first century of the church after the ascension of Christ, others asserted that the entire organization of the church must be re-thought and re-modelled as closely as possible on the New Testament church. Two re-interpretations of the Biblical texts resulted in two novel polities within Western Christendom, presbyterianism and congregationalism.

Both terms were first used in England in the late sixteenth century, the former to designate a form of church government in which authority is vested collectively in both lay and ordained elders or presbyters in a hierarchy of church councils or "courts" and the latter to designate a form of church government in which authority is vested in the local congregation alone. Whereas presbyterian church government sought to replace the authority of bishops within the church, congregationalism sought to remove the authority of a universally organized hierarchy over a local community of believers. Presbyterianism retained the notion of hierarchical authority arranged geo-politically, but congregationalism removed all notions of hierarchy from its polity.

Although the word "presbyterian" did not come into everyday use until the early seventeenth century, its theological origins are found in

---

17   Matt. 16:18–19.

John Calvin's understanding of the nature of the New Testament church and of the exclusive authority and authenticity of the New Testament in relation to church structures, in contrast to the episcopal model, which incorporated post-New Testament accretions into its understanding of ecclesiastical polity.[18] Accordingly, Calvin regarded the scriptural model of a congregation governed by elders or presbyters as the order set out in the New Testament for communities of Christian believers, but also found in the New Testament evidence for four different offices within the primitive church, reflecting the distribution of divine gifts for service within the Christian community: pastor, teacher, elder, and deacon.[19]

In contrast to the episcopal model by which authority to rule the church is derived from Christ through the apostolic succession within history, Calvin's understanding of the New Testament asserted that authority to rule the church was directly derived from Christ, the one King and Head of the earthly church and the only mediator between God and man. Since Christ promised his presence in the church through the Holy Spirit,[20] all offices are held by his appointment, and in choosing officers the church does not grant authority but merely recognizes Christ's authority and calling. This interpretation contrasted with the episcopal understanding that authority within the church was bestowed by the church through the recognition of valid bishops. Calvin acknowledged the interchangeable use of the words "elder" and "bishop" in the New Testament but thought the essential nature of the role to be that of the exercise of authority derived from Christ's calling, not from membership in an apostolic succession that was without scriptural basis.

This understanding of authority and government within the church, of a community of believers directed by elders with a variety of gifts and roles, required greater elaboration if it was to be adapted to a state larger than the small city-state of sixteenth century Geneva with its population of about 12,000 people. This adaptation occurred primarily in Scotland,[21]

---

18 For the following, see John T. McNeill and Ford Lewis Battles, eds., *Institutes of the Christian Religion*, (1559) IV. 3. 1–16. 2 vols. (Philadelphia: The Westminster Press, 1967).

19 1 Cor. 12:4–11, 28; Eph. 4:11–13; 1 Tim. 3:8, 5:17.

20 Matt. 28:18–20.

21 John Douglas, John Knox, John Row, John Spottiswoode, John Willock, John Winram, *The First Book of Discipline* (1560), F.K. Cameron, ed. (Edinburgh: Saint Andrew Press, 1972); Andrew Melville, *The Second Book of Discipline*

although similar adaptations also occurred in the Reformed communities elsewhere in Europe including in England, France, and Moravia, and resulted in the normal pattern of presbyterian church government in which the congregational model is adapted to regional and national bodies. The local congregation governed by a kirk session (consistory) comprised of elders including the teaching elder, or minister, remains the core community. Regional and national organization is based on representation from the kirk sessions in presbyteries (colloquy, classis); synods, for a number of presbyteries; and general assemblies, which are the supreme legislative, judicial, and administrative bodies and are comprised of equal numbers of ministers and elders commissioned by the presbyteries.

The four-tiered hierarchy of "church courts" — kirk sessions, presbyteries, synods, general assemblies — is characteristic of virtually all presbyterian churches worldwide, with some smaller churches foregoing either synods or general assemblies. In contrast to episcopal orders of church government in which authority is normally understood to descend from bishops, authority to govern in presbyterian church government is understood to come directly from Christ and the work of the Holy Spirit, expressed when congregations call and ordain their teaching and ruling elders. Thus, even the authority of the higher courts rests ultimately in the local congregations, as demonstrated by the so-called "Barrier Act"[22] procedure whereby general assemblies are not permitted to change doctrine, government, or worship until ratified by a majority of presbyteries.

Although congregationalism is normally said to have begun in late sixteenth-century England as a response to Queen Elizabeth I's efforts to create a uniform national church governed by crown and bishop, congregationalism, broadly defined as a form of church polity that insists on the independence and autonomy of every local congregation as a community of believers, may be said to date to the Anabaptist Reformation in the Low Countries, which eschewed hierarchy and human authority within the church as unscriptural. These most radical advocates of the Reformation took the New Testament evidences of the primitive Christian communities alone as models for Christian life in society and found no

---

(1578), James Kirk, ed. (Edinburgh: Saint Andrew Press, 1980); and Westminster Assembly of 1645, *The Form of Presbyterial Church Government*, numerous modern editions.

22 Enacted by the General Assembly of the Church of Scotland in 1697 and adopted by presbyterian churches worldwide.

evidence in scripture either of episcopacy or of presbyterian hierarchy. Congregationalism was essentially decentralized Calvinism insofar as it retained the focus on the local community directly under the guidance of Christ as the source of authority. The congregation was Christ's "gathered community" and under the guidance of the Holy Spirit selected its own minister and elders or deacons and conducted its affairs independently from other gathered communities. The congregational meeting of all admitted members gathered under the guidance of the Holy Spirit was thought to be the truest interpretation of the church of the New Testament. Bishops and presbyters were simply irrelevant and unscriptural.

Congregationalism as a discrete denomination of loosely collected congregations grew up in England in the late sixteenth century and flowered in New England in the seventeenth and eighteenth centuries, but the concept of congregational polity as a form of church government is widespread and found to a greater or lesser degree among Baptists, Methodists, Pentecostals, Mennonites, and Hutterites as well as being the characteristic mode of organization for the various Evangelical congregations that have grown up in North America in this century. Rigid and law-ridden governing structures are eschewed by congregational-style churches, once it is accepted that the church consists of those who respond personally to the call of Christ and through believer's baptism covenant with him and with one another to live together in community.

While these three historic theologies and models for church government predominate in Christendom and correctly characterize most Christian denominations — the Roman Catholic Church, Anglicans, Lutherans, Presbyterians, Mennonites — virtually all denominations have experienced the influence of one or more of these three in the past century so that some elements of each may be found to have infiltrated the historic polities, changing their character although not necessarily their outward forms. Churches are dynamic organizations and their evolving self-understandings require sensitivity on the part of those acting for them.

C. CHRISTIAN DISPUTE RESOLUTION

All Christian denominations share certain basic New Testament principles for the resolution of disputes within the church.[23] Indeed, Paul asserted

---

23　The concern here is with internal disputes not disputes involving the state or civil matters.

that disputes arising within the church should be resolved within the church only. When writing to the early congregation at Corinth, he admonished the community for permitting disputes at all and advised against appeals to civil courts since they were staffed by unbelievers, recommending instead that internal disputes be resolved internally before believers.[24]

The fundamentals of Christian dispute resolution are found in the words of Christ himself, at Matthew 18:15–17:

> If another member of the church sins against you, go and point out the fault when the two of you are alone. If the member listens to you, you have regained that one. But if you are not listened to, take one or two others along with you, so that every word may be confirmed by the evidence of two or three witnesses. If the member refuses to listen to them, tell it to the church; and if the offender refuses to listen even to the church, let such a one be to you as a Gentile and a tax collector.

Dispute resolution was to be informal then, as the few examples suggest as found in the New Testament.[25] It is believed that an early role for bishops in the post-New Testament church was to resolve disputes within their communities, although the earliest references to this practice date from the writings of Cyprian, Bishop of Carthage, in the mid third century. Over the succeeding centuries, both substantive and procedural law became more sophisticated and codified, borrowing heavily from Roman law and dictated to the Western Christian church by the bishops, most especially by the pontiff, the Bishop of Rome.[26]

This edifice of canon law and church courts came under attack at the time of the Reformation, particularly on the Continent. In England, both were more slowly revised to reflect the polity and theology of the evolving state church, but the concept remained that a church ruled by bishops required also a canon law and courts to enforce uniformity of belief and practice. By contrast, those branches of the Reformation inspired by Calvin and by the Anabaptists eradicated both Roman canon law and formal church courts from their polities. Thus, within presbyterian polities even today, rules of procedure of a relatively unsophisticated sort exist to regulate the relatively informal relationships and practices of sessions,

---

24   1 Cor. 6:1–7.
25   Acts 5:1–12; 1 Tim. 1, 20; 2 Tim. 2:24–25.
26   Below section D.

presbyteries, synods, and general assemblies. Most congregational polities operate without laws or courts, preferring to rely instead directly on Matthew 18:15–17 for the informal resolution of disputes, failing which, removal from the congregation remains the final sanction. Internal dispute resolution processes, then, generally reflect the polities and the understanding of the sources of authority within the church of the three different styles of Christian denominations.

It remains then, to introduce briefly the polities, dispute resolution procedures, and their sources within the largest Christian denominations in Canada today.

D. THE ROMAN CATHOLIC CHURCH

The largest religious institution in Canada is the Roman Catholic Church with an estimated membership of 12.5 million members nationwide.[27] Since the Canadian church is simply one part of the worldwide Roman Catholic Church, administered from the Holy See in Rome and under the temporal and spiritual direction ultimately of the Pope, its polity, laws, customs, and judicial processes are those established by the Holy See for all branches of the church worldwide and are hierarchical in nature.

The Holy See, which is the official senior bureaucracy of the Roman Catholic Church considered as a community of faith, is distinguishable from the City of the Vatican, but the status in international law of Vatican City is ambiguous.[28] By a treaty and concordat in 1929, Italy recognized the "sovereignty of the Holy See in the international domain" and its exclusive sovereignty over the City of the Vatican. Since then a number of states have recognized the Vatican as a state by entering into diplomatic relations with it, including Canada. Vatican City exists as a territorial organization inside the city of Rome for the sole function of supporting the Holy See as a religious bureaucracy but it has few features

---

27   Eileen W. Lindner, ed., *Yearbook of American and Canadian Churches* (Nashville: Abingdon Press, 2001) at 343. Most denominations publish annual membership statistics and may be contacted directly to ascertain these. This volume is used in this chapter because it cumulates these scattered figures in one volume and although the numbers recorded are often two to three years out of date, they remain approximately current for present purposes.

28   For what follows, see Ian Brownlie, *Principles of Public International Law*, 4th ed. (Oxford: Clarendon Press, 1990) at 65–66.

of a normal civil state. The legal personality of the Holy See apart from the Vatican is uncertain but it seems clear that with the exception of accredited diplomatic representatives such as a papal nuncio, the religious personnel under the spiritual direction of the Holy See are not entitled to diplomatic immunity nor is the Holy See entitled to shelter behind Vatican City to avoid legal liability for the acts and omissions of its religious personnel in Canada or elsewhere.

The principal source within the church of authority for and a description of the polity, law, and judicatories of the Roman Catholic Church is the Code of Canon Law[29] promulgated on 25 January 1983 by Pope John Paul II. The practice of codifying the canons of the church is ancient, dating from the early centuries of the church; however, the first comprehensive collection of ecclesiastical laws was that compiled by Gratian in the mid twelfth century, the *Corpus iuris canonici* (or *Decretum Gratiani*) modelled after the *Corpus iuris civilis* of Justinian. As a collection of existing laws, the principles often contradicted one another, but were, in subsequent centuries, added to by various other collections of laws as part of the *Corpus iuris canonici*, including the *Liber Extra* of Pope Gregory IX (1234), the *Liber Sextus* of Pope Boniface VIII (1298), the *Clementiae* of Pope Clement V (1305–1314) promulgated by Pope John XXII (1331), as well as the *Extravagantes* of Pope Clement V and the *Extravagantes communes*, decretals of various popes that had never been gathered into a single collection.

After the Middle Ages, ecclesiastical legislation continued to be enacted but was never gathered into a single code. Thus, the bishops convened at the First Vatican Council in 1870 requested that a new collection of canon laws be compiled and this finally appeared in 1917, promulgated with effect from 19 May 1918 by Pope Benedict XV. The object of this first, modern Code since the Middle Ages was to collect and

---

29 E. Caparros, M. Theriault, and J. Than, eds., *Code of Canon Law Annotated* (Montreal: Wilson and Lafleur Ltee, 1993). For other annotated versions, see *The Canon Law: Letter and Spirit* (Collegeville, MN: The Liturgical Press, 1995); and *New Commentary on the Code of Canon Law* (New York: Paulist Press, 2000). The Ukrainian Catholic Church, as an Eastern Rite institution, is largely subject to the same Code of Canon Law in respect to its eparchies in Canada and is administered as a separate part of the universal Catholic Church. Additionally, there is a diocese of the Polish National Catholic Church in Canada, which is administered separately but still under the authority of Rome.

codify in one place all of the previous legislation, not to create new law. The need for a more complete revision became increasingly evident in the twentieth century and Pope John XXIII declared in 1959 that a renewal of the Code was required. A pontifical commission was established in 1963 to draft the Code, which was ultimately promulgated in 1983.

Comprised of seven major parts covering over a thousand pages in a dual Latin-English version, the Code aims to provide for virtually all aspects of life within the Roman Catholic Church worldwide, both theological and juridical. Thus, after Book I, which is primarily the definition and interpretation part, Book II sets out the position, obligations, and rights of the laity and the clergy, including the hierarchy, and sources of authority within the worldwide church. Book III defines the teaching authority of the church and Book IV the sacramental authority in relation to the seven sacraments of the church, as well as the liturgy, the cult of saints, relics, and other related matters. Book V deals with the administration of church property and contracts, while Book VI deals with offences and penalties and Book VII with legal processes.

Although the Code of Canon Law is the primary and most comprehensive source of law, it is supplemented by a variety of laws, norms, and customs applicable both to the worldwide church as well as for national or "particular" churches, promulgated by the conferences of bishops for those areas.

The ecclesiastical polity prescribed by the Code of Canon Law[30] is hierarchical, with authority vested primarily in the Pope as the successor of Peter but shared also with the College of Bishops meeting in ecumenical council as the successors in apostolic succession from the apostles. Final authority in the church resides in the Pope. Since ecumenical councils are rare, the Synod of Bishops, a group of bishops representative of the worldwide church, meets at specified times when convened by the Pope to discuss matters proposed to it and to make recommendations to him for ratification as church law. A permanent secretariat of the Synod at the Holy See carries out the day to day administration of these decisions.

In addition to the Synod of Bishops, the College of Cardinals, who may be bishops, priests, or deacons, exists as a special college to elect the Pope in accordance with the laws and practices of the church. Only a validly elected Pope is vested with supreme authority. The conduct of the

---

30   The following precis is drawn from Book II.

business of the church on a daily basis is vested in the Roman Rota, which is composed of a variety of Congregations and Tribunals at the Holy See.

The Code further sets out the structures and norms of practice for the particular churches in each country of the world where the Roman Catholic Church is found. The Roman Catholic Church is organized into approximately four thousand dioceses worldwide, each under a bishop who is responsible to the Pope directly for its affairs. There are about sixty dioceses in Canada. In addition, particular institutions, such as religious institutes (or "orders"), are under their own head such as an abbot, superior, or a territorial prelate. The bishop is the highest authority in his diocese but must conform to the higher laws of the church established by Rome. Groups of neighbouring dioceses may be constituted as provinces with a metropolitan or archbishop having administrative authority over those provinces and responsible to the Pope. In addition, in most countries there is a national conference of bishops with its own administration to co-ordinate the national life of the church in that country, under the authority of Rome. Bishops, archbishops, and bishops' conferences are sources of law applicable within their respective territories provided they comply with higher laws in the church.

Within each diocese are a number of parishes or local congregations entrusted to a parish priest under the authority of the diocesan bishop. In each parish and diocese a variety of councils and committees carry out the day-to-day work of the church, assisted by a variety of persons, lay and clergy, voluntary and paid. Essentially, however, authority is hierarchical and downward flowing within the church, although consultative processes are common and involve both clergy and laity.

The Roman Catholic Church claims jurisdiction over its members in relation to all cases of violation of church law and in relation to all spiritual matters.[31] It leaves to the civil courts jurisdiction over property and contract as well as over the civil effects of matrimony and annulment (divorce). While disputes concerning the property and civil rights of the laity are regarded as civil matters, disputes concerning the property of the church are regarded as matters for the ecclesiastical courts.

Essentially, the hierarchy of courts within the church is comprised of three levels: First Instance Tribunals and Second Instance Tribunals within a "national" church, with final appeal to the Roman Rota or Apostolic

---

31   The following precis is drawn from Book VII.

Signatura in Rome. However, because of the final authority of the Pope, any litigant may refer a case directly to him at any time in the process.

The First Instance Tribunal is essentially the bishop of the diocese who will usually exercise this judicial power through others. The tribunal members are constituted as a permanent body headed by a judicial vicar or *officialis* and staffed by associate judicial vicars or *vice-officiales*, who must be priests. Occasionally the First Instance Tribunal may serve several dioceses or even provinces, as the local situation warrants. In addition, for religious orders or institutions directly under the authority of Rome, the First Instance Tribunal will be struck from within the institution where the dispute occurs.

The First Instance Tribunal may consist of one, three, or five judges as the bishop may deem appropriate. One of these may be chosen to be the *auditor* whose function is to gather the "proofs" or written pleadings and generally to know the facts of the case, although the *auditor* does not define the issues for the Tribunal. The Tribunal is also assisted by the *ponens* or *relator* who is the secretary but also, more importantly, presents the cases to the judges and assists in writing the judgment. In reaching judgment, the Tribunal may also rely on "assessors" who are essentially expert witnesses relevant to some aspect of the matter before the court; the "promoter of justice" or prosecutor whose function is to safeguard the public good; and, in matrimonial cases and cases relating to ordained persons, the "defender of the bond," whose role is to protect the bond of matrimony or of ordination. The First Instance Tribunal comes to its decision primarily on the basis of written depositions and decisions of the court are collegial, with only the majority decision reported to higher tribunals.

The Second Instance Tribunal is usually the national tribunal for a particular church and may be organized on a variety of regional bases. It is constituted in the same way as the First Instance Tribunal but drawn from a larger regional base. In Canada, the Canadian Conference of Catholic Bishops has constituted one national appeal tribunal, as have a number of other countries. While the Second Instance Tribunal may act as an appeal court, reviewing lower court decisions, it often acts to ratify the sentence of the First Instance Tribunal by decree, after considering the documentation sent from it and hearing the observations of the defender of the bond. Decisions are normally made by a bench of at least three judges. Approximately ninety-eight percent of cases heard at First and Second Instance are marriage annulment cases, which typically end with the decree of the Second Instance Tribunal. The remaining cases are largely concerned with clergy discipline and administrative errors.

The ordinary Third Instance Tribunal of the Roman Catholic Church is the Roman Rota, presided over by the Dean of the Rota and usually sitting in benches of three judges. There are no specific norms regarding the composition although all judges are required to be priests and leading authorities on canon law. The other Third Instance Tribunal is the Apostolic Signatura, which is the supreme court of the church and primarily hears rare cases of appeals against the Rota. Approximately four hundred cases annually are appealed to the Rota from the church worldwide, most concerning marriage annulments.[32]

The paucity of reported cases in the civil law reports in Canada suggests how self-contained and disciplined the judicatory process is in the Roman Catholic Church, in contrast to other religious institutions, whose disputes often spill out into the civil courts. However, the Roman Catholic Church and its members are obliged to conform to the law of Canada, both in respect to criminal and civil matters since, from the perspective of the civil law, it is merely a voluntary association like any other in the country.

As a voluntary association, the Roman Catholic Church is obliged to hold and manage its property through civil bodies corporate to have civil legal status. Each diocese, school, college, university, charitable institution, and religious order is incorporated either federally or provincially as is appropriate to its circumstances. The property of that entity is then vested in the body corporate, which can sue or be sued. In a diocese, typically all parish properties are vested in the bishop and the bishopric is incorporated as the civil body corporate.[33] There is no federally incorporated entity for the entire Roman Catholic Church in Canada; the universal church as is present in Canada is present in the dioceses directly subject to the Holy See, and the civil property of those dioceses together with the property of

---

32 For a highly critical study of this process, see Robert H. Vasoli, *What God Has Joined Together: The Annulment Crisis in American Catholicism* (Oxford: Oxford University Press, 1997). See also a highly critical review: Lynda A. Robitaille, (1999) 33 Studia Canonica 265.

33 *An Act to Incorporate the Roman Catholic Bishops of Toronto and Kingston in Canada* (1845) 8 Vict. c. 82. This model is followed by other bishoprics nationally.

the other entities constitutes the entire property devoted to the propagation of Roman Catholicism in Canada. At most, the civil legal characterization of the "national" church would be as an unincorporated association
suable through a representative party such as a diocese or the Canadian
Conference of Catholic Bishops, which is incorporated.[34]

E. THE ANGLICAN CHURCH OF CANADA

The second largest religious institution in Canada with an episcopal polity is the Anglican Church of Canada,[35] whose historical predecessor
denomination, the Church of England in Canada, has been present since
the early eighteenth century. Although today an autonomous member of
the worldwide Anglican Communion, from the appointment of Bishop
Charles Inglis in Nova Scotia in 1787, Canadian dioceses were originally
subject to the jurisdiction of the Archbishop of Canterbury.[36] From the
mid nineteenth century onward, regional organization proceeded in the
various colonies with synods, a form of regional government, for the
church developing (as they were in England at the same time). Prompted by Confederation in 1867, the Anglican community within Canada
moved toward the creation of a national church, with a General Synod as
its highest governing body being created in 1893.

---

34 At the time of writing the status of the "national" church in the civil law is
    under consideration in the courts in numerous cases in relation to civil legal
    liability for the abuses in the Indian residential schools. See for example *Re
    Residential Schools*, unreported decision of 28 August 2001 (Alta. C.A.); *Sev-
    eright v. A.-G. Canada*, unreported decision of 14 September 2001 (Sask. Q.B.).
    See also *J.R.S. v. Glendinning* (2000), 191 D.L.R. (4th) 750 (Ont. S.C.J.). Con-
    versely, the courts have been willing to grant intervener status to the Canadian
    Conference of Catholic Bishops in relation to various issues in which the
    Roman Catholic Church is said to have an interest. See for example *Chamber-
    lain v. Surrey School District No. 36* (2000), 191 D.L.R. (4th) 128 (B.C.C.A.);
    and *Trinity Western University v. B.C. College of Teachers* (2001), 199 D.L.R.
    (4th) 1 (S.C.C.).

35 Total membership in 1996, the last year reported, was 739,699: above note 27.

36 See generally R.V. Harris, *An Historical Introduction to the Study of the Canon
    Law of the Anglican Church of Canada* (Toronto: Anglican Church of Canada,
    1965); and H.R.S. Ryan, *Aspects of Constitutional History: The General Synod of
    the Anglican Church of Canada* (Toronto: Anglican Book Centre, 1993).

From the first meeting of the General Synod in 1893, the Church of England in Canada (known as the Anglican Church of Canada from 1955) became an independent denomination with an episcopal polity and judicatories. The sources of law for these are found in its own canon law as well as in civil legislation, both federal and provincial, incorporating various bodies within the church for the purpose of holding and using temporal property and entering into contractual relationships.

While the Canons of the General Synod[37] are clearly drafted for the Canadian church, it is understood by the church that they are in historical continuity with the English church both before and after the Reformation in England, and therefore in continuity with the earliest canons of the Western Christian church and its understanding of the so-called mandate of Christ handed down through the apostolic succession of bishops to govern the church as his authentic interpreters. The first post-Reformation compilation of canons for the Church of England were the Canons of 1603, which embodied many of the principles of previous canons relating to doctrine, liturgy, polity, and the relationship with the Crown-in-Parliament. The Canons of 1603 were framed by the Convocation of 1603 within the authority of the *Act for the Submission of the Clergy* of 1534,[38] and therefore as subject to Parliament, which has retained final legislative authority for the Church of England to the present day. With the autonomy of the Canadian church in 1893, the General Synod became the final authority within the Canadian church, enacting its laws and establishing its structures and organization. Since its first bishops were ordained in succession to the bishops of the English church, the authentic teaching authority associated with the apostolic succession is assumed.

However, it is equally important to state that the national structure of the church provides for additional sources of authority for changes in polity, doctrine, and liturgy, in both the ordinary clergy and the laity, who

---

37 *Handbook of the General Synod of the Anglican Church of Canada*, 12th ed. (Toronto: Anglican Church of Canada, 1999). For a general background on Anglican Canon Law, see Norman Doe, *The Legal Framework of the Church of England* (Oxford: Clarendon Press, 1996); Rupert D.H. Bursell, *Liturgy, Order and the Law* (Oxford: Clarendon Press, 1996); Lynne Leeder, *Ecclesiastical Law Handbook* (London: Sweet and Maxwell, 1997); Norman Doe, ed., *Canon Law in the Anglican Communion* (Oxford: Clarendon Press, 1998); and Mark Hill, *Ecclesiastical Law*, 2d ed. (Oxford: Oxford University Press, 2001).

38. (Eng.) 25 Henry VIII c. 19 (1534).

not only hold offices within the church but are represented in General Synod, as well as in lower legislative assemblies. The Anglican Church of Canada is comprised of four levels of organization: nationally, in the General Synod, which meets triennially under the leadership of the Primate of Canada and is composed of all the bishops and of members chosen from the clergy and laity; regionally, in four ecclesiastical provinces — Canada, Ontario, Rupert's Land, and British Columbia, each with its own metropolitan and provincial synod; locally, in thirty dioceses across the country, each with its own bishop and diocesan synod; and finally, in local parishes or congregations.

The General Synod consists of three orders meeting in a common assembly: the Order of Bishops, the Order of Clergy, and the Order of Laity, the latter two chosen on a representative basis but the former comprising all bishops holding active office. The Primate, who is the temporal head of the Church, is the president and is assisted by certain officers, including the Prolocutor (and Deputy Prolocutor), who is chosen by the General Synod; the General Secretary, who is responsible for the day to day oversight of the committees, councils, boards, and commissions of the national church; and the Chancellor (and Vice Chancellor), who is either a judge of a civil court or lawyer of ten years' standing and communicant member of the church and who serves as legal adviser to the Primate and is responsible for the law of the church.

The General Synod operates through the national Executive Council and a variety of standing committees, boards, and commissions on a daily basis and between its triennial meetings. The General Synod has authority and jurisdiction over all matters affecting the general interest of the national church including its doctrine, liturgy, polity, and judicatories. Decisions are made by a two-thirds majority vote of each Order and the approval of all three Orders is required; however, special voting rules govern changes in the constitution of the church and in the canons relating to doctrine, worship, or discipline. All alterations to these canons must be passed by a two-thirds majority in each Order voting at two successive sessions of the General Synod, with the proposed alterations having been referred for consideration to dioceses and provincial synods following the first approval of the General Synod.

Regional government for the church is organized into the four ecclesiastical provinces, for which provision is made in the Canons of the General Synod — Ontario, British Columbia (including the Diocese of Yukon), Rupert's Land (the civil provinces of Alberta, Manitoba,

Saskatchewan, and the Northwest Territories), and Canada (the remaining civil provinces of Canada).[39] A province is under the general authority of a metropolitan archbishop, who is assisted like the Primate at the national level by Prolocutors, Chancellors, and an Executive Officer and Executive Council. The jurisdiction and authority of the provincial synod, which also meets triennially and is comprised of laity and clergy, is to provide for the general interest and well-being of the church within its own jurisdiction and in compliance with the provisions enacted by the General Synod. A provincial synod is not concerned with doctrine, liturgy, or polity, but rather with administrative matters, especially the appointment and discipline of clergy and bishops within the province, and the administration of property within the province. Each ecclesiastical province has its own constitution and canons that constitute the law for the province in relation to matters within its jurisdiction.

Within each Ecclesiastical Province there are a number of dioceses, with a total of thirty nationally.[40] Headed by a bishop, and meeting in diocesan synod, typically on an annual basis, the authority and jurisdiction of the diocese is more specifically the general well-being of the parishes and congregations within the diocese. The bishop is assisted by one or more coadjutor bishops or suffragan bishops, an administrator of the diocese, Chancellor, Vice-Chancellor, and Executive Committee. The diocese is an administrative unit, governed by its own constitution and canons, with no authority over polity, doctrine, or liturgy.

Finally, within each diocese are the local congregations or parishes, under the supervision of the local minister or priest. Each parish may have its own bylaws and conducts its local activities in general meeting of all communicant members, known as the vestry. Two churchwardens are appointed annually, one by the vestry and one by the minister, and they are responsible, as prescribed by the bylaws, for property matters generally.

---

39 Each of the four provinces has its own canons and what follows is based on the Constitution and Canons for the Ecclesiastical Province of Ontario, but again, there is considerable uniformity among the four provinces.

40 What follows is based on the Constitution and Canons for the Diocese of Ottawa but there is considerable uniformity among all Canadian dioceses. It is necessary to consult the local diocese to ascertain local practices precisely. These are unpublished but available in looseleaf from local dioceses or parishes. Bylaws may also be available. For the role of the chancellor, see William J. Hemmerick, "The Role of the Chancellor in the Anglican Church" (1996) 2 J.C.L.A.C. 72.

Judicial and disciplinary processes within the Anglican Church of Canada reflect the hierarchical nature of the spiritual and administrative structures. The right to legal representation is permitted at all levels. Canon XVIII of the Canons of the General Synod provides that the bishop of a diocese has ecclesiastical jurisdiction, authority, and power of discipline over all clergy and laity within the diocese by virtue of the office of bishop.[41] The bishop also has jurisdiction to determine the membership, practice, and procedure of the Bishop's Court, and provision for these is normally made in the canons and bylaws of each diocese. Offences for the purposes of church law include clergy discipline for a wide variety of matters such as neglect of duties, immoral conduct, or conviction on an indictable offence under the civil law, as well as violation of the principles and practices of the church and differences between an incumbent of a parish and the parishioners.[42]

The membership of the Bishop's Court includes the Bishop, the Chancellor, three members of the clergy, and two lay members, with five being the usual quorum to include either Bishop or Chancellor, who presides. The court may also be assisted by assessors who may be theologians. The process is not fixed nor is it complex, being largely established by the Bishop as the case requires, although it appears to be generally adversarial in nature. The sanctions permitted include admonition, either public or private, suspension, deprivation or deposition from office, or deposition from a position of ministry within the church.

Appeal is to the Court of Appeal for the ecclesiastical province and the canons for the province make provision for the membership, practice, and procedure for that court. The court is composed of five members. Where the trial is of a bishop, three members of the court are bishops, plus one member each of the clergy and laity. Where the trial is of a priest or deacon, one member is a bishop, one is a member of the laity, and three are members of the clergy. Where the trial is of a member of the laity, the court is composed of three members of the laity, one bishop, and one member of the clergy. The court is advised by two assessors, one of whom is the Chancellor of the province and their role is to advise on practice and procedure. Appeal from a Bishop's Court is by right.

---

41 Above note 37.
42 See also Christopher G. Riggs, "The Non-Disciplinary Termination of Clerical Appointments in the Anglican Diocese of Toronto" (1999) 3 J.C.L.A.C. 33.

The final appeal is to the Supreme Court of Appeal for the Anglican Church of Canada.[43] It is composed of nine members with members of the same Order of the person being tried predominating the membership, as was the case in the Provincial Court of Appeal. The Supreme Court is advised by at least four assessors including the Chancellor of the General Synod and provincial or diocesan chancellors; however, if doctrine is at issue at least two assessors must be theologians. Appeal is by right and the court sits wherever in the country is appropriate to the case. The Supreme Court may hear witnesses *viva voce* and it may also hear "special cases" sent to it directly from a diocese for its opinion on questions of law.

These courts meet very rarely. Indeed, since 1893 the Supreme Court has met only once, in 1989, to consider a challenge to the Book of Alternative Services, and in which it upheld the ordination of a bishop using a service in that book.[44] Even Bishops' Courts so rarely meet that their procedures are not fixed in many dioceses.[45]

Finally, it should be noted that Canon XXI of the Canons of the General Synod[46] also provides for the establishment in each diocese of an Ecclesiastical Matrimonial Commission to deal with applications from divorced persons for re-marriage within the church and that a relatively detailed procedure is set out for such commissions.

It remains to consider how the Anglican Church of Canada holds its property. Essentially, each diocese is incorporated pursuant to provincial legislation, usually by private act, and all the property in the diocese is vested in the bishop as trustee who holds and manages it as provided by the legislation, bylaws, and the constitution and canons and their bylaws, if any, of the diocese. The General Synod was incorporated by federal legislation in 1921[47] for the purposes of holding and managing the property and assets of the national church.[48] In addition, specific institutions associated with the Anglican Church of Canada, such as schools, colleges, or universities, as well as specific boards, societies, or assets may

---

43 Above note 37, Canon XX.
44 Ryan, above note 36 at 101–106.
45 "The Ferry Case" (1992) 1 J.C.L.A.C. 3.
46 Above note 37.
47 S.C. 1921, c. 82; as amend. S.C. 1951, c. 55 and S.C. 1956, c. 57.
48 Since many were first incorporated in the nineteenth century, subsequent amending legislation is also likely to be in place.

also be incorporated by private legislation, federal or provincial, as the case may be.[49]

Although episcopal in outward structure and subscribing to the doctrine of the apostolic succession of its bishops, the Anglican Church of Canada has moved toward a system of church government in the second half of the twentieth century that has been characterized as "episcoposynodical or synodico-episcopal" in style.[50] Whether the source of authority remains exclusively with the bishops in the House of Bishops or is now shared with the General Synod has become elusive.

F. LUTHERAN CHURCHES

Lutheran denominations worldwide as well as in Canada are episcopal in polity, however bishops tend to be understood more as senior administrators than as exclusive authorities on doctrine and discipline within the church. Lutheran congregations were first organized in Nova Scotia in 1749 and for most of the past two centuries Canadian Lutherans were organized with American Lutheran synods on a North American-wide basis. However, in the second half of the twentieth century autonomous Lutheran bodies were established in Canada, of which the largest is the Evangelical Lutheran Church in Canada with approximately 140,000 members and adherents.[51] The second largest, with approximately 60,000 members and adherents,[52] is the Lutheran Church – Canada, which tends to be found primarily in the Western provinces.[53] The following description is of the polity and judicatories of the Evangelical Lutheran Church ("ELCC") and while these are approximated in the Lutheran Church – Canada ("LCC") and other Lutheran bodies worldwide, it is necessary to consult the constitutional documents of those bodies should legal advice be required.

---

49   It is necessary to search for specific legislation for each such body and to
     ensure that all amendments are found prior to advising the body concerned.
50   Ryan, above note 36 at 106.
51   Above note 27 at 340 (1999 figures reported).
52   Ibid. at 341 (1999 figures reported).
53   Two tiny Lutheran Churches are also found in Canada: the Church of the
     Lutheran Brethren with approximately 600 members and adherents and the
     Estonian Evangelical Lutheran Church with approximately 5,000 members and
     adherents: above note 27 at 340 (1997 figures reported).

In contrast to other episcopal polities, it is understood within the ELCC that the focus of church life and the primary source of authority resides within the community of believers in the local congregation rather than in the office of bishop and in the ecclesiastical hierarchy. Each congregation is incorporated pursuant to provincial legislation for non-profit corporations and has its own written constitution, reflecting a model constitution provided by the national church. Congregational property is vested in the congregation, as is the right to enter contracts provided a two-thirds majority approval is granted by the congregational meeting.[54]

The authority of the congregation is vested in the congregational meeting, which calls the pastor, after consultation with the bishop of the synod in which it is located; makes significant decisions about buying or selling property; and elects the Congregational Council of approximately six to twenty-four members (usually twelve to fifteen), who are the trustees of the congregation with general oversight over both the temporal and spiritual life of the congregation. A variety of congregational committees are responsible to the Council and congregation for various aspects of congregational life.

Regionally, the ELCC is divided into five synods across Canada (British Columbia, Alberta, Saskatchewan, Manitoba, and Eastern) and each synod is also incorporated pursuant to the appropriate legislation, federal and provincial, and has its own constitution and bylaws.[55] The head of each synod is a bishop who is its chief executive officer with a synod staff responsible for co-ordination of synod activities and carrying out the decisions of the synod convention. The bishop is elected from the pastors within the synod by the convention for four-year terms. However, the highest authority in each synod is the synod convention, which meets at least once annually. Its membership consists of all the pastors in the synod and one lay delegate from each congregation, chosen by the congregation. Between conventions, a synod council comprised of the officers of the synod and twelve additional members, six lay and six clergical, is responsible for carrying out the work of the synod through the synod office. The synod also has a variety of standing committees.

Some synods are also subdivided into conventions, as is the Eastern Synod because of its large geographical size. Its structures and represen-

---

54 The Constitution of St. Peter's Church, Ottawa was used in what follows. These documents are unpublished but available from local congregations.
55 *Constitution and Bylaws of the ELCC* (unpublished).

tation patterns reflect those of the synod but for a smaller area and its head is a dean who is elected by the convention conference.[56]

The highest legislative authority in the national church is the Biennial Convention whose membership consists of two hundred pastors elected by synod conferences and a lay delegate elected by each congregation whose pastor is not a delegate. This convention has general oversight over all temporal and spiritual matters and is headed by the national bishop of the ELCC. Between meetings, responsibility for carrying out the work of the national church is vested in the National Church Council, which is composed of the officers from the national office as well as one pastor and one lay person from each synod. The national office is divided into various divisions responsible for implementing the policies of the national church.

While authority in the ELCC is vested in its three (or four) tiers of representative institutions, and therefore ultimately in its membership, the bishop's role in discipline within the church is more than that of merely an administrative nature.

Provision is normally made by congregational constitutions for discipline and dispute resolution within the congregation, usually either of members who advocate doctrines contrary to those of the church or who are involved in an internal dispute. Constitutions typically provide that the provisions of Matthew 18:15–18 quoted above shall be followed, normally with the involvement of the pastor in an informal setting. If no resolution is found, then discipline is to be administered by the Congregational Council, which meets privately and must reach a two-thirds majority vote prior to imposing a sanction, which may be censure before the Council or the congregation, suspension from membership, repentance and amendment, or expulsion from membership and the sacraments. Right of appeal exists to the congregational meeting and from there to the synod.

Where it is the pastor whose preaching, life, or conduct is the cause for conflict, then the bishop of the synod, who is responsible for the clergy within the synod, is involved from the outset. The bishop personally may informally make inquiries and seek resolution but where that approach fails, will appoint an investigating committee composed of the bishop, two pastors, and two lay members. This committee investigates and if it finds that there is reason to believe the charges have substance,

---

56   *Constitution and Bylaws of the Eastern Synod* (unpublished).

the bishop will then convene a committee on discipline as soon as possible. The committee on discipline consists of uneven numbers, four clergy and three laity, appointed by the synod council, and the national bishop. The accused has a right to legal counsel and to a full hearing. The committee reports its findings in writing with a recommendation for action and six of its members must concur. The sanctions permitted are private censure and admonition by the bishop; censure and admonition before the synod council; suspension from office for a designated period or until there is satisfactory evidence of repentance and amendment; or removal from the roster of ordained ministers.

The decision of the committee on discipline may be appealed to the court of adjudication of the national church, which consists of seven members, four lay and three clergy, who are elected by the biennial convention for not more than two consecutive four-year terms. The court may establish its own rules of procedure and it may hear, in addition to appeals from lower tribunals, references of questions in relation to doctrine or conscience. A two-thirds majority is required to either sustain or reverse an appeal. Its decision is final.

These tribunals have rarely met and most disputes are quietly resolved within the congregation through the informal intervention of the pastor, or occasionally the bishop.

As stated earlier, property in the ELCC is vested in the congregation, synod, and national church respectively with the appropriate body incorporated pursuant either to provincial or federal law, as the case may be. Each level of organization has its own constitution and bylaws, available from its governing body but not otherwise published.

G. ORTHODOX CHURCHES

There are a large number of Orthodox denominations operating in Canada that are also episcopal in polity, including the Antiochian Orthodox Christian Archdiocese of North America, the Armenian Holy Apostolic Church, the Greek Orthodox Metropolis of Toronto, Orthodox Church in America (Canada Section), the Russian Orthodox Church in Canada, the Romanian Orthodox Church in America, the Romanian Orthodox Episcopate of America, the Serbian Orthodox Church, the Syrian Orthodox Church of Antioch, and the Ukrainian Orthodox Church of Canada. Some of these are autonomous Canadian denominations, some are parts of an American parent church, while others are directly under the authority of the church in their country of origin. All are episcopal and traditionally hierarchical in organization but incorporate for the purposes of holding and managing property, usually federally.[57]

H. METHODIST CHURCHES

Methodism has been present in Canada since the late eighteenth century, in a variety of strains, of both British and American origin. These strains came together in 1884 to form the Methodist Church, which in 1925 merged with Congregationalists and Presbyterians to form the United Church of Canada. Methodism continues, however, today in Canada as new Methodist bodies have come into existence after 1925, which are primarily American in origin. Two of the three Methodist bodies organized in Canada are episcopal in polity; these are the British Methodist Episcopal Church of Canada, which has several congregations in Ontario, and the Free Methodist Church in Canada, which became autonomous in 1990 and has a membership of approximately 11,000 members and adherents.[58] The Wesleyan Church of Canada with about 6,000 members and adherents[59] is part of the American parent church and its polity does not have bishops, rather superintendents, who serve much the same function. Both the Free Methodist Church and the Wesleyan Church of Canada are organized along historic Wesleyan lines with three layers of organization (congregation, district, and general conference), but unlike other Protestant denominations, authority appears to flow downward as reflected by their respective *Disciplines*,[60] which provide in very great detail for church life at all levels. These Books of Discipline constitute the comprehensive sources of law within these churches, providing as well for judicial and disciplinary procedures,

---

57 The number of these Orthodox communities, each with its unique polity, made it impossible to choose one as typical for current purposes. Legal advisers should ensure that they have the appropriate constitutional documents and legislation for the church with which they are dealing.

58 Above note 27 at 341 (1998 figures reported).

59 *Ibid.* at 344 (1999 figures reported).

60 For the Free Methodist Church, see *The Manual of the Free Methodist Church in Canada* (Mississauga: Light and Life Press, 1999); and for the Wesleyan Church see *The Discipline of the Wesleyan Church* (Indianapolis: Wesleyan Publishing House, 2000).

resort to which is rare, since disputes are dealt with informally by local pastors and excommunication is the sanction employed for members and clergy who do not comply with the pastor's decision.

Both denominations are federally incorporated,[61] but individual congregations are not. All church property in the Wesleyan Church, including all congregational property, is vested in the Wesleyan Church of Canada while all property in the Free Methodist Church, including all congregational property, is vested in the General Conference of that denomination.

I. THE PRESBYTERIAN CHURCH IN CANADA

The two largest denominations in Canada that are the historical descendants of Calvinism insofar as their polities are presbyterian rather than episcopal in nature are the Presbyterian Church in Canada (PCC)[62] and the United Church of Canada (UCC). Of these, the purer presbyterian polity is found in the former while the polity of the latter also shows influences of both the Methodist and Congregational churches, which merged with about sixty percent of Presbyterians in 1925 to form the United Church of Canada.[63] This section will deal with the PCC while the next section will deal with the UCC.

Created in 1875 by the merger of all of the Presbyterian groups in Canada at that time and continuing after the division in 1925, Presbyterians have been in Canada since the mid eighteenth century, and therefore constitute one of the oldest branches of the Christian church continuously worshipping here. The PCC presently numbers approximately 140,000 members.[64] Since 1875, it has been an autonomous denomination, although it looks to its European, and especially Scottish, forebears for historical continuity, and this is reflected in its understanding of its sources of church law.

---

61 For the Free Methodists: S.C. 1926–27, c. 107, as am. 1959, c. 67. For the Wesleyan Church: S.C. 1944–45, c. 62.

62 Presbyterian polity is also characteristic of the tiny (c. 11,000 member) Synod of the Presbyterian Church in America (Canadian Section) in Canada.

63 See N. Keith Clifford, *The Resistance to Church Union in Canada 1904–1939* (Vancouver: U.B.C. Press, 1985).

64 Above note 27 at 342 (1999 figures reported).

The polity, practice, and procedure of the PCC is found primarily in its own *The Book of Forms*,[65] but this is supplemented by historic documents of presbyterian polity including *The First Book of Discipline*,[66] *The Second Book of Discipline*,[67] the Westminster Standards,[68] and *Cox's Practice and Procedure in the Church of Scotland*.[69]

The fundamental unit of presbyterian polity is the local congregation. While election by the local congregation to church office is the sole means for membership in the higher councils of the church, final authority in all matters of doctrine, discipline, and worship is vested in the highest council, the General Assembly. Therefore, it may be said that while representation selection flows upward, authority flows downward within presbyterian polity. The congregation is governed by its minister (the "teaching elder") and its kirk session (the "ruling elders"), who are theoretically chosen by the congregation and ordained for life, and who together enjoy spiritual and temporal oversight over congregational life. The chairman or "moderator" of the kirk session is the minister. Specific responsibility for the management of congregational property and contracts is vested either in a board of managers or trustees, or in an incorporated board, if the congregation has been incorporated.[70] These board members are elected by the congregation in general meeting and are responsible to the congregation, as well as, in most cases, to the kirk session for the management of congregational property. A variety of congregational committees whose membership is typically appointed by the kirk session are responsible for the conduct of congregational activities to the kirk session.

The next level of organization, the presbytery, is regional and consists of a number of congregations. There are forty-six presbyteries

---

65   (Don Mills: The Presbyterian Church in Canada, 2002). Updated annually.

66   Above note 21.

67   *Ibid.*

68   *Ibid.*

69   (Edinburgh: The Church of Scotland, 1976), 6th ed. Now overtaken for the Church of Scotland by *The Constitution and Laws of the Church of Scotland* (Edinburgh: Church of Scotland, 1997). See also Andrew Herron, *The Law and Practice of the Kirk: A Guide and Commentary* (Glasgow: Chapter House Ltd., 1995).

70   It would appear that most Presbyterian congregations continue to vest their property in trustees; however, some have incorporated either by private act or pursuant to provincial non-profit corporation legislation.

nationally. Typically a presbytery will meet monthly, and membership is restricted to ministers within that area plus one representative elder from each kirk session chosen by the kirk session. The member of presbytery chosen annually to chair its meetings is known as the moderator, who is, effectively, the chief executive officer of the presbytery. Whereas kirk session meetings are secret and their deliberations not usually disclosed to the congregation, presbytery meetings are open to all members of the church. Presbytery enjoys a supervisory role over all ministers and congregations within its bounds in all spiritual and temporal matters, and is responsible for such decisions as the erection or winding down of congregations and the approval of a congregation's choice of minister, as well as the approval of candidates for ministry from within its bounds.

The next level of organization is the synod, which is comprised of a number of presbyteries, of which there are eight in Canada. Synods meet on average once a year and are composed of all ministers and the representative elders to presbyteries within their bounds. The role of a synod is to supervise the work of the presbyteries within its bounds in all spiritual and temporal matters. Again, its chairperson is known as the moderator.

The highest organ of government within the PCC is the General Assembly, which meets for one week annually. For the rest of the year, the management of the national church vests in the General Assembly Office and the Principal Clerk of the General Assembly, who is responsible for carrying out and co-ordinating the decisions of the General Assembly. Its membership consists of one-sixth of the total number of ministers in the church chosen by presbyteries on a revolving basis, together with an equal number of elders. Approximately three hundred commissioners are selected annually to attend. The General Assembly enjoys oversight over the church in all matters, both temporal and spiritual, and acts as the highest legislative, executive, and judicial authority within the church. The sole restriction on the power of the General Assembly is the so-called "Barrier Act" procedure, which must be followed if a change in the law of the church is contemplated. This procedure requires that changes in relation to matters of doctrine, discipline, government, and worship be approved by a majority of presbyteries prior to final approval by the General Assembly. Both Synods and General Assemblies are open assemblies. The chairman of the General Assembly is its Moderator.

In addition to being responsible for administrative matters, kirk sessions, presbyteries, synods, and General Assembly are also regarded as and usually referred to as "church courts," since discipline of both clergy and laity occurs in these bodies. Disciplinary proceedings against a member or elder will normally commence in the kirk session, which constitutes itself as a "court" with formalities relating to witnesses, evidence, and so on. Somewhat unusually, the parties are not permitted to have legal counsel but must either represent themselves or be represented by a friend who may not be a lawyer. The procedures set out in *The Book of Forms* are detailed. The process is inquisitorial rather than adversarial in nature, reflecting its Scottish civil law origins. Sanctions include admonition, rebuke, suspension, removal from office, and excommunication.

Appeal is to the higher courts in order of the hierarchy with the same procedures applying there when constituted as a court. The General Assembly usually does not meet in full session as a court, rather it will appoint a judicial committee of not more than ten commissioners from that Assembly to hear final appeals. It may also appoint a Commission or a Special Commission to investigate disciplinary matters and that Commission's decision is final, unless it has acted *ultra vires*, in which case appeal may be made to the next General Assembly. In contrast to other Protestant denominations where formal disciplinary proceedings are rare, informal discussions would suggest that at least ten to fifteen judicial proceedings are underway nationally at various judicial levels within the PCC annually.

Property owned at the local, regional, and national levels of the PCC is held in a variety of ways. The national church is incorporated[71] and property owned by the national church is vested by legislation in the Trustee Board of the Church.[72] Generally speaking, property at the congregational, presbytery, and synod level is vested in trustees, sometimes for the local congregation and sometimes for the national church; however, some presbyteries and congregations have been incorporated with their property vested in the body corporate. As well, the colleges and some other institutions have been incorporated and hold their own property as bodies corporate.[73]

---

71 S.O., 1874, c. 75.

72 S.C. 1939, c. 64 as am. S.C. 1962, c. 23; and S.C. 1966, c. 116.

73 Legal advisors should be careful to establish precisely how these issues are dealt with by the particular Presbyterian body they are advising, since a wide variety of property-holding practices are found, usually reflecting the historical origins of the body concerned.

J. THE UNITED CHURCH OF CANADA

The largest religious institution in Canada whose polity may be broadly characterized as presbyterian in nature is the United Church of Canada, with a 1999 membership of 1,589,886.[74] Formed in 1925 as the result of the union of all Congregationalists, Methodists, and approximately sixty percent of the membership of the Presbyterian Church in Canada, the polity also reflects, but to a lesser extent, the more congregational practices of its other two uniting members.[75] The polity, practice, and procedure of the United Church of Canada is found in *The Manual*, revised and published periodically by the denomination. While it may be necessary in unusual circumstances to consult the historic constitutional documents of predecessor denominations, this is rare because *The Manual* is intended to be comprehensive.

The United Church of Canada came into existence by virtue of the *United Church of Canada Act*,[76] federal legislation enacted to avoid the property disputes that had resulted in the House of Lords decision in *General Assembly of Free Church of the Scotland v. Lord Overtown*,[77] occasioned by a church union in Scotland. Pursuant to the Act, the basic law of the United Church is the Basis of Union, which sets out the doctrine, polity, ministry, and administrative structure for the church. The Basis can be changed only by the General Council with the consent of the presbyteries, and is supplemented by the Bylaws, which fill out the details for the day-to-day implementation and running of the church. The Bylaws may be changed by the General Council or the General Council Executive without notice or consent of the presbyteries and carry less weight than the Basis of Union as the fundamental law of the UCC.

The fundamental unit of United Church polity is the pastoral charge[78] under a minister, which may consist of one congregation only, or of several, depending on size, geography, or other local factors. Three alternative organizational models are available for pastoral charges. The first is composed of a session, consisting of elders elected by the congre-

---

74 Above note 27 at 343.
75 See generally Clifford, above note 63 and *The Manual: The United Church of Canada 2001* (Toronto: United Church Publishing House, 2001) at 7–12.
76 S.C., 1924, c. 100.
77 [1904] A.C. 515 (H.L.).
78 *The Manual*, ss. 101–295.

gation, a committee of stewards also elected by the congregation and an official board. The session enjoys spiritual oversight over the congregation, while the stewards are responsible for securing funds and the board is responsible for the management of the temporal property of the congregation. The second model is of a unified board structure, under a church board, elected by the congregation with spiritual and temporal oversight, while the third model is of a unified council structure, under a church council, again with spiritual and temporal oversight of the pastoral charge. These three reflect the local organizational models of the uniting denominations, although the first is the most prevalent in the modern UCC. A variety of congregational committees exist to conduct the activities of the congregation, all ultimately under the supervision of the appropriate governing body of the pastoral charge.

The next level of organization is the presbytery,[79] which is regional in nature, consisting of representatives of a number of pastoral charges, both ordained and lay, in equal numbers. Presbyteries meet regularly, typically monthly, and their main responsibility is the oversight of both the spiritual and temporal affairs of the pastoral charges in that presbytery. The member of presbytery responsible for convening meetings is the chairperson, who is assisted by a secretary. Presbytery oversight includes responsibility for the erection and the winding down of pastoral charges, the approval of ministerial appointments to pastoral charges within the presbytery, and oversight of the relationship between minister and pastoral charge, including ministerial discipline as necessary. A variety of presbytery standing committees are responsible for carrying out these duties.

Above the presbytery is the conference,[80] which is comprised of a number of presbyteries and meets either annually or biennially, depending on need or local practice. Conference membership is composed of all ministers within the bounds of the conference and an equal number of lay members elected by presbyteries. The role of the conference is to have spiritual oversight over all within its bounds, to deal with matters referred to it by the General Council and to deal with any appeals or petitions made to it from within its bounds. In addition, conference is responsible for electing both lay and ministerial members to the General Council and for ordaining candidates for ministry recommended by the presbyteries.

---

79 *Ibid.* ss. 300–393.
80 *Ibid.* ss. 400–470.

The conference is headed by a president, who is assisted by an executive, a small staff, and a variety of conference standing committees.

The highest court of the UCC is the General Council,[81] which meets biennially for two weeks and consists of an equal number of clerical and lay commissioners selected by conferences across the country. The General Council has authority to legislate on all matters relating to doctrine, worship, membership, and government of the church and to legislate on all matters relating to property. As in the Presbyterian Church in Canada, so too in the UCC each level of government combines legislative, executive, and judicial functions, and the General Council, like the General Assembly, is the highest legislative, executive, and judicial authority. However, also in keeping with presbyterian custom, where a change is proposed to a fundamental law of the church, that change must be approved by the majority of presbyteries prior to final approval by the General Council. The chairperson of the General Council is its moderator, who holds the appointment for two years and acts as the chief executive officer of the church, to conduct the business of the church when the General Council is not in session. The Moderator is assisted by a national staff under the direction of a general secretary, who is the chief administrative officer. All meetings of all levels of government within the UCC are open, in contrast to the usual presbyterian practice of closed meetings for kirk sessions.

Sessions, presbyteries, conferences, and General Council also serve as "church courts" and are referred to as such in relation to matters of discipline for both clergy and laity. Where the person under discipline is a member of the laity, the session, church board, or church council is the appropriate forum for resolution; however, where the person under discipline is a member of the clergy, the presbytery is the first forum for resolution. Both laity and clergy have a right of appeal through the higher courts to the General Council. Parties may be represented by legal counsel at all levels and a relatively sophisticated code of procedure is found in *The Manual* to govern the proceedings at all levels.

At the highest level, the General Council does not meet in full session as a court; rather, appeals are heard and disposed of by a Judicial Committee,[82] whose members serve for terms of appointment and who

---

81   *Ibid.* ss. 500–554.
82   *Ibid.* ss. 540–549.

sit in panels, like an ordinary civil court. Appeals are subject to final review and affirmation by the General Council, if requested, although the General Council does not re-hear the appeal. In contrast to other Protestant denominations, the UCC generally has a larger number of judicial proceedings at all levels underway nationally, although the numbers vary annually.

Property owned at the local, regional, and national levels of the UCC is held in a variety of ways. The national church is federally incorporated[83] and property held for national church purposes is vested in it. Generally speaking, property at the congregational, presbytery, and conference level is vested in trustees for the purposes of that level, although there would also appear to be increasing use of corporations with the property vested in the body corporate. Church colleges and other institutions are also incorporated, so that legal advisers are required to investigate precisely how property is held in respect to every individual entity of the church prior to giving advice.

K. BAPTIST CHURCHES

A number of denominations in Canada are the historical descendants of the Anabaptist Reformation and have church polities of a congregational rather than episcopal or presbyterian nature. The largest of these groups are the various Baptist fellowships in Canada, but others include the Mennonites, the Brethren in Christ, the Old Order Amish, and the Hutterites. (The Congregational Church, *per se*, disappeared in Canada in 1925 when it merged with Methodists and Presbyterians to form the United Church of Canada. There is a small denomination, the Congregational Christian Church in Canada, with about 5,000 members that has been revived.[84]) Demographically, the Baptist and Mennonite groups constitute the largest and the most "structured" of these Anabaptist heirs. Other groups are not only small in numbers but also highly decentralized with little denominational structure, if any, beyond the local community, which is typically self-governing and possessed of few assets.

While some of these groups are incorporated, others are unincorporated, with local property vested in trustees pursuant to trust deeds. The

---

83   Above note 76.
84   Above note 27 at 340 (1997 figures reported).

Hutterian Brethren is an example of a community that has incorporated both federally and provincially in respect to individual bruderhofs, appreciating the value of the body corporate as a means of holding property in common in keeping with its doctrine.[85] On the other hand, the preference for poverty and the distribution of assets in excess of immediate personal requirements are reflected in the virtual absence of the use of legal property-holding devices in other groups.[86]

There are a number of different Baptist fellowships across the country, some quite small, such as the Free Will Baptists (c. 700 members) and the Canadian Convention of Southern Baptists (c. 9,600 members), while the remaining groups are of modest size, such as the Baptist Convention of Ontario and Quebec (c. 58,000 members), the Baptist Union of Western Canada (c. 20,000 members), and the United Baptist Convention of the Atlantic Provinces (c. 63,000 members).[87] Although separate denominations with their own institutional structures, most Baptist groups within Canada have become members of two umbrella organizations, the Canadian Baptist Federation with approximately 131,000 members and the Evangelical Baptist Fellowship with approximately 62,000 members.[88] Whether the fellowship is large or small, a member of one of these two federations or not, the polity, nature of authority, and its exercise are virtually the same. The description that follows is based on the Baptist Convention of Ontario and Quebec.

The focus for Baptists is the local congregation, which is not only regarded as autonomous, but also is regarded as a complete Christian society in itself. The "Baptist church" is the congregation, and membership in a larger geographical grouping is regarded as largely for facilitation of joint mission and outreach work beyond the financial or geographical reach of individual communities. Baptists are non-hierarchical in both theology and polity. The congregational meeting, of which one becomes a member only through believer's baptism, is the focus for authority and initiative. The emphasis in Baptist theology on believer's baptism is the key to understanding why a gathered community of such believers is the primary focus of Baptist institutional life. While practices

---

85   Below chapter 8.
86   Legal advisers must research how each group operates and holds property prior to giving advice.
87   Above note 27 at 338–343 (1999 figures reported).
88   *Ibid.*

differ somewhat from congregation to congregation, oversight of a congregation is vested in its pastor, whom it calls, and in the deacon's board. Ranging in size in relation to the size of the congregation, the deacon's board is elected by the congregation for fixed terms and has both spiritual and temporal oversight of the congregation, including the pastor. Deacons are not ordained and occasionally honorary deacons (not more than three) may be elected to recognize special services rendered over time to the congregation. Some congregations also elect elders who focus on worship and evangelism, leaving the deacons with responsibility for benevolent work and visitation. In addition to the deacons' board, congregations also appoint three trustees for the purpose of vesting property and a variety of congregational committees with responsibility for various aspects of congregational life.

Congregations are typically federated in larger regional groups called either associations or areas. These have no authority in any matter whatsoever over individual congregations but exist to facilitate co-ordination of various projects within their region. It is also the practice, though not necessary, of associations to examine and ordain pastors and to maintain a roll of suitable pastors for congregational call.

Finally, congregations may also be members of larger territorial units, conventions, which meet in annual assembly but again have no authority, rather serve as co-ordinating bodies for matters such as overseas missions, preparation of Sunday school curricula, and running divinity colleges. Delegates to the conventions are chosen directly by their congregations and while a convention is headed by a president, who is assisted by a small full-time staff, the purpose of these persons is to carry out the wishes of the local congregations not to dictate to them. Effectively, then, there is no hierarchy of authority among Baptists.

The congregational focus of Baptist church life is also reflected in the way in which property is held. Local congregations own their own property and vest it in trustees pursuant to a trust deed. However, increasingly, some congregations are incorporating and vesting their property in the body corporate. Local congregations also have their own constitutions, which set out the practices, procedures, and duties for the officers and committees of the congregation. Conventions and particular institutions such as missions, colleges, and universities are incorporated, federally or provincially, as the case may be, and have bylaws pursuant to such legislation.

Baptist churches have no judicatories, church courts, rules of procedure, or formal disciplinary processes. Rather, where a dispute or disciplinary matter arises in relation to a member of the congregation, it may be dealt with informally by the pastor or be referred to the deacon's board, which will deal with it as it sees fit. There is no avenue for appeal whatsoever and dissatisfaction with the outcome must either be borne in silence or expressed by withdrawal from the congregation. Where the controversy involves an ordained pastor, the area minister, who is an employee of the area, will be called in to resolve it informally, with appeal to the executive minister of the convention, who effectively runs the day-to-day operations of the convention office. The decision of the executive minister is final, and appeal to the annual assembly of the convention is not available. "Separation" is regarded as the only viable alternative for a dissatisfied member or pastor.

L. MENNONITE COMMUNITIES

Among those religious groups who are the historical descendants of the Anabaptist Reformation and congregational in polity, the Mennonite communities in Canada are even less connected than the Baptists.[89] A Mennonite congregation is entirely free-standing and need not be federated with or in any way attached to one of the dozen or so conferences in Canada or approximately twenty conferences in North America. Historically, Mennonites have modelled themselves more closely than any of the other Christian groups discussed above on the primitive church of the New Testament, as one consisting entirely of discrete local communities of believers, entered solely by believer's baptism.

However, most congregations are associated with a conference, indeed may be a member of several conferences, which tend to be organized on a regional basis, although some are also organized on historical lines, reflecting the European place of origin or particular theological grouping. Conferences exist primarily to promote social programs, and run missions and bible colleges — they are not ecclesiastical administrative units within the Mennonite community. They are usually incorporated pursuant to federal or provincial legislation, as appropriate, with constitutions, for the purpose of holding and managing property used for

---

89 For a history of Mennonite, Hutterite, and Doukhobor conflicts with the law, see William Janzen, *Limits on Liberty: The Experience of Mennonite, Hutterite and Doukhobor Communites in Canada* (Toronto: U. of T. Press, 1990).

conference initiatives. Within Canada the largest conferences are the Conference of Mennonites in Canada (c. 28,000 members) and the Canadian Conference of Mennonite Brethren Churches (c. 33,000 members); smaller conferences are the Evangelical Mennonite Conference (c. 7,000 members), the Evangelical Mennonite Mission Conference of Canada (c. 4,600 members), the Mennonite Church (c. 8,000 members), and the Reinland Mennonite Church (c. 900 members).[90]

As self-standing communities of faith, each congregation is entirely self governing and each has its own constitution. Most congregations are incorporated pursuant to provincial non-profit corporation legislation and their congregational constitutions are effectively bylaws pursuant to this incorporation.[91] Authority within a congregation is vested in the congregation in general meeting. The pastor is called by the congregation and may be dismissed as well (being employed by a contract of employment that is for a fixed term). The council of the congregation, which is charged with the general supervision of both temporal and spiritual matters, is also elected by the congregation. The council typically consists of ten to twelve members, who chair various congregational committees or groups. The members are not ordained and are not understood to be "elders." In addition, the congregation elects several deacons to be responsible specifically for the welfare of congregational members. Various sub-committees also exist to look after various aspects of congregational life. When congregations are members of conferences, they may select delegates to attend any activities or meetings but the selection process is informal and often on the basis of availability. No authority is vested in these persons whatsoever. Simplicity is the paramount characteristic of Mennonite organizations.

Congregational constitutions rarely contain provisions to govern disciplinary processes, nor are there any courts or tribunals struck to deal with such matters. Rather, where the dispute involves members, the pastor will simply deal with it on an informal basis or arrange for some form of third-party mediation, as is appropriate in the circumstances. While shunning and excommunication remain, by custom, the ultimate sanc-

---

90   Above note 27 at 339–342 (1999 figures reported). In 2001, the larger conferences in North America realigned themselves to form the Mennonite Church Canada and the Mennonite Church USA, each responsible for its own international mission work.

91   The constitution of the Ottawa Mennonite Church is relied on here.

tions available, they are rarely used today; issues are normally resolved quietly. When the dispute involves a minister, which is very rare, again, the normal route would be informal, internal resolution, although if this fails, an outside minister from the conference will be called in to mediate. Since Mennonite pastors are employed by contracts of employment, terms for dismissal are provided that may be invoked in appropriate circumstances. There are no routes of appeal outside the congregation.

M. OTHER CHRISTIAN COMMUNITIES

In addition to the major denominational groups represented in the discussion above, two other categories of Christian communities may be identified, virtually all of the individual examples of which are intensely congregational in polity — a veritable forest of single instances. The first category may be said to include those communities that have fragmented from main-line Protestantism between the sixteenth and the early twentieth centuries and include the Moravians, the Society of Friends, the Christadelphians, and the Plymouth Brethren. Some observers might also include within this category, religious groups that themselves claim to be Christian but whose teachings are so different from the main branches of Christianity that many Christians would dispute that claim; these include the Mormons, Jehovah's Witnesses, and Seventh Day Adventists, as well as the Doukhobors, who began as a small sect of Russian Orthodoxy.

The second category may be said to consist of the Evangelical denominations that have grown up, especially in the second half of the twentieth century, some of which are organized denominations with national or North American administrative structures, but many of which are autonomous congregations, some of which may be loosely associated. These include the Salvation Army, Christian and Missionary Alliance, Evangelical Free Church, Associated Gospel Churches, Fellowship Baptists, the Bible Church, and the Pentecostal Assemblies of Canada, as well as some Reformed communities such as the Christian Reformed Church and the Reformed Church in Canada (although some observers might not agree with this last group being classified as "Evangelical").[92]

---

92   For a taxonomy of Evangelicals, see Lloyd Mackey, *These Evangelical Churches of Ours* (Winfield, B.C.: Wood Lake Books, 1995).

Most of these communities are congregational rather than hierarchical in structure, although individual congregations are usually members of national or international associations of similar congregations. Most have come into existence recently, and use non-profit corporations to hold and manage property. Legal advisers should regard each congregation as unique and consider its incorporating legislation, constitution, and bylaws when rendering advice. The historical standards, customs, texts, and oral traditions found in the older Christian denominations are largely irrelevant to these theologically and legally sleek communities.

N. NON-CHRISTIAN RELIGIOUS INSTITUTIONS

According to the 1991 Religion Census, approximately one million Canadians claim membership in the other world religions found in Canada today. Of these, approximately 318,000 people are Jews, while approximately 747,000 people subscribe to a variety of "Eastern non-Christian,"[93] religions, including Baha'i (c. 15,000), Buddhism (c. 163,000), Confucianism (c. 400), Hinduism (c. 157,000), Islam (c. 253,000), Jainism (c. 1,400), Shintoism (c. 450), Sikhism (c. 147,000), Taoism (c. 1,700), and Zoroastrianism (c. 3,200).[94]

Most of these religions are not characterized, from a legal perspective, as hierarchical, nor do many of them possess, generally speaking, the complex structures of administration and courts with codes of law and legal procedure characteristic of the historical branches of Christianity. Within Canada, they are largely community based, with each congregation incorporated as a non-profit corporation and carrying out its community life in accordance with its own constitution, bylaws, religious texts, and practices of ancient, foreign origin. Legal advisers must take each individual community as they find them in giving advice, as with the proliferation of Evangelical Christian congregations.

---

93 The umbrella category language of the Census.
94 See generally Geoffrey Parrinder, ed., *World Religions: From Ancient History to the Present* (New York: Hamlyn, 1985).

Chapter Four

Constitutional Fundamentals

A. CONSTITUTIONAL FUNDAMENTALS

The constitutional relationship of the governments of Canada, both federal and provincial, to religious institutions is, as in most other countries, the consequence of history. It reflects the constitutional inheritance of a specifically English[1] understanding of parliamentary government, as

---

1   Scots constitutional law differs from English constitutional law in regarding church and state as two separate kingdoms, each sovereign within its own realm, and this is ultimately reflected in the *Church of Scotland Act*, 1921 (11 & 12 Geo. 5, c. 29) and the Articles Declaratory thereto. The principle of separate but equal kingdoms enshrined in that Act is the consequence of four centuries of struggle by the established Church of Scotland for such recognition. See generally Francis Lyall, *Of Presbyters and Kings: Church and State in the Law of Scotland* (Aberdeen: Aberdeen University Press, 1980); and the *Stair Memorial Encyclopedia of the Laws of Scotland* V. 136–162, 357–372. See also Anon., "The Legal Position of Dissenting Churches in Scotland" (1887) 31 Journal of Jurisprudence 616; R. King Murray, "The Constitutional Position of the Church of Scotland" [1958] P.L. 155; T.B. Smith, "The Union of 1707 as Fundamental Law" [1957] P.L. 99; T.M. Taylor, "Church and State in Scotland" [1957] J.R. 121; Michael Upton, "Marriage Vows of the Elephant: The Constitution of 1707" (1989) 105 L.Q.R. 79; Rodney Brazier, "The Constitution of the United Kingdom" [1999] Camb. L.J. 96; and Elizabeth Wicks, "A New Constitution for a New State? The 1707 Union of England and Scotland" (2001) 117 L.Q.R. 109.

modified by indigenous Canadian constitutional requirements and arrangements, reflecting in turn Canadian historical experience. It also reflects historical British[2] understandings of the proper relationship of "church and state," again as modified by the historical evolution of those understandings in Canadian history and contemporary experience.

Although Canada is, and has been from its inception, a country with an overwhelming, if nominal, Christian majority, Christian theologies of the two kingdoms, which assert the independence of the spiritual from the temporal realm, have never been accepted in constitutional law, although they have enjoyed tacit acceptance in practice.[3] Rather, the inheritance of the English theory of parliamentary sovereignty means that in Canada, Parliament has supreme and sovereign authority over the affairs of all individuals and institutions within its geographical jurisdiction, including all religious institutions and the religious practices of individual citizens, subject only to the generally applicable constitutional limitations on its sovereign legislative power. Parliamentary sovereignty means that Parliament has the power, as Dicey stated, "to make or unmake any law whatsoever."[4]

In England the sovereignty of Parliament was first asserted in the legislation of the English Reformation, which threw off the universal claims of the Roman pontiff over England and created the Church of England as the state church whose earthly head was the Crown-in-Parliament.[5] While the conflict for supremacy within the realm of England between Crown and Parliament was not finally resolved until a century and a half later, after the Glorious Revolution of 1688–89,[6] it was never doubted from the 1530s onward that whichever contestant won the tussle for supremacy in the state, the state enjoyed authority over the church. The

---

2   The reluctance, until recently, of Canadian legislatures and courts to make law for religious institutions is surely a reflection of the greater respect for Christianity found in the United Kingdom historically in contrast to the anti-clericalism characteristic of French history and society.

3   See above chapter 1 for this theological background.

4   A.V. Dicey, *The Law of the Constitution*, 10th ed. (London: MacMillan, 1959) at 39.

5   22 Henry VIII, c. 15 (1531); 23 Henry VIII, c. 20 (1532); 24 Henry VIII, c. 12 (1533); 26 Henry VIII, c. 1, 19, 20, 21 (1534); and 28 Henry VIII, c. 10 (1536).

6   *Bill of Rights*, 1 Will. & Mary, c. 2 (1689); *Mutiny Act*, 1 Will. & Mary, c. 5 (1689); *Toleration Act*, 1 Will. & Mary, c. 18 (1689); *Triennial Act*, 6 & 7 Will. & Mary, c. 2 (1694); *Civil List Act*, 9 & 10 Will. III, c. 23 (1697); *Treasons Act*, 7 & 8 Will. & Mary, c. 3 (1696); and *Act of Settlement* 12 & 13 Will. III, c. 2 (1701).

English Reformation, from a legal perspective, was first and foremost about the assertion of the primacy of the English state over the church and the assimilation of that church with the state. Once a sovereign Parliament emerged as the supreme authority within the state, that sovereignty was as much over the church as the state.

From the Reformation legislation of the 1530s onward, Parliament asserted the constitutional right to determine all ecclesiastical matters not just in relation to property and contract but also all matters of doctrine, polity, and liturgy. The Westminster Parliament continues to enjoy and occasionally to exercise that constitutional right today in relation to the established church. While such intervention has become increasingly rare in the past century and is unlikely ever again to be exercised without the clear request of the church, Parliament retains sovereignty over the Church of England, and the Crown-in-Parliament is the "supreme governor" of the church.

However, it is also the case that Parliament simply by virtue of its sovereignty over all persons and institutions within the state also enjoys sovereignty over all other non-established Christian denominations and all other non-Christian religious institutions within the British state. With the growth of religious toleration in England[7] in the course of the eighteenth century, Parliament enacted legislation not only to permit religious pluralism but also to facilitate property-holding and the enjoyment of civil status by non-established churches and religious institutions by public statutes of general application as well as by private legislation of particular application, and at the request of the concerned church. By virtue of residence within the geographical jurisdiction of Parliament, all religious institutions and persons are subject to Parliament.

This constitutional inheritance means that in Canada[8] Parliament theoretically enjoys sovereign and supreme authority over all religious institutions and individuals engaged in religious practices. However, in

---

7   Again, historically Scotland had a different religious history.

8   The understanding and analysis of Canadian constitutional law in this chapter is derived from the leading text: Peter W. Hogg, *Constitutional Law of Canada* (Toronto: Carswell, 2001 Student Edition). See also for *Charter*-related issues: Gerald A. Beaudoin and Ed Ratushny, eds., *The Canadian Charter of Rights and Freedoms*, 2d ed. (Toronto: Carswell, 1989); and Gerald A. Beaudoin and Errol Mendes, eds., *The Canadian Charter of Rights and Freedoms*, 3d ed. (Toronto: Carswell, 1996).

contrast to the United Kingdom, where sovereignty may only be limited by the overriding law of the European Union,[9] in Canada there are at least three major limitations on the exercise by Parliament of its sovereignty generally and more specifically in relation to religion. Federalism curtails the power of Parliament as found within a unitary state by dividing and distributing it between federal and provincial legislatures, each with certain exclusive jurisdictions. When each level of government enjoys exclusive jurisdiction, the plenary authority inherent in the concept of a single national supreme legislature is thereby constrained.

Secondly, the entrenchment of the *Canadian Charter of Rights and Freedoms*, which creates standards against which legislation and administrative actions must be measured by the courts, curtails the exclusive sovereignties of federal and provincial legislatures when courts strike down legislation failing to meet these standards. This restriction is not absolute, however, for two reasons. Section 33 permits both Parliament and the provincial legislatures to override most of the provisions of the *Charter* by including in legislation an express declaration that the statute is to operate notwithstanding a provision in section 2 or sections 7 to 15 of the *Charter*. Moreover, Part V of the *Constitution Act, 1982*, provides for five different amending procedures for the *Constitution*,[10] thereby ensuring the supremacy of the legislatures over the *Charter*.

Thirdly, the amending procedures also ensure legislative sovereignty generally over all legislation including constitutional legislation such as the *Charter*.

The principal division of sovereignty within Canada is found in the *Constitution Act, 1867*. However, that statute is silent in relation to jurisdiction over religion, religious institutions, and religious practice in Canada. Since issues of religion constituted one of the most acrimonious political issues in the pre-Confederation colonies, it may be wondered why they were left out of the *Constitution Act, 1867*, other than in relation to section 93 denominational school rights. The First Amendment in the American *Bill of Rights*, which had already been passed by Con-

---

9 The Westminster Parliament retains its sovereignty to legislate notwithstanding the delegation of that sovereignty in 1998 to the statutory assemblies: *Government of Wales Act 1998* (U.K.), 1998, c. 38; *Scotland Act 1998* (U.K.), 1998, c. 46; and *Northern Ireland Act 1998* (U.K.), 1998, c. 47.

10 *Canada Act, 1982* (U.K., 1982, c. 11), Schedule B, ss. 38–49. Also found in R.S.C. 1985, App. II, No. 44.

gress in 1789 and ratified by three-fourths of the states in 1791, had provided the fathers of Confederation with an example of a written constitution providing both for jurisdiction over religion and protection for freedom of religion.

Two reasons may be suggested for this lacuna in the *Constitution Act, 1867*. First, the preamble to the Act states that Canada was to have "a Constitution similar in principle to that of the United Kingdom" so that the protection of liberties in relation to religion, expression, assembly, and association could be left to the common law, inherited as part of the United Kingdom constitutional arrangement. The historical position of the English common law is that every subject is free to do as he or she wishes provided the positive law, whether judge-made or legislative, does not expressly prohibit that conduct. While English legislation in the sixteenth and seventeenth centuries had restricted the common law rights of Protestant Dissenters and Roman Catholics, most of that legislation had been repealed prior to the reception dates for the common law in the Canadian colonies, which had, in any case, enacted local legislation in relation to matters of religion from early on.

Some of this pre-Confederation legislation may constitute the second reason why the *Constitution Act, 1867*, was silent both as to jurisdiction over religion and the protection of freedom of religion. In 1851 the legislature of Canada[11] enacted legislation guaranteeing "... the free exercise and enjoyment of Religious Profession and Worship, without discrimination or preference, so as the same be not made an excuse for acts of licentiousness, or a justification of practices inconsistent with the peace and safety of the Province."[12] Moreover, this typically Canadian legislative approach reflected the practice of religious freedom in the four original provinces by 1867 insofar as numerous religious groups flourished in an open religious marketplace, if equally subject to the law. It seems likely, then, that the fathers of Confederation regarded freedom of religion to be protected already and to be a matter of local or provincial concern.[13]

---

11 Now modern Ontario and Quebec: *Act of Union*, 3 & 4 Vict., c. 35 (1840).

12 *Freedom of Worship Act*, 14 & 15 Vict., c. 175 (1851). This legislation continues in force in Ontario: *Religious Freedom Act*, R.S.O. 1990, c. R. 22.

13 The intensely local nature of religious life in each of the four colonies, Nova Scotia, New Brunswick, Canada East, and Canada West, in 1867 is demonstrated by the large body of historical writing about nineteenth-century Canadian ecclesiastical history, which is itself fragmented into local or provincial studies.

Section 129 of the *Constitution Act, 1867*, further provided for the continuance in force of all pre-Confederation legislation until repealed or altered. The enactment of legislation later in the nineteenth century by the provinces to regulate secular activities on Sunday reflected the contemporary widespread belief that the power to legislate for religious matters resided with the provinces.[14]

B. RELIGION IN THE WRITTEN CONSTITUTION

1) *Constitution Act, 1867*

While there are no express provisions in the *Constitution Act, 1867*, dealing with jurisdiction over religion or the protection of freedom of religion, certain sections may be said to be concerned with religion either by virtue of their inherent nature or by virtue of subsequent judicial interpretation. Section 91 grants to Parliament the exclusive right to legislate in relation to marriage and divorce,[15] criminal law,[16] and "such Classes of Subjects as are expressly excepted in the Enumeration of the Classes of Subjects by this Act assigned exclusively to the Legislatures of the Provinces."[17]

The Act further grants the exclusive right to legislate to the provincial legislatures in relation to the "Establishment, Maintenance and Management of Hospitals, Asylums, Charities, and Eleemosynary Institutions in and for the Province,"[18] the solemnization of marriage,[19] "Property and Civil Rights in the Province,"[20] and "all Matters of a merely local or private Nature in the Province."[21] Section 93 makes additional provision for provincial jurisdiction over denominational schools in existence at the time of Confederation or thereafter created,[22] and further similar provi-

---

14 Hogg, above note 8 at 469.
15 Section 91(26).
16 Section 91(27).
17 Section 91(29).
18 Section 92(7).
19 Section 92(12).
20 Section 92(13).
21 Section 92(16).
22 Section 93. This applied in 1867 to Ontario, Quebec, New Brunswick, and Nova Scotia and was extended to British Columbia and Prince Edward Island when they joined Confederation: British Columbia Terms of Union (Order in

sions are found in the constitutional legislation of the *Manitoba Act*,[23] the *Alberta Act*,[24] the *Saskatchewan Act*,[25] and the *Newfoundland Act*[26] in relation to constitutional guarantees for denominational schools in those provinces. Section 93 was amended in 1997 by the addition of section 93A to provide that the denominational school provisions no longer apply to Quebec.[27] In 1998, Term 17 of the *Newfoundland Act* was amended to remove denominational school privileges in Newfoundland.[28]

2) *Constitution Act, 1982*

While the *Constitution Act, 1867*, may be said to focus on jurisdiction, the *Constitution Act, 1982*, may be said to focus on explicit protection for religious freedom and other associated freedoms. The preamble to the Act states that "Canada is founded upon principles that recognize the supremacy of God and the rule of law,"[29] a phrase included as a result of lobbying by evangelical Christians and to ensure Western Canadian support for the entire constitutional package.[30] The *Canadian Charter of Rights and Freedoms* further states that everyone has certain fundamental freedoms: "freedom of conscience and religion,"[31] "freedom of thought, belief, opinion, and expression,"[32] "freedom of peaceful assembly,"[33] and "freedom of association."[34] The *Charter* also guarantees "the right to life,

---

Council, 16 May 1871); and Prince Edward Island Terms of Union (Order in Council, 26 June 1873).

23 (1870) R.S.C. 1985, App. II, No. 8, s. 22.
24 (1905) R.S.C. 1985, App. II, No. 20, s. 17.
25 (1905) R.S.C. 1985, App. II, No. 21, s. 17.
26 (1949) R.S.C. 1985, App. II, No. 32, Sched., Term 17.
27 Constitution Amendment, 1997 (Quebec), SI/97–141.
28 Constitution Amendment, 1998 (*Newfoundland Act*), SI/98–25.
29 R.S.C. 1985, App. II, No. 44, Preamble.
30 For a comprehensive account of the historical background see George Egerton, "Trudeau, God, and the Canadian Constitution: Religion, Human Rights, and Government Authority in the Making of the 1982 Constitution" in David Lyon and Marguerite Van Die, eds., *Rethinking Church, State, and Modernity: Canada between Europe and America* (Toronto: University of Toronto Press, 2001) at ch. 5.
31 Section 2(a).
32 Section 2(b).
33 Section 2(c).
34 Section 2(d).
35 Section 7.

liberty and security of the person"[35] and guarantees to every individual the right to equality before and under the law and not to be discriminated against on the basis of religion.[36] The *Charter* further provides for the "preservation and enhancement of the multicultural heritage of Canadians"[37] and guarantees the rights and privileges for which constitutional provision had previously been made in respect of denominational schools.[38] All these sections are subject to the overriding provision of section 1, that is, "to such reasonable limits prescribed by law as can be demonstrably justified in a free and democratic society."[39]

3) Human Rights Legislation

Although not constitutionally entrenched, legislative protection for freedom of religion is also found in provincial human rights legislation and in the *Canadian Bill of Rights*.[40] Prior to 1982, these sources of law together with the common law constituted the legal protections for freedom of religion in Canada.

Concern for the protection of civil liberties by legislation grew up in Canada, as in other Western countries, after the Second World War, as an international response to the newly-named "crimes against humanity" perpetrated during the War as well as those perpetrated by various socialist regimes in the course of the twentieth century. This heightened sensitivity extended to discriminations long tolerated within individual jurisdictions in relation to such matters as employment and accommodation, prompting legislation to prohibit future discrimination on a variety of grounds, including religion. Human rights legislation protects religion negatively by prohibiting the denial of rights on religious grounds.[41]

Prior to the enactment of human rights legislation in the second half of the twentieth century, civil liberties had been protected in common law countries by the common law itself, and by the existence of an inde-

---

36   Section 15.
37   Section 27.
38   Section 29.
39   Section 1.
40   (1960) R.S.C. 1985, App. III.
41   For the history of this legislation see W.S. Tarnopolsky and W.F. Pentney, *Discrimination and the Law* (Toronto: Carswell, 1985), ch. 2; and R.St.J. MacDonald and John Humphrey, eds., *The Practice of Freedom* (Toronto: Butterworths, 1979) chs. 3, 4, 5, 15, 16.

pendent judiciary, which had historically not only favoured the individual over the state but also had favoured a society characterized by less law rather than more, leaving the individual free to pursue his or her own goals in life. The high-water mark for the protection of religious liberty in Canada was reached by the judiciary without the assistance of legislation in the so-called "implied bill of rights" cases resulting from the persecution of Jehovah's Witnesses by the Duplessis regime (1936–1959) in Quebec.[42] In *Saumur v. City of Quebec*,[43] Rand J. described freedoms such as religion, expression, and association as fundamental rights because they are inherent in being human and a prior condition for society; as such they could only be cut down by the positive law in exceptional situations for the common good. Once these rights became enshrined in legislation, the courts came to see them less in the common law tradition as an essential attribute of humanity and more in the French civil law tradition as a gift of the state and legally unstable for that reason.

The earliest statutory protection for civil liberties, including freedom of religion, is found in statutory bills of rights enacted by several provinces.[44] These are less important after the adoption of the *Charter* in 1982, but remain in force, and are effective to the extent that their provisions may be found to be broader than the *Charter*.

More important in relation to the extent to which religious freedom is protected in the provinces pursuant to section 92(13),[45] are the provincial human rights codes. The first provincial human rights code was enacted in Ontario in 1962[46] with the other provinces following suit,[47] and the federal government finally enacting its own code in 1977.[48] These codes set out the right to equal treatment in respect of goods, services, facilities, accommodation, employment, and contracts generally without discrimination on the basis of a wide range of characteristics including

---

42 R. v. *Boucher*, [1951] S.C.R. 165; *Saumur v. City of Quebec*, [1953] 2 S.C.R. 299; *Chaput v. Romain*, [1955] S.C.R. 834; *Lamb v. Benoit*, [1959] S.C.R. 321; and *Roncarelli v. Duplessis*, [1959] S.C.R. 121.

43 *Ibid.* at 329. See also *Chaput v. Romain, ibid.* per Taschereau J. at 840.

44 Saskatchewan *Bill of Rights Act*, S.S. 1947, c. 35; Alberta *Bill of Rights Act*, S.A. 1972, c. 1; and Quebec *Charter of Human Rights and Freedoms*, S.Q. 1975, c. 6.

45. *Constitution Act*, 1867.

46 S.O. 1961–62, c. 93; now R.S.O. 1990, c. H-19 as am.

47 For a history of rights legislation, see generally W.S. Tarnopolsky, *The Canadian Bill of Rights*, 2d ed. (Toronto: McClelland & Stewart, 1975).

48 *Canadian Human Rights Act*, R.S.C. 1985, c. H-6.

religion or creed. These codes also contain provisions exempting certain types of institutions from the anti-discrimination requirement, including religious, philanthropic, educational, fraternal, and social institutions primarily engaged in serving the interests of persons who identify with them. Such provisions permit religious institutions to engage in practices that would otherwise be discriminatory. Each province has a human rights commission set up pursuant to the provincial code, which is statutorily mandated to investigate and adjudicate discrimination complaints, with right of appeal to the courts. Since these codes apply to private companies and to individuals, they complement the *Charter*, which is restricted in application to governmental activity.

Although rendered insignificant by the adoption of the *Charter* in 1982,[49] the *Canadian Bill of Rights*[50] was an important step in the provision of legislative protection of freedom of religion. The Bill remains in force but most of its provisions have been duplicated and extended by the *Charter*. The Bill was not entrenched as constitutional legislation as a benchmark for the assessment of all other governmental activities; it could be amended or repealed as ordinary legislation at any time; and it applied only to the federal government. Although still in force, it was largely overtaken by the *Charter* with two exceptions for which the *Charter* does not provide: (i) section 1(a) extends "due process" to the protection of property; and (ii) section 2(e) guarantees a fair hearing for the determination of rights and obligations. Since 1982, neither has been the subject of litigation.

The preamble to the *Canadian Bill of Rights* was the first piece of legislation to give "God" statutory status and must be one of only very few pieces of legislation in the common law tradition to refer to "God." The preamble provides:

> The Parliament of Canada, affirming that the Canadian Nation is founded upon principles that acknowledge the supremacy of God, the dignity and worth of the human person and the position of the family in a society of free men and free institutions.
>
> Affirming also that men and institutions remain free only when freedom is founded upon respect for moral and spiritual values and the rule of law.

---

49 See Peter W. Hogg, "A Comparison of the *Charter of Rights* with the *Canadian Bill of Rights*" in Beaudoin and Ratushny, above note 8, ch. 1.

50 S.C. 1960, c. 44; R.S.C. 1985, Appendix III.

The Bill further provides both for freedom from discrimination on the basis of religion[51] and "freedom of religion,"[52] "freedom of speech,"[53] and "freedom of assembly and association."[54] It also guarantees equality before the law.[55] In contrast to the *Charter*, these protections were rendered less potent by two factors, the non-entrenchment of the Bill, as stated earlier, and the restraint with which the Supreme Court of Canada interpreted it in the two cases relating to religion.[56] Since 1982, the exclusive use of the *Charter* by litigants to promote freedom of religion has cast doubt on the continuing value of the Bill in that regard.

4) Delegation of Constitutional Authority

The absence of provision in the written constitution for jurisdiction over religion in Canada has resulted in a history of litigation to determine authority in relation to legislation about temperance[57] and Sunday observance[58] in the nineteenth century and the extent of the denominational schools[59] jurisdiction in the twentieth century. As with other subject-matters for which no express provision is made in the written constitution, it has come to be accepted that both federal and provincial governments may enact legislation affecting religion, subject to judicial determination in any resulting litigation as to whether or not the legislation is appropriate to its enacting jurisdiction.[60]

Where a court has determined that a specific matter falls within federal jurisdiction, it may be that federal legislation enacted within the authority of the federal government will effectively enlarge the scope of the powers of a provincial legislature by a conditional delegation of

---

51   Section 1.
52   Section 1(c).
53   Section 1(d).
54   Section 1(c).
55   Section 1(b).
56   Compare *Robertson and Rosetanni* v. *R.*, [1963] S.C.R. 651, which upheld the federal *Lord's Day Act* and *R.* v. *Big M Drug Mart Ltd.*, [1985] 1 S.C.R. 295, which struck down that Act. In the other case, *Walter* v. *Alberta (A.G.)* (1969), 3 D.L.R. (3d) 1 (S.C.C.), the court upheld Alberta legislation implicitly aimed at restricting communal land ownership by Hutterite colonies.
57   Below section D(1).
58   Below section D(2).
59   Below section D(3).
60   Hogg, above note 8 at chs. 14 and 16 generally.

power to enact legislation to the provinces.[61] After the decision of the Privy Council in *A.G. Ont.* v. *Hamilton Street Railway Co.*,[62] which struck down the Ontario *Lord's Day Act*[63] on the ground that the regulation of secular activity on Sundays was an exclusive federal power within section 91(27) over criminal law, the federal government enacted the federal *Lord's Day Act*,[64] prohibiting various activities on Sunday but also permitting provinces to opt out of any prohibition if they chose.[65]

The effect of this opting out clause, which resulted in provincial legislation regulating Sunday activities, was re-considered in *Lord's Day Alliance of Canada* v. *A.G. B.C.*,[66] where the issue was the validity of a British Columbia bill to amend the Vancouver City Charter to allow the city to enact a bylaw permitting fee-paying spectator sports on Sunday afternoons. The Supreme Court upheld the provincial legislation, but further decided that the legislation was independently valid within both section 92(13), property and civil rights, and section 92(16), matters of a merely local or private nature. While the latter part of this decision may be doubtful in light of the *Hamilton Street Railway Co.* finding that Sunday observance regulation is exclusively within the federal criminal power, the former part may show that it is permissible for the federal government to delegate jurisdiction to the provinces, at least in relation to Sunday observance legislation.[67]

That such delegation of authority to enact legislation in relation to religion must be express is suggested by two other lower court cases. In *Kent (District)* v. *Storgoff*,[68] a municipal bylaw enacted to prohibit a group of Doukhobors from entering the municipality was found to be invalid as

---

61   Hogg, above note 8 at 349–352.

62   [1903] A.C. 524 (P.C.).

63   R.S.O. 1897, c. 246.

64   S.C. 1906, c. 27.

65   *Ibid.* s. 6: "It is not lawful for any person, on the Lord's Day, except as provided in any provincial Act or law now or hereafter in force, to engage in...."

66   [1959] S.C.R. 497.

67   *Cf. A.G. N.S.* v. *A.G. Canada*, [1951] S.C.R. 31. See also W.R. Lederman, "Some Forms and Limitations of Co-operative Federalism" (1967) 45 Can. Bar Rev. 409; P.C. Weiler, "The Supreme Court and the Law of Canadian Federalism" (1973) 23 U.T.L.J. 307; Gerald V. LaForest, "Delegation of Legislative Power in Canada" (1975) 21 McGill L.J. 131; and E.A. Driedger, "The Interaction of Federal and Provincial Laws" (1976) 54 Can. Bar Rev. 695.

68   (1962), 38 D.L.R. (2d) 362 (B.C.S.C.).

an invasion of the exclusive federal criminal law power over unlawful assemblies and possible breaches of the peace, a power which had not been delegated to the province in respect to religious assemblies. Again, when a Quebec statute purported to incorporate a national board for a church, the legislation was held to be *ultra vires* by the Privy Council; however, a subsequent federal act confirming and ratifying the Quebec Act was held to be *intra vires*,[69] thereby implying that had federal authority been granted initially, the provincial legislation may have been found valid.

C. THE CHARACTERIZATION AND INTERPRETATION OF CONSTITUTIONAL PROVISIONS

Since no express provision is made in the written constitution for constitutional jurisdiction over religion and since the protection of freedom of religion and freedom from discrimination on religious grounds are provided for in both federal and provincial legislation, the first step in determining the applicability of legislation in relation to religion is that of judicial review on the ground of constitutionality within the division of powers pursuant to the *Constitution Act, 1867*. Once the court has determined that the legislation under consideration is *intra vires* the legislating jurisdiction, then the second step is that of judicial review on *Charter* grounds to ensure that the legislation does not offend the rights and freedoms entrenched constitutionally by the *Charter*.

Nowhere does the written constitution of Canada stipulate that constitutional review should precede *Charter* review when determining the validity of legislation. However, in the earliest decisions from the Supreme Court of Canada after 1982, the Court adopted this two-step procedure in respect to legislation to amend the Ontario *Education Act* to extend public funding of denominational schools;[70] to determine the validity of the federal *Lord's Day Act*;[71] and the validity of the Ontario *Retail Business Holidays Act*.[72] It is also clearly the case, however, that leg-

---

69   *St. Andrew's Church v. Presbyterian Temporalities Fund* (1883), 6 L.N. 27 (Que. C.A.).

70   *Reference Re Bill 30, An Act to Amend the Education Act (Ontario)*, [1987] 1 S.C.R. 1148.

71   *R. v. Big M Drug Mart Ltd.*, above note 56.

72   *R. v. Edwards Books and Art Ltd.*, [1986] 2 S.C.R. 713.

islation that is contrary to the "Constitution of Canada" is, pursuant to section 52 of the *Charter*, of no force or effect, so that it may be possible to proceed directly to such a conclusion when the impugned legislation clearly contravenes the Constitution. In less obvious cases, the two-step process practised by the Supreme Court reflects the relationship of the *Constitution Act, 1867* and the *Charter* — the *Charter* assumes the logical existence of legislative power to enact legislation, therefore that authority ought to be subject first to judicial review. Legislation may be struck down on either ground.[73]

To determine whether legislation in relation to religion is *intra vires* the powers of the enacting jurisdiction, it is necessary to identify the "matter" or the "pith and substance" of the legislation, that is, its essential character or nature, and then to assign it accordingly to either a federal or provincial category of authority as set out in the *Constitution Act, 1867*. Since many statutes contain features that may be both federal and provincial, the task of the courts is to identify the dominant feature of the legislation and then to categorize it as federal or provincial accordingly.

The most frequently considered legislation in relation to religion that the courts have been obliged to characterize for constitutional purposes is legislation relating to Sunday observance. To discuss the dominant feature of this legislation, the Privy Council[74] and the Supreme Court of Canada[75] have determined the purpose of such legislation and then placed it in the appropriate class of matter pursuant to the *Constitution Act, 1867*. Thus, in R. v. *Big M Drug Mart*, the Supreme Court found the purpose of the federal *Lord's Day Act*, which prohibited various social and commercial activities on Sunday, to be the preservation of the sanctity of the Christian Sabbath as required by the Fourth Commandment.[76] This

---

73   See generally Hogg, above note 8 at ch. 15 for a full analysis of the applicable principles. The following discussion focuses only on those cases explicitly dealing with religion. Since the principles applied in these cases are those applied in respect to other subject-matters, there is every reason to believe that the other principles for judicial review on constitutionality grounds would apply in future religion cases where appropriate.

74   *Hamilton Street Railway Co.*, above note 62; and *Lord's Day Alliance of Canada* v. *A.G. Man.*, [1925] A.C. 384 (P.C.).

75   *Henry Birks & Sons (Montreal) Ltd.* v. *City of Montreal*, [1955] S.C.R. 799; R. v. *Big M Drug Mart*, above note 56; and R. v. *Edwards Books and Art Ltd.*, above note 72.

76   Exodus 20:8–11 (N.S.R.V.).

purpose was discerned from the title and history of the Act. Since the earlier case, *Hamilton Street Railway Co.*, had defined a breach of the Ten Commandments[77] as a criminal matter, the power to enact legislation that sought to enforce such fell within the federal section 91(27) criminal power.[78]

Conversely, where legislation regulating Sunday activities has the purpose of observing a secular common pause day to provide a day of rest and recreation for workers, then its dominant purpose will predict its characterization as within provincial section 92(13) jurisdiction over property and civil rights. Thus, in R. v. *Edwards Books and Art*, the Supreme Court of Canada also looked to the title and history of the Ontario *Retail Business Holidays Act* to decide that it had an exclusively secular purpose and fell within section 92(13). The characterization of the legislation in *Edwards Books* as secular was made by the Court despite the fact that the legislation contained an exemption for retailers, who closed on Saturday for religious reasons, to open on Sunday. Dickson C.J.C. explained this away by suggesting that the purpose of the religious exemption was to neutralize or maximize the adverse effects of an otherwise valid piece of provincial human rights legislation. Therefore its characterization was governed by the legislation's context as valid provincial legislation in relation to property and civil rights.[79]

In *Big M Drug Mart*, the Supreme Court of Canada did not have to consider the effects of the legislation as well as the purpose to determine its pith and substance since they were identical; however, in *Edwards Books* the effect of the legislation might fairly be said to differ from the secular purpose, insofar as Sunday closing arguably compelled retailers to observe a religious holiday, which might have prompted the conclusion that the legislation was at least concurrently religious and secular in nature. The point was not explored, but there have been cases concern-

---

77 Exodus 20:1–17.

78 See also the following cases where the courts considered whether or not provincial legislation constituted a proper opting out of the federal power: *Ouimet v. Bazin* (1912), 46 S.C.R. 502; *Lord's Day Alliance v. A.G. Man.*, above note 74; *R. v. Epstein*, [1931] O.R. 726 (H.C. in chambers); *Henry Birks & Sons (Montreal) Ltd. v. City of Montreal*, above note 75; *Lord's Day Alliance of Canada v. A.G. B.C.*, above note 66; *Lieberman v. R.*, [1963] S.C.R. 643; and *R. v. Top Banana Ltd.* (1974), 4 O.R. (2d) 513 (H.C.).

79 Above note 72 at 750–751. The reasoning here is very weak.

ing religion where the courts have looked to the effect of legislation to assist in the classification of the matter for constitutional purposes.

In *Saumur v. City of Quebec*,[80] a municipal bylaw that created an offence to distribute literature on the streets of Quebec without the written permission of the chief of police was found to be *ultra vires* and an infringement of federal jurisdiction over religion because while it was *prima facie* enacted for a valid municipal purpose of controlling litter on the streets or protecting pedestrians, the chief of police actually exercised his discretion to restrict the attempts of Jehovah's Witnesses to proselytize. The Supreme Court of Canada looked to the effect of the implementation of the bylaw in order to characterize it for constitutional purposes.

How a court characterizes legislation determines its constitutional validity, and it is clear from these examples that unspoken assumptions and implicit policy choices are made in relation to legislation concerning religion as much as in relation to other matters.

Where a court decides that legislation is *ultra vires* the enacting jurisdiction, it has the option of severing the parts of the statute deemed to be unconstitutional and then of enforcing the remainder.[81] Severance has never been applied to any legislation relating to religion on constitutional grounds; on the other hand, the striking down of the entire *Lord's Day Act* in *Big M Drug Mart* on *Charter* grounds is the only example of a statute relating to religion being struck down in its entirety.[82]

Once legislation relating to religion has been found to be *intra vires* the enacting jurisdiction by virtue of judicial review of the constitutionality issue, the second step is judicial review pursuant to the *Charter* to determine whether the legislation abridges a *Charter* right. *Charter* review is a two-step process requiring first, a determination of whether or not the legislation at issue abridges a *Charter* right and, secondly, a determination of whether that legislation may be justified under section 1, if it does abridge a *Charter* right, as a reasonable limit prescribed by law demonstrably justifiable in a free and democratic society.

Whereas the characterization of laws in relation to judicial federalism review focuses on the dominant purpose and largely ignores the effect of a law in order to determine its pith and substance, the characterization of laws for judicial *Charter* review will look not only to the

---

80   [1953] 2 S.C.R. 299.
81   Hogg, above note 8 at 374–376 for the non-religion cases.
82   Below section D for a more extensive discussion of the cases by topic.

purpose but will regard even the effect of the law alone as sufficient to abridge a *Charter* right subject to section 1.[83] That either the purpose or the effect of legislation may render it in breach of a *Charter* right was established in *R. v. Big M Drug Mart*.

In that case, Dickson C.J.C., for the majority, looked to the history of the legislation as well as its title to determine the purpose as a religious one requiring the observance of the Christian Sunday and found that purpose to abridge the *Charter* right to religious freedom. In his view it was not necessary to find that the effect of the legislation also breached the *Charter* because effects can never be relied upon to save legislation with an invalid purpose. Nor could legislation with an invalid purpose ever be justified under section 1.[84]

While Dickson C.J.C. thought the appropriate focus of judicial *Charter* review to be on the purpose of legislation and that effects should be examined secondarily only when the purpose failed to disclose a *Charter* breach, Wilson J. thought the *Charter* to be an effects-oriented document so as to place a less heavy evidentiary burden on the plaintiff. The purpose need not matter if the effect alone was to abridge an entrenched right.[85]

In the subsequent case, *R. v. Edwards Books*, Dickson C.J.C. affirmed the view that the primary focus should be on the purpose of the impugned legislation and found that the *Retail Business Holidays Act* had no religious purpose, again by looking at the history of the legislation. The Court was also required, however, to examine the effects of the legislation since the retailers had argued that the effect of the Act was to require them to comply with the Christian Sabbath and also to place a religious burden on those who wished to observe a different Sabbath. Dickson C.J.C. dismissed the former argument by stating that the legislation did not compel actual Sunday observance, merely Sunday closing, and noted in respect to the latter argument that retailers who closed on a second day did so not because of the legislation but because of their

---

83 See generally the following: W.W. Black, "Intent or Effects: Section 15 of the *Charter of Rights and Freedoms*" in J.M. Weiler and R.M. Elliott, eds., *Litigating the Values of a Nation: The Canadian Charter of Rights and Freedoms* (Toronto: Carswell, 1986) at 120; and William F. Pentney, "Interpreting the *Charter*: General Principles" in Beaudoin and Ratushny, above note 8 at 21.

84 Above note 56 at 334, 353.

85 *Ibid.* at 361. See also *R. v. Videoflicks Ltd.* (1984), 48 O.R. (2d) 395 (C.A.) per Tarnopolsky J.A.

religious beliefs.[86] Nevertheless, he agreed that the net effect of the legislation was to place an economic burden on non-Sunday observers
obliged by their beliefs to close on another day; however, this breach was
demonstrably justifiable in the majority's view, pursuant to section 1, in
order to protect the rights of the non-unionized retail workers.[87]

When either the purpose or the effect of legislation is to abridge a
Charter right, the Supreme Court of Canada further asserted in *Edwards
Books* that not every trivial or insubstantial burden on religious freedom
would justify a finding of breach of section 2(a), otherwise the *Charter*
could be used to protect even innocuous secular legislation such as a taxation act imposing a sales tax even on products used in religious worship.[88] The view that there is no breach of the *Charter* if the effect of a law
on a *Charter* right is trivial or insubstantial was also stated in another
early religion case, *R. v. Jones.*[89]

In *Jones*, the accused, a Baptist pastor, was charged with a breach of
the Alberta *School Act*[90] because he refused to apply for a certificate of
efficient instruction required by the province for the small school he was
running in the basement of his church on the ground that to do so would
be at variance with his belief that God had placed him in direct authority over the upbringing and education of his children. For the majority,
Wilson J. found there to be no violation of freedom of religion because
the effect of the legislation was "trivial or insubstantial";[91] LaForest J., for
the minority, found that the Act had violated Mr. Jones' freedom of religion but was sustainable pursuant to section 1. A test for distinguishing
a trivial from a substantial infringement has yet to be devised by the
courts in relation to religion, although the distinction is now made in
many religion cases.[92] Without greater judicial clarification, the distinction may simply come to reflect personal judicial views as to what is

---

86 Above note 72 at 758 ff. Beetz and McIntyre JJ. adopted this view but found
  there to be no abridgement of freedom of religion: at 788–792.

87 For a trenchant critique of this reasoning, see Andrew J. Petter and Patrick J.
  Monahan, "Developments in Constitutional Law: The 1986-87 Term" (1988)
  10 Sup. Ct. L.R. 61 at 78–86.

88 Above note 72 per Dickson C.J. at 759.

89 [1986] 2 S.C.R. 284.

90 R.S.A. 1980, c. S-3.

91 Above note 89 at 314.

92 Virtually all of them in fact.

important or unimportant in life rather than the actual impact of the infringement on the complainant's life.

In asserting the primacy of a purposive approach to *Charter* interpretation in relation to freedom of religion, the Supreme Court of Canada reasserted the position it took in the early *Charter* case, *Hunter v. Southam Inc.*,[93] that unlike ordinary statutes, which are drafted for short-term purposes and can be amended or repealed, the *Charter* is meant to provide a continuing framework for governmental action and must, therefore, be capable of growth and development to deal with the unimagined future.[94] In *Big M Drug Mart*, the Court further expounded, however, on the need to examine the language, the historical origins, and the context of any legislation under *Charter* consideration,[95] not to search out a frozen concept but rather to "draw inspiration and guidance from our legal tradition"[96] so as to place the legislation in its proper context. But in *Big M Drug Mart*, Dickson C.J.C. rejected the American "shifting purpose" approach,[97] which would assert a contemporary purpose for legislation quite different from its original purpose in order to uphold that legislation.[98] Thus, the Court rejected the position that a Sunday observance law could be upheld as a secular pause day law, which merely happened to designate Sunday as the most convenient day; the historical purpose and goal of the legislation was to ensure widespread social observance of the Christian sabbath. In *R. v. Butler*,[99] a unanimous Supreme Court suggested that by formulating the original purpose of a *Criminal Code* provision relating to obscenity as generally protecting society from harm caused by obscene materials, it was possible to uphold the provision as a permissible shift in emphasis from the promotion of morality to the promotion of sexual equality. However, in *R. v. Zundel*,[100] the Court retreat-

---

93 [1984] 2 S.C.R. 145.

94 *Ibid.* per Dickson C.J.C. at 155.

95 Above note 56 per Dickson C.J.C. at 344.

96 Pentney, above note 83 at 25.

97 *McGowan v. Maryland*, 366 U.S. 40 (1961); *Two Guys from Harrison Allentown v. McGinley*, 366 U.S. 582 (1961); *Braunfield v. Brown*, 366 U.S. 599 (1961); and *Gallagher v. Crown Kosher Super Market*, 366 U.S. 617 (1961).

98 Above note 56 at 335.

99 [1992] 1 S.C.R. 452.

100 [1992] 2 S.C.R. 731, where the court refused to interpret the "false news" provisions in the *Criminal Code* by shifting the emphasis from protection from malicious lies to promoting social harmony.

ed from an approach that would interpret laws as generally as possible and allow a changing emphasis, to the approach in *Big M Drug Mart*, which rejected the shifting purpose position.

Moreover, the Supreme Court has largely rejected the use of United States First Amendment[101] cases to interpret section 2(a). In *Big M Drug Mart*, Dickson C.J.C. surveyed a number of such cases but ultimately found them to be unhelpful in relation to freedom of religion because the First Amendment and section 2(a) are quite different in language, substance, legal context, and historical context.[102]

The Supreme Court has been equally willing to reject as interpretation guides the decisions under the *Canadian Bill of Rights*. In relation to section 2(a), this meant the rejection in *Big M Drug Mart* of *Robertson* on the ground that the discrete effects test set out by Ritchie J.[103] was unsuitable for *Charter* interpretation when both purpose and effect might be employed to find an act in breach of a *Charter* right.[104]

Finally, reinforcement for the view that the *Charter* should be interpreted generously and as a unique document in relation to freedom of religion is found in the willingness of the Supreme Court of Canada to employ the section 27 guarantee of multiculturalism as a tool for interpreting section 2(a).[105]

---

101 "Congress shall make no law respecting an establishment of religion, or prohibiting the free exercise thereof."

102 Above note 98. In several other early s. 2(a) cases, the courts attempted to adapt First Amendment jurisprudence, but with little success and the practice quickly died out; see for example *R. v. Jones*, above note 89; and *Zylberberg v. Sudbury Board of Education* (1988), 65 O.R. (2d) 641 (C.A.) per Lacourciere J.A. Although Canada has signed various international treaties, these are not part of domestic law and not enforceable in Canadian courts. The most important is the *International Covenant on Civil and Political Rights* enforced by the U.N. Human Rights Committee. To date s. 2(a) cases have not acknowledged this document, nor the persuasive value of the *European Convention on Human Rights*.

103 Above note 56 at 325–327. See also *Hamilton v. Canadian Transport Commission*, [1978] 1 S.C.R. 640. *Cf. R. v. Drybones*, [1970] S.C.R. 282, per Cartwright C.J. dissenting.

104 Above note 56 at 333.

105 *Big M Drug Mart*, above note 56 and *Re Bill 30*, above note 70. For a most comprehensive analysis of s. 27 see Joseph Eliot Magnet, "Multiculturalism in the *Canadian Charter of Rights and Freedoms*" in Beaudoin and Mendes, above note 8 at ch. 18.

Once a legislative provision has been found to abridge a *Charter* right, it may only be upheld pursuant to section 1 of the *Charter* if it is reasonable and demonstrably justifiable in a free and democratic society, as assessed by the courts.[106] Thus, in *Big M Drug Mart*, the Supreme Court found that legislation whose purpose was to compel Sunday observance was unconstitutional since it could not satisfy the criteria of section 1.[107] Conversely, in *Edwards Books* the Court found the legislation to be justifiable because not only did it provide a common pause day for retail employees who enjoyed few legal protections but it also contained exemptions for retailers who observed Saturday as the Sabbath. It is widely accepted that how section 1 will be applied to the facts of any case is largely a matter of the values of the court, which will be reflected in the policies expressed or implicit in the final decision. Although the earlier *Charter* cases worked through the criteria prescribed by *R. v. Oakes*, recently the courts have largely abandoned that convoluted process in favour of a simple declaration that the abridgement of a right is either justified or not justified without explanation for the decision.[108]

D. SPECIFIC CONSTITUTIONAL ISSUES INVOLVING RELIGION

In the light of the foregoing principles for the construction of the written constitution, this section will examine five specific areas in which the courts have, since 1867, been required to interpret both constitutional and *Charter* provisions in relation to religion. Judicial review on constitutional jurisdiction grounds has focused on three specific issues pursuant to the *Constitution Act, 1867*: temperance legislation, Sunday

---

106 *R. v. Oakes*, [1986] 1 S.C.R. 103. See Hogg, above note 8 at chs. 33 and 35 generally for a full discussion of s. 1.

107 See also *Zylberberg v. Sudbury Board of Education* (1988), 65 O.R. (2d) 641 (C.A.); and *Canadian Civil Liberties Association v. Ontario* (1990), 71 O.R. (2d) 341 (C.A.).

108 Of the large literature on s. 1, the following articles focus most cogently on the question of values: William R. Lederman, "Assessing Competing Values in the Definition of *Charter* Rights and Freedoms" in Beaudoin and Ratushny, above note 8 at 127; and Errol P. Mendes, "The Crucible of the *Charter*: Judicial Principles v. Judicial Deference in the Context of Section 1" in Beaudoin and Mendes, above note 8 at ch. 3.

observance legislation, and denominational schools. Judicial review on *Charter* grounds has focused on two specific issues: the meaning and extent of the section 2(a) fundamental right to freedom of conscience and religion, and the section 2(b) fundamental right to freedom of expression. Both constitutional review and *Charter* review have been conducted in relation to Sunday observance legislation and denominational school rights.

While it is the case that the courts have also considered sections 1, 7, 15, 27, and 29 in relation to religious issues, this consideration has typically occurred as secondary to consideration of section 2(a), and these sections will, therefore, be dealt with within the context of the discussion of section 2(a).

1) Temperance

The earliest constitutional difficulty in relation to religion arose from the temperance legislation enacted from the mid nineteenth century onwards in Canada as a result of Christian campaigns for the moral reform of Canadian society. The absence of statutory regulation of the production and sale of alcohol and the widespread drunkenness found in Canada as elsewhere in Western societies resulted in campaigns for temperance legislation largely led by evangelicals. The evangelical revivals of the nineteenth century were characterized by increased social activism and willingness to use secular laws to secure moral reform.[109]

---

109 See generally Richard Allen, *The Social Passion: Religion and Social Reform in Canada 1914–1928* (Toronto: University of Toronto Press, 1973); Carl Berger, *Science, God and Nature in Victorian Canada* (Toronto: University of Toronto Press, 1983); Nancy Christie and Michael Gauvreau, *A Full-Orbed Christianity: The Protestant Churches and Social Welfare in Canada, 1900–1940* (Montreal: McGill-Queen's University Press, 1996); Ramsay Cook, *The Regenerators: Social Criticism in Late Victorian English Canada* (Toronto: University of Toronto Press, 1985); Sharon Cook, *Through Sunshine and Shadow: The Women's Christian Temperance Union, Evangelicalism and Reform in Ontario, 1874–1930* (Kingston: McGill-Queen's University Press, 1995); Brian Fraser, *The Social Uplifters: Presbyterian Progressives and the Social Gospel in Canada, 1875–1915* (Waterloo: Waterloo University Press, 1988); Michael Gauvreau, *The Evangelical Century: College and Creed in English Canada from the Great Revival to the Great Depression* (Kingston: McGill-Queen's University Press, 1991); David B. Marshall, *Secularizing the Faith: Canadian Protestant Clergy and the Crisis of Belief, 1850–1940* (Toronto: University of Toronto Press, 1992); Jan Noel,

Since the *Constitution Act, 1867*, does not provide for jurisdiction over the subject-matter of temperance, some confusion resulted as to whether the federal or provincial governments had the power to enact temperance legislation, and litigation ultimately ensued to determine the issue. The constitutionality of the *Canada Temperance Act*,[110] which contained a local option provision was considered in *Russell v. R.*,[111] where the Privy Council upheld the legislation as within federal jurisdiction because it did not fall under any provincial head of legislative power. The purpose of the legislation was to promote temperance throughout Canada and not in any one province, and legislation intended to be national in scope must, the Privy Council reasoned, be within federal jurisdiction.[112]

In the subsequent case, *A.G. Ontario v. A.G. Canada*,[113] the Privy Council concluded that the federal power to enact the temperance legislation was found in the "peace, order and good government" (POGG) clause of section 91 of the *Constitution Act, 1867*, because of its national dimensions. This so-called *Local Prohibition* case was concerned with provincial temperance legislation enacted for Canada West in 1864,[114] which also contained a local options clause and was largely similar to the later federal Act that purported to repeal it. Lord Watson found that the provincial legislation was *intra vires* both section 92(13) and section 92(16) and could not be repealed by Parliament. Thus, concurrent federal and provincial legislation on temperance was permitted, although *Russell* suggested otherwise. The significant advance in the *Local Prohibition* case was, however, the Privy Council's view that the POGG power granted Parliament constitutional jurisdiction to enact legislation that is national in scope, in relation to temperance as well as in relation to other matters.

Confirmation that the federal government enjoys jurisdiction to enact temperance legislation within a national dimensions interpretation

---

Canada Dry: Temperance Crusades Before Confederation (Toronto: University of Toronto Press, 1995); Marguerite Van Die, *An Evangelical Mind: Nathaniel Burwash and the Methodist Tradition in Canada, 1839–1918* (Kingston: McGill-Queen's University Press, 1989); and Mariana Valverde, *The Age of Light, Songs and Water: Moral Reform in English Canada, 1885–1925* (Toronto: University of Toronto Press, 1991).

110 R.S.C. 1927, c. 196 and *Temperance Act*, S.C. 1864, c. 18.

111 (1882), 7 App. Cas. 829 (P.C.).

112 *Ibid.* per Sir Montague Smith at 841.

113 [1896] A.C. 348 (P.C.).

114 *Temperance Act*, 27 & 28 Vict., c. 18 (1864). The so-called "Dunkin Act."

of the POGG power came in *A.G. Ontario v. Canada Temperance Federation*.[115] Two arguments were made attacking the constitutional validity of the *Canada Temperance Act*: either that *Russell* was wrongly decided because it did not understand the POGG power to encompass only national emergencies, or if *Russell* did so, then the emergency of nation-wide drunkenness had passed. Despite constitutional decisions since *Russell* with regard to other subject-matters that had asserted that the POGG power was restricted to emergencies and did not grant jurisdiction to Parliament to enact legislation with a national dimension,[116] the Privy Council upheld *Russell*, opining that it had not been decided on the basis of an emergency and that the POGG power was not confined to emergencies. Thus, the *Canada Temperance* case upheld the Act and the power of the federal government to enact temperance legislation with national dimensions.[117]

While both federal and provincial legislation may be enacted in relation to temperance, in the former case pursuant to the POGG power, and in the latter case pursuant to section 92(13) and section 92(16) of the *Constitution Act, 1867*, federal local option legislation is paramount over provincial local option legislation where both are purportedly adopted in the same district.[118] Where subsequent provincial legislation conflicts with pre-Confederation temperance legislation, that provincial legislation is invalid, since it cannot repeal or modify legislation which must be repealed or modified by Parliament.[119] Where a defendant is charged with selling liquor in contravention of provincial legislation, the proper forum is a provincial court since the matter does not come within the federal criminal power.[120]

2) Sunday Observance

In addition to temperance, the other major social cause promoted by Christians, especially those influenced by the evangelical social gospel,

---

115 [1946] A.C. 193 (P.C.).
116 See generally Hogg, above note 8 at 427–434.
117 The Act has never been formally repealed.
118 *Local Prohibition Case*, above note 113.
119 *Compton v. Simoneau* (1891), 14 L.N. 347 (Que.). *Cf. Local Prohibition Case*, above note 113.
120 *City of Montreal v. Doyle* (1880), 2 L.Th. 182 (Que. Recorder's Ct.).

was the regulation of Sunday activities through legislation.[121] Sunday observance legislation was not new in the nineteenth century, Sabbath observance being first enforced by legislation in early seventeenth century England.[122] However, its enforcement had fallen into desuetude by the mid nineteenth century and historical accounts of that period indicate that Sunday activities did not differ from those of other days of the week — in fact, sports, fairs, and taverns seemed to be especially popular on Sundays.[123] Legislation to enforce Sunday as a day of religious observance was originally premised on the Fourth Commandment[124] and the judicial construction of the Ten Commandments as "criminal" in nature was reflected in constitutional decisions as to jurisdiction to enact Sabbath legislation since the *Constitution Act, 1867* was silent on the matter.

In the decades after Confederation, it was widely thought that the provinces enjoyed jurisdiction in relation to Sunday observance pursuant to section 91(13) and section 92(16),[125] and many provinces enacted Sunday legislation.[126] However, this view was superseded by the Privy Council decision in *A.G. Ontario v. Hamilton Street Railway Co.* that Sun-

---

121 See generally the references above note 109. See also George S. Holmstead, *The Sunday Law in Canada* (Toronto: Poole, 1912); Christopher Armstrong and H.V. Nelles, *The Revenge of the Methodist Bicycle Company: Sunday Streetcars and Municipal Reform in Toronto, 1888–1897* (Toronto: Peter Martin Associates, 1977); Paul Laverdure, "Canada's Sunday: The Presbyterian Contribution, 1875–1950" in William Klempa, ed., *The Burning Bush and a Few Acres of Snow* (Ottawa: Carleton University Press, 1994) at 83; and Alan Metcalfe, *Canada Learns to Play: The Emergence of Organized Sport, 1807–1914* (Toronto: University of Toronto Press, 1987).

122 *An Act for Punishing diverse Abuses committed on the Lord's Day called Sunday*, 1625, (1 Car. I c. 1.).

123 Above note 121.

124 Exodus 20:8–11.

125 Douglas Schmeiser, *Civil Liberties in Canada* (Toronto: Oxford University Press, 1974) at 101–110. See also J.A. Barron, "Sunday in North America" (1965) 79 Harvard L. Rev. 42; Mike Brundrett, "Demythologizing Sunday Shopping: Sunday Retail Restrictions and the *Charter*" (1992) 50 U.T. Fac. L.Rev. 1; T.J. Christian and K.D. Ewing, "Sunday Trading in Canada" [1987] 46 Camb. L.J. 4; Robert Curtis, "Sunday Observance Legislation" (1974) 12 Alta. L.Rev. 236; and Kenneth M. Lysyk, "Constitutional Aspects of Sunday Observance Law" (1966) 2 U.B.C.L. Rev. 59.

126 See generally for a history of the legislation: *Lord's Day Alliance of Canada v. A.G. Manitoba*, [1925] A.C. 384 (P.C.) per Lord Blanesburgh at 390–392.

day observance was a federal criminal matter within section 91(27), apparently because the Board regarded the Ten Commandments as criminal or penal in nature.[127] In response, the federal *Lord's Day Act* was enacted in 1906 and provincial legislation repealed. However, this legislation contained provisions permitting the provinces to opt out of the federal provision, clearly to circumvent the Privy Council decision and to permit the continuation of the original Canadian understanding that the regulation of Sunday activities was a local matter and ought to be attuned to local circumstances.[128]

These provisions were upheld by the Privy Council in *Lord's Day Alliance of Canada* v. *A.G. Manitoba*,[129] on the grounds that the provincial legislation permitting Sunday excursions was not prohibitory or penal in character and that Sunday excursions had not been prohibited by any federal legislation. The Supreme Court of Canada followed this reasoning in *Lord's Day Alliance of Canada* v. *A.G. B.C.*[130] in relation to permitting sports for gain on Sundays.

Despite lingering ambiguity as to whether Parliament could delegate its jurisdiction to the provinces or the opting out provisions could be properly construed as delegation,[131] subsequent decisions upheld provincial legislation when it was framed within the opting out sections of the *Lord's Day Act* and satisfied the criteria set down in *Lord's Day Alliance of Canada* v. *A.G. Manitoba*. Where legislation was exclusively provincial in nature, it was struck down as *ultra vires*. Thus, in *Ouimet* v. *Bazin*,[132] Quebec legislation prohibiting, *inter alia*, theatrical performances on Sunday was found to be *ultra vires* because the legislation was criminal in nature. On the other hand, provincial legislation permitting the sale of fruits, sweets, and cigars on Sunday was upheld as within the delegation to the province to enact Sunday legislation.[133]

---

127 See also *Re Legislation Respecting Abstention from Labour on Sunday* (1905), 35 S.C.R. 581.

128 Above note 64, ss. 4, 6, 7.

129 Above note 126. See also *Roch* v. *Cour Municipale de Montreal*, [1963] Que. S.C. 1; and *Montreal* v. *Salle de danse "Danse Le Vent"*, [1966] R.L. 365 (Tribunal de Montreal).

130 Above note 66.

131 Above section B(4).

132 Above note 78. *Cf. R.* v. *Epstein*, [1931] O.R. 726 (H.C.).

133 *Spiliotopulas* v. *R.* (1917), 30 C.C.C. 123 (Que. C.A.). See also *Clarke* v. *Wawken* (1930), 2 D.L.R. 596 (Sask. C.A.).

Since the provinces have authority pursuant to section 92(13) and section 92(16) to regulate business, recreation, and labour relations generally, provincial legislation characterized as essentially about such matters has been upheld as within provincial powers, even though Sundays may be involved. Provincial jurisdiction over hours of work for labour as a matter of property and civil rights or as a local matter within the province,[134] has been extended to uphold the enactment by the province of legislation regulating the closing of pool halls and bowling alleys, including Sunday closing.[135] Again, a municipal closing bylaw that included Sunday has been found to be secular in nature if the bylaw as a whole shows an intention to regulate closing times for local trade purposes and applies to holidays generally, most of which have no religious significance.[136] Finally, a municipal bylaw regulating the hours of closing of a miniature golf course was also upheld on the ground that it was permissible to enact legislation whose object was the securing of a reasonable degree of quiet at the times when naturally people would not wish to be disturbed, including after 11:45 p.m. on weeknights and all day on Sunday.[137]

The scope of the federal power pursuant to section 91(27) over the regulation of religious holidays has been explored in one case, *Henry Birks v. City of Montreal*,[138] in which Quebec legislation purporting to authorize municipalities to pass bylaws to close stores on five Roman Catholic feast days was found to be *ultra vires* the province as an infringement of the federal criminal power.

That Parliament retains, in constitutional theory at least, exclusive jurisdiction over the regulation of Sunday as a day of religious observance was upheld after the enactment of the *Canadian Charter of Rights and Freedoms* by the Supreme Court of Canada in *R. v. Big M Drug Mart*.[139] However, this explicit religious characterization of the *Lord's Day Act*, which gave it its criminal character for constitutional review purposes, proved fatal for *Charter* review purposes, insofar as it dictated the

---

134 *Reference Re Legislative Jurisdiction over Hours of Labour*, [1925] S.C.R. 505; and *A.G. Canada v. A.G. Ontario*, [1937] A.C. 326 (P.C.).

135 *Lieberman v. R.*, [1963] S.C.R. 643. See also *Cusson v. Philion*, [1959] Que. S.C. 248, aff'd [1961] Que. Q.B. 566 (C.A.).

136 *R. v. Top Banana Ltd.* (1974), 4 O.R. (2d) 513 (H.C.).

137 *R. v. Epstein*, above note 132.

138 Above note 75.

139 See also *R. v. W.H. Smith Ltd.*, [1983] 5 W.W.R. 235 (Alta. Prov. Ct.).

conclusion, in *Big M. Drug Mart*, that the Act infringed section 2(a) of the *Charter* and could not be saved by section 1.

While provincial legislation compelling Sunday observance is still beyond provincial jurisdiction because it falls within the federal criminal power, provincial legislation setting aside Sunday as a common pause day is within provincial jurisdiction over property and civil rights, as found by the Supreme Court of Canada in *R. v. Edwards Books*.[140] Moreover, the secular purpose of a common pause day is sufficiently important to be upheld within section 1 of the *Charter*.[141] Secular pause day legislation, which eliminates special exemptions for non-Christians by permitting them, in effect, to choose one other pause day a week, is permitted by section 2(a) of the *Charter* and valid without recourse to section 1,[142] although the presence of very wide exemptions might also be found to be valid within section 2(a).[143] Further consideration of the impact of the *Charter* on Sabbath and other holy day observance is considered in a later chapter.[144]

3) Education

a) Denominational School Rights

Prior to Confederation, legislation had been enacted by the Province of Canada permitting both Roman Catholic minorities in Canada West[145] and Protestant minorities in Canada East[146] to enjoy publicly-funded schools separate from their respective public school systems.[147] The protection of

---

140 Above note 72; and *R. v. Hy & Zel's Supermarket Drug Store* (2000), 194 D.L.R. (4th) 375 (Ont. S.C.J.).

141 *Ibid.*

142 *Peel v. Great Atlantic & Pacific Co.* (1991), 78 D.L.R. (4th) 333 (Ont. C.A.); and *R. v. Westfair Foods Ltd.* (1989), 65 D.L.R. (4th) 56 (Sask. C.A.).

143 *London Drugs Ltd. v. City of Red Deer*, [1988] 6 W.W.R. 173 (Alta. C.A.), leave to appeal to S.C.C. refused [1988] 6 W.W.R. lxix (S.C.C.).

144 Below chapter 13.

145 *Common Schools Act*, 4 & 5 Vict., c. 18 (1841); *An Act respecting Separate Schools*, 22 Vict., c. 65 (1859); and *An Act to restore to Roman Catholics in Upper Canada certain rights in respect to Separate Schools*, 26 Vict., c. 5 (1863).

146 8 Vict., c. 41 (1845); 9 Vict., c. 27 (1846); and *An Act respecting Provincial Aid for Superior Education*, 24 Vict., c. 15 (1861).

147 See generally R.D. Gidney and W.P.J. Miller, *Inventing Secondary Education: The Rise of the High School in Nineteenth Century Ontario* (Kingston: McGill-Queen's University Press, 1990).

these hard-earned denominational schools constituted one of the most significant issues for negotiation in the years before 1867, and section 93 of the *Constitution Act, 1867*, contains the compromise about education that has been said to be at the heart of the union, even without which Confederation might not have occurred.[148] Section 93 is the only provision in the *Constitution Act, 1867*, that deals expressly with religion and it has proven to be one of the most litigated sections in the Act.[149]

Section 93 confers exclusive power to the provinces to make laws in relation to education, subject to four qualifications: (i) no provincial law may prejudicially affect any right or privilege with respect to denominational schools that any class of persons had at the time of Confederation; (ii) denominational schools for Protestants and Roman Catholics in Quebec are placed on the same footing as denominational schools for Roman Catholics in Ontario; (iii) a Protestant or Roman Catholic "minority" has a right of appeal to the Governor General in Council from any decision by any provincial authority affecting any right or privilege in relation to

---

148 *Re Bill 30*, above note 70 per Wilson J. at 1173–1174.

149 See generally Gordon Bale, "Constitutional Values in Conflict: Full Funding for Ontario's Catholic High Schools" (1986) 18 Ott. L. Rev. 533; Richard W. Bauman and David Schneiderman, "The Constitutional Context of Religious Practices in Saskatchewan Public Schools: God was in the Details" (1996) 60 Sask. L.R. 265; A.S. Brent, "The Right to Religious Education and the Constitutional Status of Denominational Schools" (1976) 40 Sask. L. Rev. 239; Greg M. Dickinson, "Looking into the Mirror of Denominational School Rights in Ontario" (1998) 9 Educ. & L.J. 115; William F. Foster and William J. Smith, "Religion and Education in Canada" (2000) 10 Educ. & L.J. 393, (2001) 11 Educ. & L.J. 1 and (2001) 11 Educ. & L.J. 203; John P. McEvoy, "Denominational Schools and Minority Rights" (2001) 12 N.J.C.L. 449; Christopher Richter, "Separation and Equality: An Argument for Religious Schools within the Public System" (1996–97) 28 Ott. L. Rev. 1; Schmeiser, above note 125 at ch. 4; B. Sokhansarj, "Our Father Who Art in the Classroom: Exploring a Charter Challenge to Prayer in the Public Schools" (1992) 56 Sask. L. Rev. 47; Jonathan Stainsby, "Plus ça change...: Education and Equality Rights in the Supreme Court" (1988) 46 U.T. Fac. L.Rev. 259; Adam Stephens, "Privilege for Few, Equality for None: Constitutional Protection for Roman Catholic Separate School Funding in Ontario" (2000) 10 Educ. & L.J. 179; Carol A. Stephenson, "Religious Exercises and Instruction in Ontario Public Schools" (1991) 49 U.T. Fac. L.Rev. 82; and L.E. Weinrib, "The Religion Clauses: Reading the Lesson" (1986) 8 Sup. Ct. L.R. 507.

education; and (iv) Parliament may enact remedial legislation to give effect to any such decision of the Governor General in Council.[150]

Section 93 was applicable to the four original provinces, was extended to British Columbia and Prince Edward Island, and in slightly different versions was made part of the terms on which Manitoba, Alberta, Saskatchewan, and Newfoundland entered Confederation.[151] Today, section 93 no longer applies in Quebec and the variation for Newfoundland no longer applies in that province.[152] Since neither New Brunswick nor Nova Scotia had publicly funded denominational schools in 1867, section 93 has always been irrelevant in those provinces, as well as in British Columbia, which had no publicly funded denominational schools in 1871.

Professor Hogg has noted[153] that section 93 is anomalous in two respects. First, it amounts to a "small bill of rights"[154] for minority religious groups by restraining the otherwise plenary power of the provinces over education; and secondly, it subordinates the exercise of provincial powers over education by the right of appeal to Parliament and the Governor General in Council.

In *Adler* v. *Ontario*,[155] the majority in the Supreme Court of Canada stated that section 93 is a "comprehensive code" concerning the provincial educational power. On strict construction, it provides expressly only for denominational schools and only implicitly for public schools since public school funding is the benchmark assumed in the section for establishing the appropriate level of state support for denominational schools. Section 93 cannot be enlarged by section 2(a) in order to mandate the establishment or funding of other religious schools or school systems but the plenary nature of the province's educational jurisdiction under section 93 means that a province enjoys a discretion, but not an obligation,

---

150 Section 93(1)–(4).

151 Above notes 23–26.

152 Above notes 27–28.

153 Above note 8 at 638, n. 41.

154 *Cf. Greater Montreal Protestant School Board* v. *Quebec (A.G.)*, [1989] 1 S.C.R. 377 per Beetz J. at 401 who disapproved of the use of this phrase by Professor Hogg because s. 93(1) should be interpreted strictly, not liberally as a bill of rights would be.

155 (1996), 140 D.L.R. (4th) 385 (S.C.C.). For an analysis, see M.H. Ogilvie, "Adler v. Ontario: Preconceptions, Myths (or Prejudices) About Religion in the Supreme Court of Canada" (1997) 9 N.J.C.L. 79.

to establish and fund other schools. The section 93 right of funding for denominational schools is immune from *Charter* review.

Section 93 denominational school rights are not, however, immune from constitutional amendment or repeal. Pursuant to the amending formula in section 43 of the *Charter*, section 93A was enacted in 1997 so that section 93 no longer applies to Quebec;[156] and in 1998, after provincial referenda,[157] Term 17 of the Newfoundland *Treaty of Union* was redrafted to remove public funding for denominational schools although non-denominational religion courses are required to be taught and religious observances permitted where requested by parents.[158] The use of referenda to assess public support for the repeal of minority religious constitutional rights has been upheld by the courts.[159]

The protection afforded to denominational schools by the four qualifications in section 93 is confined to such schools; otherwise, provincial power over non-denominational or public schools is unlimited. Thus, in

---

156 Constitution Amendment, 1997 (Quebec) S.I./97–141: "93A. Paragraphs (1) to (4) do not apply to Quebec."

157 For a history of the referenda and litigation prior to the amendment, see John P. McEvoy, "Denominational Schools and Minority Rights: *Hogan v. Newfoundland (Attorney General)*" (2001) 12 N.J.C.L. 449. For the complete litigation record, see *Hogan v. Newfoundland (School Boards for Ten Districts)* (1997), 154 Nfld. & P.E.I.R. 121, 479 A.P.R. 121 (Nfld.T.D.); and (1999), 173 Nfld. & P.E.I.R. 148, 530 A.P.R. 148 (Nfld.T.D.), rev'd (2000), 189 Nfld. & P.E.I.R. 183, 571 A.P.R. 183 (Nfld. C.A.), leave to appeal refused [2000] 2 S.C.R. ix (S.C.C.). For the litigation relating to a possible injunction to prevent the Governor General from issuing the proclamation, see *Hogan v. Newfoundland (A.G.)* (1998), 162 Nfld. & P.E.I.R. 132, 500 A.P.R. 132 (Nfld. T.D.). For the challenge to the referenda procedure, see *Hogan v. Newfoundland (A.G.)* (1998), 166 Nfld. & P.E.I.R. 161, 511 A.P.R. 161 (Nfld. T.D.), aff'd (1998), 172 Nfld. & P.E.I.R. 185, 528 A.P.R. 185 (Nfld. C.A.).

158 Constitution Amendment, 1998 (*Newfoundland Act*) S.I./98–25:

   17.(1) In lieu of s. ninety-three of the *Constitution Act, 1867*, this term shall apply in respect of the Province of Newfoundland.

   (2) In and for the Province of Newfoundland, the Legislature shall have exclusive authority to make laws in relation to education, but shall provide for courses in religion that are not specific for a religious denomination.

   (3) Religious observances shall be permitted in a school where requested by parents.

159 Above note 157.

Hirsch v. Montreal Protestant School Board[160] the Privy Council held that while Jews could not be defined as "Protestants" for the purposes of section 93, the province was free to establish other schools for religious groups that were not set out in section 93. However, the protections for denominational schools do not extend to non-denominational subjects taught in such schools in Quebec, in relation to which general provincial educational standards are applicable. In *Greater Montreal Protestant School Board v. Quebec (A.G.)*,[161] the Supreme Court of Canada found that a common curriculum for the province in relation to non-denominational subjects could be enforced in denominational schools without detriment to the section 93 protection. This protection is extended on the basis of religious belief alone and regardless of language[162] and covers only those rights and privileges established by legislation.[163] An exception to this restriction on legislation is found in the *Manitoba Act*,[164] where section 22 defines the protected rights as those existing "by law or practice"; however, subsequent judicial interpretation has ignored the phrase "or practice."

The only rights and privileges protected are those that were in existence at the time of entry into Confederation;[165] and these will, accordingly, vary from province to province.[166] Thus, where a province decides to change the language of instruction in a denominational school from the language at the time of union to the other official language, it may do so, because the choice of language of instruction is not protected under section 93. In *Mackell*,[167] the Privy Council upheld Regulation 17 pursuant to which the Ottawa separate school trustees were require to change from

---

160 [1928] 1 D.L.R. 1041 (P.C.).

161 [1989] 1 S.C.R. 377.

162 *Ottawa Roman Catholic Separate School Board v. Mackell* (1917), 32 D.L.R. 10 (P.C.).

163 *Maher v. Town of Portland* (1874), cited in G.J. Wheeler, *Confederation Law of Canada* (London: Eyre and Spottiswoode, 1896) at 338 (P.C.).

164 *Barrett v. City of Winnipeg*, [1892] A.C. 445 (P.C.); and *Brophy v. Manitoba (A.G.)*, [1895] A.C. 202 (P.C.).

165 *Jacobi v. Newell (No. 4)* (1994), 112 D.L.R. (4th) 229 (Alta. Q.B.).

166 *Greater Montreal Protestant School Board v. Quebec Min. of Education* (1976), 83 D.L.R. (3d) 645 (Que. S.C.), leave to appeal to S.C.C. refused (1978), 83 D.L.R. (3d) 679n (C.A.).

167 Above note 162.

French to English-speaking instruction. Moreover, a province may reorganize its school boards from a system based on religion to a system based on language provided the reorganization does not prejudicially affect the rights and privileges of the denominational schools.[168]

A province may reorganize its school board system to reduce the number of boards and such reorganization will not infringe denominational school rights provided provision is made for effective and representative management in the new denominational school boards.[169] Nor are denominational school rights under section 93 infringed where a provincial commission to reorganize school board systems enjoys extensive powers to require existing boards to produce business records, make new regulations, and impose more extensive conflict of interest guidelines,[170] provided such guidelines do not infringe section 15 equality rights; by, for example, disqualifying spouses of school board employees from election to a board without clear evidence that spousal conflicts were a pressing or substantial problem.[171]

In *Public School Boards Association of Alberta* v. *Alberta (A.G.)*,[172] the Supreme Court considered the related issues of whether the section 93 denominational guarantees included a guarantee of reasonable autonomy for public and separate school boards; whether section 93 precluded a province from reorganizing funding for school boards by centralizing taxation so that the province disbursed funds to school boards on an equal amount per student basis in place of local direct taxation by school boards; and whether statutory permission to separate school boards to opt out so as to continue direct taxation, but topped up by the province to achieve the same per student amount, amounted to discrimination against public boards. The Court decided that section 93 did not include a guarantee of reasonable autonomy but did imply a principle of proportionality as between public and separate boards. This standard of fairness in the distribution of moneys to schools was a general one that did not

---

168 *Reference Re Quebec Education Act*, [1993] 2 S.C.R. 511.
169 *Berthelot v. Ontario (Educational Improvement Commission)* (1998), 168 D.L.R. (4th) 201 (Ont. Div. Ct.).
170 *Ontario Public School Boards Association v. Ontario (A.G.)* (1997), 151 D.L.R. (4th) 346 (Ont. Gen Div.) rev'd on other grounds (1999), 175 D.L.R. (4th) 609 (Ont. C.A.).
171 *Ibid.* (Ont. C.A.).
172 (2000), 191 D.L.R. (4th) 513 (S.C.C.).

prohibit distinctions in funding provided they were fair. The funding changes the provincial legislation prescribed were fair because they were based on equal amounts per student distributed to all boards.

In a similar case, *Ontario English Catholic Teachers Association v. Ontario (A.G.)*,[173] the Court also applied the principle that a province could restructure the educational funding system without prejudicing denominational school rights provided equity was maintained between the public and separate boards. Provincial legislation was upheld, which removed taxing powers from local boards, imposed various restrictions on spending, and provided for closer supervision of boards' financial affairs; the legislation did not impact on the denominational aspects of the Roman Catholic schools and the new funding structure treated those schools in the same way as the public schools. The Supreme Court also confirmed the position first stated in *Adler* that the public school system has no express constitutional status; therefore, since the Roman Catholic school system had no absolute right to independent management, control, or taxation, neither has the public school system.

On the other hand, section 93 does not prohibit the creation of new rights and privileges in relation to denominational schools, although it expressly protects only those in existence at the time of entry into Confederation. Thus, in *Re Bill 30*,[174] the Supreme Court of Canada found that a provincial legislature is not precluded by section 2(a) of the *Charter* from conferring new denominational school rights, through the extension of funding to the end of high school, on Roman Catholics only, since section 93(3) expressly contemplates the establishment of new denominational school systems and therefore implicitly authorizes additions to existing denominational school systems. Additionally, four of the seven members of the Court also thought that section 93 did not preclude the return of rights thought to be possessed by Roman Catholics at Confederation. Moreover, the Court regarded discrimination on the basis of religion in relation to denominational schools to be permissible under the *Charter*.

Since section 93 applies only to laws that prejudicially affect denominational rights and privileges, legislation with a beneficial effect has been upheld, such as legislation improving the method of election of sep-

---

173 (2001), 196 D.L.R. (4th) 577 (S.C.C.).
174 Above note 70.

arate school trustees from that at Confederation[175] and legislation altering the school taxes paid by corporations so as to increase the separate school share.[176] When legislation has been characterized as neutral, such as the statutory imposition of liabilities assumed by a provincially-appointed commission operating separate schools, the Privy Council has found the legislation not to be prejudicial,[177] thereby suggesting a presumption against a finding of prejudicial effect. Where legislation permits both Roman Catholic and public school boards to impose education development charges as part of the entire provincial funding scheme for schools, there is no prejudicial effect on Roman Catholic school rights where the legislation treats both school systems equally and does not amount to an attempt to make Roman Catholic school supporters pay rates for the support of the public schools.[178]

In addition to the regulation of the non-denominational portions of their curriculum, denominational schools are also subject to provincial regulation of other non-denominational aspects, including municipal zoning bylaws and building codes[179] and the right to collective bargaining for teachers in such schools.[180] Moreover, language rights pursuant to section 23 of the *Canadian Charter of Rights and Freedoms* are applicable to denominational schools as long as they amount to the regulation of the non-denominational aspects of education.[181]

The provincial power to regulate does not include the power to abolish denominational schools, although it may extend to the power to restrict the duration of denominational education, as the Privy Council

---

175 *Belleville Roman Catholic Separate School Board v. Grainger* (1878), 25 Gr. 570 (Ch.).

176 *Calgary Board of Education v. A.G. Alberta* (1981), 28 A.R. 359 (C.A.), leave to appeal to S.C.C. refused (1981), 30 A.R. 180 (S.C.C.).

177 *Ottawa Roman Catholic Separate School Board v. Quebec Bank*, [1920] A.C. 230 (P.C.).

178 *Ontario Home Builders' Association v. York Region Board of Education* (1996), 137 D.L.R. (4th) 449 (S.C.C.).

179 *City of Toronto v. Toronto Roman Catholic Separate School Board*, [1925] 3 D.L.R. 880 (P.C.).

180 *Moose Jaw School District No. 1 v. A.G. Saskatchewan* (1975), 57 D.L.R. (3d) 315 (Sask. C.A.). For a larger discussion of the extension of denominational privilege over teachers in Roman Catholic schools, see below chapter 10, section B(5).

181 *Mahe v. Alberta*, [1990] 1 S.C.R. 342.

found in *Tiny Roman Catholic Separate Trustees v. R.*[182] Where such restrictions have occurred, they may subsequently be lifted and the level of rights existing or believed by the court to have existed at Confederation be restored, as was ordered by the Supreme Court of Canada in *Re Bill 30*.[183]

The provincial power to regulate the non-denominational aspects of denominational schools does not include the power to decline to form a Roman Catholic school board where the statutory requirements are satisfied; a minister of education is required to consider only those materials stipulated by the legislation.[184] A public school board has no constitutional right to prevent a separate school board from establishing a separate school district by amalgamation with a regional public school system.[185]

The provincial power to regulate denominational schools in their non-denominational aspects may be limited. Thus, another Regulation 17 case decided that the right of denominational schools to be managed by denominational trustees, which existed at Confederation, cannot be removed by provincial legislation even where the matter in dispute is the language of instruction rather than denominational education.[186] However, legislation providing for the mere temporary suspension of denominational trustees should they not respect the law in relation to non-denominational aspects, is not prejudicial to denominational rights and privileges.[187]

Again, provincial legislation forcing denominational schools to accept children of other religious groups has been struck down as prejudicial. Thus, in *Hirsch*, Quebec legislation deeming Jews to be Protestants for these purposes was found to be unconstitutional by the Privy Council, which emphasized the importance of exclusivity in denominational school systems to ensure the retention of their denominational character.

A final restriction by the courts on provincial legislative power to cut down denominational school privileges is in relation to funding. In *Tiny*,

---

182 [1928] 3 D.L.R. 753 (P.C.).

183 Above note 70.

184 *Saskatchewan Rivers School Division No. 119 v. Saskatchewan (Minister of Education)* (2000), 197 Sask. R. 218 (Q.B.).

185 *Sturgeon School Division No. 24 v. Alberta* (2000), 272 A.R. 190 (Q.B.).

186 *Ottawa Roman Catholic Separate School Board v. City of Ottawa*, [1917] A.C. 76 (P.C.).

187 *Re Ottawa Separate School Board* (1917), 40 D.L.R. 465 (C.A.).

the Privy Council upheld a reduction in the proportion of provincial education funding available to separate schools in Ontario. However, doubt was cast on this in *A.G. Quebec v. Greater Hull School Board*,[188] where the Supreme Court of Canada struck down Quebec legislation that had repealed a pre-Confederation statute providing that denominational schools share in provincial grants in proportion to the number of their pupils. That case also struck down a provision requiring a referendum on taxation for denominational school purposes in which those who were not denominational school supporters were permitted to vote. In the subsequent *Re Bill 30*, the majority in the Supreme Court of Canada struck down the part of the *Tiny* decision that had sustained the authority of provincial legislatures to reduce funding to denominational schools.

After 1985 when section 15 of the *Charter* came into force, the issue of whether section 93 denominational privileges could be struck down on equality grounds in respect to denominational school funding or whether provinces are constitutionally required to fund other religious school systems pursuant to section 15(1) has been considered. In *Re Bill 30*, the Supreme Court of Canada decided that the privileges enjoyed under section 93 could not be removed pursuant to the equality provisions. The Court stated that the *Charter* could not be used to amend or repeal earlier constitutional documents although it admitted that section 93 created inequality in relation to school funding that could be denied to other religious groups.[189] The Court confirmed this position in *Adler*, on the ground that one section of the Constitution could not be used to strike down another.

Where denominational school rights are believed to be prejudicial, the aggrieved party has a right both to appeal to the Governor General in Council pursuant to section 93(3) and to request remedial legislation from Parliament pursuant to section 93(4). This power has never been used, although it almost was in 1896 when the Conservative federal government introduced a remedial bill to restore denominational school rights removed by Manitoba legislation in 1890.[190] The Privy Council upheld the legislation.[191] Before the federal legislation was enacted, a general election was held in 1896 in which the "Manitoba schools question"

---

188 [1984] 2 S.C.R. 575.

189 See Dale Gibson, "Comment" (1988) 67 Can. Bar Rev. 142.

190 *Public Schools Act*, 53 Vict. c. 38 (1890).

191 Above note 164.

was the main issue. The winning Liberal government persuaded the province to repeal the legislation, which it did in 1897.[192] Sections 93(3) and 93(4) have not been appealed to since.

b) Religion in Public Schools

With the coming into effect of the *Charter* in 1982, certain aspects of education have also become matters of constitutional law as subject to judicial *Charter* review; in particular, religious exercises and religious instruction. In *Zylberberg* v. *Sudbury Board of Education*,[193] an Ontario regulation providing for religious exercises including "the reading of the Scriptures or other suitable readings and the repeating of the Lord's Prayer or other suitable prayers" was found to be in breach of section 2(a) of the *Charter* because it imposed Christian observances upon non-Christian pupils, despite a provision for exemption from participation. This was construed as indirect coercion since peer pressure would compel students to conform by attending, rather than making a public religious statement not required of the majority by invoking the exception.

In a subsequent decision, *Canadian Civil Liberties Association* v. *Ontario*,[194] the other part of the same Ontario regulation providing for two periods per week of religious instruction also came under scrutiny in the Ontario Court of Appeal, which struck it down pursuant to section 2(a) because its purpose was Christian indoctrination. Again, the regulation was not saved by an exemption from participation because of the likelihood that peer pressure would render it nugatory. The court rejected arguments under section 1 that the regulations could be saved because religious instruction was a means to teach children about morality. The court thought there were other ways of doing so than by Christian "indoctrination," but did not state what these were.

In response to the suggestion of the Ontario Court of Appeal in these decisions that education about religion was permissible in the public schools provided it was not indoctrinational, the Ontario government issued the so-called "Policy Memorandum 112" to permit education about religion. This approach was challenged by a multi-faith parents'

---

192 60 Vict., c. 26 (1897).

193 Above note 107. See also *Manitoba Association for Rights & Liberties* v. *Manitoba* (1992), 94 D.L.R. (4th) 678 (Man. Q.B.).

194 *Ibid.*

coalition in *Bal v. Ontario (A.G.)*,[195] on the ground that the secular values implicit in this approach imposed a world view inimical to their religious values on their children and constituted an infringement of their section 2(a) freedom. The Ontario Court of Appeal characterized secular as neutral and rejected their argument entirely. However, religion has not been entirely erased by the courts from public schools. In *Islamic Schools Federation of Ontario v. Ottawa Board of Education*,[196] in which Muslims sought the closure of two public high schools with large Muslim student populations on two Muslim holy days, the Ontario Divisional Court declined to do so but did note that the religious exemption provisions in provincial legislation and the practices of the schools in accommodating individual student holy day absences were evidence that there was no infringement of section 2(a).

To ensure that their children receive a religious and moral education, parents have increasingly turned to independent schools whose numbers have grown considerably since 1982. However, it appears that these schools are also subject to judicial *Charter* review, as found by the Supreme Court of Canada in *R. v. Jones*.[197] While parents are free to fulfil their legal duty to provide education for their children in the educational forum of their choice, where provincial legislation requires certification of schools as providing efficient instruction in secular subjects, managers of such schools may be subject to penalty for failure to comply, although their religious beliefs do not encompass a role for the state in the education of their children. Thus, in *Jones*, four of the seven judges found there to be no violation of section 2(a) by requiring certification, while the other three thought the section 2(a) violation reasonable under section 1 because of the state's compelling interest in the education of all future citizens. The Court was unanimous in the view that the state was obliged to accommodate religious diversity in education under section 2(a).

However, in *Adler*, the Supreme Court of Canada also clearly held that the state was not obliged to go the next step and fund religious schools under the *Charter*, other than those already constitutionally privileged pursuant to section 93.[198] Five of the nine justices thought the reason to be that section 93, as a comprehensive education code, imposed

---

195 (1994), 21 O.R. (3d) 682 (Gen. Div.), aff'd (1997), 101 O.A.C. 219 (C.A.).
196 (1997), 145 D.L.R. (4th) 659 (Ont. Div. Ct.).
197 Above note 89.
198 Above note 155.

no such requirement. But Sopinka and Major JJ. thought that the failure to fund did not constitute a section 2(a) infringement — although parents had a constitutional right to educate their children as they wish, the state was under no duty to fund religious schools. Their costs flowed from religious belief not state action; religious schools are really private schools to which the section 15 equality guarantee does not apply either as a listed or analogous ground of discrimination. McLachlin and L'Heureux-Dubé JJ. thought that the failure to fund religious schools was a breach of section 15 because there was adverse effect discrimination in the imposition of a disproportionate burden on parents whose religious beliefs required them to send their children to religious schools. McLachlin J. thought this discrimination was justified under section 1 because public schools promoted a more tolerant society but L'Heureux-Dubé J. thought the discrimination to be unjustified and that there was a constitutional obligation to fund, at least partially, religious schools.[199]

The constitutional position for religious parents and children who do not enjoy the school funding privileges flowing from section 93 is that they have the right pursuant to section 2(a) to education in a religious context, whether at home or in a religious school. However, there is no constitutional right pursuant to either section 2(a) or section 15 to state funding of religious education. It must be funded either privately, or by voluntary provincial allocations to religious schools or parents pursuant to ordinary provincial legislation, which is subject to future amendment or repeal.[200]

4) Freedom of Conscience and Religion

Section 2(a) of the *Charter* is the first time a Canadian constitutional document has expressly provided protection for freedom of religion. The

---

199 In 1999, the U.N. Human Rights Committee decided that the failure to fund other religious schools in Ontario than Roman Catholic schools put Canada in breach of the *International Covenant on Civil and Political Rights: Waldman's Case*, CCPR/C/67/D/694/1996 (3 Nov. 1999). See also the later failed case where the complainant sought to remove funding from the Roman Catholic school system: *Todman's Case*, CCPR/C/67/D/816/1998 (5 Nov. 1999).

200 In most provinces this legislation is structured to provide funding directly to schools on the basis of administrative criteria; exceptionally, in Ontario the funding is by way of a tax deduction available to parents to offset partially the fees for attending religious schools: *Responsible Choices for Growth and Accountability Act*, S.O. 2001, c. 8, s. 40 (Equity in Education Tax Credit).

common law had been the source of protection prior to 1982, not only through the English common law inheritance but also from consideration by the Canadian courts of the nature of freedom of religion in pre-*Charter* Canada.

After the conquest of Quebec in 1759, which ended the Roman Catholic religious monopoly in that colony, and despite assertions of establishment by other denominations in the colonies that became Canada, all religious groups in Canada have been regarded in law as being on an equal footing, enjoying identical legal rights, with the exception of section 93 denominational school rights.[201] While Canadian history, particularly in the mid nineteenth century, is replete with denominational disputes over a wide variety of issues,[202] after Confederation there would appear to have been widespread acceptance of the position that all religious groups enjoy freedom of belief and expression, although some smaller, marginal groups like the Mennonites and Hutterites ran into problems with the state over issues of importance to them, such as military conscription, taking oaths, and schooling.[203] There is very little case law about the meaning of freedom of religion prior to the cases involving the Jehovah's Witnesses in the mid twentieth century. Generally, there were simply few cases coming before the courts.[204]

It remains uncertain whether the protection of religious freedom in Canada is a federal or provincial or a shared jurisdiction. The enactment of human rights legislation by the provinces in relation to matters within section 92(13) and section 92(16) and of federal human rights legislation in relation to matters within federal jurisdiction suggests that there

---

201 For judicial expression of equal footing in law, see below chapter 8.

202 M.H. Ogilvie, "What is a Church By Law Established" (1990) 28 O.H.L.J. 179.

203 See generally William Janzen, *Limits on Liberty: The Experience of Mennonite, Hutterite and Doukhobor Communities in Canada* (Toronto: University of Toronto Press, 1990).

204 See generally Schmeiser, above note 125 at 71–95; 113–117. See also William W. Black, "Religion and the Right of Equality" in A. Bayefsky and M. Eberts, eds., *Equality Rights and the Canadian Charter of Rights and Freedoms* (Toronto: Carswell, 1985); Paul Horwitz, "The Sources and Limits of Freedom of Religion in a Liberal Democracy: Section 2(a) and Beyond" (1996) 54 U.T. Fac. L.R. 1; William Klassen, "Religion and the Nation: An Ambiguous Alliance" (1990) 40 U.N.B.L.R. 87; and Patrick Macklem, "Freedom of Conscience and Religion in Canada" (1984) 42 U.T. Fac. L.R. 50.

is a widespread understanding that the jurisdiction is shared in accordance with the same constitutional principles used to assess jurisdiction over other subject-matters for which no express provision is made in the written constitution. The express provisions of the *Charter*, likewise, are as extensive as the jurisdiction of the *Charter* itself. In short, there is no single constitutional document nor is there a single jurisdiction in Canada with authority to define the nature of freedom of religion in Canada.

Canadian courts had addressed the issue of the legal content of the concept of freedom of religion prior to the first *Charter* case, *R. v. Big M Drug Mart*, in which the Supreme Court of Canada interpreted section 2(a). Early cases considered the nature of public expression of religious views; thus, in *City of Montreal* v. *Madden*,[205] charges of disturbing the peace against the Salvation Army were dropped because the defendant had not acted wilfully. On the other hand, in *Re Cribbin and the City of Toronto*,[206] a Toronto bylaw prohibiting speeches, lectures, or sermons in a public park on Sundays was upheld when challenged by the Salvation Army, on the ground that such activities might provoke ill-feeling and breaches of the peace.

Freedom of expression as a component of freedom of religion was considered subsequently on several occasions by the Supreme Court of Canada in appeals from Quebec by Jehovah's Witnesses who were persecuted by the Duplessis government.[207] In *Boucher* v. *R.*,[208] charges of seditious libel against a Witness who had distributed highly inflammatory pamphlets about Roman Catholics and the government in Quebec were struck down on the ground that while the pamphlets might cause agitation, they were not written with the intention of causing hostility or of overthrowing established authority, thereby suggesting the outer limits within which freedom of religious expression might be enjoyed.

Although two earlier lower court decisions[209] had decided that distributing religious literature on the streets was part of the free exercise of religion for which no licence could be required, in *Saumur* v. *City of Que-*

---

205 (1884), 29 L.C.J. 134 (S.C.).

206 (1891), 21 O.R. 325 (H.C.).

207 William Kaplan, *State and Salvation: The Jehovah's Witnesses and their Fight for Civil Rights* (Toronto: University of Toronto Press, 1989).

208 [1951] S.C.R. 265.

209 *R. v. Kite* (1949), 2 W.W.R. 195 (B.C. Co. Ct.); and *R. v. Naish* (1950), 1 W.W.R. 987 (Sask. Police Ct.).

bec,[210] concerning a city bylaw prohibiting the distribution of pamphlets on the street without police permission, the Supreme Court of Canada upheld both the bylaw and Saumur's right to distribute Witnesses' literature in a decision in which seven of the nine justices delivered separate opinions. The rights to distribute literature,[211] to assemble in peaceful assembly,[212] and to post bail for arrested co-religionists[213] were also upheld by the Supreme Court in subsequent cases in which the courts repeatedly re-asserted that freedom of religion encompassed belief, expression, assembly, and proselytizing.

In other cases involving Jehovah's Witnesses, freedom of religious expression has been held to include the rights of Witnesses' school children to decline to take oaths of allegiance or to participate in other patriotic school activities.[214] Moreover, Mennonites were able to push this decision even further in a pre-*Charter* case, *R. v. Wiebe*,[215] which overturned earlier Mennonite cases,[216] by deciding that freedom to educate children without state interference was also protected by provincial bill of rights legislation as an expression of freedom of religion.

While Canadian courts did not construct a commonly accepted and comprehensive definition of the legal content of freedom of religion prior to the *Charter*, their responses on those occasions when invited to consider the issue suggested a liberal, generous, and expansive approach expressed on a case-by-case basis. Again, Canadian courts did not construct a constitutional theory about jurisdiction over freedom of religion yet clearly indicated that proper judicial review on constitutional grounds involved the application of the same principles applied in respect to other disputed subject-matters.

The basic guarantee of religious freedom is contained in section 2(a). In contrast to the American First Amendment where the free exercise of

---

210 [1953] 2 S.C.R. 299.

211 *Lamb v. Benoit*, [1959] S.C.R. 321.

212 *Chaput v. Romain*, [1955] S.C.R. 834.

213 *Roncarelli v. Duplessis*, [1959] S.C.R. 121.

214 *Donald v. Hamilton (City) Board of Education*, [1945] 3 D.L.R. 424 (Ont. C.A.); and *Chabot v. School Commissioners of Lamorandiere* (1957), 12 D.L.R. (2d) 796 (Que. C.A.).

215 (1978), 3 W.W.R. 36 (Alta. Prov. Ct.).

216 *R. v. Hildebrand*, [1919] 3 W.W.R. 286 (Man. C.A.); *R. v. Ulmer*, [1923] 1 D.L.R. 304 (Alta. C.A.); and *Perepolkin v. B.C. Superintendent of Child Welfare (No. 2)* (1957), 11 D.L.R. (2d) 417 (B.C.C.A.).

religion is expressed as an absolute right, the *Charter*, itself, qualifies the religious freedom guarantee in five ways: (i) section 2(a) creates an equivalence between religion and conscience, which need not be religious; (ii) section 15 reduces religion to one of many categories vying for "equality"; (iii) section 27 suggests that religion may be subsumed under culture and that all multicultural heritages are to be preserved and enhanced in the interpretation of the *Charter*; (iv) section 29 privileges existing denominational schools and, therefore, certain denominations; and (v) section 1 gives courts discretion to qualify the fundamental freedom of religion by "such reasonable limits prescribed by law as can be demonstrably justified in a free and democratic society." Effectively, the *Charter* reduces and relativizes religious freedom and gives courts the power to select and balance other countervailing claims.

One other part of the *Charter* might originally have been considered to be a source of interpretation of the freedom of religion guarantee; that is, the preamble, which states that "Canada is founded on principles that recognize the supremacy of God and the rule of law." From the outset, the difficulty in distilling meaning from the phrase "the supremacy of God" has been conceded,[217] and the possibility that the preamble might be used to interpret the religion guarantee to favour any specific religious perspective has been repeatedly denied by the courts, which apply the usual rules of statutory interpretation when considering the value of the preamble as an interpretative guide to the *Charter*.[218]

The courts have consistently rejected the use of the preamble to interpret the *Charter* for a number of reasons: (i) the preamble is too ambiguous;[219] (ii) the preamble is inconsistent with the democratic principles that undergird the entire Constitution;[220] (iii) the preamble conflicts with the fundamentally secular nature of the Canadian state and

---

217 P.W. Hogg, *Canada Act 1982 Annotated* (Toronto: Carswell, 1982) at 9; and Dale Gibson, *The Law of the Charter* (Toronto: Carswell, 1986) at 65–66. See also an early attempt at explication: Brayton Polko, "The Supremacy of God and the Rule of Law in the *Canadian Charter of Rights and Freedoms*: A Theologico-Political Analysis" (1987) 32 McGill L.J. 854.

218 Ruth Sullivan, *Driedger on the Construction of Statutes*, 3d ed. (Toronto: Butterworths, 1994) at 259–263.

219 *Zylberberg*, above note 107 per the court at 657.

220 *R. v. Morgentaler*, [1988] 1 S.C.R. 30 per Wilson J. at 178.

society;[221] and (iv) the preamble has the potential to cut down other provisions of the *Charter*[222] that guarantee conscience and religion generally (section 2(a)), equality on the basis of religion (section 15), multiculturalism (section 27), and constitutionally privileged denominational schools (section 29). The preamble has been judicially pronounced "a dead letter ... [which] can only be resurrected by the Supreme Court of Canada,"[223] which has shown no inclination to do so.[224]

The four fundamental freedoms set out in section 2 of the *Charter*, of conscience and religion, expression, peaceful assembly, and association, are all required for people of faith to enjoy some measure of religious freedom. To date only section 2(a) has been subject to extensive consideration by the courts, especially by the Supreme Court of Canada, and while there is some case law in relation to section 2(b) and freedom of religion, the relationship of section 2(a) and section 2(b) has yet to be explored, while section 2(c) and section 2(d) have not yet been seriously considered in relation to freedom of religion.[225]

In *R. v. Big M Drug Mart*, Dickson J. defined freedom of religion in section 2(a) as follows:[226]

> The essence of the concept of freedom of religion is the right to entertain such religious beliefs as a person chooses, the right to declare religious beliefs openly and without fear of hinderance or reprisal, and the right to manifest belief by worship and practice or by teaching and dissemination. But the concept means more than that.

---

221 *O'Sullivan v. M.N.R.* (1991), 84 D.L.R. (4th) 124 (F.C.T.D.) per Muldoon J. at 139; *Rodriguez v. A.G. B.C.* (1993), 107 D.L.R. (4th) 342 (S.C.C.) per Lamer C.J.C. at 366; *Lethbridge RCMP Veterans' Court Challenge Committee v. A.G. Canada* (1994), 94 C.L.L.C. 14, 035 (F.C.T.D.) per Reed J. at 12, 220–12, 221; *Adler v. Ontario*, above note 154 per Sopinka J. at 447; and *Freitag v. Penetanguishene (Town)* (1999), 179 D.L.R. (4th) 150 (Ont. C.A.), *passim*.

222 *Zylberberg*, above note 107 per the court at 657.

223 *R. v. Sharpe* (1999), 175 D.L.R. (4th) 1 (B.C.C.A.) per Southin J.A. at 47.

224 For discussions of the philosophical and political values that appear to undergird this approach to the religion provisions in the *Charter*, see M.H. Ogilvie, "The Unbearable Lightness of *Charter* Canada" (2002) 3 *Journal of the Church Law Association* 201; and M.H. Ogilvie, "Between *Liberté* and *Égalité*: Religion and the State in Canada" in R. Atherton, D. Meyerson, and P. Radan, eds. [untitled collection] (Oxford: Oxford University Press, 2003).

225 For s. 2(b), below section D(5).

226 Above note 56 at 336–37.

Freedom can primarily be characterized by the absence of coercion or constraint. ... Freedom in a broad sense embraces both the absence of coercion and constraint, and the right to manifest belief and practices. Freedom means that, subject to such limitations as are necessary to protect public safety, order, health, or morals or the fundamental rights and freedoms of others, no one is to be forced to act in a way contrary to his beliefs or his conscience.

Dickson J. justified this restrictive definition of freedom of religion by reference to the alleged historical divisiveness of religion and the post-Reformation evolution of toleration and of the "centrality of individual conscience" to belief, uncoerced by the state.[227] Section 27 was also invoked in favour of respecting religious minorities, so that the Sunday observance legislation could be struck down as "fundamentally repugnant,"[228] as an attempt to impose the beliefs of a Christian "majority."

Dickson J. further suggested that in section 2(a) "religion" is really to be assimilated to "conscience," and this position was further clarified in *R. v. Edwards Books*. In *Big M Drug Mart* this view seems implicit in his linking, historically, the growth of religious toleration and the growth of parliamentary democracy and the requirement for individual judgment and individual conscience if democracy is to operate. Thus, he further stated:

> ... the purpose of freedom of conscience and religion [is] clear. The values that underlie our political and philosophic traditions demand that every individual be free to hold and to manifest whatever beliefs and opinions his or her conscience dictates, provided, *inter alia*, only that such manifestations do not injure his or her neighbours or their parallel rights to hold and manifest beliefs and opinions of their own. Religious belief and practice are historically prototypical and, in many ways paradigmatic of conscientiously-held beliefs and manifestations and are therefore protected by the Charter.[229]

That freedom of religion as a separate fundamental value is assimilated with freedom of conscience in section 2(a) is suggested by Dickson C.J.C. in *Edwards Books*:[230]

---

227 *Ibid.* at 361.
228 *Ibid.* at 366.
229 *Ibid.* at 346–47.
230 Above note 72 at 759.

The purpose of section 2(a) is to ensure that society does not interfere with profoundly personal beliefs that govern one's perception of one-self, human kind, nature, and, in some cases, a higher or different order of being. These beliefs, in turn, govern one's conduct and practices. The Constitution shelters individuals and groups only to the extent that religious beliefs or conduct might reasonably or actually be threatened. For a state-imposed cost or burden to be prescribed by section 2(a) it must be capable of interfering with religious belief or practice. In short, legislative or administrative action which increases the cost of practis-ing or otherwise manifesting religious beliefs is not prohibited if the burden is trivial or insubstantial.

The Court did not identify the criteria for distinguishing which belief system is to be favoured when religious and non-religious belief systems make competing claims. Nor did the Court identify the criteria for distin-guishing when a state-imposed burden is more than trivial or insubstan-tial. It seems unavoidable that the criteria chosen would be secular and therefore not likely neutral, once the Court is obliged to frame criteria.

Early confirmation by the Supreme Court of Canada that religion for section 2(a) purposes is to be secularized and privatized as just another belief system is found in Wilson J.'s statement in R. v. Morgentaler that section 2(a) should extend to "conscientiously held beliefs, whether grounded in religion or in a secular morality"[231] as well as in her dissent in Jones where she opined that the Charter intended "the freedom of the individual to realize and develop his potential to the full, to plan his own life to suit his own character, to make his own choices for good or ill, to be non-conformist, idiosyncratic and even eccentric — to be, in today's parlance, 'his own person' and accountable as such. John Stuart Mill described it as 'pursuing our own good in our own way.'"[232] Perhaps another insight into how the Supreme Court of Canada conceptualized the content of section 2(a) may be gained from the list of activities given by Dickson C.J.C. in Edwards Books in which individuals might indulge on the common pause day; these include only secular activities such as

---

231 Above note 220 at 34.
232 Above note 89 at 318. Although LaForest J. in Jones emphasized that the valid-ity of and sincerity with which beliefs are held should not be explored, it is arguable that the courts do so; see M.H. Ogilvie, "Who Do You Say that You Are? Courts, Creeds and Christian Identity" (2000) 3 Journal of the Church Law Association 140.

family visits and recreational pastimes but do not include worship or any other religious activity.[233]

The content of section 2(a) as expressed in the foundational decisions in *Big M Drug Mart* and *Edwards Books* are widely cited and are widely regarded as the comprehensive statement of the legal nature of freedom of religion in later cases.[234] Freedom of religion is not absolute but limited, and the courts will determine its limits. How they do so will be explored in the chapters that follow in the context of specific issues; however, recent case law has explored the more difficult issue of balancing the section 2(a) religious freedom guarantees with competing claims made under the section 15 equality provisions. The outcome of these decisions is that the Supreme Court of Canada now draws very narrowly the constitutional parameters within which freedom of religion can be exercised.

In *R. v. Big M Drug Mart*, Dickson J. defined the content of section 2(a) to include the right to declare openly, manifest, practise, teach, and disseminate religious beliefs. Although much greater clarification is still required, it would appear that the courts deal with religious expression under section 2(a) and with hate speech against religious groups or perspectives under section 2(b). The line between religious expression that is a legitimate expression of beliefs, and expression with a religious connotation that is critical of others to the point of inciting hate or even violence, has not been drawn and will likely prove impossible to draw with any predictable accuracy by the courts.

As the Supreme Court of Canada acknowledged in *Big M Drug Mart*, religious expression has traditionally been regarded as an element of religious freedom. Expression, generally, has also been regarded as an element of democracy. Many religions, including the two largest in Canada, Christianity and Islam, place a duty to evangelize on believers so that public free expression is required if believers are to be fully religious. Public religious expression is also required if religious people are to enjoy full democratic rights as citizens; to suggest otherwise is a denial of democracy. The extent and limits of religious expression under section 2(a) have been explored by the courts in the context of expression said to be hateful of a religious group in relation to section 2(b) and also in the context of expression said to be offensive and hurtful of a sector of

---

233 Above note 72 at 770.

234 See for example *Zylberberg*, above note 107; *C.C.L.A.*, above note 107; and *Adler*, above note 155.

Canadian society whose claims to equality under section 15 have been consistently upheld by the courts.

In *Ross v. New Brunswick School District No. 15*,[235] the Supreme Court upheld the section 2(a) religious expression rights of a public school teacher who had disseminated anti-Semitic writings outside the classroom. Although Ross never clarified how his anti-Semitic activities were justified in Christian teaching, the Court accepted the sincerity of his beliefs and upheld his right to express them.[236] However, it agreed with a lower tribunal's decision to remove him from the classroom to an administrative position as an appropriate measure under section 1 because his views had somehow become known in the classroom and poisoned the teaching environment there. The Court adopted the position in *Big M Drug Mart* that section 2(a) rights were limited where a religious belief "denigrates and defames"[237] the religious beliefs of others, thereby denying their equality right to equal respect and dignity.[238] The Court appeared to treat Ross's activities as hate propaganda under section 2(b) and may not, for that reason, have given sufficient attention to the issues of what degree or type of religious expression is permissible. If all religious expression must be free from criticism of others, then there can be no public religious expression. Further clarification is required.

One way in which the courts have limited religious expression under section 2(a) is to favour the section 15 equality rights of homosexuals when competing claims have been made. "Equality" is by its very nature tautologous and empty until content is poured into it by the courts. The articulation of a definitive scope and content for section 15 has eluded the courts;[239] however, in relation to determining which groups or individuals may make equality claims, the Supreme Court has decided that in addition to those expressly listed in the section, others can be implicitly added on analogous grounds.[240] Sexual orientation is one such analogous ground because like listed grounds such as gender or race, it "is a deeply personal characteristic that is either unchangeable or changeable

---

235 (1996), 133 D.L.R. (4th) 1 (S.C.C.).

236 *Ibid.* per LaForest J. at 28. See also Ogilvie, above note 232.

237 *Ibid.* per LaForest J. at 36.

238 *Ibid.* per LaForest J. at 31–42.

239 Two comprehensive studies of the options considered are William Black and Lynn Smith, "The Equality Rights" in Beaudoin and Mendes, above note 8 at ch. 14 and Hogg, above note 8 at ch. 52.

240 *Andrews v. Law Society of British Columbia* (1989), 56 D.L.R. (4th) 1 (S.C.C.).

only at unacceptable personal costs."[241] But it is not enough to be an analogous ground; in addition, any alleged discrimination must also constitute a "violation of essential human dignity."[242]

In *Trinity Western University v. British Columbia College of Teachers*,[243] the Supreme Court of Canada considered how section 2(a) religious expression and section 15 equality rights of homosexuals should be balanced. The Court decided that the Christian private university's teaching graduates should not be required to complete their teacher training for certification to teach in public schools at a secular public university as the B.C. College of Teachers had argued. The University's community standards statement requiring that the students live a Christian lifestyle while members of the university community, including refraining from homosexual activity, was insufficient evidence that the graduates would engage in discriminatory conduct toward homosexuals once teaching.

The Court squarely stated the core issue as balancing section 2(a) and section 15 equality rights and defined the test for resolving the proper balance as the distinction between belief and conduct; the former may be exercised within a religious community but the latter may not be exercised outside a religious community.[244] The eight to one majority thought that the university's community standards were not discriminatory as understood by current section 15 jurisprudence, which upheld the validity of the exemptions for religious institutions contained in provincial human rights codes from the general requirement of equality as defined by the courts.[245] The majority upheld the right of the licensing body to discipline graduates who engaged in discriminatory conduct but did not define what conduct might be discriminatory.[246] By failing to endorse the

---

241 *Egan v. Canada* (1995), 124 D.L.R. (4th) 609 (S.C.C.) per LaForest J. at 619. In *Vriend v. Alberta* (1998), 156 D.L.R. (4th) 385 (S.C.C.), the court read "sexual orientation" into the prohibited grounds in s. 15(1).

242 *Law v. Canada* (1999), 170 D.L.R. (4th) 1 (S.C.C.) per Iacobucci J. at 37–41. This approach was adopted to require that same-sex benefits be extended to same-sex couples in *M. v. H.* (1999), 171 D.L.R. (4th) 577 (S.C.C.).

243 (2001), 199 D.L.R. (4th) 1 (S.C.C.). See also M.H. Ogilvie, "After the *Charter*: Religious Freedom and Other Legal Fictions in Canada" (2003) 2 O.U.C.L.J. forthcoming.

244 *Ibid.* per Iacobucci J. at 30.

245 *Ibid.* per Iacobucci J. at 33–34.

246 *Ibid.* per Iacobucci J. at 31–33. The sole dissenting judge, L'Heureux-Dubé J. had no doubt that the only issue in the case was discrimination against homo-

permissibility of expressing what may be unpopular religious beliefs out-side a religious community, the Supreme Court cast considerable doubt over the extent to which religious expression is exercisable in public spaces in Canada, thereby trimming the content of section 2(a) further.[247]

In *R. v. Big M Drug Mart*, Dickson J. framed the fundamental freedom of conscience and religion as one guaranteeing freedom for and freedom from religion. The first two decades of *Charter* jurisprudence suggest that the section 2(a) guarantee is considered by the courts to be primarily one guaranteeing freedom from religion in all public spaces in Canada. Con-firmation that the trajectories running through the section 2(a) cases are the trinity of state neutrality, secular society, and private religion may be found in the Ontario Court of Appeal's decision in *Freitag* v. *Penetan-guishene (Town)*,[248] in which the court upheld the removal of all religious observance from public deliberations as a valid application of the section 2(a) religion guarantee.[249]

5) Freedom of Expression

Prior to 1982 Canadian courts had rarely considered either constitution-al jurisdiction over freedom of expression or its substantive nature. As with the other types of civil liberties, it was generally assumed that the right to free expression was protected by the common law and that if issues of jurisdiction over its regulation were to arise, then the normal

---

sexuals and refused to consider whether s. 2(a) religious freedom should be bal-anced against s. 15 equality rights in concluding that the community standards statement is discriminatory and the graduates should be considered biased.

247 That religious (in all cases, Christian) expression may not be made publicly under s. 2(a) where the other right to be balanced is the s. 15 equality right of homosexuals is also suggested by recent human rights tribunal decisions: *Brillinger* v. *Brockie (No. 3)* (2000), 37 C.H.R.R. D/15 (Ont. Bd. Inq.); in only one case to date, currently under appeal to the Supreme Court of Canada, has a court upheld the right to public religious expression: *Chamberlain* v. *Surrey School District No. 36* (2000), 191 D.L.R. (4th) 128 (B.C.C.A.).

248 Above note 221. *Cf. Ontario (Speaker of the Legislative Assembly)* v. *Ontario (Human Rights Commission)* (2001), 54 O.R. (3d) 595 (C.A.) where legislative privilege permitted the provincial legislature to continue to say the Lord's Prayer. See also Michael D. Mysack, "Houses of the Holy? Reconciling Parlia-mentary Privilege and Freedom of Religion" (2001) 12 N.J.C.L. 353.

249 For a more extensive analysis of these decisions, see the two articles by Ogilvie, above note 224.

principles of constitutional adjudication would determine which level of government had authority. The few cases considered by the Supreme Court of Canada prior to 1982 were concerned primarily with the issue of political speech, which the Court was quick not only to protect to the fullest extent possible, but also to assign to Parliament pursuant to its criminal law powers.[250]

Section 2(b) guarantees to everyone the fundamental freedom of "thought, belief, opinion and expression, including freedom of the press and other media of communication." While no rationale is given for the protection of freedom of expression, in *Irwin Toy* v. *Quebec*,[251] Dickson C.J.C., Lamer, and Wilson JJ. stated the reasons as follows:

> (1) seeking and attaining the truth is an inherently good activity; (2) participation in social and political decision-making is to be fostered and encouraged; and (3) the diversity in forms of individual self-fulfil-ment and human flourishing ought to be cultivated.[252]

This statement does not define what or how extensive freedom of expression is nor does it offer much indication of the nature of the values underlying free expression. Subsequent cases have not explored these issues further so that the theoretical foundations for freedom of expression remain unarticulated, if even implicitly present, in the case law.[253] In relation to religion, freedom of expression has been most frequently considered by the Supreme Court of Canada in cases involving hate propaganda against religious minorities. The *Criminal Code* makes it an indictable offence to engage in conduct that amounts to wilfully promoting hatred against any section of the public distinguished by religion,[254] or to spread views known to be false that causes injury to a public interest.[255]

---

250 *Saumur*, above note 42. *Switzman* v. *Elbling*, [1957] S.C.R. 285. See also Clare Beckton, "Freedom of Expression" in Beaudoin and Ratushny, above note 8, ch. 6; Clare Beckton, "Freedom of Expression in Canada — 13 Years of Charter Interpretation" in Beaudoin and Mendes, above note 8, ch. 5; and Victor V. Ramraj, "*Keegstra, Butler,* and Positive Liberty: A Glimmer of Hope for the Faithful" (1993) 51 U.T. Fac. L.R. 304.

251 [1989] 1 S.C.R. 927.

252 *Ibid.* at 976.

253 For a recent comprehensive study, see Keith Dubick, "The Theoretical Foundation for Protecting Freedom of Expression" (2001) 13 N.J.C.L. 1.

254 R.S.C. 1985, c. C-46, s. 319.

255 *Ibid.* s. 181.

In *R. v. Keegstra*,[256] a school teacher who had been found guilty of making anti-Semitic comments in the classroom challenged the *Criminal Code* provision as to promoting hatred as a violation of freedom of expression pursuant to section 2(b). The Court unanimously held that the promotion of hatred against a religious group was protected by section 2(b), which covered all messages no matter how unpopular, distasteful, or contrary to mainstream thinking they may be. Nor, in the view of the Court, could this protection of expression be narrowed by reference to the equality rights in section 15 or the multicultural guarantees in section 27. The Court further upheld the provisions of the Code pursuant to section 1 by a margin of four to three.

In the companion case, *R. v. Zundel*,[257] the Supreme Court of Canada, also by a margin of four to three, struck down the spreading false news provision of the *Criminal Code* on the ground that it was not a reasonable limit on freedom of expression. The accused had published pamphlets alleging that the Holocaust was an invention of an international Jewish conspiracy, but was finally acquitted because the *Criminal Code* provision was unconstitutional. The Court unanimously held that the activity of publishing deliberate falsehoods was protected under section 2(b) on the ground that the protection covered both false and true statements, but decided to strike down the Code provision on section 1 grounds.

Since *Keegstra* and *Zundel*, the application of the hatred propaganda provisions of the *Criminal Code* in relation to religion has been considered only in *R. v. Harding*,[258] where the accused was alleged to have promoted hatred against Muslims by pamphlets and telephone messages that said that all Muslims were dangerous, violent, and cruel; posed a threat to all other religions; and planned to take over Canada. While the court upheld the right of the accused to express opinions about religions including criticism of other religions as wrong, the imbedding of wilful messages of hate in permitted expressions will not protect the maker of the message of hate from conviction. Moreover, the wilful blindness requirement for the offence was satisfied where the accused deliberately refrained from obtaining final confirmation of suspect facts so as to be able to deny knowledge.

---

256 [1990] 3 S.C.R. 697.
257 (1992), 95 D.L.R. (4th) 202 (S.C.C.).
258 (2001), 52 O.R. (3d) 714 (S.C.J.).

A second means of limiting freedom of expression, in addition to the use of the hate propaganda provisions of the *Criminal Code*, is human rights code violations. In *Taylor* v. *Canadian Human Rights Commission*,[259] which was concerned with the promotion of anti-Semitic hatred through a telephone message service, the Court again found that section 2(b) protected the form of expression found in the telephone messages. However, the Court also found that a ban on the telephone service ordered by the Canadian Human Rights Commission pursuant to section 13(1) of the *Canadian Human Rights Act*,[260] which characterized such messages as discriminatory, was justified on the ground that the legislation was a reasonable limit within section 1 of the *Charter*. The result for Taylor was that he remained in prison for contempt by continuing to transmit the messages after being forbidden to do so once the order was entered as an order of the Federal Court.[261]

Whether it is possible to erode the prohibitions in the *Canadian Human Rights Act* against telephone hate messages by inviting callers to a Canadian telephone number to dial a number in a foreign country promoting discriminatory messages relating to Canada was considered by the Supreme Court of Canada in *Canadian Human Rights Commission* v. *Canadian Liberty Net*.[262] Again, in relation to anti-Semitic messages, the Court found that there was a contempt of court after an injunction had been entered as an order of the Federal Court; part of the contempt occurred in Canada when callers were directed to a telephone line in a foreign country. Although the Court has not yet heard a case involving discriminatory internet communications from foreign web sites, there would appear to be no reason why such communications would not be treated in the same way as telephone communications from a foreign telephone line, as unreasonable under section 1.[263]

Provincial human rights codes have also been considered in relation to the expression of hate against religious minorities. In *Ross* v. *New*

---

259 [1990] 3 S.C.R. 892. See also *Chilliwack Anti-Racism Project Society* v. *Scott* (1996), 27 C.H.R.R. D/446 (C.H.R. Bd. of Inq.).

260 S.C. 1976–77, c. 33.

261 *Taylor* has also been applied where the telephone message service exposed people to hatred by virtue of sexual orientation: *McAleer* v. *Canadian Human Rights Commission* (1999), 175 D.L.R. (4th) 766 (Fed. C.A.).

262 (1998), 157 D.L.R. (4th) 385 (S.C.C.).

263 *Zundel* v. *Canada (Attorney-General)* (2000), 195 D.L.R. (4th) 394 (Fed. C.A.).

Brunswick School District No. 15,[264] a teacher whose anti-Semitic writings were published outside the classroom was found to have had his freedom of expression pursuant to section 2(b) abridged by an order made by a provincial human rights board of inquiry that he be assigned to non-classroom duties, on the ground that to uphold that order would amount to condonation of the suppression of views that are politically unpopular at any given time. However, the Supreme Court also held that the abridgement of his freedom of expression under section 2(b) was reasonable under section 1 because his views had become known in the school and had poisoned the classroom environment, despite the fact that Ross had not published his views there.[265]

Section 2(b) has also been considered in several other quite distinct contexts. First, the Manitoba Court of Appeal has held that a provincial election expenditures act providing for partial reimbursement of election expenditures was not a breach of either section 2(a) or 2(b) because no taxpayer is compelled to agree with the views of the candidates or parties nor forbidden to express a contrary view.[266]

Secondly, a bookstore in Ontario was held not to be able to rely on a breach of section 2(b) to resist Sunday closing pursuant to provincial secular pause day legislation designed to protect retail workers.[267] The legislation did not abridge the store's right to stock and sell the books it wished, rather it protected retail workers.

Thirdly, the arguments of a multi-faith coalition in *Bal* that provincial education regulations requiring that classroom instruction be non-doctrinal and not give primacy to any particular faith were an abridgment of section 2(b), were not accepted by the Ontario courts on the ground that the purpose of the regulations was to secularize the public school system and not to restrict freedom of expression. No restrictions were

---

264 (1996), 133 D.L.R. (4th) 1 (S.C.C).

265 For a decision relating s. 2(b) and the B.C. *Human Rights Code* and the jurisdiction of the tribunal, see *Abrams v. North Shore Free Press Ltd. (No. 3)* (1999), 33 C.H.R.R. D/435 (B.C. Trib.), aff'd 2001 BCCA 22 (C.A.).

266 *Re MacKay and Government of Manitoba* (1985), 24 D.L.R. (4th) 587 (Man. C.A.). Why freedom of expression and religion were not abridged indirectly was not considered.

267 *Re Coles Book Stores Ltd. and A.G. Ontario* (1991), 88 D.L.R. (4th) 312 (Ont. Gen. Div.).

placed on expression by the regulation and a student was not prevented from expressing his or her beliefs.[268]

Fourthly, freedom of expression is also limited in relation to protests at abortion clinics. Whether the situation is one in which a "bubble zone" is created by a court[269] or by provincial legislation,[270] the courts have upheld the use of bubble zones to prevent distress to staff and patients at abortion clinics. The courts have found that where the reason for protest is the expression of religious beliefs about abortion, restraints on protest constitute an infringement of both section 2(a) and section 2(b) but these infringements are justifiable to ensure access to abortion, privacy, and dignity for patients, and security for both patients and staff.

Finally, freedom of expression has also been considered in relation to the exercise of mayoral discretion to proclaim "gay and lesbian pride" events such as marches, days, or weekends when the mayor and/or municipal council have objections to such publicly sanctioned events based on religious beliefs about homosexuality. A series of decisions by human rights tribunals in several provinces has established that the discretion to make proclamations is subject to human rights laws and that there is a requirement to proclaim gay and lesbian events, which overrides any freedom of religious expression pursuant to section 2(b) of the mayor or council involved. Under section 1, any violation of freedom of expression is reasonable to ensure freedom from discrimination on grounds of sexual orientation as a pressing and substantial concern.[271]

Issues of expression have also been considered pursuant to section 15 of the *Charter*. In *Deptuch* v. *Saskatchewan Government Insurance*,[272] an application for a personalized licence plate to read "BLZBUB" was refused on the ground that it contained religious connotations. The court dismissed an application for a declaration that the refusal constituted a denial of equality rights under section 15, because the province treated

---

268 Above note 195.
269 *Ontario (Attorney-General)* v. *Dieleman* (1994), 117 D.L.R. (4th) 449 (Ont. Gen. Div.).
270 *R.* v. *Lewis. Elizabeth Bagshaw* (1996), 139 D.L.R. (4th) 480 (B.C.S.C.), appeal dismissed *R.* v. *Lewis* (1997), 153 D.L.R. (4th) 184 (B.C.C.A.).
271 *Hudler* v. *London (City)* (1997), 31 C.H.R.R. D/500 (Ont. Bd. Inq.); *Hill* v. *Woodside* (1998), 33 C.H.R.R. D/349 (N.B. Bd. Inq.); and *Hughson* v. *Kelowna (City)* (2000), 37 C.H.R.R. D/122 (B.C.H.R.T.).
272 (1992), 101 Sask. R. 193 (Q.B.).

everyone the same insofar as no one was granted licence plates conveying religious messages.

Finally, in *Kane v. Church of Jesus Christ Christian Aryan-Nations*,[273] an Alberta Board of Inquiry found that the display of a burning cross and KKK signs constituted a message of discrimination against non-Christians pursuant to provincial human rights legislation, and banned it as a result.

Section 2(a) and 2(b) cases demonstrate that the courts make findings of violation of the fundamental freedoms of religion and religious expression in the context of those sections, but decide whether or not such violations should be balanced against conflicting claims and how that balance should be tipped under section 1. The political criteria articulated by the courts in determining how any balance is to be struck are becoming clearer now, twenty years after the entrenchment of the *Charter*. These are a neutral state, a secular public sphere, and the privatization of religion to the extent that public expression must give way to the *Charter* values devised by the courts for public life. The net effect, to date, has been to remove public expressions of Christianity from public life and institutions. Whether this approach will achieve the stated purpose of a tolerant, religiously pluralistic country remains to be seen.

---

273 (1992), 18 C.H.R.R. D/268 (Alta. Bd. Inq.).

Chapter Five

Criminal Law

A. INTRODUCTION

At one time, a description of the criminal law in a book about law and religion might have entailed discussion of the entire criminal law because that law so closely reflected divine law, and was patently understood to do so and was expected to do so by most people. While the criminal law in Canada continues to reflect the moral commands of Christianity, especially in relation to offences against the person. The law also now permits, through its regulation, conduct once forbidden by both divine and civil law, but now forbidden by divine law alone to Christians, as well as to adherents of other religious faiths more recently established in Canada who either share the same religious texts or other religious texts that enjoin believers to similar standards of personal conduct.

In this chapter, the topics covered are those sections of the *Criminal Code*[1] that either expressly deal with religion *per se* or that would be recognized, still, by most people in Canada as having a religious background and context. The latter category is potentially large, if crimes such as murder or manslaughter were included, so these obvious categories have been excluded in favour of categories in which religious actors in Canadian society have sought a role, such as suicide, abortion, the right to life,

---

1   R.S.C. 1985, c. C-46.

and the duty to preserve life. Nor is consideration given to criminal categories such as sexual assault, even when committed by clergy, because there is no specifically religious significance to the normal application of the criminal law to such offenders. Civil law implications of criminal conduct, such as vicarious liability on the part of the employer religious institution, are considered in later chapters.

B. SUNDAY OBSERVANCE

Although no provision in the *Criminal Code* either expressly regulates the religious observance of Sunday or prescribes what may or may not be done on Sunday, the Privy Council[2] established that legislation relating to Sunday falls within federal jurisdiction over criminal law within section 91(27) of the *Constitution Act, 1867*.[3] Parliament still retains exclusive legislative authority over Sunday observance; however, federal legislation in this area would very likely be struck down pursuant to section 2(a) of the *Canadian Charter of Rights and Freedoms*, after the federal *Lord's Day Act* was struck down in its entirety by the Supreme Court of Canada in *R. v. Big M Drug Mart*.[4]

Provincial Sunday observance legislation that purports to regulate Sunday activities as a matter of exclusive provincial jurisdiction is *ultra vires*, thus provincial legislation prohibiting theatrical performances on Sunday,[5] permitting Sunday movies,[6] horse racing,[7] and dance halls[8] has been declared invalid. Moreover, a somewhat extended construction of the federal criminal law power over Sunday regulation has also led the Supreme Court of Canada to find that provincial legislation purporting to regulate the observance of certain Roman Catholic feast days was also an unconstitutional infringement of the federal criminal power.[9]

2   *A.G. Ontario v. Hamilton Street Railway Co.*, [1903] A.C. 524 (P.C.). For a full discussion, see above chapter 4, section D(2).

3   R.S.C. 1985, App. II, No. 5.

4   [1985] 1 S.C.R. 295.

5   *Ouimet v. Bazin* (1912), 46 S.C.R. 502.

6   *Marin v. United Amusement Corp.* (1929), 47 Que. K.B. 1 (C.A.).

7   *Connaught Park Jockey Club v. District Magistrate's Court* (1966), 51 D.L.R. (2d) 559 (Que. S.C.).

8   *Montreal (City) v. Salle de danse "Dans le Vent"*, [1966] R.L. 365 (Tribunal de Montreal).

9   *Henry Birks & Sons (Montreal) Ltd. v. City of Montreal*, [1955] S.C.R. 799.

On the other hand, and despite lingering doubts as to whether Parliament may delegate its jurisdiction to the provinces or that the opting out clauses in the federal *Lord's Day Act* were properly construed as delegation, provincial legislation has been found to be *intra vires* in relation to Sunday sports.[10] In addition, provincial legislation pursuant to section 92(13) or section 92(16) in relation to the regulation of the hours of work for labour,[11] and to securing a reasonable degree of quiet in the neighbourhood of a miniature golf course,[12] have been found to be *intra vires* the provinces.

The courts have been unwilling to extend the criminal law power over Sundays, and possibly other days of religious observance, to nonreligious holidays; thus in *R. v. Southland Corp.*,[13] the Manitoba Court of Appeal affirmed a decision of the Provincial Court that Remembrance Day legislation should not be classified as criminal law and that its regulation falls within provincial jurisdiction pursuant to section 92(13).

While these cases stand and continue to define the contents and contours of federal jurisdiction pursuant to section 91(27) over Sunday regulation, it is doubtful after *Big M Drug Mart* that this jurisdiction will be exercised in the foreseeable future.

C. LEGAL PROCESS ON SUNDAY

The common law prohibited the issuance and execution of legal process on holidays, including Sundays.[14] However, section 20 of the *Criminal Code* has reversed that rule and provides that a warrant or summons authorized by the Code, or an appearance notice, promise to appear, undertaking or recognizance issued, given, or entered into in accordance with the Code, may be issued, executed, given, or entered into on

---

10 *Lord's Day Alliance of Canada* v. *A.G. B.C.*, [1959] S.C.R. 497.

11 *Reference Re Legislative Jurisdiction over Hours of Labour*, [1925] S.C.R. 505; *A.G. Canada* v. *A.G. Ontario*, [1937] A.C. 326 (P.C.); *Cusson* v. *Philion*, [1961] Que. Q.B. 566 (C.A.); *Lieberman* v. *R.*, [1963] S.C.R. 643; and *R. v. Top Banana Ltd.* (1974), 4 O.R. (2d) 513 (H.C.).

12 *R. v. Epstein*, [1931] O.R. 726 (H.C.).

13 [1978] 6 W.W.R. 166 (Man. Prov. Ct.), aff'd [1979] 2 W.W.R. 171 (C.A.).

14 *Ex parte Frecker* (1897), 33 C.L.J. 248 (N.B.S.C.); and *R. v. Lawlor* (1916), 44 N.B.R. 347 (K.B.).

a holiday,[15] including a Sunday.[16] An arrest under warrant on a Sunday is also valid.[17]

Where the *Criminal Code* is silent as to the holidays to be observed in the criminal courts, then days that were *dies non juridicus* in England, such as New Year's Day, should also be so in Canada.[18] Easter Monday, although it is a statutory holiday, is not a *dies non juridicus*, and judicial acts performed on that day, such as taking a plea, or pronouncing conviction and sentence, are therefore valid.[19]

Taking the verdict of a jury and any proceeding incidental thereto is not invalid simply because it is done on a Sunday or a holiday.[20] Thus, where a jury commenced its deliberations on a Friday and continued on Saturday, it may be permitted to continue its deliberations on Sunday and to be assisted by having the evidence read back on Sunday, since this is incidental to the taking of the verdict.[21] A preliminary inquiry held on a Sunday is invalid, since such an inquiry does not involve a jury.[22] However, an accused charged with an indictable offence may be committed for trial on a Sunday.[23]

D. UNLAWFUL ASSEMBLY

In England legislation has been enacted from time to time to prohibit or restrict meetings for religious purposes, including meetings in private houses of only a few people.[24] Such legislation was generally enacted to inhibit the practices and growth of churches outside the established Church of England and was particularly directed at Protestant Dissenters. After the growth of religious toleration from the mid eighteenth century,

---

15   *R. v. McGillivray* (1907), 41 N.S.R. 321 (C.A.).

16   *Interpretation Act*, R.S.C. 1985, c. I-21, s. 35.

17   *R. v. Leahy* (1901), 35 N.B.R. 509 (C.A.); and *R. v. Smith*, [1927] 2 D.L.R. 982 (Man. C.A.).

18   *R. v. Sawchuk*, [1923] 2 W.W.R. 824 (Man. K.B.).

19   *R. v. Kay* (1907), 38 N.B.R. 231 (C.A.); and *Kinch v. R.* (1961), 131 C.C.C. 342 (P.E.I. S.C.).

20   Section 654.

21   *R. v. Baillie* (1991), 66 C.C.C. (3d) 274 (B.C.C.A.).

22   *R. v. Cavelier* (1896), 11 Man. R. 333 (Q.B.).

23   *R. v. Leahy*, above note 17.

24   See for example the *Conventicles Act*, 22 Car. II., c. 1 (167).

this legislation was repealed; however, the criminal law in both common law countries and in the *Criminal Code* makes provision for unlawful assemblies, which may apply to religious as well as other assemblies.

Section 63(1) defines an unlawful assembly as an assembly of three or more persons who, with intent to carry out a common purpose, assemble in such a manner or so conduct themselves when they are assembled as to cause persons nearby to fear, on reasonable grounds, that they will disturb the peace tumultuously or needlessly, and without reasonable cause provoke other persons to disturb the peace tumultuously. Persons who are lawfully assembled may become an unlawful assembly if they conduct themselves with a common purpose in a manner that would have made the assembly unlawful if they had assembled in that manner and for that purpose.[25] Persons are not unlawfully assembled by reason only of being assembled to protect the dwelling-house of any one of them against persons threatening to break and enter for the purpose of committing an indictable offence therein.[26]

To date there are no cases pursuant to section 63 in relation to meetings for a religious purpose. It would appear that a religious meeting held within a private building is unlikely to be an unlawful assembly, although there is no judicial authority to that effect.[27]

E. DISTURBING WORSHIP

It was long an offence at common law to interfere with or disturb a minister of the established Church of England in the performance of divine worship[28] or to strike him in a church or a graveyard.[29] This protection is now extended to all clergy of any religious institution by virtue of section 176 of the *Criminal Code*, which provides that a person is guilty of an indictable offence punishable by a term of imprisonment not exceeding two years who, by threats or force, unlawfully obstructs or prevents, or attempts to obstruct or prevent a minister or member of the clergy from

---

25 Section 63(2).
26 Section 63(3). See also the related sections concerning riots: ss. 32–33, 64–69, 175 and 786–787.
27 Section 63(1) has been found not to violate ss. 2(b), (c), (d), or 7 of the *Charter* in *R. v. Lecompte* (2000), 149 C.C.C. (3d) 185 (Que. C.A.).
28 *R. v. Parry* (1686) Trem. P.C. 239.
29 *Wilson v. Greaves* (1757), 1 Burr. 240, 97 E.R. 293.

celebrating divine service or performing any other function in connection with that calling, or who assaults or offers any violence to a minister or member of the clergy or arrests him or her on a civil process, knowing that the minister or member of the clergy is about to perform, on the way to perform, or is returning from the performance of clerical duties.[30] Where a priest who is not entitled to conduct a service in a particular building attempts to do so and is so prevented by a member of the congregation, as occurred in R. v. *Wasyl Kapij*[31] where the priest had seceded from the congregation and was trespassing, there is no offence under the Code.

It is also an offence punishable on summary conviction to disturb or interrupt an assemblage of persons met for religious worship or for a moral, social, or benevolent purpose.[32] This latter phrase has been subject to an expansive judicial interpretation in R. v. *Cardinal*,[33] in which the court decided that it was an offence within the section to disturb a meeting held for a Metis community for the purposes of instruction in driving regulations and procedures, on the ground that learning to distinguish between right and wrong conduct fitted within the word "moral." On the other hand, a meeting held purely for political purposes has been found not to be within the definition of assemblage and its disturbance not an offence within the section.[34]

Finally, it is an offence punishable on summary conviction wilfully to do anything that disturbs the order or solemnity of religious worship.[35] At common law, behaviour that disturbed religious worship included indecent behaviour, such as brawling in the churchyard;[36] shouting about idolatry during the prayer of consecration in Holy Communion;[37] shouting about hypocrisy when certain ministers of state attended divine worship;[38] the loud singing of hymns throughout the service so as to make

---

30 Section 176(1).
31 (1905), 1 W.L.R. 130 (Man. C.A.).
32 Section 176(2).
33 (1969), 70 W.W.R. 699 (Alta. Mag. Ct.).
34 R. v. *Lavoie* (1902), 6 C.C.C. 39 (Que. S.C.).
35 Section 176(3).
36 *Vallancey* v. *Fletcher*, [1897] 1 Q.B. 265.
37 *Girt* v. *Fillingham*, [1901] P. 176 (Consistery Ct. of St. Albans); and *Jones* v. *Catterall* (1902), 18 T.L.R. 367 (Q.B.D.).
38 *Abrahams* v. *Carey*, [1967] 3 All E.R. 179 (Q.B.D.).

the officiating cleric's voice inaudible;[39] exhorting participants to leave the service;[40] creating a noise with a loud-hailer outside the place of worship and wearing placards calculated to disturb congregants;[41] refusing to sit in the pew indicated by the ushers;[42] and generally, shouting during the service.[43]

What amounts to improper behaviour was said, at common law, to depend on the circumstances, so that an act done during a church service may not be considered improper or indecent in other contexts.[44] Nor does "indecent" or "improper" mean conduct that tends to deprave or corrupt, nor does it have any necessary sexual connotation; rather, it may mean simply creating a disturbance in church.[45] It is no defence to a charge of disturbing religious worship that the statements made by the disturber were correct or that the conduct amounted to a *bona fide* claim of right.[46] Moreover, a clergyman can be convicted of disturbing religious worship in his own church or churchyard.[47]

Where a person refuses to sit in the pew indicated by an usher and sits elsewhere, such as on a campstool beside the pew in which he wishes to sit so as to disturb worship, that person may lawfully be removed by church officials, who are not thereby disturbing worship.[48] Moreover, church officials have the authority to regulate seating so as to prevent disorder and crowding, including removing a member from an accustomed pew to another.[49]

When a person is barred from entering a place of worship, a court will not make an order at that person's request for a police officer to

---

39 *Matthews v. R.*, [1934] 1 K.B. 505.
40 *R. v. Gauthier* (1905), 11 C.C.C. 263 (Que. K.B.).
41 *R. v. Reed* (1985), 19 C.C.C. (3d) 180 (B.C.C.A.).
42 *Reid v. Inglis* (1862), 12 U.C.C.P. 191.
43 *Girt v. Fillingham*, above note 37; *Jones v. Catterall*, above note 37; and *Abrahams v. Carey*, above note 38.
44 *Worth v. Terrington* (1845), 13 M. & W. 781, 153 E.R. 328.
45 *Palmer v. Roffey* (1824), 2 Add. 141, 162 E.R. 246; *Girt v. Fillingham*, above note 37; *Jones v. Catterall*, above note 37; *Abrahams v. Carey*, above note 38.
46 *Asher v. Calcraft* (1887), 18 Q.B.D. 607. *Cf. Kensit v. Dean & Chapter of St. Paul's*, [1905] 2 K.B. 249.
47 *Vallancey v. Fletcher*, above note 36.
48 *Reid v. Inglis*, above note 42.
49 *Carleton Place Methodist Church v. Keyes* (1902), 3 O.L.R. 165 (C.A.).

accompany him to worship, nor will a higher court grant a mandamus to compel a lower court to make such an order.[50]

The constitutionality of section 176 has been tested both in respect to jurisdiction over the issue of disturbing worship as well as in respect to the guarantees of freedom of religion and freedom of expression pursuant to section 2(a) and section 2(b) of the *Canadian Charter of Rights and Freedoms* respectively.

In *Skoke-Graham* v. *R.*,[51] parishioners in a Roman Catholic church attempted to receive communion while kneeling, but were refused since the liturgy had been changed to require communion to be received while standing. After being refused communion, the parishioners stood and walked back to their pews in an orderly manner. The Supreme Court of Canada found that this conduct did not violate section 176(2) because although the conduct was wilful and produced annoyance for the congregation, it did not disturb the order or solemnity of the worship service since the acts were brief, passive in nature, and desisted from upon request by the priest. The Court further found that the section fell clearly within the criminal law powers of Parliament because the provision is penal in nature and designed to protect persons who have gathered for a socially beneficial activity from being purposefully disturbed or interrupted.

In *R.* v. *Reed (No. 2)*,[52] the defendant was convicted of two counts under section 176(3) for standing outside a place of worship wearing a placard that was offensive and profane to the congregation and also for making comments to worshippers as they entered. On appeal of his suspended sentence and probation for two years, including a term that he not attend within one block of the congregation when it assembled for worship, it was argued that these terms infringed his *Charter* rights under sections 2(a) and (b). However, the B.C. Court of Appeal stated that in an area such as this of competing rights and freedoms, the exercise of *Charter* rights had to take account of the freedom of religion rights of the congregation as well. It regarded the sentence as an appropriate balance of the competing rights and section 176 as likewise striking a reasonable balance, so that section 176 was valid legislation and did not offend section 2 of the *Charter*.

---

50   *R.* v. *Reed*, [1999] 3 W.W.R. 550 (B.C.C.A.).

51   [1985] 1 S.C.R. 106.

52   (1994), 91 C.C.C. (3d) 481 (B.C.C.A.).

F. BLASPHEMY

The *Criminal Code* provides that it is an indictable offence punishable by a term of imprisonment not exceeding two years to publish a blasphemous libel.[53] Whether or not any published matter is a blasphemous libel is a question of fact.[54] No count for publishing a blasphemous libel is insufficient only because it does not set out the words alleged to be libellous,[55] although further particulars may be ordered.[56] While it is sufficient to prove that the published matter was libellous with or without innuendo,[57] a court may charge that the published matter was written in a sense that, by innuendo, made the publication criminal.[58]

Section 295 of the Code does not define the word "publisher" but it may be that the definition of "publish" in section 299 applies to blasphemous libel as well as to defamatory libel as set out in section 298. Section 299 states that a person publishes a libel when it is exhibited in public, caused to be seen or read, or is shown or delivered, or caused to be shown or delivered, with the intent that it should be seen or read by the person whom it defames or by any other person.

Nor does section 296 define "blasphemous libel"; however, a number of cases have considered the matter. Historically, blasphemy was one of four forms of criminal libel, including defamatory, seditious, and obscene libel. It was an extension of seditious libel at a time when its purpose was to protect the established church in its intimate constitutional arrangement with the English state. Its close relationship to heresy and the protection of morality, as part of the political order of early modern England, is no longer a feature of blasphemous libel; the modern secular state no longer regulates morality or heresy, leaving the concept of blasphemous libel without any certain legal content. Its original function in the common law of protecting Christianity, especially the established Church of England, can no longer be said to apply and its adaptation to a multi-religious society is unclear.[59] At common law, blasphemy and

---

53   Section 296(1).
54   Section 296(2).
55   Section 584(1).
56   Section 587(1)(e).
57   Section 584(3).
58   Section 584(2).
59   G.D. Nokes, *A History of the Crime of Blasphemy* (London: Sweet & Maxwell, 1928).

blasphemous libel consisted of the publication of contemptuous, reviling, scurrilous, or ludicrous matter relating to God, Jesus Christ, the Bible, or the formularies of the Church of England;[60] that is, the common law extended its protection only to Christianity and more especially to the legally established church. It was not a blasphemy at common law to attack any religion except Christianity,[61] and attacks on Judaism were not protected.[62] Nor, in *Ex parte Choudhury*[63] was the English Queen's Bench willing to extend the protection to cover Islam, or any religion other than Christianity, because it would be virtually impossible to set clear limits to the offence if it were to be extended. Attacks on the Christian religion, however, have to be such as tend to lead to a breach of the peace.[64]

There is too little case law in Canada to determine whether the scope of the protection against blasphemous libel is more extensive than in England. While it has been found that attacks upon God are blasphemous,[65] it may no longer be blasphemous to publish attacks against the doctrines of Christianity[66] or upon the Christian clergy.[67] To date Canadian courts have not been asked to consider the extension of blasphemous libel to other religions and it may be that such consideration will be found to be more appropriate under the hate propaganda sections of the

---

60   R. v. *Taylor* (1676), 1 Vent. 293, 86 E.R. 189; R. v. *Woolston* (1729), 1 Barn K.B. 162, 94 E.R. 112; R. v. *Williams* (1797), 26 State Tr. 653; R. v. *Hetherington* (1841), 4 State Tr. N.S. 563; R. v. *Gathercole* (1838), 2 Lew. C.C. 237, 168 E.R. 1140; R. v. *Ramsay and Foote* (1883), 15 Cox C.C. 231; *Bowman* v. *Secular Society Ltd.*, [1917] A.C. 406 (H.L.); R. v. *Gott* (1922), 16 Ct. App. R. 87 (C.C.A.); *Whitehorse* v. *Lemon*, [1979] A.C. 617 (H.L.); and R. v. *Chief Metropolitan Stipendiary Magistrate, ex parte Choudhury*, [1991] 1 All E.R. 306 (Q.B.D.).

61   *Whitehorse* v. *Lemon*, ibid.

62   R. v. *Gathercole*, above note 60. For the English position, see D.W. Elliott, "Blasphemy and Other Expressions of Offensive Opinion" (1993) 3 Eccl. L.J. 70; Clive Unsworth, "Blasphemy, Cultural Divergence and Relativism" (1995) 58 M.L.R. 658.

63   Above note 60.

64   R. v. *Waddington* (1822), 1 B. & C. 26, 107 E.R. 11; R. v. *Hetherington*, above note 60; R. v. *Gathercole*, above note 60; R. v. *Ramsey*, above note 60; *Bowman* v. *Secular Society*, above note 60; and R. v. *Gott*, above note 60.

65   R. v. *Pelletier* (1901), 6 R.L.N.S. 116 (Que. S.C.); R. v. *Kinler* (1925), 63 Que. S.C. 483; and R. v. *St. Martin* (1933), 40 R. de Jur. 411 (Que. S.C.).

66   R. v. *Kinler*, ibid.; and R. v. *St. Martin*, ibid.

67   Ibid.

Code.[68] If the blasphemous libel provision is still restricted to the protection of Christianity, it is unlikely to survive a *Charter* challenge.

Whatever the content of the phrase "blasphemous libel," it does not matter whether the words are spoken or written for an offence to occur.[69] Moreover, while the publisher of the words must intend to publish, it need not be intended that the publication amount to blasphemy.[70] Finally, the *Criminal Code* provides that a person may not be convicted of blasphemous libel for expressing in good faith and in decent language, or for attempting to establish by argument used in good faith and conveyed in decent language, an opinion upon a religious subject.[71]

G. OFFENCES AGAINST MARRIAGE

1) Bigamy

Bigamy is regarded by many religious groups as morally wrong and is an indictable offence that may be committed in Canada or by a Canadian citizen resident in Canada who travels abroad for that purpose.[72] Section 290(1) of the *Criminal Code* provides that a person commits bigamy in Canada if he or she is married and goes through a form of marriage with another person; if he or she knows that another person is married and goes through a form of marriage with that person; or, if he or she goes through a form of marriage with more than one person on the same day or simultaneously.[73] A Canadian citizen resident in Canada commits bigamy if he or she leaves Canada with the intent to do any of these things.[74]

The Code further provides that a person does not commit bigamy by going through a form of marriage if that person in good faith and on reasonable grounds believes that his or her spouse is dead; if the person's spouse has been continuously absent from him or her for seven years immediately preceding the form of marriage; if the person has been

---

68 Sections 318–320.
69 *R. v. Boulter* (1908), 72 J.P. 188 (C. Crim. Ct.); and *R. v. Gott*, above note 60.
70 *Whitehorse v. Lemon*, above note 60.
71 Section 296(3). See also *R. v. Ramsay and Foote*, above note 60; *R. v. Boulter*, above note 69; *R. v. Sterry*, unreported decision noted (1926), 48 C.C.C. 1 (Ont. C.A.); and *R. v. St. Martin*, above note 65.
72 Section 290(1).
73 Section 290(1)(a).
74 Section 290(1)(b).

divorced from the bond of the first marriage; or, if the former marriage has been declared void by a court of competent jurisdiction.[75] It is not a defence that the parties would, if unmarried, have been incompetent to contract marriage under the law of the place where the marriage is alleged to have occurred.[76] The onus is on the accused to establish that a marriage or a form of marriage was invalid.[77] No act or omission by an accused charged with bigamy invalidates a marriage or form of marriage that is otherwise invalid.[78]

A "form of marriage" is further defined as a ceremony of marriage that is valid by the law of the place where it was celebrated; or, by the law of the place where the accused is tried, even if it is not valid by the law of the place where it was celebrated.[79] Thus, the lack of a marriage licence is irrelevant if the ceremony is recognized as one producing a valid marriage.[80]

The constitutionality of the *Criminal Code* provisions in relation to bigamy have been upheld as within federal jurisdiction by the Supreme Court of Canada.[81] The purpose of the provisions relating to forms of marriage outside Canada is not to give extramarital application to Canadian law but to compel Canadian citizens who are resident in Canada to obey the law and not elude it by foreign marriages.[82] However, to prove the offence, intention to leave Canada to commit bigamy must be shown.[83]

To prove bigamy, the Crown must prove: i) that the accused was previously married; ii) that the first spouse was still living when the second form of marriage was gone through; and iii) that there was a second form of marriage.[84] Whether or not the Crown must also prove that the accused actually knew that the first spouse was still alive at the time of the second marriage depends on the circumstances of the case,[85] with an absence of

---

75 Section 290(2).
76 Section 290(3).
77 Section 290(4).
78 Section 290(5).
79 Section 214; and *R. v. Robinson* (1938), 26 Ct. App. R. 124 (C.C.A.).
80 *R. v. Howard* (1966), 3 C.C.C. 91 (B.C. Co. Ct.).
81 *Reference Re Criminal Code, 1892* (1897), 27 S.C.R. 461.
82 *R. v. Brinkley* (1907), 14 O.L.R. 434 (C.A.); and *R. v. Earl Russell*, [1901] A.C. 446 (H.L.).
83 *R. v. Pierce* (1887), 13 O.R. 226 (C.A.).
84 *Queneau v. R.* (1949), 8 C.R. 235 (Que. C.A.).
85 *R. v. Curgerwen* (1865), L.R. 1 C.C.R. 1.

evidence that the parties to the first marriage had been separated being fatal to the defendant.[86] Where the issue is absence or separation from the spouse for seven years, the Crown must prove that the spouse was alive during those seven years, unless the accused fails to prove such a period of absence, in which case there is no burden on the Crown.[87]

Neither cohabitation nor reputation of marriage is sufficient proof of a prior marriage.[88] To be of value, the proof should show a marriage in fact and not merely the performance of a marriage ceremony.[89] The same strictness of proof is also required in relation to the second marriage for a successful charge of bigamy.[90] If a copy of an entry in a marriage register is produced, the accused's identity with the person named in it may be proved by any means, including photographs,[91] and a witness to the register need not be called.[92] It is sufficient to call a person who was present at the ceremony, who can describe it and identify the parties.[93] A certificate of marriage given by a district registrar may be simply proof of what is entered in the register and not of the performance of a valid marriage.[94]

Since the guilt or innocence of the accused depends on the legality of the first marriage, it must be strictly proved in law.[95] Compliance with provincial laws regarding the solemnization of marriage should be established — in particular, that the officiating minister is authorized.[96] The person conducting the marriage should be presumed to be entitled so to

86 R. v. *Jones* (1883), 11 Q.B.D. 118; and *Queneau* v. R., above note 84.
87 R. v. *Curgerwen*, above note 85; R. v. *Jones*, above note 86; R. v. *Dwyer* (*McGuire*) (1883), 27 L.C. Jur. 102; *Queneau*, above note 84; and R. v. *Taylor*, [1950] 2 K.B. 368 (C.A.).
88 *Morris* v. *Miller* (1767), 4 Burr. 2057, 98 E.R. 73; *Catherwood* v. *Caslon* (1844), 13 M. & W. 261, 153 E.R. 108; and R. v. *Naguib*, [1917] 1 K.B. 359 (C.C.A.).
89 R. v. *Naguib*, ibid.
90 R. v. *Hutchins* (1913), 6 Sask. L.R. 220 (C.A.). Cf. R. v. *Brown* (1843), 2 Car. & K. 504, 175 E.R. 209; R. v. *Brierly* (1887), 14 O.R. 525 (C.A.); and R. v. *Robinson*, above note 79.
91 R. v. *Tolson* (1864), 4 F. & F. 103, 176 E.R. 488.
92 Ibid.; and R. v. *Birtles* (1911), 75 J.P. 288 (C.C.A.).
93 R. v. *Allison* (1806), Russ. & Ry. 109, 168 E.R. 709; R. v. *Mainwaring* (1856), Dears. & B.; 169 E.R. 948; and R. v. *Brooks*, [1944] 2 D.L.R. 558 (N.S.C.A.).
94 R. v. *Lafreniere* (1910), 12 Que. P.R. 83; R. v. *Brooks*, ibid.
95 R. v. *Ray* (1890), 20 O.R. 212 (C.A.); R. v. *Roop*, [1924] 3 D.L.R. 985 (N.S.S.C.); and s. 291(2) provides for the authority of marriage certificates.
96 R. v. *Cameron* (1917), 29 C.C.C. 113 (N.S. Co. Ct.).

do,[97] and it is not necessary that proof be submitted that the minister was validly ordained.[98] A member of the clergy who performed the prior marriage is competent to give evidence that he or she was duly ordained and cognisant of the law pursuant to which the marriage ceremony was performed.[99] A marriage "ceremony" so regarded is a "form of marriage."[100]

Where a prior marriage has occurred abroad, its validity must be proved by expert evidence.[101] A mere witness to the marriage who is neither a lawyer nor an inhabitant of the foreign country is not such an expert.[102] However, a member of the clergy who performed the ceremony and was authorized to do so in the foreign jurisdiction may give such expert evidence.[103] An extract from a parish register of marriages abroad, authenticated and signed by the Registrar, is sufficient proof.[104]

An admission by the accused of a prior marriage is admissible in evidence against him or her, although it must be received with caution.[105] However, where there is no evidence connecting the admission with the time and place mentioned in the charge, and no indication of what the form of marriage was, then the admission is not proven.[106] Nor is an admission proven merely because a deed, whereby the accused conveys property in trust for an alleged spouse, is offered in support of it.[107] A mere admission will rarely be proof of a prior marriage,[108] although in one case, where the accused had admitted to close companions the existence of a prior marriage, that marriage was found to be sufficiently proven.[109] Where evidence was given by persons present at the wedding of cohabitation and the birth of children, and that the spouse was cur-

---

97 R. v. Debard (1918), 44 O.L.R. 427 (C.A.).

98 R. v. Cameron, above note 96.

99 R. v. Brierly, above note 90; and R v. Bleiler (1912), 1 D.L.R. 878 (Alta. C.A.).

100 R. v. Grant, [1924] 3 D.L.R. 985 (N.S.C.A.).

101 R. v. Naoum (1911), 24 O.L.R. 306 (C.A.); R. v. Debard, above note 97; R. v. Moscovitch (1927), 20 Cr. App. R. 121; and R. v. Foster, [1935] 1 D.L.R. 252 (N.B.C.A.).

102 R. v. Smith (1857), 14 U.C.Q.B. 565 (C.A.).

103 R. v. Brierly, above note 90.

104 R. v. Innes, [1933] 2 D.L.R. 110 (Ont. C.A.).

105 R. v. Allan (1867), 7 N.S.R. 5 (C.A.); and Queneau v. R., above note 84.

106 R. v. Hutchins, above note 90.

107 R. v. Duff (1878), 29 U.C.C.P. 25.

108 R. v. Ray, above note 95.

109 R. v. Creamer (1860), 10 Low Can. R. 404 (C.A.).

rently living with the accused's parents, such evidence has been found to be of value, although not conclusive, in determining whether there was a prior marriage.[110]

Once a prior marriage is proved, there is a presumption as to its validity in the absence of adverse evidence.[111] Where a jury entertains any doubt as to the validity of a prior marriage, the accused must be acquitted.[112]

Where sufficient evidence of the prior marriage is proven, the *Criminal Code* provides for four defences for the accused person: an honest belief in the death of the spouse; continuous absence of the spouse for seven years; dissolution of the prior marriage; and a judicial declaration that the prior marriage is void. The first defence has been accepted in several cases where the court found that the accused in good faith and on reasonable grounds believed a spouse to be dead.[113] These cases date from the nineteenth century when accurate information about persons at a distance was harder to attain than today, so it may be that the standards to be satisfied in pleading this defence successfully today are higher.

When the accused relies upon the defence of continuous absence for seven years, the onus is on the Crown to prove that the accused knew the other party to be alive within that period.[114] It is, however, sufficient for the Crown to prove that the accused had the means of ascertaining such knowledge,[115] and circumstantial evidence may be relied upon to determine that the accused had such knowledge.[116] Continuous absence means absence from the person and is required, although both spouses may live within the same province.[117]

With respect to the third defence to a charge of bigamy, that is, the dissolution of the prior marriage, the Canadian courts have consistently

---

110 R. v. *Naoum*, above note 101.
111 R. v. *Cresswell* (1876), 1 Q.B.D. 446 (C.C.R.).
112 R. v. *Morrison*, [1938] 3 All E.R. 787 (C.A.).
113 R. v. *Briggs* (1856), Dears. & B., 164 E.R. 933; and R. v. *Tolson* (1889), 23 Q.B.D. 168 (C.C.R.). Cf. *Queneau*, above note 84.
114 R. v. *Jones*, above note 86; R. v. *Heaton* (1863), 3 F. & F. 818, 176 E.R. 374; R. v. *Curgerwen*, above note 85; R. v. *Lund* (1921), 16 Cr. App. Rep. 31 (C.C.A.); R. v. *Peake* (1922), 17 Cr. App. Rep. 22 (C.C.A.); R. v. *Debay* (1875), 9 N.S.R. 540 (C.A.); R. v. *Dwyer*, above note 87; *Re Tomes*, [1927] 2 D.L.R. 864 (Man. K.B.); R. v. *McCrory*. R. v. *Eddy* (1931), 66 O.L.R. 530 (C.A.); *Queneau*, above note 84.
115 R. v. *Briggs*, above note 113.
116 R. v. *Welch* (1931), 57 C.C.C. 202 (N.B.C.A.); and R. v. *Brooks*, above note 93.
117 R. v. *Rafuse* (1915), 49 N.S.R. 391 (C.A.).

held that the accused does not commit bigamy by going through a form of marriage when a foreign divorce is recognized as valid by Canadian courts.[118] Moreover, the courts have been willing to extend somewhat the defence of divorce in relation to the prior marriage by finding that an honest belief held on reasonable grounds that the prior marriage has been dissolved by divorce[119] or was otherwise invalid,[120] is a defence to a charge of bigamy. However, the position is not entirely clear since there have been several cases in which the courts have found that an honest belief reasonably held, but mistaken, that the prior marriage has been dissolved by divorce, is not a defence to a charge of bigamy.[121] A guilty mind is said to be an essential ingredient for bigamy.[122]

A person who commits bigamy is guilty of an indictable offence and liable to a term of imprisonment not exceeding five years.[123] However, the personal character of the accused, the desirability of giving the accused the opportunity to redeem him or herself, and the desirability of protecting those who have suffered should all be taken into consideration in determining the sentence.[124]

2) Procuring a Feigned Marriage

A person who procures or knowingly aids in procuring a feigned marriage with another person is guilty of an indictable offence and liable to imprisonment for a term not exceeding five years.[125] A person shall not be convicted of this offence on the evidence of only one witness unless

---

118 R. v. *Bleiler*, above note 99; and R. v. *Tucker* (1953), 8 W.W.R. (N.S.) 184 (B.C.C.A.).

119 R. v. *Gould*, [1968] 2 Q.B. 65 (C.A.); R. v. *Woolridge* (1979), 49 C.C.C. (2d) 300 (Sask. Prov. Ct.); *cf. R. v. Wheat and Stocks*, [1921] 2 K.B. 119 (C.C.A.).

120 R. v. *King*, [1964] 1 Q.B. 285 (C.A.); *cf. R. v. Connatty* (1919), 83 J.P. 292 (Recorder); R. v. *Dolman*, [1949] 1 All E.R. 813 (C.C.A.); R. v. *Brinkley* (1907), 14 O.L.R. 434 (C.A.); R. v. *Bleiler*, above note 99; R. v. *Morgan* (1942), 4 D.L.R. 321 (N.S.C.A.); and *Queneau*, above note 84.

121 R. v. *Haugen*, [1923] 2 W.W.R. 709 (Sask. C.A.); R. v. *Simard* (1931), 56 C.C.C. 296 (Que. C.S.P.); and R. v. *Woolridge*, above note 119.

122 R. v. *Sellars* (1905), 9 C.C.C. 153 (N.S. Co. Ct.).

123 Section 291(1).

124 R. v. *Clarke* (1959), 124 C.C.C. 284 (Man. C.A.). For a case under English legislation that bigamy cannot found a claim to financial support, see *Whiston v. Whiston*, [1998] 1 All E.R. 423 (C.A.).

125 Section 292(1).

the evidence of that witness is corroborated in a material particular by evidence that implicates the accused.[126]

3) Polygamy

Although polygamy is morally permitted to and practised by the members of some religious organizations in Canada today, it is prohibited by both the common law and the *Criminal Code*. A person is guilty of an indictable offence and liable to a term of imprisonment not exceeding five years who practises, enters into, or in any manner agrees or consents to practise or enter into any form of polygamy or any kind of conjugal union with more than person at the same time, whether or not such union is legally recognized as a binding form of marriage, or if that person celebrated, assists, or is a party to a rite, ceremony, contract, or consent that purports to sanction such a union.[127] Where an accused is so charged, no averment or proof of the method by which the alleged relationship was entered into, agreed to, or consented to is necessary, nor is it necessary to prove that the persons who are alleged to have entered into the relationship had or intended to have sexual intercourse.[128]

The purpose of this provision is to punish polygamy, not adultery, and therefore it is not applicable to two people married to other spouses who cohabit and have children.[129] Although the provision has been applied to couples who are adulterous,[130] it has been said that it was intended to apply only to Mormons, who at one time openly practised polygamy.[131] The original section in the *Criminal Code* was headed "Polygamy and Spiritual Marriages" and was enacted following similar legislation in the United States.[132] The provision has also been held to be applicable to "Blood Indians," whose traditional customs permitted a man to be married to two women simultaneously.[133] An essential ingredi-

---

126 Section 292(2).
127 Section 293(1).
128 Section 293(2).
129 *R. v. Labrie* (1891), 15 L.N. 31 (C.A.); *R. v. Liston* (1893), 34 C.L.J. 546n (Ont. S.C.); and *R. v. Tolhurst*, [1937] 3 D.L.R. 808 (Ont. C.A.).
130 *R. v. Harris* (1906), 11 C.C.C. 254 (Que. C.S.P.); and *Dionne v. Pepin* (1934), 72 Que. S.C. 393.
131 *R. v. Liston*, above note 129; and *R. v. Tolhurst*, above note 129.
132 *R. v. Tolhurst*, *ibid.*
133 *R. v. Bear's Shin Bone* (1899), 3 C.C.C. 329 (N.W.T. C.A.).

ent of a "conjugal union" for the purpose of the prohibition is that the accused be living with a person already married.[134]

H. UNLAWFUL SOLEMNIZATION OF MARRIAGE

Section 294 of the *Criminal Code* provides that it is an indictable offence punishable by a term of imprisonment not exceeding two years to solemnize or pretend to solemnize a marriage without lawful authority, the proof of which lies on the defendant, or to procure a person to solemnize a marriage knowing that that person is not lawfully authorized to do so. Lawful authority is bestowed pursuant to provincial marriage legislation,[135] which typically bestows such authority on the duly ordained clergy of every religious denomination.[136] In addition, it has been specifically held that Mormon clergy also have legal authority to solemnize marriages.[137]

Where an independent congregation possesses no rites or ceremonies whereby ministers are ordained or appointed, the person acting as the pastor who solemnizes marriages does so unlawfully.[138] This defect may be overcome by obtaining registration to solemnize marriage pursuant to the applicable provincial legislation,[139] and it is not necessary that such a person be ordained.[140]

A marriage celebrated by an unregistered minister is a nullity.[141] Where a marriage is solemnized in a foreign jurisdiction, the legal

---

134 *Trudeau v. R.*, [1935] 2 D.L.R. 786 (Que. C.A.).

135 *Marriage Act*, R.S.A. 1980, c. M-6; *Marriage Act*, R.S.B.C. 1979, c. 251; *Marriage Act*, R.S.M. 1987, c. M-50; *Marriage Act*, R.S.N.B. 1973, c. M-3; *Solemnization of Marriage Act*, R.S.N. 1990, c. S-19; *Solemnization of Marriage Act*, R.S.N.S. 1989, c. 436; *Marriage Act*, R.S.O. 1990, c. M-3; *Marriage Act*, R.S. P.E.I. 1988, c. M-3; and *Marriage Act*, R.S.S. 1978, c. M-4.

136 *Re Marriage Legislation in Canada*, [1912] A.C. 880 (P.C.); and *Ross v. Mac-Queen*, [1948] 2 D.L.R. 536 (Alta. S.C.). Also *Constitution Act, 1867*, s. 92(12).

137 *R. v. Dickout* (1893), 24 O.R. 250 (C.A.).

138 *R. v. Brown* (1908), 17 O.L.R. 197 (C.A.).

139 *Re Marriage Act. Re Application of Victoria City Temple*, [1934] 3 W.W.R. 761 (B.C.S.C.).

140 Above note 135.

141 *Gilham v. Steele*, [1953] 2 D.L.R. 89 (B.C.C.A.).

authority of the person who solemnized it is determined in accordance with the local law of that foreign jurisdiction.[142]

Finally, anyone who is lawfully authorized to solemnize marriage and who knowingly and wilfully solemnizes a marriage in contravention of the laws of the province in which it is solemnized is guilty of an indictable offence and liable to a term of imprisonment not exceeding two years.[143]

I. ADULTERY AND SEXUAL IMMORALITY

Adultery, that is, voluntary sexual intercourse of a married person with another person to whom he or she is not lawfully married, is regarded by many religious organizations as morally impermissible to their members. At one time, it was also prohibited by the criminal law, but is no longer. It was also a crime in New Brunswick under pre-Confederation legislation[144] prohibiting adultery, which was occasionally enforced after Confederation[145] until repealed in 1954.[146] It was not necessary under this legislation that both parties be married — a married person may be convicted of adultery with an unmarried person.[147] On a charge of adultery, marriage had to be proved with the same degree of strictness as for the offence of bigamy.[148] Condonation was not a defence to a charge of adultery.[149] A jury was to be warned about the dangers of convicting on the basis of uncorroborated evidence.[150]

Although the *Criminal Code* does not prohibit adultery, it does provide that a person may be guilty of an indictable offence and liable to imprisonment for up to two years, who, in the home of a child, participates in adultery or sexual immorality or habitual drunkenness or any other form

---

142 *R. v. Naoum*, above note 101; *R. v. Ellis* (1883), 22 N.B.R. 440 (C.A.); and *Johnson v. Hazen* (1914), 43 N.B.R. 154 (Ch.D.).

143 Section 295.

144 *Offences Against Public Morals Act*, R.S.N.B. 1854, c. 145, s. 3.

145 *R. v. Strong* (1915), 43 N.B.R. 190 (N.B.C.A.); and *R. v. Foster* (1935), 8 M.P.R. 10 (N.B.C.A.).

146 *Criminal Code*, S.C. 1953–54, c. 57, s. 8; now s. 9.

147 *R. v. Egre* (1877), 17 N.B.R. 189 (C.A.).

148 *R. v. Ellis* (1833), 22 N.B.R. 440 (C.A.); and *R. v. Foster*, above note 145.

149 *R. v. Strong*, above note 145.

150 *R. v. Akerley* (1918), 46 N.B.R. 195 (C.A.).

of vice, and thereby endangers the morals of the child or renders the home an unfit place for a child.[151] A "child" is a person who is or who appears to be under eighteen years.[152] Such proceedings require the consent of the Attorney General, unless they are instituted by a recognized society for the protection of children or an officer of a juvenile court.[153]

In interpreting this section, the courts have held that mere living together does not constitute immorality within the provision,[154] without additional evidence of danger to the child's morals.[155] Nor is there an offence within the section when the child is too young to appreciate the immoral nature of the conduct.[156] It must be shown that the result of the conduct is to endanger the morals of the child, not that the accused intended the conduct to have this result.[157] Although no reported case deals with adulterous conduct under this section, where there is sexual immorality there must be proof that the accused intentionally engaged in the conduct with knowledge or wilful blindness that the children were aware of the sexually immoral conduct.[158]

---

151 Section 172(1).

152 Section 172(3).

153 Section 172(4).

154 R. v. *Okrainets*, [1930] 1 W.W.R. 826 (Sask. Dist. Ct.); R. v. *Eastman*, [1932] O.R. 407 (S.C.); and R. v. *Vahey* (1932), 58 C.C.C. 401 (Ont. C.A.).

155 R. v. *Okrainets, ibid.*

156 R. v. *X.*, [1969] R.L. 65 (Que. C.S.P.).

157 R. v. *E. and F.* (1981), 61 C.C.C. (2d) 287 (Ont. Co.Ct.), where photographing a child in sexually provocative poses was found to endanger her morals.

158 In R. v. *B.E.* (1999), 139 C.C.C. (3d) 101 (Ont. C.A), sexual morality was required to be measured by reference to community standards of tolerance: a child was said to be harmed by sexual immorality where the sexual conduct creates the risk that the child will never understand that exploitative or non-consensual activity is wrong; where conduct degrading to women will imperil the child's ability to understand that all persons are equal and worthy of respect regardless of gender; where the conduct reduces the child's understanding of parental responsibilities to protect and nurture children; and where the conduct involves the child and may leave that child without a proper sense of self-worth and autonomy. This case also found the offence to violate s. 2(b) of the *Charter* but to be a reasonable limit under s. 1. How this would apply to adultery within s.172 remains to be seen.

J. INCEST

Most religions forbid incest, as does the *Criminal Code*. A person who commits incest is guilty of an indictable offence and liable to a term of imprisonment not exceeding fourteen years.[159] "Incest" is defined as sexual intercourse with a person one knows to be by blood relationship one's parent, child, brother or sister (including one's half-brother or half-sister),[160] grandparent, or grandchild.[161] An accused is not guilty of this offence where he or she was, at the time the sexual intercourse occurred, under restraint, duress, or fear of the person with whom the intercourse occurred.[162]

The constitutionality of section 155 was upheld in *R. v. S.(M.)*,[163] which was concerned with a charge of incest against a father who lived in a sexual relationship with his daughter, producing two children. The B.C. Court of Appeal refused to overturn his conviction or to accept his defence of consent.[164] The word "child" in the section is not limited by age, but rather is intended to prohibit behaviour within certain blood relationships, the inherent power of a parent over a child negating any notion of genuine consent regardless of the child's age. There was no discrimination against the father under section 2(d) of the *Charter* because freedom of association is designed to protect an individual's right to participate in collective, social activities not intimate or sexual relationships. Nor was there discrimination under section 2(a); the fact that incest is rooted in a moral principle developed within a religious tradition is no support for a claim that there is interference with freedom of religion when the accused purports to express religious freedom by disagreement with the criminal law. Finally, the court also found there to be no discrimination under section 15 of the *Charter* because the father could not bring himself within a discrete and insular minority that has suffered historical prejudice in Canadian society.

---

159 Section 155(2).
160 Section 155(4).
161 Section 155(1) and s. 4(5) "sexual intercourse."
162 Section 155(3). In addition to s. 155, several other sections of the Code prohibit related activities, including sexual interference (s. 151); invitation to sexual touching (s. 152); sexual exploitation (s. 153); and anal intercourse (s. 159).
163 (1996), 111 C.C.C. (3d) 467 (B.C.C.A.), leave to appeal to S.C.C. refused 113 C.C.C. (3d) vii.
164 On consent, see also *R. v. F.(R.P.)* (1996), 105 C.C.C. (3d) 435 (N.S.C.A.).

K. BESTIALITY

Most religions forbid bestiality, as does the *Criminal Code*. A person who commits bestiality is guilty of an indictable offence and liable to a term of imprisonment not exceeding ten years, or is guilty of an offence punishable on summary conviction.[165] A person who compels another person to commit bestiality[166] and a person who commits bestiality in the presence of a person under fourteen years of age or incites a person under that age to commit bestiality[167] is also guilty of an indictable offence and liable to a term of imprisonment not exceeding ten years, or is guilty of an offence punishable on summary conviction. Bestiality may be committed although the accused and the animal are of the same sex, and drunkenness is no defence to a charge of bestiality or of attempted bestiality.[168]

L. ABORTION

Most religions forbid abortion, regarding the destruction of a foetus as murder of the unborn. However, while the *Criminal Code* contains a provision relating to abortion,[169] that provision has been found to be of no force or effect by the Supreme Court of Canada in *R. v. Morgentaler*,[170] on the ground that it violates section 7 of the *Charter*, insofar as the denial of a right to an abortion, which forces a woman to carry a foetus to term, is an interference with her body and an infringement of the security of her person, both physically and psychologically. Moreover, the Supreme Court has since repeatedly decided that a foetus has no rights in law that can be protected pursuant to section 7 of the *Charter*. Thus, in *Winnipeg*

---

165 Section 160(1).

166 Section 160(2).

167 Section 160(3).

168 *R. v. Triller* (1980), 55 C.C.C. (2d) 411 (B.C. Co. Ct.).

169 Section 287. See also s. 288, which prohibits unlawfully procuring or supplying noxious things for the purpose of procuring miscarriage. The *Criminal Code* also makes provision for infanticide (ss. 233, 237, 238) and neglect in relation to childbirth (ss. 242–243).

170 [1988] 1 S.C.R. 30. See also on the issue of standing to sue to enforce s. 287: *Borowski v. A.G. Canada* (1987), 39 D.L.R. (4th) 731 (Sask. C.A.), aff'd on other grounds (1989), 57 D.L.R. (4th) 231 (S.C.C.); and *Campbell v. A.G. Ontario* (1987), 42 D.L.R. (4th) 383 (Ont. C.A.), leave to appeal to S.C.C. refused (1987), 42 D.L.R. (4th) 383n (S.C.C.).

Child and Family Services v. *G.(D.F.)*,[171] the Court declined to order that a pregnant woman who was addicted to glue-sniffing be detained in a medical centre until after the birth of the child on the ground that the foetus possessed no legal rights because it was not a legal person. Again, in *Dobson* v. *Dobson*,[172] a child born alive who had suffered serious and permanent injuries *in utero* unsuccessfully sued his mother by his litigation guardian for compensation because of her negligent driving. The Court declined to impose a duty of care on the mother because any duty would result in extensive and unacceptable intrusions into the bodily integrity, privacy, and autonomy rights of women and because of the difficulty in articulating a legal standard of care in a situation where almost every action of a pregnant woman was capable of affecting the well-being of the foetus. In a parallel case under Quebec civil law, *Tremblay* v. *Daigle*,[173] the Court also held that a foetus has no right to life, so that the father could not be granted an injunction to restrain an abortion. Several lower courts have followed this direction.[174]

The power to regulate abortion is within the exclusive criminal law jurisdiction of Parliament pursuant to section 91(27) of the *Constitution Act, 1867*.[175] Thus, provincial legislation that required the consent of a husband or of parents to an abortion before the procedure could be carried out has been struck down as an *ultra vires* attempt to enact criminal law.[176] Moreover, provincial legislation designed to prevent the establishment within a province of free-standing abortion clinics has also been struck down as *ultra vires* since the province was attempting to restrict access to a procedure found to be socially desirable as within federal jurisdiction.[177]

---

171 (1997), 152 D.L.R. (4th) 193 (S.C.C.).
172 (1999), 174 D.L.R. (4th) 1 (S.C.C.). *Cf. Breau (Litigation Guardian of)* v. *General Accident Assurance Co. of Canada* (2000), 194 D.L.R. (4th) 105 (N.B.C.A.). See also Mitchell McInnes, "Pre-Natal Injuries in the Supreme Court of Canada" (2000) 116 L.Q.R. 26.
173 [1989] 2 S.C.R. 530. See also Glanville Williams, "The Fetus and the 'Right to Life'" [1994] 53 Camb. L.J. 71.
174 *R.* v. *Demers* (1999), 176 D.L.R. (4th) 741 (B.C.S.C.).
175 *R.* v. *Morgentaler*, [1976] 1 S.C.R. 616.
176 *Reference Re Freedom of Informed Choice (Abortions) Act* (1985), 25 D.L.R. (4th) 751 (Sask. C.A.).
177 *R.* v. *Morgentaler*, [1993] 3 S.C.R. 463.

The question of whether or not peaceful picketing outside hospitals, publicly-funded abortion clinics, or doctors' private houses constituted breaches of section 2(a) or section 2(b) of the *Charter* was considered in *A.G. Ontario v. Dieleman*.[178] After finding that the Attorney-General has standing to request an injunction on the basis that he or she has a duty to ensure the delivery of publicly-funded medical services, the Ontario General Division found that picketing on public property was protected pursuant to section 2(b) of the *Charter* as a lawful exercise of freedom of expression; however, the privacy interests of the women undergoing abortions as well as those of doctors and private clinics overrode the section 2(b) freedom so that an injunction could be granted to prohibit picketing within five hundred feet of homes and clinics as a reasonable limit under section 1. The court found further that section 2(a) was not infringed because the picketers were not denied freedom of religion.

M. SUICIDE

Most religions forbid suicide, and although the common law once did likewise,[179] only counselling suicide or aiding or abetting a person to commit suicide is now prohibited by the *Criminal Code*. Under section 241, a person is guilty of an indictable offence and liable to a term of imprisonment not exceeding fourteen years if that person counsels, or aids or assists another to commit suicide, whether suicide ensues or not. Intention to assist in a suicide must be proven and drunkenness is a defence.[180] The survivor of a suicide pact may be liable to be convicted of aiding suicide but may have a defence if the parties were in such a mental state that they had formed a common and irrevocable intent to commit suicide together simultaneously and by the same act, where the risk of death is identical and equal for both.[181] It is not an offence for prison

---

178 (1994), 117 D.L.R. (4th) 449 (Ont. Gen. Div.); R. v. Lewis. *Elizabeth Bagshaw* (1996), 139 D.L.R. (4th) 480 (B.C.S.C.), appeal dismissed *R. v. Lewis* (1997), 153 D.L.R. (4th) 184 (B.C.C.A.); and *R. v. Demers*, above note 174.

179 *Stone v. World Newspaper Co.* (1918), 30 C.C.C. 292 (Ont. S.C.); and *London Life Insurance Co. v. Lang Shirt Co.*, [1929] S.C.R. 117.

180 *R. v. Loomes*, unreported decision of 6 January 1975 (Ont. C.A.).

181 *R. v. Gagnon* (1993), 84 C.C.C. (3d) 143 (Que. C.A.).

officials to observe a prisoner's hunger strike to the point of suicide without preventing it by force-feeding.[182]

The constitutionality of the suicide provision in the Code was considered in *Rodriguez v. A.G. B.C.*,[183] in which a terminally ill person sought a declaration that the provision violated sections 7, 12, and 15(1) of the *Charter* and therefore was of no effect. The Supreme Court of Canada decided the suicide provision was valid because it expressed the state's interest in protecting the vulnerable and reflects fundamental values in Canadian society.

The majority found that section 241 of the Code did not deprive a person of security in a manner that does not accord with the principles of fundamental justice under section 7 of the *Charter*; the purpose of the Code provision is to protect life and to ensure that no other person actively participates in taking life. Nor is the *Charter's* section 12 guarantee of protection against cruel and unusual treatment or punishment violated either, because there is no active state involvement in prolonged suffering leading to a natural death in the situation. Finally, even if there was a violation of section 15 of the *Charter* because a physical disability deprives a person of a benefit or subjects him or her to a burden, the legislation is still saved by section 1 because of the overriding interest of the state in protecting the vulnerable and protecting life. The minority found section 7 to be infringed by section 241 because the Code imposed a limit on the right of a person to deal with his or her own body; moreover, the limit was not one shared by a physically able person who is also determined to take his or her own life. This limit was found not to be reasonable under section 1 of the *Charter*. Nor was the minority persuaded that allowing assisted suicide would lead to killing others without their free consent because of the other provisions in the *Criminal Code*.

N. DUTY TO PRESERVE LIFE

A parent, foster parent, guardian, or head of family is under a legal duty to provide necessaries of life for a child under sixteen years of age.[184] A married person is also under a legal duty to provide necessaries of life for

---

182 *A.G. B.C. v. Astaforoff*, [1993] 6 W.W.R. 322 (B.C.S.C.), aff'd [1984] 4 W.W.R. 385 (B.C.C.A.).

183 [1993] 3 S.C.R. 519.

184 Section 215(1)(a), (2), and (4).

his or her spouse.[185] A person is also under a legal duty to provide necessaries of life for a person under his or her charge if that person is unable by reason of detention, age, illness, mental disorder, or other cause to withdraw him or herself from that charge, and is unable to provide him or herself with necessaries of life.[186] Where the parent of a child in need of medical assistance refuses to obtain such assistance, it is no lawful excuse that it is contrary to the tenets of the parent's religious faith to do so. The guarantee of freedom of religion pursuant to section 2(a) of the *Charter* may not be relied upon as a defence by the parent.[187] A person who fails to perform the legal duty to preserve life is guilty of an indictable offence and liable to imprisonment for not more than two years or of a summary offence punishable on summary conviction.[188]

O. "RIGHT TO DIE"

Section 45 of the *Criminal Code* protects persons from criminal responsibility in relation to surgical operations performed with reasonable skill and care in the particular circumstances and where it is reasonable to perform the operation having regard to all the circumstances at the time of the operation. This provision has been found not to apply to situations in which a patient has made a voluntary choice to stop a medical procedure so as to allow nature to take its course. Thus, where a completely paralysed patient decides to discontinue medical treatment that would keep him or her alive for a long time, the conduct of the physician in halting the treatment is not unreasonable within the section and would not result in criminal liability.[189]

P. INJURING ANIMALS

Animal sacrifice, often involving cruelty to animals, is prescribed for certain ceremonies of some religious groups. However, the *Criminal Code* contains provisions designed to protect animals from cruelty and these

---

185 Section 215(1)(b).

186 Section 215(1)(c).

187 *R. v. Tutton* (1985), 18 C.C.C. (3d) 328 (Ont. C.A.), aff'd (1989), 48 C.C.C. (3d) 1 (S.C.C.).

188 Section 216(3).

189 *Nancy B. v. Hotel-Dieu de Quebec* (1992), 86 D.L.R. (4th) 385 (Que. S.C.).

provisions apply to religious uses of animals as much as to other acts of cruelty to animals.

A person who wilfully kills, maims, wounds, poisons, or injures cattle, or who places poison where it may easily be consumed by cattle, is guilty of an indictable offence and liable to a term of imprisonment not exceeding five years.[190] Wilful intent is not limited to evil intent.[191] Stray cattle not shown to have been owned by anyone are also covered by this section.[192]

A person who wilfully and without lawful excuse kills, maims, wounds, poisons, or injures dogs, birds, or other animals that are not cattle and are kept for a lawful purpose, or who places poison where it may easily be consumed by such animals, is guilty of an offence punishable on summary conviction.[193]

A person commits an offence punishable on summary conviction[194] who: i) wilfully causes or permits to be caused unnecessary pain, suffering, or injury to an animal or bird; ii) by wilful neglect causes damage or injury to animals or birds while they are being driven or conveyed; iii) abandons an animal or bird he or she owns or controls so as to leave it in distress, or fails to provide suitable or adequate food, water, shelter, or care for it; iv) encourages, aids, or assists at the fighting or baiting of animals or birds; v) wilfully and without reasonable excuse administers a poisonous or injurious substance to a domestic animal or bird or to an animal or bird wild by nature that is kept in captivity, or wilfully permits such a substance to be administered to such an animal or bird owned by him or her; vi) promotes, arranges, conducts, assists in, receives money for, or takes part in any meeting, competition, exhibition, pastime, practice, display, or event at or in the course of which captive birds are liberated by hand, traps, contrivance, or any other means for the purpose of being shot when they are liberated; or vii) is the owner, occupier, or person in charge of any premises and permits those premises, or any part of them, to be used for a purpose mentioned in (vi).[195]

---

190 Section 444.
191 *R. v. Dupont*, [1978] 1 S.C.R. 1017.
192 *R. v. Brown* (1984), 11 C.C.C. (3d) 191 (B.C.C.A.).
193 Section 445.
194 Section 446(2).
195 Section 446(1).

Pursuant to a charge of either of the offences in (i) or (ii), evidence that a defendant failed to exercise reasonable care or supervision of an animal or bird, thereby causing it pain, suffering, damage, or injury, will in the absence of evidence to the contrary be proof that such pain, suffering, damage, or injury has been caused or permitted to be caused — either wilfully, or by wilful neglect, as the case may be.[196]

Pursuant to a charge of the offence in (iv), evidence that the defendant was present at the fighting or baiting of animals or birds will in the absence of evidence to the contrary be proof that he or she encouraged, aided, or assisted in such fighting or baiting.[197] The court may, upon conviction of a person for any of the offences above, make an order prohibiting him or her from owning or having custody or control of an animal or bird for up to two years,[198] and breach of such an order is an offence punishable on summary conviction.[199]

Q. WITCHCRAFT

Section 365 of the *Criminal Code* makes it an offence punishable on summary conviction fraudulently to pretend to exercise or use any kind of witchcraft, sorcery, enchantment, or conjuration,[200] or fraudulently to pretend from one's skill in or knowledge of an occult or crafty science to discover where or in what manner anything that is supposed to have been stolen or lost may be found.[201] "Fraudulently" in the criminal law, generally, means any conduct that is dishonest and morally wrong.[202]

This provision in the Code originates in the *Witchcraft Act, 1735*,[203] and is to be construed with reference to that Act, which made it an offence merely to undertake to engage in the conduct prohibited.[204] Having an honest belief in an occult or crafty science is not a defence.[205]

---

196 Section 446(3).
197 Section 446(4).
198 Section 446(5).
199 Section 446(6); see also s. 446(7) for keeping a cockpit.
200 Section 365(a).
201 Section 365(c).
202 *R. v. DeMarco* (1973), 13 C.C.C. (2d) 364 (Ont. C.A.).
203 9 Geo. II, c. 5 (1735).
204 *R. v. Milford* (1890), 20 O.R. 306 (C.A.); and *R. v. Duncan*, [1944] K.B. 713.
205 *R. v. Pollock* (1920), 54 D.L.R. 155 (Ont. C.A.).

R. FORTUNE-TELLING

It is also an offence punishable on summary conviction fraudulently to undertake to tell fortunes for a consideration.[206] The mere telling of a fortune is not illegal, rather the Crown must also prove an intention to delude or defraud.[207] It is sufficient to establish intention that the claim of the accused to tell fortunes is made with the intention that the person to whom it is made shall believe in the existence of the power.[208] It is not required that the predictions were false or that the accused claimed a power to predict the future.[209] An honest belief by the accused in his or her power to predict the future is not a defence.[210]

It is the telling of a fortune that constitutes the offence, not the method of doing so, and reading palms, for example, is an offence.[211] In some instances, the use of a contractual document to indicate consent to a palm reading has been held to be a sham and no defence to the charge;[212] but in other instances the accused has been found not guilty because of the presence of contractual consent to the palm reading.[213] No municipal, provincial, or other authority can give a valid licence to engage in fortune-telling in breach of the *Criminal Code*.[214]

S. GAMING, BETTING, AND LOTTERIES

Many religions prohibit their adherents from participation in games of chance, gaming, betting, and lotteries, and the *Criminal Code* contains a number of provisions that regulate these activities.[215] The reasons for

---

206 Section 365(b).
207 *R. v. Marcott* (1901), 2 O.L.R. 105 (C.A.); *R. v. Monsell* (1916), 28 D.L.R. 275 (Ont. C.A.); *R. v. Dazenbrook* (1975), 23 C.C.C. (2d) 252 (Ont. Prov. Ct.); and *R. v. Corbeil* (1981), 65 C.C.C. (2d) 570 (Que. C.A.).
208 *R. v. Larin*, [1974] R.L. 238 (Que. Prov. Ct.); and *R. v. Labrosse*, [1987] 1 S.C.R. 310.
209 *R. v. Labrosse, ibid.*
210 *R. v. Pollock*, above note 205.
211 *R. v. Best*, [1935] 1 D.L.R. 158 (Man. C.A.).
212 *R. v. Monsell*, above note 207.
213 *R. v. Chilcott* (1902), 6 C.C.C. 27 (Ont. Co. Ct.).
214 *Stonehouse v. Masson*, [1921] 2 K.B. 818; and *R. v. Stanley* (1952), 6 W.W.R. (N.S.) 574 (Alta. T.D.).
215 Sections 201–209.

their regulation today, however, appear to be entirely secular rather than religious, so no further consideration of these provisions will be given.

T. HATE PROPAGANDA

Advocating or promoting genocide is an indictable offence punishable by a term of imprisonment not exceeding five years.[216] "Genocide" means either killing members of an identifiable group or deliberately inflicting on such a group conditions of life calculated to bring about its physical destruction in whole or in part.[217] "Identifiable group" means any section of the public distinguished by colour, race, religion, or ethnic origin.[218] The *Criminal Code* provisions relating to seizure by warrant of communications facilities or equipment[219] apply, with such modifications as the circumstances require, to the provisions relating to advocating or promoting genocide.[220] A proceeding for advocating or promoting genocide requires the consent of the Attorney General for the jurisdiction in which the proceeding is sought.[221]

A person who incites hatred against any identifiable group by communicating statements in any public place where such incitement is likely to lead to breach of the peace is guilty of an indictable offence punishable by a term of imprisonment not exceeding two years or of an offence punishable on summary conviction.[222] A person who wilfully promotes hatred against any identifiable group by communicating statements other than in private conversation is also guilty of an indictable offence punishable by a term of imprisonment not exceeding two years or of an offence punishable on summary conviction.[223]

There is no offence where the defendant establishes that the statements were true; where the defendant in good faith expressed or attempted to establish by argument an opinion on a religious subject; where the defendant made statements, which he or she believed on reasonable

---

216 Section 318(1).
217 Section 318(2).
218 Section 318(4).
219 Sections 199(6), (7).
220 Section 319(5); see also s. 320.
221 Section 318(3).
222 Section 319(1); see also s. 319(7).
223 Section 319(2); *R. v. Keegstra*, [1991] 2 W.W.R. 1 (S.C.C.).

grounds to be true, relevant to any subject of public interest, the discussion of which was for the public benefit; or where the defendant in good faith intended to point out, for the purpose of removal, matters producing or tending to produce feelings of hatred toward an identifiable group in Canada.[224]

Where a person is convicted of the offences under section 319 of the Code, the court may order anything by means of or in relation to which the offence was committed to be forfeited for disposal, as the Attorney General for the jurisdiction in which the conviction occurs may direct.[225] The *Criminal Code* provisions relating to seizure by warrant of communications facilities or equipment[226] apply, with such modifications as the circumstances require, to the provisions relating to public incitement of hatred.[227] A proceeding for public incitement of hatred requires the consent of the Attorney General for the jurisdiction in which the proceeding is sought.[228]

The constitutionality of these provisions has been upheld by the Supreme Court of Canada, which has found that although they infringe freedom of expression pursuant to section 2(b) of the *Charter*, they constitute a reasonable limit within section 1.[229] In addition to the criminal action for hate propaganda, actions pursuant to human rights legislation may also be brought against a person who disseminates hate propaganda by means of telecommunication systems.[230]

U. CRIMINAL PROCEDURE

The mere fact that an organization claims to be a religion does not bar the Crown or any other litigant from seeking a search warrant under the *Criminal Code*,[231] and it is not the function of a court to pass judgment on the validity of religious beliefs sincerely held in deciding whether to

---

224 Section 319(3).
225 Section 319(4).
226 Sections 199(6), (7).
227 Section 319(5); see also s. 320.
228 Section 319(6).
229 For the cases and discussion, see above chapter 4, section D(5).
230 *Ibid.*
231 Section 487.

issue a warrant.[232] Since there is no absolute legal privilege accorded to the relationship between a member of the clergy and a parishioner, a warrant may be obtained to seize files allegedly made in the course of such a relationship, and section 2(a) of the *Charter* may not be relied upon in this circumstance.[233] The other procedural sections of the *Criminal Code* have yet to be challenged in relation to section 2(a) of the *Charter*.[234]

V. CRIMINAL PENALTIES

An accused who commits offences of mischief to property motivated by religious hatred cannot be sentenced for his or her beliefs, although these beliefs are relevant insofar as they explain his or her actions.[235] An offence directed against a particular religious group, such as the desecration of a place of worship, is particularly serious, because it attacks the very fabric of society and is done to cause emotional upset and injury to the members of the congregation. Such an offence deserves a more severe penalty than does mere property damage.[236]

---

232 *Church of Scientology* v. R. (1987), 31 C.C.C. (3d) 449 (Ont. C.A.), leave to appeal to S.C.C. refused 33 C.R.R. 384 (S.C.C.).

233 *Ibid.*

234 An argument that the religious concerns of parents about public trial access to videotapes depicting the rape, torture, and brutalization of their daughters was made but not determined in *French Estate* v. *Ontario (A.G.)* (1998), 152 D.L.R. (4th) 144 (Ont. C.A.).

235 *R.* v. *Lelas* (1990), 74 O.R. (2d) 552 (C.A.).

236 *Ibid.*

Chapter Six

Public Order

A. INTRODUCTION

There are a small number of legal issues that cannot easily be accommodated exclusively within either criminal or constitutional law because they partake of some elements of both categories. In this chapter, these topics are grouped together under the rubric "public order," since public order appears to be in some way a unifying feature. Many of these cases pose unique criminal or constitutional issues; however, because they appear to be out of the mainstreams of these areas, they have been collected in this chapter. Each issue considered here has typically been the topic of judicial adjudication on only one or a few instances, so it is difficult to discern general themes or policies of the law in relation to "public order" other than a determination by the courts to enforce it.

B. RELIGIOUS SOLICITATION

In *R. v. Big M Drug Mart Ltd.*,[1] the Supreme Court of Canada included freedom of expression and freedom to proselytize as constituent elements in freedom of religion pursuant to section 2(a) of the *Charter*. Although

---

1   [1985] 1 S.C.R. 295.

no post-*Charter* cases have yet considered the nature of the freedom to proselytize, several pre-*Charter* cases involving the distribution of religious pamphlets on the streets have considered the matter from the perspective of the common law. In *Saumur v. City of Quebec*,[2] the Supreme Court of Canada upheld the common law right of Jehovah's Witnesses to distribute pamphlets peacefully in public places as the exercise of freedom of religious expression, despite a city bylaw, validly enacted within provincial jurisdiction over property and civil rights.

In an earlier case, *Boucher v. R.*,[3] which was concerned with the distribution of religious pamphlets containing inflammatory comments about Roman Catholics in Quebec, the Court found that the peaceful distribution of religious pamphlets is not seditious unless there is an intention to incite to violence or to create public disturbance or disorder against the Crown or the institutions of government; the promotion of ill will and hostility between different classes of subjects is not sufficient for sedition. Subsequently, the Supreme Court of Canada further held that where an arrested person was peacefully distributing religious pamphlets in public that were not seditious, an action for false arrest and malicious prosecution will be sustained against an arresting officer who acted with malice and in the absence of reasonable and proper cause.[4]

The solicitation of money in public by religious groups has also been considered in one case. In *International Society for Krishna Consciousness (Iskon Canada) v. City of Edmonton*,[5] the court held that where a municipal bylaw required authorization to solicit funds for charities in public, and an organization solicited funds for the poor in India without authorization, no issue of freedom of religion arose and the bylaw was enforceable as *intra vires* provincial jurisdiction since it was essentially about the regulation of charities rather than religion.

---

2   [1953] 2 S.C.R. 299. See also the earlier lower court decisions: *R. v. Kite* (1949), 2 W.W.R. 195 (B.C. Co. Ct.); and *R. v. Naish* (1950), 1 W.W.R. 987 (Sask. Police Ct.).

3   [1951] S.C.R. 265.

4   *Lamb v. Benoit*, [1959] S.C.R. 321.

5   (1978), 94 D.L.R. (3d) 561 (Alta. T.D.).

C. PRIVATE MEETINGS

The attempted suppression of private religious meetings has been considered in one reported case to date in Canada, again involving the persecution of Jehovah's Witnesses by the Duplessis government in Quebec. In *Chaput v. Romain*,[6] the police broke into a private home where a religious service was in progress, ordered the minister to stop reading from the Bible, seized the Bible and other religious literature, and dispersed those assembled. The Supreme Court of Canada awarded the occupier of the house moral damages under the Quebec Civil Code and stated that the authorities of the state do not enjoy the right to disrupt a peaceful private religious meeting even where the religious views of those holding the meeting are distasteful to the majority of the public and where the public has been invited to attend.

D. PUBLIC ASSEMBLIES AND PROCESSIONS

In *Chaput v. Romain*, the Supreme Court of Canada also considered the question of whether a religious meeting in a private house to which the public is invited is, in fact, a public meeting, and deciding it to be so, found that it was protected from wrongful interference by the police, provided it was peaceful and not seditious.[7]

Public assemblies or processions held by religious groups may fall afoul of municipal bylaws, which are the typical means of regulating such events. *R. v. Harrold*[8] concerned a Hare Krishna group, which proselytized by going about the streets chanting and playing musical instruments. When charged with breach of a municipal anti-noise bylaw, the group challenged the regulation as an *ultra vires* interference with freedom of religious expression. The British Columbia Court of Appeal characterized the bylaw as one of general application, not in any way directed at interference with freedom of religion, and found it to be *intra vires* provincial jurisdiction pursuant to section 92(13) of the *Constitution Act, 1867*.

On the other hand, a municipal bylaw has been declared *ultra vires* when it was clearly directed at a particular religious group. In *District of*

---

6   [1955] S.C.R. 834. See also above chapter 5, section D.
7   Above chapter 5, section E.
8   (1971), 19 D.L.R. (3d) 471 (B.C.C.A.), leave to appeal to S.C.C. refused (1971), 19 D.L.R. (3d) 471n (S.C.C.).

Kent (District) v. *Storgoff*,[9] a municipality declared an emergency and enacted a local bylaw to prohibit a group of Doukhbours from entering the municipality, in anticipation of possible breaches of peace and unlawful assembly. The bylaw was declared invalid on the ground that it was *ultra vires* a municipality and a province to create a new crime, which on the face of it the bylaw purported to do.

In these cases the courts construe the bylaw as they do legislation pursuant to the rules of constitutional judicial review, looking for the "pith and substance" of the bylaw to determine whether it falls within provincial jurisdiction under section 92(13) or section 92(16) or federal jurisdiction pursuant to section 91(27).

E. CEREMONIAL WEAPONS

Some branches of the Sikh religion require their adherents to wear a dagger, known as a kirpan, as a religious obligation.[10] This practice has resulted in conflict when a kirpan has been misconceived as a hidden weapon and worn in situations such as schools, courts, and hospitals where public safety is particularly monitored. In the earliest reported case, *Hothi* v. *R.*,[11] the accused was not permitted by the court to wear a kirpan in court, although the court acknowledged that the kirpan was a religious symbol and not a weapon. The decision was based on the authority of a judge to maintain control of his or her courtroom and that control has historically encompassed the right to ensure that no weapons whatsoever be in a courtroom.

The right of baptised Sikhs to wear a kirpan to school has been upheld in two reported cases to date. In *Tuli* v. *St. Albert Protestant Separate School District No. 6*,[12] the Alberta Queen's Bench upheld the right of a Sikh student to wear his kirpan to school, although the school board had passed a resolution stating he would be suspended if he did. The court found that the student would be seen to have fallen from his faith

---

9   (1962), 38 D.L.R. (2d) 362 (B.C.S.C.).

10 George Parrinder, ed., *World Religion: From Ancient History to the Present* (New York: Facts on File, 1985) ch. 15 for the religious reasons for this practice.

11 [1986] 3 W.W.R. 671 (Man. C.A.), leave to appeal to S.C.C. refused (1986), 43 Man. R. (2d) 240 (S.C.C.).

12 (1985), 8 C.H.R.R. D/3906 (Alta. Q.B.).

if he was not permitted to wear the kirpan and further found that by permitting him to wear it, an opportunity would be provided for those unfamiliar with the Sikh religion to develop an understanding of another culture and religion. Again, in *Peel Board of Education* v. *Ontario Human Rights Commission*,[13] the Ontario Divisional Court sustained the right to wear a kirpan to school on several grounds including provincial human rights legislation, the absence of hardship on the board, and the absence of proof that the school would be less safe if permission was granted.

Finally, the right to wear a kirpan in a hospital or a rehabilitation clinic has also been upheld pursuant to provincial human rights legislation insofar as the practice may be reasonably accommodated without affecting public safety.[14]

F. RELIGIOUS RIGHTS OF PRISONERS

In *Maltby* v. *A.G. Saskatchewan*,[15] inmates held in a provincial correctional centre on remand pending trial brought an application for a declaration that a number of their alleged rights pursuant to the *Charter* had been violated, including their section 2(a) right of freedom of religion insofar as they had limited access to chaplains and no access to chapel services. The Saskatchewan Court of Appeal found that there was no violation of the section 2(a) guarantee since the religious programme at the centre, although not perfect, did allow for freedom of religion, and the restrictions were reasonable in the interests of security at the centre.

To prove an infringement of section 2(a), prisoners must show a connection between their religious beliefs and the alleged offensive aspect of prison life. In *Regina Correctional Centre (Inmate Committee)* v. *Saskatchewan*,[16] aboriginal inmates claimed that smoking cigarettes was a part of aboriginal religion so that a no-smoking policy violated their section 2(a) rights. The Saskatchewan Queen's Bench declined to accept that argu-

---

13 (1991), 80 D.L.R. (4th) 475 (Ont. Gen. Div.), leave to appeal to Ont. C.A. refused (1991), 3 O.R. (3d) 531n (C.A.).

14 *Singh* v. *Workmen's Compensation Board Hospital and Rehabilitation Centre* (1981), 2 C.H.R.R. D/459 (Ont. Bd. of Inq.); and *Workmen's Compensation Board of B.C.* v. *Council of Human Rights of British Columbia* (1990), 70 D.L.R. (4th) 720 (B.C.C.A.).

15 (1982), 143 D.L.R. (3d) 649 (Sask. Q.B.).

16 (1995), 133 Sask. L.R. 61 (Q.B.).

ment because it was undocumented.[17] In another lower court decision relating to the alleged sacramental use of marijuana, although not in the context of prison, the court agreed that it may be possible to prove that a ban on the practice constitutes an infringement of section 2(a); no such actual finding was made on the facts.[18]

G. MILITARY SERVICE

Conscientious objection in relation to military service is mandated for some religious groups that practise pacifism; however, the courts have not always acknowledged that obligation. Where candidates for Canadian citizenship refused to take the oath of allegiance unless it be on the condition that they are exempted from possible military duty, a court has upheld the right to refuse them citizenship on the ground that it is a fundamental aspect of citizenship that citizens be prepared to defend their country in time of war.[19]

On the other hand, where a person is a minister of a church recognized as a "religious denomination" within wartime conscription regulations, the courts have sustained the legal right of that person to be exempted from military service.[20]

H. OATHS OF ALLEGIANCE

Another objection to taking an oath of allegiance required for citizenship for reasons of freedom of religion pursuant to section 2(a) of the *Charter*, has been the fact that the oath is to the Crown, who is the head of the Church of England, by an appellant who is not of that faith. In *Roach v. Minister of State for Multiculturalism and Culture*,[21] this argument was not accepted because the Crown holds no such religious position within the constitution of Canada, which is a secular constitution and the oath is simply to the Crown as head of state in Canada.

---

17 For a denial of a vegetarian diet required by religion after a prisoner refused the vegetarian diet he was previously served, see *Maurice v. Canada (A.G.)* 2001 F.C.A. 206 (Fed. C.A.).

18 *Tucker v. R.*, unreported decision of 13 December 1944, Doc. T-1805-98 (Fed. T.D.).

19 *Re Jensen*, [1976] 2 F.C. 665 (Citizenship App. Ct.).

20 *Re Bien and Cooke* (1943), 81 C.C.C. 316 (Sask. K.B.).

21 (1992), 88 D.L.R. (4th) 225 (F.C.T.D.).

I. SANCTUARY

In recent years, some religious organizations have provided "sanctuary" in a place of worship to persons who are sought by the civil authorities, typically refugee claimants avoiding deportation on the grounds of alleged unfairness in the refugee process. These religious groups assert that a right to offer sanctuary exists in the common law and that they are simply exercising that right, with the result that law enforcement officers should not forcibly enter and seize the persons being protected. However, the right to offer sanctuary does not exist in the common law and places of worship can be entered at any time by law enforcement officers. Medieval canon law asserted the right to offer sanctuary and the pre-Reformation common law recognized sanctuary as a privilege attached to a sanctified place not a privilege attached to a person.[22] The abuses associated with sanctuary by the early sixteenth century were so considerable that its abolition at the time of the English Reformation was ensured. The abolition proceeded by steps from the 1530s on and sanctuary was completely abolished in 1624.[23]

The modern sanctuary movement may derive its moral foundations in law from various international conventions[24] that recognize the right to asylum,[25] but these provide no support in Canadian law for protecting either places of worship or those who take refuge in them. Those who harbour sanctuary seekers remain subject to the criminal law should law enforcement authorities decide to act.[26]

22　J.H. Baker, "The English Law of Sanctuary" (1990) 2 Eccl. L.J. 2; Robert Ombres, "Letter" (1990) 2 Eccl. L.J. 121; and Teresa Field, "Biblical Influences on the Medieval and Early Modern English Law of Sanctuary" (1991) 2 Eccl. L.J. 222.

23　(Eng.) 21 Jac. I, c. 28 (1624). For the earlier legislation, see Baker, *ibid.* at 12–13.

24　*Universal Declaration of Human Rights* (1948); *Convention Relating to the Status of Refugees* (1951).

25　W.C. Ryan, "The Historical Case for the Right of Sanctuary" (1987) Journal of Church and State 209; and Teresa Sutton, "Modern Sanctuary" (1996) 4 Eccl. L.J. 487.

26　The 1983 Code of Canon Law does not include any provision claiming for the Roman Catholic Church a right to offer sanctuary although the 1917 Code did. Anglican canon law has never contained such a claim.

Chapter Seven

Evidence

A. INTRODUCTION

Telling the truth, no matter the consequences, is an ideal propounded by many religions, often backed by the threat of ultimate sanctions to be determined by God who is presented as a rewarder of truth and an avenger of falsehood. For Jews, Christians, and Muslims, the religious obligation to tell the truth is found in the Ninth Commandment,[1] and the Anglo-Canadian common law reflects both that injunction and the divine sanction that backs it in a number of rules of evidence. Two of these have particular bearing on the law relating to religious institutions. Originally, the common law required all evidence to be given under oath on the assumption that no person would tempt divine retribution by telling lies. Again, the common law after the Reformation has historically been reluctant to grant an absolute privilege to protect communications made within the context of confession to a clergyperson because of the overriding policy of doing justice in this world by punishing those who break the law of God, which once constituted the core of the criminal law.

While giving evidence under oath and privileged communications are the evidentiary issues relating to religion most considered by the

---

1   Exodus 20:16: "You shall not bear false witness against your neighbour." (New Revised Standard Version – N.R.S.V.).

courts, it should be noted that conceptually related to the issue of privileged communication is the recent statutory duty imposed on clergy to report child abuse regardless of the context within which this information was gained.[2]

B. EVIDENCE UNDER OATH

At common law, the general rule was that evidence in a trial could only be given under oath, so that where a potential witness either refused to take an oath[3] or was too young to understand the importance of doing so,[4] their evidence could not be taken. The practice grew up of permitting an accused person to give an unsworn statement at the close of the prosecution's case, since an accused was not permitted to give evidence on his or her own behalf; but that practice was disallowed after the *Canada Evidence Act*,[5] which permitted an accused to give evidence under oath, was passed in 1893. While there are instances where an unrepresented accused person has been permitted to make unsworn statements of fact,[6] the normal practice for a person who refuses to take an oath or to give evidence in accordance with any procedure that would bind his or her conscience is to give evidence on affirmation.[7]

Oath-taking is regulated by the federal and the various provincial Evidence Acts,[8] and although the *Canada Evidence Act* does not prescribe any particular form of oath, leaving the matter either to the common law or to provincial legislation, legislation in many provinces contains provisions relating to the ordinary form of oath and permitted alternatives. A variety of forms of words and gestures are prescribed by the various provincial legislation, but permission is also given generally to permit a

---

2   Below chapter 11, section F.

3   *Maden v. Catanach* (1861), 7 H. & N. 360, 158 E.R. 512.

4   *R. v. Brasier* (1779), 1 Leach, 168 E.R. 202.

5   R.S.C. 1985, c. C-5; *R. v. Krafchenko*, [1914] 6 W.W.R. 836 (Man. K.B.).

6   *R. v. Kelly* (1917), 54 S.C.R. 220.

7   *R. v. Bluske*, [1948] 1 D.L.R. 843 (Ont. C.A.).

8   *Alberta Evidence Act*, R.S.A. 1980, c. A-21; *Evidence Act*, R.S.B.C. 1996, c. 124; *Evidence (Manitoba) Act*, R.S.M. 1987, c. E-150; *Evidence Act*, R.S.N.B. 1973, c. E-11; *Evidence Act*, R.S.N. 1990, c. 115; *Evidence Act*, R.S.N.S. 1989, c. 154; *Evidence Act*, R.S.O. 1980, c. E-23; *Evidence Act*, R.S.P.E.I. 1988, c. E-11; and *Saskatchewan Evidence Act*, R.S.S. 1978, c. S-16.

witness to take an oath in a form, manner, and ceremony that he or she declares to be personally binding. It is a criminal offence knowingly to give a false statement either under oath or under affirmation.[9]

A person taking an oath must understand its nature and its consequences.[10] Historically, the common law required a witness to believe in God or in a supreme being, and to believe that God is a rewarder of truth and avenger of falsehood.[11] The belief could be in rewards and punishment in this world[12] or in the world to come.[13] The same criteria are required for children as for adults.[14] A belief in the existence of a God who does not reward or punish was insufficient to qualify a prospective witness to take an oath; rather, a belief in future rewards and punishments was required,[15] although a belief in divine punishment for falsehoods in this world might be sufficient.[16] A person who felt a moral obligation to be truthful but who lacked a religious belief could not be sworn.[17] An atheist could not be a witness.[18] It was not necessary to believe in the Christian God to be sworn; rather, a person who believed in a god and in future rewards and punishments could be sworn as a witness.[19]

---

9 *Criminal Code*, R.S.C. 1985, c. C-46, ss. 131–132.

10 *R. v. Brasier*, above note 4; and *R. v. Hill* (1851), 2 Den. 254, 169 E.R. 495.

11 *Omychund v. Barker* (1745), 1 Atk. 21, 26 E.R. 15; *Miller v. Salomons* (1852), 7 Ex. 473, 155 E.R. 1036; *Bell v. Bell* (1899), 34 N.B.R. 615 (C.A.); *Farrell v. Portland Rolling Mills Co.* (1907), 3 E.L.R. 244 (N.B.S.C.), aff'd (1908), 38 N.B.R. 364 (C.A.), rev'd on other grounds (1908), 40 S.C.R. 339; *Crown Lumber Co. v. Hickle*, [1925] 1 D.L.R. 625 (Alta. C.A.); and *R. v. Defillipi*, [1932] 1 W.W.R. 545 (Alta. C.A.).

12 *Crown Lumber Co. v. Hickle*, ibid.

13 *Farrell v. Portland Rolling Mills Co.*, above note 11.

14 *R. v. Antrobus*, [1947] 1 W.W.R. 157 (B.C.C.A.); *R. v. Bannerman* (1966), 55 W.W.R. 257 (Man. C.A.), aff'd (1966), 57 W.W.R. 736 (S.C.C.); *R. v. Dawson* (1968), 64 W.W.R. 108 (B.C.C.A.); and *R. v. Hanna* (1993), 80 C.C.C. (3d) 289 (B.C.C.A.), leave to appeal to S.C.C. refused (1994), 91 C.C.C. (3d) vi (S.C.C.).

15 *Bell v. Bell*, above note 11.

16 *Attorney-General v. Bradlaugh* (1885), 14 Q.B.D. 667 (C.A.).

17 *Maden v. Catanach*, above note 3.

18 *Omychund v. Barker*, above note 11; and *Gray v. Macallum* (1892), 2 B.C.R. 104 (C.A.).

19 *Omychund v. Barker*, ibid.; *R. v. Pah-Mah-Gay* (1860), 20 U.C.Q.B. 195 (C.A.); and *Gray v. Macallum*, ibid.

More recently, it has been held that if a witness says that he or she regards an oath as binding upon his or her conscience, then that is tantamount to affirming that God is his or her witness and it is unnecessary and irrelevant to question further that belief.[20] Moreover, a witness may be sworn if he or she understands the moral obligation to tell the truth,[21] and the witness may then take the oath if he or she feels it will bind his or her conscience,[22] even in the absence of a belief in any spiritual consequences of lying.[23]

No particular form of oath is prescribed at common law.[24] All that is required is that the witness takes an oath in a form that binds his or her conscience.[25] Any form of oath considered binding by the witness is sufficient.[26] Oaths that have been allowed include a Chinese chicken oath,[27] or Chinese paper oath,[28] and a Chinese saucer-breaking oath.[29] A "Mahometan" has been permitted to take an oath on the "Alcoran."[30] And North American Indians have been permitted to take oaths[31] or affirm[32] by words or ceremonies significant to them. However, where the faith to which the witness adheres prescribes a particular form of oath,

---

20   *Ram v. R.* (1915), 51 S.C.R. 392.

21   *Reference Re R. v. Truscott*, [1967] S.C.R. 309.

22   *R. v. Taylor* (1970), 75 W.W.R. 45 (Man. C.A.); *R. v. Dinsmore*, [1974] 5 W.W.R. 121 (Alta. T.D.); *R. v. Walsh* (1978), 45 C.C.C. (2d) 199 (Ont. C.A.); *Lind v. Sweden* (1987), 40 C.R.R. 250 (Ont. C.A.), leave to appeal to S.C.C. refused (1978), 40 C.R.R. 250n (S.C.C.).

23   *R. v. Bannerman* (1966), 55 W.W.R. 257 (Man. C.A.), aff'd (1966), 57 W.W.R. 736 (S.C.C.); and *Lind v. Sweden, ibid.*

24   *Frank v. Carson* (1865), 15 U.C.C.P. 135; and *R. v. Tuck* (1912), 5 D.L.R. 629 (Alta. C.A.).

25   *Omychund v. Barker*, above note 11.

26   *Omychund v. Barker, ibid.*; *Atcheson v. Everitt* (1776), 1 Cowp. 382, 98 E.R. 1142; *R. v. Tuck*, above note 24.

27   *R. v. Wooey* (1902), 9 B.C.R. 569 (C.A.).

28   *R. v. Ping* (1904), 11 B.C.R. 102 (C.A.).

29   *R. v. Entrehman* (1842), Car. & M. 249, 174 E.R. 493.

30   *R. v. Morgan* (1764), 1 Leach 54, 168 E.R. 129.

31   *R. v. Born with a Tooth* (1994), 25 W.C.B. (2d) 10 (Alta. Q.B.); *cf. R. v. Butler and Butler* (1984), 63 C.C.C. (3d) 243 (B.C.C.A.).

32   *R. v. Agawa*, unreported decision of 14 May 1993 (Ont. Gen. Div.).

33   *Omychund v. Baker*, above note 11; *R. v. Pah-Mah-Gay*, above note 19; and *R. v. Tuck*, above note 24.

then that form must be used,[33] otherwise any form binding the witness's conscience may be used.[34] A witness may take a religious oath other than that of swearing on the Bible.[35]

Where the witness is a Christian, a variety of forms of oath have been accepted, reflecting the variety of denominational or national origins of the witness in question. Thus, witnesses have been permitted to swear the oath on the Bible by uplifted hand without touching or kissing the Bible;[36] to swear on the Old Testament only;[37] and to swear by using only the words, "So help me, God."[38]

It is no defence to a charge of perjury that the accused was directed to swear in a particular form if he or she made no objection to doing so,[39] but where a witness states that he or she is a Christian and is nevertheless instructed by the judge to swear a non-Christian form of oath, no binding form of oath has been administered. A charge of perjury will not lie for testimony given under an invalid form of oath.[40] Where a witness takes an oath and subsequently commits perjury, an argument that the form of the oath was ineffective to bind his or her conscience is irrelevant.[41]

The refusal by some prospective witnesses to swear oaths for either religious or non-religious reasons led to the enactment of legislation, first in England[42] and subsequently in Canada,[43] permitting witnesses to affirm that they will be truthful, and providing for the form of such an affirmation. Thus, religious persons whose religion forbids the taking of

---

34 R. v. *Pah-Mah-Gay*, *ibid.*

35 R. v. *Kalevar* (1991), 4 C.R. (4th) 114 (Ont. Gen. Div.).

36 *David Mildrone's Case* (1786), 1 Leach 412, 168 E.R. 308; *William Walker's Case* (1788), 1 Leach 498, 168 E.R. 351, *Mee v. Reid* (1791), Peake 32, 170 E.R. 69.

37 *Edmonds v. Rowe* (1824), Ry. & Mood. 76, 171 E.R. 949.

38 R. v. *Cummiskey* (1930), 54 C.C.C. 306 (P.E.I. S.C.).

39 *Curry v. R.* (1913), 48 S.C.R. 532; and R. v. *Cummiskey*, *ibid.*

40 R. v. *Tuck*, above note 24.

41 *Queen's Case* (1820), 2 Brod. & B. 234, 129 E.R. 976; *Ram v. R.*, above note 20; and R. v. *Tuck*, *ibid.*

42 *Quakers and Moravians Act*, 3 & 4 Will. 4 (1833), c. 49; *Quakers and Moravians Act*, 1 & 2 Vict. (1838), c. 77; and *Oaths Act*, 1 & 2 Vict. (1838), c. 105.

43 See various Evidence Acts, above note 8. See also R. v. *Fletcher* (1982), 1 C.C.C. (2d) 370 (Ont. C.A.). For a debate about the value of continuing to use oaths and affirmations, see A. Peter Nasmith, "High Time For One Secular 'Oath'" (1990) 24 L.S.U.C. Gaz. 230; Michael Bennett, "The Right of the Oath" (1995) 17 Adv. Q. 39 and "No Time to Swear" (1997) 19 Adv. Q. 444.

oaths, such as Quakers[44] or Mennonites,[45] may affirm instead. An atheist may affirm,[46] as may a Satanist.[47] However, when a Sikh wished to swear an oath on the Granth, a sacred book of the Sikhs, he was not permitted to do so because a copy was not available.[48] A witness who admits to having religious beliefs but who is unable to say what form of oath would bind his or her conscience may not affirm.[49]

A witness who wishes to affirm on grounds of conscientious scruples must state a statutory ground for doing so.[50] It is the duty of the presiding trial judge to examine the witness to ascertain that the witness holds no religious beliefs before deciding to permit him or her to affirm.[51] The judge must also ascertain whether the witness understands the importance of telling the truth.[52] Where a witness takes an oath and afterwards states that he or she does not regard the oath as binding, an opportunity should be afforded to affirm.[53] While some courts scrupulously examine the religious views of the witness to ensure that an objection to an oath is not frivolous,[54] others assume that an adult who does not appear to suffer from a mental disorder or defect and who appreciates the importance of telling the truth should be permitted to do so.[55]

C. PRIVILEGED COMMUNICATIONS

Before the Reformation in England, clergy were bound by canon law not to reveal communications made to them within the context of confession and were subject to deprivation should they violate the seal of the con-

---

44   *Atcheson v. Everitt*, above note 26.
45   *R. v. Sveinsson* (1950), 102 C.C.C. 366 (B.C.C.A.).
46   *Maden v. Catanach*, above note 3; and *R. v. Dawson*, above note 14.
47   *R. v. Walsh*, above note 22.
48   *R. v. Pritam Singh*, [1958] 1 W.L.R. 143 (Leeds Assizes).
49   *Nash v. Ali Khan* (1892), 8 T.L.R. 444 (Q.B.D.).
50   *R. v. Deakin* (1911), 19 W.L.R. 43 (B.C.C.A.).
51   *R. v. Tuck* (1912), 5 D.L.R. 629 (Alta. C.A.); *R. v. Hawke* (1975), 7 O.R. (2d) 145 (C.A.); *R. v. Walsh*, above note 22; and *R. v. Kalevar* (1991), 4 C.R. (4th) 114 (Ont. Gen. Div.).
52   *R. v. Hawke*, ibid.
53   *Roberts v. Poitras* (1962), 32 D.L.R. (2d) 334 (B.C.S.C.).
54   *R. v. Braumberger* (1967), 62 W.W.R. 285 (B.C.C.A.).
55   *R. v. Deakin*, above note 50; and *R. v. Walsh*, above note 22.

fessional.[56] Since the canon law was enforced in the church courts, it was uncertain what the position might be in the common law courts, although it was clear in canon law that a violation at the insistence of the common law courts would result in punishment for the priest. The common law position remained uncertain after the Reformation, although by the nineteenth century it was clear that while clergy of the Church of England were still obliged by the canon law to remain silent, the common law did not recognize any absolute privilege for "priest-penitent communications."[57] The position in Canada was similar insofar as clergy did not enjoy any absolute privilege at common law,[58] although a number of churches required their clergy to resist attempts to disclose the confidences of confession.[59]

---

56 See generally Rupert D.H. Bursell, "The Seal of the Confessional" (1990) 2 Eccl. L.J. 84, reprinted (1993) 1 Journal of the Church Law Association 152; and D.W. Elliott, "An Evidential Privilege for Priest-Penitent Communications" (1995) 3 Eccl. L.J. 272, reprinted (1998) 2 Journal of the Church Law Association 409. See also William C. Wantland, "The Seal of Confession and the Episcopal Church in the United States of America" (1996) 4 Eccl. L.J. 580.

57 The strict position of the common law restricting absolute privilege to state privilege and solicitor-client privilege is set out in *Alfred Crompton Amusement Machines Ltd. v. Customs and Excise Commissioners*, [1974] A.C. 405 (H.L.); and *D. v. National Society for the Prevention of Cruelty to Children*, [1978] A.C. 171 (H.L.). In one English case, an assize court held in contempt a priest who remained silent: *R. v. Hay* (1860), 2 F. & F. 3, 175 E.R. 933 (Durham Assizes). But the disclosures here were not made in the context of confession. The common law regarded it a matter for the discretion of a court as to whether or not to compel the disclosure of general conversations of a spiritual nature with clergy: *R. v. Griffen* (1853), 6 Cox C.C. 219.

58 *Re Church of Scientology and The Queen (No. 6)* (1987), 31 C.C.C. (3d) 449 (Ont. C.A.). See also Robert Chambers and Mitchell McInnes, "Evidence - Privilege - Priest - Penitent Privilege" (1989) 68 Can. Bar. Rev. 176; Barbara Cotton, "Is there a Qualified Privilege at Common Law for Non-Traditional Classes of Confidential Communications? Maybe" (1990) 12 Advocates Q. 195; H.R.S. Ryan, "Obligation of the Clergy Not to Reveal Confidential Information" (1991) 73 C.R. (3d) 217, reprinted in (1993) 1 Journal of the Church Law Association 201; and J.A. Epp, "Recognition of Religious Advisor Privilege in Canada's Supreme Court" (1992) 56 Mod. L. Rev. 233.

59 See a sampling of these instructions in (1993) 1 Journal of the Church Law Association 102–111.

However, the position in Canada was clarified in *R. v. Gruenke*[60] in which the Supreme Court of Canada decided that there is no absolute privilege in relation to religious communications; rather, the determination of whether or not disclosure should be required is to be made on a case-by-case basis by the courts. *Gruenke* concerned statements made by the accused to her pastor two days after the victim's murder, that she had killed the victim, and the Supreme Court agreed with the lower courts that these statements were admissible because they had not been made in confidence, an essential element of privilege. Although both Quebec[61] and Newfoundland[62] have enacted legislation protecting clergy-penitent absolute privilege, the absence of legislation and of clear case law in the other jurisdictions enhances the importance of *Gruenke* as the definitive statement of the common law in relation to religious communications.

Speaking for the majority, Lamer C.J.C. adopted the four-fold test formulated by Wigmore[63] as necessary conditions for the establishment of a privilege in relation to religious communications: (i) the communications must originate in a confidence that they will not be disclosed; (ii) this confidentiality must be essential to the full and satisfactory maintenance of the relations between the parties; (iii) the relation must be one that in the opinion of the community ought to be fostered; and (iv) the injury that would result from the disclosure must be greater than the benefit that would be gained for the correct disposition of the litigation.[64] Thus, the Court adopted a case-by-case approach to the issue of privileged communications and rejected both the concept of an absolute privilege and the idea that there should never be any such privilege.

In the view of the Court, these criteria were broad enough to encompass all the policy considerations in determining whether to grant a priv-

---

60 (1991), 67 C.C.C. (3d) 289 (S.C.C.). *Cf. R. v. Spence* (1990), 95 Sask. R. 58 (Q.B.), aff'd on other grounds (1991), 89 Sask. R. 276 (C.A.), leave to appeal to S.C.C. refused (1991), 93 Sask. R. 159 (S.C.C.).

61 *Charter of Human Rights and Freedoms*, R.S.Q. 1977, c. C-12, s. 9. See generally David M. Eramian, "The Confidentiality of Information Revealed to a Priest or Other Minister of Religions Under the Civil Law of Quebec" (1993) 1 Journal of the Church Law Association 219.

62 *Evidence Act*, R.S.N. 1990, c. E-16, s. 8.

63 *Evidence in Trials at Common Law* (Boston: Little Brown, 1961) vol. 8 at 527, para. 2285.

64 *Gruenke*, above note 60 at 306.

ilege in a particular case, including the section 2(a) guarantee of freedom of religion; the *Charter* did not create a *prima facie* privilege on religious freedom grounds. The Court was also of the opinion that the paramount principle remains that all relevant evidence must be available to a court unless there are compelling reasons to the contrary.[65] The application of the Wigmore criteria to the facts resulted in the conclusion that the communication to the pastor was not privileged. It did not satisfy the first criterion of originating in confidence; rather, it was made more to relieve emotional stress than for any religious purpose. The Court further noted that the absence of a formal practice of confession in the evangelical church of the accused was not determinative provided there was an expectation of confidentiality. The Court also found that there was no infringement of freedom of religion as a result of the admission into evidence of the communication.

Prior to the adoption of the Wigmore criteria in *Gruenke* by the Supreme Court of Canada, the Ontario Court of Appeal had suggested this approach in an earlier case about religious communications,[66] and this suggestion was followed in the only case to date other than *Gruenke* to deal with religious communications, *R. v. Medina.*[67] The court in *Medina* found that the privilege did not arise because the disclosures were made in the context of a casual conversation and there was no indication of repentance on the part of the accused; there was real doubt that the pastor was consulted *qua* pastor.

Since *Gruenke*, the courts have been committed to developing the law relating to clergy/penitent privilege on a case-by-case basis; few cases come before the courts so it will be a long time before the scope and content of the privilege, if any, will be known. It will not be absolute, but how qualified it might be remains to be seen.

D. SEARCH WARRANTS

Closely related to the question of privilege for religious communications is that of whether a similar privilege may apply in respect to the seizure of church documents by the police pursuant to a search warrant issued

---

65   *Ibid.* at 303. L' Heureux-Dubé J. (Gonthier J. concurring) thought there should be a category of priest-penitent privilege.

66   Above note 58.

67   [1988] O.J. No. 2348 (H.C.J.).

under section 487 of the *Criminal Code*. In *Re Church of Scientology and the Queen*,[68] the Ontario Court of Appeal concluded that there was no privilege and no protection pursuant to section 2(a) of the *Charter* and upheld the seizure of 850 boxes containing 39,000 files and books by the police from the Church of Scientology offices.

The courts have repeatedly stated in Canada that religious institutions enjoy no absolute protection by or exemption from the law of the land, and the decisions in *Gruenke* and *Church of Scientology (No. 6)* demonstrate that principle. Moreover, the case-by-case approach adopted by the Supreme Court of Canada creates great uncertainty for clergy in the performance of their clerical duties and as well as the potential for conflict when their clerical duties require disobedience to the law of the land.

---

68   Above note 58.

Chapter Eight

Religious Organizations

A. INTRODUCTION

Although churches and religious institutions exist primarily for spiritual and moral purposes, as human institutions existing in time and place, they require both real and personal property in order to carry out and promote their spiritual and moral goals in this world. Thus, religious organizations employ the vehicles and techniques of the common law to hold and use property necessary for their work. The interaction of religious institutions with the civil law encompasses virtually all those areas of the law that deal in any way with property. This is reflected in this chapter, which will consider the legal status of religious institutions and the role of the civil courts in relation to civil law issues, incorporation, trusts and trustees, church officers, real property issues, taxation, municipal zoning, wills and bequests, and the resolution of church property disputes on the merger or dissolution of a religious institution.

Historically, virtually all religious organizations in Canada have been Christian and virtually all branches of the Christian church have been represented here since the early nineteenth century. Therefore, the law, both legislation and common law, relates almost entirely to Christian denominations. It reflects both problems that arise from the three broad organizational patterns into which Christian denominations can be placed, episcopal, presbyterian, and congregational, and certain phenomena in the religious history of Canada.

The dominance of Anglicanism and the temporal wealth of that church in the nineteenth century is reflected in a separate section,[1] exploring the large volume of cases in which the courts considered peculiarly Anglican legal issues. The major schism within the Protestant community caused by the creation of the United Church of Canada in 1925 is also reflected in the bitter property dispute cases that followed.[2] Finally, the role of the civil courts in adjudicating disputes within religious organizations remains an ever-present theme in a country without an established church but that has a legal inheritance established at the time of the English Reformation in which it is understood that churches are to be subject to the state. The common law inheritance of Canada is not one of strict separation, but rather of the sovereignty of Parliament over all persons and institutions within Canada.[3]

Since legal textbooks are largely exercises in historical writing, this chapter necessarily reflects Canada's Christian religious and legal inheritances. While the 1991 Religion Census re-confirmed the demographic predominance of Christianity in Canada, it may be anticipated that future editions will reflect the growing religious diversity of the country, should disputes erupt into the courts.

B. MEANING OF "CHURCH" AND "RELIGIOUS" INSTITUTION

The courts have been required to consider the meaning of the word "church" for the purposes of interpretation in a contract or conveyance and for the purposes of determining the application of legislation. In 1887 in *Bliss* v. *Christ Church, Fredericton*,[4] the court stated that "church" signified either a place of Christian worship or a collective body of Christian people having a common faith and doctrine, associated together for

---

1   Below section E(1).

2   Below section M.

3   See M.H. Ogilvie, "The Legal Status of Ecclesiastical Corporations" (1989) 74 Can. Bus. L.J. 74 at 80–88; "Ecclesiastical Law-Jurisdiction of Civil Courts - Status of Clergy: *McCaw* v. *United Church of Canada*" (1992) 71 Can. Bar Rev. 597 at 601–610; and "Ecclesiastical Law - Jurisdiction of Civil Courts - Governing Documents of Religious Organizations - Natural Justice: *Lakeside Colony of Hutterian Brethren* v. *Hofer*" (1993) 72 Can. Bar Rev. 238 at 245–249.

4   (1887), Tru. 314 (N.B. Q.B.).

worship under a creed and discipline. Limitation of the use of the word "church" to Christian denominations was consistently found in succeeding cases as is the dual application to both an individual congregation and a collective body, or denomination defined by doctrine and discipline. Thus, in *Huegli v. Pauli*,[5] the word "church" was found to be used in these two distinct senses in a conveyance, to refer to the Evangelical Lutheran Church and to a single congregation of that church. To receive recognition in law as a "church," an organization is required to have established rites and ceremonies and must also provide for some regular ordination or appointment of those who minister; a mere isolated or single congregation may not satisfy such requisites.[6]

Judicial consideration of the meaning of "church" has been largely superceded in the course of the twentieth century by amendment of provincial legislation to encompass expressly an increasing number of religious institutions beyond the original number of Christian denominations and congregations, provided such societies are characterized by a common set of beliefs and goals. Such legislation is to be construed liberally and not restrictively limited to Christianity.[7] Thus, the meanings of the legislative language, whether of "church," "religious society," "religious institution" or "religious organization," or other equivalent legislative language,[8] have been considered by the courts in three contexts.

First, the expansion of provincial legislation to permit a variety of religious institutions to hold and use property for religious purposes was interpreted liberally at the beginning of this century to find that the Salvation Army was a Christian religious institution within the applicable act, although on the facts of the case it was not a society answerable in tort.[9] Secondly, provincial legislation in relation to authority to solemnize marriages has been interpreted to recognize the ministers of independent

---

5   (1912), 4 D.L.R. 319 (Ont. H.C.).

6   *R. v. Brown* (1908), 17 O.L.R. 197 (C.A.).

7   *R. v. Dickout* (1893), 24 O.R. 250 (C.A.).

8   Each province uses its own terminology; see, in relation to land-holding: *Religious Societies' Land Act*, R.S.A. 1980, c. R-14; *Trustee (Church Property) Act*, R.S.B.C. 1996, c. 465; *Religious Societies' Lands Act*, R.S.M. 1987, c. R-70; *Religious and Charitable Corporations Property Act*, R.S.N.S. 1989, c. 394; *Religious Congregations and Societies Act*, R.S.N.S. 1989, c. 395; *Religious Organizations' Lands Act*, R.S.O. 1990, c. R-23; and *Religious Societies' Land Act*, R.S.S. 1978, c. R-19.

9   *Kingston v. Salvation Army* (1904), 7 O.L.R. 681 (C.A.).

Protestant congregations[10] and of the Mormons.[11] Thirdly, federal conscription legislation has been interpreted to exempt from conscription a duly recognized minister of a small Protestant denomination, the Church of Christ, although it was the practice of that denomination for its ministers to earn their living from secular occupations; in this case, farming.[12] Whether or not the courts will recognize the practice of some religious institutions of regarding all adult, male members as "ministers" is undecided.[13]

A related question is the recognition in law of Roman Catholic religious societies, which are not incorporated within a Canadian jurisdiction; rather, they are incorporated elsewhere but have communities here. In *Archer v. Society of the Sacred Heart of Jesus*,[14] in which a dismissed religious wished to sue the society for wrongful dismissal and a *quantum meruit* for past service, the Ontario Court of Appeal found that the society "resided" in the province and could be sued, although the action itself was dismissed on other legal grounds.

Whether or not a non-Christian religious organization will be recognized *qua* religious organization for legal purposes appears to be largely of historical interest, since all Canadian jurisdictions have expanded specific legislative enactments to encompass the religious pluralism of Canadian society. In this, the Canadian situation differs from that prevailing in the common law in England where the word "religion" has been considered by the courts on several occasions in relation to "the advancement of religion" as a head of charity pursuant to *Income Tax Special Purposes Commissioners* v. *Pemsel*.[15] The courts have limited "religion" by stipulating two requirements: (i) "religion" requires some form of deism or worship of a god, which need not be the Christian God;[16] and (ii) "reli-

---

10   R. v. *Brown* (1908), 17 O.L.R. 197 (C.A.); and *Victoria City Temple* v. *Thompson*, [1934] 3 W.W.R. 761 (B.C.S.C.).

11   R. v. *Dickout*, above note 7.

12   *Bien* v. *Cooke*, [1944] 2 D.L.R. 187 (Sask. K.B.).

13   Religious groups, such as the Jehovah's Witnesses and Hutterites, regard all adult, male members as ministers and have asserted their right to be exempt from conscription and to clergy privilege in relation to evidence.

14   (1905), 9 O.L.R. 474 (C.A.).

15   [1891] A.C. 531 (H.L.).

16   *Bowman* v. *Secular Society*, [1917] A.C. 406 (H.L.); and R. v. *Registrar-General, ex parte Segerdal*, [1970] 2 Q.B. 697 (C.A.).

gion" rather than ethical systems of belief is required.[17] An exception may be made to include Buddhism as a religion although Buddhists do not believe in a god.[18] Whether Canadian law will require either condition generally and not just in relation to charities law is uncertain.[19]

C. LEGAL STATUS OF RELIGIOUS INSTITUTIONS

In some common law jurisdictions, religious institutions are not treated equally insofar as one may have the status of an established church while the others are accorded a less privileged and not necessarily equivalent status in law, either in relation to the established church or in relation to one another. Thus, in England, the Church of England has enjoyed the status of established state church since the English Reformation, while other Christian and non-Christian institutions have been granted legal rights in different measures from time to time since the sixteenth century. In most other common law jurisdictions, religious institutions, whether Christian or non-Christian, are equal before the law. Thus, in the United States, after the abolition of the last established church in Massachusetts in 1833, all religious institutions are treated equally in law; by virtue of the constitutional requirement in the First Amendment[20] for separation of church and state, governments are not permitted to favour one religion over any other.[21]

---

17 *Re South Place Ethical Society*, [1980] 1 W.L.R. 1565 (C.A.). For earlier similar cases involving freemasons and theosophists respectively, see *United Grand Lodge of Ancient Free and Accepted Masons of England and Wales* v. *Holbourn B.C.*, [1957] 1 W.L.R. 1080 (C.A.); and *Berry* v. *St. Marylebone B.C.*, [1958] Ch. 406 (C.A.).

18 *Ex parte Segerdal*, above note 16 per Lord Denning.

19 For a discussion challenging whether "religion" should be a head of charity, see Jim Phillips, "Religion, Charity, and the Charter of Rights" in Jim Phillips, Bruce Chapman, and David Stevens, eds., *Between State and Market: Essays on Charities Law and Policy in Canada* (Montreal: McGill-Queen's University Press, 2001) ch. 10.

20 "Congress shall make no law respecting the establishment of religion, or prohibiting the free exercise thereof."

21 Ensuring strict separation and equality of treatment before the law is in practice extremely difficult to achieve. See R.S. Alley, *The Supreme Court on Church and State* (New York: Oxford University Press, 1988) for a selection of American cases struggling with the problem; John J. Patrick and Gerald P. Long, *Consti-*

Both historically and currently, the legal status of religious institutions in Canada, both in relation to the state and to one another, encompasses elements of establishment and of equality.[22] Prior to the Conquest of Quebec in 1759, the Roman Catholic Church was the only church permitted in the French colony and enjoyed the intimate relationship with the government of New France characteristic of an established church. After the *Constitutional Act, 1791*,[23] the Church of England in "Canada" enjoyed certain property rights not accorded to other religious denominations, although its assertions of establishment status were never formally recognized in law. Indeed, it may still be the case that the Anglican Church of Canada is still in law the established church in Nova Scotia,[24] New Brunswick,[25] and Prince Edward Island[26] by virtue of late eighteenth-century legislation making its predecessor denomination, the Church of England, the established church in those colonies, with certain statutory privileges, which remain in force in the absence of disestablishment legislation.[27] More-

---

tutional Debates on Freedom of Religion (Westport, CT: Greenwood Press, 1999); and John Witte, *Religion and the American Constitutional Experiment* (Boulder, CO: Westview, 2000).

22   See M.H. Ogilvie, "What is a Church By Law Established?" (1990) 28 O.H.L.J. 179; and M.H. Ogilvie, "Ecclesiastical Law - Strict Separation of Church and State - Parliamentary Sovereignty: *Logan* v. *Presbytery of Dumbarton*" (1997) 76 Can. Bar Rev. 529.

23   (Eng.) 31 Geo. III, c. 31, (1791) ss. 36–40. See generally A.H. Young, "A Fallacy in Canadian History" (1934) 15 Can. Hist. Rev. 351; J.J. Talman, "The Position of the Church of England in Upper Canada, 1791–1840" (1934) 15 Can. Hist. Rev. 361; J.S. Moir, "The Settlement of the Clergy Reserves 1840–1855" (1956) 37 Can. Hist. Rev. 46; J.S. Moir, *Church and State in Canada West: Three Studies in the Relation of Denominationalism and Nationalism, 1841–1867* (Toronto: University of Toronto Press, 1959); A. Wilson, *The Clergy Reserves of Upper Canada: A Canadian Mortmain* (Toronto: University of Toronto Press, 1968); J.L.H. Henderson, "The Abominable Incumbus: The Church as by Law Established" (1969) 10 Journal of the Canadian Church History Society 58; and Curtis Fahey, *In His Name: The Anglican Experience in Upper Canada, 1791–1854* (Ottawa: Carleton University Press, 1991).

24   (N.S.) 32 Geo. II, c. 5 (1758).

25   (N.B.) 26 Geo. III., c. 4 (1786); see also *Doe d. St. George's Church* v. *Cougle* (1870), 13 N.B.R. 96 (S.C.).

26   (P.E.I.) 43 Geo. III, c. 6 (1802).

27   *Constitution Act, 1867*, R.S.C. 1985, App. II, No. 5, s. 129 provides that pre-Confederation legislation remains in force unless specifically repealed.

over, the provisions in the Constitution of Canada relating to the funding of denominational schools might arguably entrench a quasi-established status for those denominations funded in certain provinces,[28] and the provision in the preamble to the *Constitution Act, 1982*,[29] relating to the "supremacy of God" might also be said to accord some constitutional privilege on those religious institutions that acknowledge "God" in contrast to those that do not, although the courts have repeatedly resisted this conclusion.[30]

The issue of legal establishment has yet to be addressed squarely by the Canadian courts.[31] In England, two early twentieth century decisions have attempted to define "establishment" in law. In *Marshall v. Graham*,[32] Phillimore J. stated:

> A church which is established is not thereby made a department of state. The process of establishment means that the state has accepted the Church as the religious body in its opinion truly teaching the Christian faith, and given to it a certain legal position and to its decrees, if rendered under certain legal conditions certain civil sanctions.[33]

The House of Lords also considered the legal characteristics of establishment in *General Assembly of the Free Church of Scotland v. Lord Overtoun*,[34] scattering remarks throughout a 250-page decision that are best captured in the definition provided by *Halsbury's Laws of England*:[35]

> The word "established" in relation to a church is used in various senses. In one sense every religious body recognised by the law, and protected in the ownership of its property and other rights may be said to be by law established. In another sense the words "established church" are used to mean the church as by law established in any country as the

---

28 *Ibid.* s. 93 and *Constitution Act, 1982*, R.S.C. 1985, App. III, No. 44 ss. 2(a), 15, 27, and 29.
29 That Canada is "founded upon principles that recognize the supremacy of God."
30 Above ch. 4, section D(4).
31 For judicial views expressed in relation to public funding for Roman Catholic schools in Ontario that unequal treatment is constitutionally permitted in Canada in relation to school funding, see below chapter 10, section B(1)(b).
32 [1907] 2 K.B. 112.
33 *Ibid.* at 126.
34 [1904] A.C. 515 (H.L.).
35 14 Hals. (4th) para. 334 at 158–159.

public or state-recognized form of religion. The process of establishment means that the state has accepted the church as the religious body which in its opinion truly teaches the Christian faith, and has given it a certain legal position and to its decrees, if given under certain legal conditions, certain legal sanctions. What is called the "establishment" principle in relation to the church is the principle that there is a duty on the civil power to give support and assistance to the church, though not necessarily by way of endowment, and where this principle prevails a church is said to be established when it receives such support and assistance. In the fullest sense a church is said to be established when all the provisions constituting the church's system or organization receive the sanction of a law which establishes that system throughout the state and excludes any other system.

If the marks of an established church are state support and protection, it may be that a denomination which enjoys exclusive state support and protection in relation to the funding of denominational schools is at least a quasi-established church within that province.

While the legal status of religious institutions in Canada partly reflects the establishment inheritance from England, it is also subject to the equality inheritance from England accorded by the common law to all religious institutions other than the established church. In *Dunnet* v. *Forneri*,[36] the Ontario High Court stated that there is no established church in Ontario, as there is in England. Rather, in Ontario, all religious bodies are placed on a footing of equality before the law with no one denomination having preference over another. The common law protects all religious institutions equally in their enjoyment of property and unless civil rights are in question, does not interfere with their organization or faith. And in a later case, *R.* v. *Dickout*,[37] the Ontario Court of Appeal further stated that the fundamental law of the province makes no distinction between churches and denominations and that everyone is at liberty to worship God as he or she pleases. The notion of equality in relation to individuals expressing religious faith is further reflected in sections 2 and 15 of the *Canadian Charter of Rights and Freedoms*.[38]

---

36 (1877), 25 Gr. 199 (Ont. H.C.).

37 Above note 7.

38 Above chapter 4. See also the comments about "establishment" in the dissenting opinion of Lacourciere J.A. in *Zylberberg* v. *Sudbury Board of Education* (1988), 65 O.R. (2d) 641 (C.A.) at 668–678.

In several late nineteenth-century cases, the Ontario courts expressed the view that while all religious institutions enjoy equality before the law, Christianity, alone of all religions, is a part of the common law of the province and deserving of special protection. In *Pringle* v. *Town of Napanee*,[39] the court refused to enforce a contract for the rental of a hall for the purposes of public lectures attacking the fundamental doctrines of Christianity, and in *Kinsey* v. *Kinsey*,[40] the court found a bequest to be void that provided for annual lectures against Freemasonry on the ground that this was equivalent to opposing Christianity.[41] Although never overruled in Canada, it is likely that the decision of the House of Lords in *Bowman* v. *Secular Society*,[42] which enforced a contract for the rental of a hall for public lectures promoting atheism, would be applied in the light of modern circumstances.[43]

If all religious organizations are equal in the eyes of the common law, the question arose in the nineteenth century as to the status of the Church of England in the colonies since it could be argued by virtue of the reception of the common law in the colonies that the established church enjoyed the same status as in England. However, in a series of cases appealed from the Colony of the Cape of Good Hope and the Colony of Natal concerned with episcopal succession and discipline in the 1860s, the Privy Council decided that the status of the Church of England was the same as that of any other religious body.[44]

Moreover, these cases further stated that the common law regarded all religious organizations as voluntary associations. The authority of a religious organization over its members is based on their voluntary membership and mutual contractual consent to the doctrine and discipline of the association. Since contract is the legal basis for the authority of the

---

39   (1878), 43 U.C.R. 285 (Q.B.).

40   (1895), 26 O.R. 99 (Ch. D.). See also *R.* v. *Dickout*, above note 7 in relation to the recognition of Mormon clergy.

41   It should be noted that many Christian denominations today regard Freemasonry as antithetical to Christianity and require that their members not belong to the Freemasons.

42   [1917] A.C. 406 (H.L.).

43   See earlier cases with the same facts, below note 513.

44   *Long* v. *Bishop of Cape Town* (1863), 1 Moore N.S. 411, 15 E.R. 756 (P.C.); *Re Bishop of Natal* (1864), 3 Moore N.S. 114; 16 E.R. 43 (P.C.); *Bishop of Natal* v. *Gladstone* (1867), L.R. 3 Eq. 1 (P.C.); and *Bishop of Cape Town* v. *Bishop of Natal* (1869), 6 Moore N.S. 202, 16 E.R. 702 (P.C.).

organization over its membership, the courts should interpret internal rules according to the principles for the interpretation of contracts and should interfere only when these rules interfere with civil rights. The tribunals of religious organizations are not civil courts, having no authority derived from the Crown; rather, to give effect to their decisions, church tribunals must apply to the courts, which should treat their decisions like those of arbitrators.[45]

These principles treating all religious institutions as voluntary associations based on contract and equal under the law were accepted in subsequent late nineteenth-century cases in Canada.[46] Thus, in *Johnson v. Glen*,[47] canons requiring consultation by a bishop with churchwardens prior to the appointment of a rector were enforced as a matter of contract; while in *Jones v. Dorland*,[48] the Supreme Court of Canada refused to permit dissentient members of the Canada Yearly Meeting of the Society of Friends from controlling property in breach of the book of discipline; and in *Itter v. Howe*,[49] the Ontario Court of Appeal insisted that changes to the constitution of the United Brethren of Christ be made in accordance with the constitutional procedure for changes. Thus, courts consistently treat all religious institutions as voluntary associations in law and seek to enforce their respective contractual bases.[50]

---

45   *Long v. Bishop of Cape Town, ibid.* at E.R. 774. See also in relation to the Dutch Reformed Church in the colony as a voluntary organization *Murray v. Burgers* (1866), 4 Moore N.S. 250, 16 E.R. 311 (P.C.). In Canada, the association of ecclesiastical tribunal decisions and arbitration decisions for purposes of enforcement by the civil courts is first suggested in *Bishop of Columbia v. Cridge* (1874), 1 B.C.R. (Pt. 1) 5 (S.C.).

46   *Lyster v. Kirkpatrick* (1866), 26 U.C.Q.B. 217 (C.A.); and *Bliss v. Christ Church, Fredericton*, above note 4. Cf. *Doe d. St. George's Church v. Cougle*, above note 25.

47   (1879), 26 Gr. 162 (Ch.).

48   (1886), 14 S.C.R. 39.

49   (1896), 23 O.A.R. 256 (C.A.).

50   See also generally *General Assembly of the Free Church of Scotland v. Lord Overtoun*, above note 34. For more recent examples of enforcement of the contract in the constitution, see *Gill v. Bhandal* (1998), 165 D.L.R. (4th) 151 (B.C.S.C.), involving enforcement of constitution and bylaws of a Sikh Society in relation to voting at meetings; *Montreal & Canadian Diocese of the Russian Orthodox Church outside of Russia Inc. v. Protection of the Holy Virgin Russian Orthodox Church (outside of Russia) in Ottawa Inc.* (2001), 141 O.A.C. 285 (C.A.), involving enforcement of bylaws requiring bishop's and synod's consents for bylaw changes; and *Jeon v. Presbytery of Northwest America Korean American Presbyterian Church* 2000 B.C.S.C. 1218 (S.C.).

Recognition by the courts that religious institutions can be voluntary associations based on contract has extended beyond the enforcement of constitutions and bylaws for internal purposes to consideration of the implications of voluntary association in relation to third parties seeking to sue religious institutions that have not incorporated. The issue has arisen in relation to the vicarious liability of "national" church associations for actions of employees or officers of local parts of that larger association. Thus, in actions relating to the liability of the "Roman Catholic Church" in claims brought by aboriginal former residential school students in contract, tort, and fiduciary obligation, against various parts of that national body, the actions against the national body have failed on the ground that it is an unincorporated religious association and not a legal entity capable of being sued.[51] Nor is it permitted to appoint a diocesan bishop as a representative of the association for purposes of suit.[52] Presumably, this principle would also apply to other unincorporated religious associations, although it may be possible to find representative parties in trustees or other parts of the larger organization for the purpose of suing or being sued.[53]

D. JURISDICTION OF CIVIL COURTS

Although many religious institutions and their members would argue that civil authorities, whether legislative or judicial, have no jurisdiction over them in Canada, there can be little doubt, from the perspective of those civil authorities, that they enjoy as much civil jurisdiction over religious institutions as over any other individual or group of individuals within the jurisdiction. Subject to any protections accorded to individuals and religious groups pursuant to the *Canadian Charter of Rights and Freedoms*, which have yet to be worked out in detail by the courts, religious institutions and persons in Canada are subject to the sovereignty of Parliament and the sanctioning powers of the state invoked by the courts when disputes concerning religion are brought for resolution.[54]

---

51 *J.R.S. v. Glendinning* (2000), 191 D.L.R. (4th) 750 (Ont. S.C.J.); and *Re Residential Schools* (2001), 204 D.L.R. (4th) 80 (Alta. C.A.).

52 *Ibid.*

53 Below section F.

54 Above note 3.

Nevertheless, the courts have expressed reluctance to consider issues relating to religious institutions, evidencing some embarrassment that internal church disputes should be determined by secular courts and doubting the appropriateness of judicial intervention.[55] The courts have stated that they will not consider matters that are strictly spiritual[56] or narrowly doctrinal[57] in nature, but will intervene where civil rights[58] or property rights[59] have been invaded. However, the distinction may be difficult to draw because doctrine, polity, and discipline frequently impact on issues of property and civil rights, particularly when ecclesiastical and civil standards conflict. Thus, some courts have recognized that they have civil jurisdiction to intervene[60] and that such intervention may require consideration of doctrine, polity, and discipline in the adjudication of disputes concerning property, contract, or civil rights.[61] Moreover,

---

55 *Dunnet v. Forneri*, above note 36; *Pinke v. Bornhold* (1904), 8 O.L.R. 575 (H.C.); *Wetmon v. Bayne*, [1928] 1 D.L.R. 848 (Alta. C.A.); *Ukrainian Greek Orthodox Church v. Ukrainian Greek Orthodox Cathedral of St. Mary the Protectress*, [1940] S.C.R. 586; *Lindenberger v. United Church of Canada* (1985), 17 C.C.E.L. 143 (Div. Ct.), aff'd (1987), 17 C.C.E.L. 172 (Ont. C.A.); *Balkou v. Gouleff* (1989), 68 O.R. (2d) 574 (C.A.); *McCaw v. United Church of Canada* (1991), 82 D.L.R. (4th) 289 (Ont. C.A.); *Lakeside Colony of Hutterian Brethren v. Hofer*, [1992] 3 S.C.R. 165; *Pederson v. Fulton* (1994), 11 D.L.R. (4th) 367 (Ont. Gen. Div.); and *Jeon*, above note 50.

56 *Bishop of Columbia v. Cridge*, above note 45.

57 *Bishop of Columbia v. Cridge*, *ibid*; and *Balkou v. Gouleff*, above note 55.

58 *Tully v. Farrell* (1876), 23 Gr. 49 (Ch. D.); and *Dunnet v. Forneri*, above note 36.

59 *Itter v. Howe*, above note 49.

60 *Bishop of Columbia v. Cridge*, above note 45; *McPherson v. McKay* (1880), 4 O.A.R. 501 (C.A.); *Ex parte Currie* (1886), 26 N.B.R. 403 (C.A.); *Ex parte Little* (1895), 33 N.B.R. 210 (C.A.); *Lindenburger v. United Church of Canada*, above note 55; *McCaw v. United Church of Canada*, above note 55; *Davis v. United Church of Canada* (1992), 92 D.L.R. (4th) 678 (Ont. Gen Div.); and *Lakeside Colony of Hutterian Brethren v. Hofer*, above note 55.

61 *Ukrainian Greek Orthodox Church*, above note 55; *Hofer v. Hofer*, [1970] S.C.R. 958; and *Lakeside Colony of Hutterian Brethren v. Hofer*, above note 55. It should be noted that civil courts examine doctrine in relation to external disputes as well. For an example in relation to claims for exclusion from statutory pension provisions: *Salvation Army, Canada East v. Ontario (A.G.)* (1992), 88 D.L.R. (4th) 238 (Ont. Gen. Div.). Also in relation to *Charter* claims: *R. v. Jones*, [1986] 2 S.C.R. 284 per LaForest J. at 318. See generally M.H. Ogilvie, "Who Do You Say That You Are? Courts, Creeds and Christian Identity" (2000) 3 Journal of the Church Law Association 140.

where a religious institution is incorporated pursuant to civil legislation that regulates its polity and internal tribunals, such internal tribunals are as subject to civil court supervision as are any other inferior courts.[62]

Despite judicial reluctance to intervene, and self-imposed judicial restrictions on the types of issues with which the civil courts should deal, courts *qua* courts are obliged to resolve disputes brought to them and do so when those disputes emanate from religious institutions. Civil court cases involving religious institutions break down into two broad categories: property-ownership disputes when schism or merger of churches occurs, and disputes involving discipline, usually of clergy but occasionally also of laity. Each of these categories of cases will be discussed discretely later in this book,[63] but it is also possible to abstract from them, considered together, seven general principles by which the courts have been guided in making decisions about intervention and about the scope and extent of intervention. They may be listed as follows.

First, church tribunals are required to follow their own substantive and procedural rules,[64] and where they do not do so the civil courts will either refer litigants back to the church tribunal[65] or strike down its decision on the ground that it did not follow its own rules.[66] Secondly, civil courts may actively review the decisions of church tribunals; they normally prefer to sustain such decisions, especially the decisions of the highest tribunal in any religious organization.[67]

---

62 *Ex parte Currie*, above note 60; and *Lindenburger* v. *United Church of Canada*, above note 55.

63 For property disputes, see below section L and for discipline cases, below chapter 9.

64 *Halliwell* v. *Synod of Ontario* (1884), 7 O.R. 67 (Ch. D.); *Ex parte Currie*, above note 60; *Ex parte Little*, above note 60; *Huegli* v. *Pauli* (1912), 4 D.L.R. 319 (Ont. H.C.); *Holiness Movement Church in Canada* v. *Horner* (1917), 13 O.W.N. 29 (Div. Ct.); *McCharles* v. *Wyllie* (1927), 32 O.W.N. 202 (H.C.); *Orr* v. *Brown*, [1932] 3 D.L.R. 364 (B.C.C.A.); *Davis* v. *United Church of Canada*, above note 60; *Pederson* v. *Fulton*, above note 55; *Jeon*, above note 50; and *Wigglesworth* v. *Phipps* (2001), 7 C.C.E.L. (3d) 37 (Alta. Q.B.).

65 *Ash* v. *Methodist Church* (1901), 31 S.C.R. 497; *McCharles* v. *Wylie*, above note 64; *Davis* v. *United Church of Canada*, above note 60; *Pederson* v. *Fulton*, above note 55; and *Jeon*, above note 50.

66 *Halliwell* v. *Synod of Ontario*, above note 64; *Ex parte Currie*, above note 60; *Ex parte Little*, above note 60; and *McCaw* v. *United Church of Canada*, above note 55.

67 *Itter* v. *Howe*, above note 49; and *Ash* v. *Methodist Church*, above note 65.

Thirdly, church tribunals are required to comply with the rules of natural justice — in particular, the rights of the parties to know the case, to reply to the case, and to have an unbiased tribunal — and judicial intervention will occur where there has been failure to comply with these rights.[68] Fourthly, church tribunals should not act in an *ultra vires* fashion; that is, there should be no evidence of malice, *mala fides*, or of any other vitiating factor in the final decision, and if there is, judicial intervention may occur.[69]

Fifthly, civil courts may intervene, regardless of any other factors, where a church is incorporated pursuant to civil legislation that regulates its polity and internal tribunals, so that such internal tribunals are made subject to the supervision of the civil courts to the same extent as are any other inferior courts.[70] Sixthly, civil courts will intervene where property or civil rights are at stake,[71] particularly where property interests of an individual are so tied up with a religious institution that they are prejudiced by a decision of an internal tribunal.[72] Seventhly, it appears to be the case that when a punishment has been determined by an internal tribunal, the offender may be handed over to the civil courts for its enforcement.[73] Finally, Canadian civil courts will exercise jurisdiction over a foreign religious society, incorporated elsewhere, if it is resident in Canada.[74]

---

68 *Bishop of Columbia v. Cridge*, above note 60; *Wetmon v. Bayne*, above note 55; *Ukrainian Greek Orthodox Church v. Ukrainian Greek Orthodox Cathedral of St. Mary the Protectress*, above note 55; *Lindenburger v. United Church of Canada*, above note 55; *McCaw v. United Church of Canada*, above note 55; *Lakeside Colony of Hutterian Brethren v. Hofer*, above note 55; *Davis v. United Church of Canada*, above note 60; and *Levitt Kosher Foods Ltd. v. Levin* (1999), 175 D.L.R. (4th) 471 (Ont. S.C.J.).

69 *Ex parte Currie*, above note 60; *Ex parte Little*, above note 60; *Wetmon v. Bayne*, above note 55; and *Ukrainian Greek Orthodox Church v. Ukrainian Greek Orthodox Cathedral of St. Mary the Protectress*, above note 55.

70 *Ex parte Currie*, above note 60; *Lindenberger v. United Church of Canada*, above note 60.

71 *Tully v. Farrell*, above note 58; *Dunnet v. Forneri*, above note 36; and *Itter v. Howe*, above note 49.

72 *Tully v. Farrell*, above note 58; *Dunnet v. Forneri*, above note 36; *Pinke v. Bornhold* (1904), 8 O.L.R. 575 (H.C.); *Patillo v. Cummings* (1915), 24 D.L.R. 775 (N.S.T.D.); *Heinrichs v. Wiens*, [1917] 1 W.W.R. 306 (Sask. T.D.); *Cohen v. Hazen Avenue Synagogue* (1920), 47 N.B.R. 400 (Ch.); and *Zawidoski v. Ruthenian Greek Catholic Parish of St. Vladmir & Olga*, [1937] 2 D.L.R. 509 (Man. K.B.). *Cf. Christensen v. Bodner* (1976), 65 D.L.R. (3d) 549 (Man. Q.B.).

73 *Bishop of Columbia v. Cridge*, above note 60.

74 *Archer v. Society of the Sacred Heart of Jesus*, above note 14.

Civil courts have exercised jurisdiction over the internal affairs of religious institutions by means of injunctions,[75] writs of certiorari[76] and prohibition,[77] and awards of damages.[78]

E. ORGANIZATION AND CHURCH GOVERNMENT

1) The Anglican Church of Canada

While the legal status of the Anglican Church of Canada in succession to the Church of England in Canada is no different from that of any other religious organization,[79] there is a sufficiently large body of case law, dating primarily from the nineteenth century, relating to its status and episcopal polity to justify separate discussion prior to the discussion of the law relating to religious organizations generally. This section will consider the common law relating to the Anglican polity, while the section that follows will consider together the common law relating to other polities in Canada, differentiating these where distinctive factors were at issue.

Since the Anglican Church of Canada enjoys the same legal status as other religious organizations as a voluntary association,[80] the enforcement of its polity rests on the mutual contract of its members[81] and is, therefore, subject to the common law and to legislation of general application to religious organizations.[82] It is also subject to specific legislation enacted for its own purposes and for the various dioceses, schools, colleges, and other entities of which it is comprised. What follows here are common law principles that must be considered within the entire legal framework relating to any specific legal issues and accordingly may not be the

---

75 *Huegli v. Pauli* (1912), 4 D.L.R. 319 (Ont. H.C.); and *McCharles v. Wylie*, above note 65.

76 *Ex parte Little*, above note 60; and *Lindenburger v. United Church of Canada*, above note 60.

77 *Ex parte Currie*, above note 60.

78 *McCaw v. United Church of Canada*, above note 55.

79 Above section C.

80 *Dunnet v. Forneri*, above note 36; *Johnson v. Glen*, above note 47; and *Kinsey v. Kinsey*, above note 40.

81 *Johnson v. Glen*, ibid.

82 *Johnson v. Glen*, ibid.; and *Bliss v. Christ Church, Fredericton*, above note 4.

answer to a specific legal problem. Many of the common law principles discussed here have now been incorporated into, if they did not reflect original Anglican practice, but others may have been superceded either by Anglican canon law or practice or civil legislation. While they may still be part of the common law, they may no longer relfect Anglican practice.

The ecclesiastical law of England relating to the established Church of England forms no part of the law of Canada.[83] Although it was said by the New Brunswick Queen's Bench in 1870[84] that the Queen, by virtue of being the earthly head of the Church of England, may exercise the prerogative powers, such as the right to present to a vacant rectory, in relation to the Church of England in Canada, it may now be doubted whether this opinion was correct either in the late nineteenth or early twenty-first centuries.

a) Rectors and Rectories

In Anglican polity and in civil law by virtue of legislation, the right of presentation, or advowson, to a vacant church living is not vested in the Crown; rather, it has been granted by statute to the bishop in relation to all rectories within his diocese.[85] Where a Lieutenant Governor retained the royal prerogative to present to a vacant rectory, a bishop cannot legally exercise that right.[86] The right of presentation is a property right; that is, an incorporeal hereditament, which may be conveyed by deed or devise in whole or in part. However unwise or inexpedient a particular appointment may be, the power to make it is vested unconditionally in the bishop by the legislature.[87]

Where a canon of the church provides that the bishop shall consult with the churchwardens of the parish or with mission and lay representatives, an incumbent in relation to whom there has been no such consultation is not lawfully appointed; moreover, such consultation should be by personal interview, not letter.[88] Where civil legislation requires the election of a new rector by the parishioners of a particular congregation, approval by two-thirds of the qualified voters present is sufficient, even

83   *Lyster v. Kirkpatrick*, above note 46.

84   *Doe d. St. George's Church v. Cougle*, above note 25.

85   *An Act Incorporating the Synod of the Diocese of Ontario*, S.C. 1862, c. 86.

86   *Doe d. St. George's Church v. Cougle*, above note 25.

87   *A.G. Upper Canada v. Lauder* (1862), 9 Gr. 461 (U.C. Ch.).

88   *Johnson v. Glen*, above note 47.

though unqualified persons also voted. An open vote may be taken and there is no need to record the names of those who voted for and against.[89]

A priest who has been nominated, presented, and instituted by a bishop as a rector is the lawful rector even if he or she has not been inducted. Such a person may exercise the duties and functions of a rector, such as presiding at meetings for the election of churchwardens and vestrymen, and without his or her presence the meeting has no authority. But such a priest may not be able to enjoy the temporalities of the parish because induction is required for seisin of the temporalities.[90]

An "incumbent," in the wide sense of that word, is a person who occupies or fulfils the duties of any office, and it is in this sense that all the statutes dealing with the Church of England in Ontario use the term. Thus, "incumbent" refers not just to a priest who is inducted into a benefice, but also includes a priest licensed or appointed by a bishop to the cure of souls in a parish for the time being. Therefore, where a priest serves a second congregation and is inducted into that benefice, he is entitled to share in surplus income in the diocese apportioned by the congregation. The incumbent of a particular congregation need not be separated from that of any other congregation, nor need the incumbent reside within a particular township to serve as an incumbent.[91]

The incumbent of a congregation is not a member of that congregation, therefore an action brought on behalf of all the members of the congregation is not necessarily brought on behalf of the incumbent.[92]

Remuneration levels for clergy may depend on the construction of a trust for that purpose; thus, where a trust, which was originally established in relation to commutation under the *Clergy Reserve Act*,[93] gives the trustees powers to change the bylaws from time to time as to the annual salary, and where the bylaws are so changed, a priest has no right to insist on his or her previous salary.[94] Where the commutation trust fund bylaws provide that an annuity for a priest is attached to that particular person and follows him into any parish, then it cannot be

---

89   *Ex parte Beek* (1873), 15 N.B.R. 66 (C.A.).
90   *Ex parte Chandler* (1873), 14 N.B.R. 354 (S.C.).
91   *Re Incorporated Synod of the Diocese of Ontario* (1921), 20 O.W.N. 331 (H.C.).
92   *McClenaghan v. Grey* (1883), 4 O.R. 329 (Ch.).
93   S.C. 1851, c. 2.
94   *Wright v. Incorporated Synod of Diocese of Huron* (1885), 11 S.C.R. 95.

exchanged with the incumbent of a particular parish.[95] Where participation in a clergy endowment fund is precluded if a priest's annual income exceeds a set sum, the salary of a curate is not to be considered as part of the priest's income for entitlement purposes.[96]

Where an action for ejectment in respect of glebe lands is brought by the incumbent who was presented and inducted within twenty years prior to the action, the defendant's previous possession for more than twenty years could not count as against the incumbent because the twenty-year period must run against the same incumbent. Thus, where there has been a succession of incumbents in a rectory within twenty years, the laches of the former rector cannot prejudice his successor.[97] However, where there was no valid proof of presentation, institution, and induction, an action for ejectment brought by the rector to recover possession of the glebe lands must be dismissed.[98]

Finally, the synod of a diocese may have no right to dispose of rectory lands where legislation provided that rectory lands originally the subject of a Crown Grant are vested in a rector as a "corporation sole" for his or her own use and the benefit of the adjoining rectories.[99] Where legislation authorizes the Lieutenant Governor to constitute and endow rectories by patent, such authority may be exercised until checked by subsequent instructions.[100]

b) Churchwardens

Where legislation so provides, a church corporation may be created in the style of "the Rector, Churchwardens, and Vestry," and land may be validly conveyed to such a corporation and held by it. Thus, although no rector had ever been appointed to a particular parish because it had remained in the charge of a succession of missionaries, the church corporation so created could maintain an action for ejectment in its own name.[101] The churchwardens and vestry may exercise the powers and authority of a

---

95 *Geoghegan v. Synod of Niagara* (1905), 6 O.W.R. 717 (Div. Ct.).

96 *Diocesan Synod of Nova Scotia v. Ritchie* (1890), 18 S.C.R. 705.

97 *Hill v. McKinnon* (1858), 16 U.C.Q.B. 216 (C.A.).

98 *Doe d. Creen v. Friesman* (1841), 1 U.C.Q.B. 420.

99 *Dumoulin v. Langtry* (1886), 13 S.C.R. 258, leave to appeal to P.C. refused (1887), C.R. 14 A.C. 240 (P.C.).

100 *A.G. Upper Canada v. Grasett* (1857), 6 Gr. 200 (U.C.C.A.).

101 *Doe d. Rector of Andover v. Kennedy* (1886), 26 N.B.R. 83 (C.A.).

church corporation where the rector has died or is absent, or where a rector has never been appointed, and the church corporation should still be styled "the Rector, Churchwardens, and Vestry"; thus, a grant of land to a church corporation where no rector had ever been appointed or inducted was valid.[102] Where land is mortgaged to the two churchwardens and one dies, the discharge of the mortgage by the survivor and the new churchwarden is effective as against the church corporation.[103]

Churchwardens are normally elected, but an improper or irregular election may be reviewed by the courts where the qualifications of the voters are questioned. Thus, in a late nineteenth-century case, *Tully v. Farrell*,[104] the court reviewed a number of issues no longer relevant, including the right to vote of women who were pew-owners, the rights of pew-owners to devise pews to heirs, and the rights of those who rented sittings from pew-owners to vote.

Tully also stated the legal duties of churchwardens, confining these to the care of the ecclesiastical property of the parish, over which they exercise a discretionary power for specific purposes, as is Anglican custom. In all other respects, the court found, the office of churchwarden is an office of observation and complaint, but not of control with respect to divine worship. In the service of worship, they have no formal role, other than to collect the offertory.[105] Thus, it is the duty of the church corporation to preserve the church for the legitimate purpose for which it was created, which is to say, for the performance of public worship by the duly appointed and legally inducted rector, and to enable the pewholders and parishioners to attend divine service therein.[106]

Since the churchwardens are constituted as a corporation, they may sue or be sued in relation to all matters pertaining to the church corporation; thus, where churchwardens entered an agreement to pay funds to a rector in consideration of his resignation, the court found this to be enforceable against them in their corporate capacity although they had no assets out of which to pay the amount.[107] Again, churchwardens may be sued for rent owing on a house occupied by the rector to their church

---

102 *Doe d. Rector of Queensbury v. Guiou* (1848), 6 N.B.R. 6 (C.A.).
103 *Pountney v. McBirney* (1927), 33 O.W.N. 84 (H.C.).
104 *Tully v. Farrell*, above note 58.
105 *Ibid.*
106 *Doe d. St. George's Church v. Cougle*, above note 25.
107 *Re Kirkby and All Saints' Church* (1904), 8 O.L.R. 385 (H.C.).

as successors in office to former churchwardens who entered into the lease.[108] Churchwardens may also be sued on an agreement made by their predecessors to reimburse a rector for the amount expended by him on improvements to the rectory.[109]

Where a member of a church corporation wishes to sue for an alleged illegal diversion of funds held in trust by the corporation as trustee, it is not necessary that the member have a pecuniary interest, although the suit must be brought on behalf of all the members of the corporation.[110] On the other hand, where a bequest was made to the incumbent of a church to be used for the relief of the poor of that church and dispensed by the incumbent, an action by the churchwardens on behalf of the congregation against the executors of the estate to pay over sums that ought to have been paid over, failed — they did not represent the incumbent, who was not a member of the congregation; nor did they represent the poor, who constituted only one group in the congregation.[111]

In the late nineteenth century when pewholding as a means of raising funds for congregational purposes was beginning to give way to free sittings, it was somewhat unclear as to the impact this might have on the idea that churchwardens as a corporation could sue or be sued in relation to the congregation. Thus, where an action was brought against churchwardens for work done on the building under a contract with the previous churchwardens, the action failed on the basis of a defence that because the sittings were wholly free and there were no pewholders, there was no electorate who could appoint the churchwardens and vest them with the right to sue or be sued.[112] It was further held that where a congregation had been converted from a pewed to a free congregation, and a contract was previously entered into by the churchwardens in relation to the incumbent's stipend, the churchwardens after the conversion were only required to pay the stipend to the extent that they received funds from the voluntary contributions of the congregation.[113]

Confusion also remains in the nineteenth-century case law in relation to succession issues for a church corporation. Where churchwardens

---

108 *Maynard v. Gamble* (1863), 13 U.C.C.P. 56 (C.A.).
109 *Re Kirkby and All Saints' Church*, above note 107.
110 *Armstrong v. Church Society of the Diocese of Toronto* (1867), 13 Gr. 552 (Ch.).
111 *McClenaghan v. Grey* (1883), 4 O.R. 329 (H.C.).
112 *Anderson v. Worters* (1882), 32 U.C.C.P. 659 (H.C.).
113 *Daw v. Ackerill* (1898), 25 O.A.R. 37.

gave mere undertakings to support a mission appointed by the bishop, they and their successors were not bound to pay the stipend.[114] Where an action was commenced against churchwardens and these were subsequently changed at a vestry meeting, the action was allowed to be continued against the former churchwardens in their own names.[115] It is doubtful that these cases, although never overruled (perhaps because of absence of opportunity), accurately state the law, which assumes corporations to enjoy succession for purposes of suing and being sued, as does the canon law and practice of the Anglican Church of Canada.

Churchwardens also are responsible for the maintenance of church buildings. Where there is no rector they are permitted to close up a church but where there is a rector they have no right to do so or to keep possession of church buildings. If there is no rector, the church corporation, not the churchwardens, would be entitled to possession.[116]

Finally, it is necessary to distinguish churchwardens from other church committees in relation to legal liability issues. Where a minister sought to bring an action against a church committee, elected annually by a congregation, in relation to a promised stipend, the action failed because the committee was not a corporate body, had no corporate funds, and was responsible for its own engagements only. The promise made by a previously constituted committee did not bind the current committee.[117]

2) Other Religious Institutions

Although the remaining cases in relation to organization and governance issues deal with religious institutions that are congregational, presbyterian, and episcopal, but non-Anglican, in polity, this section will discuss the law in an integrated fashion, distinguishing distinctive polity issues where required. Where particular ecclesiastical constitutions make express provision for the issue in dispute the courts will apply that provision, but in its absence the general law relating to religious organizations is applied; tailored, as required, to the polity in question. This section will focus on the legal principles outside provincial legislation of general application to religious institutions; that is, situations where the

---

114 *Carry v. Wallace* (1862), 12 U.C.C.P. 372 (C.A.).
115 *McFeeters v. Dixon* (1870), 3 Chy. Chrs. 84 (Ont. Ch.).
116 *Doe d. St. George's Church v. Cougle*, above note 25.
117 *Stewart v. Martin* (1859), 18 U.C.Q.B. 477 (C.A.).

courts have been guided by specific policy requirements and the common law in coming to their conclusions. Provincial legislation of general application will be considered below.[118]

a) Authority, Legal Status, and Powers of Bishops

Disputes about the validity of episcopal appointments occasionally occur in various Orthodox communities in Canada whose internal affairs are often affected by political and ecclesiastical events in parent overseas branches. Where appeal has been made outside the community to the civil courts to determine who is the rightfully appointed bishop, the courts have reviewed the history and internal church government of the institution to determine the issue. Thus, a person appointed as bishop by the church authority authorized to make such an appointment is to be regarded as the lawfully appointed bishop.[119] On the other hand, where a bishop has been deposed but continues to exercise the office, a court will assume that the deposition complied with the constitution and grant an interim injunction to restrain the bishop from acting as bishop pending the final outcome of the dispute.[120]

The preference of the civil courts for upholding the constitutions of religious organizations is also demonstrated in relation to the exercise by a bishop of his or her constitutional authority. Where a parish constitution made provision for an appeal to the bishop in relation to a disputed election and where the bishop exercised his constitutional power to make a final decision by ordering a new election, the court upheld his decision as valid and stated its willingness to issue the necessary orders to enforce it.[121]

Episcopal polities in Canada generally utilize the "corporation sole" as the legal device for holding property and perpetual succession placed in the bishop by virtue of private legislation.[122] The courts have consid-

---

118 Below section F.
119 *Scherbanuk v. Skorodoumov*, [1935] O.R. 342 (H.C.).
120 *Holiness Movement Church v. Horner* (1917), 13 O.W.N. 29 (Div. Ct.).
121 *Colettis v. Greek Orthodox Community of East Vancouver* (1993), 107 D.L.R. (4th) 248 (B.C.S.C.).
122 W. Blackstone, 1 *Commentaries on the Laws of England*, 1st ed. (Oxford: Clarendon Press, 1765) at 458–9. For corporations sole and aggregate, see generally Paul G. Kauper and Stephen C. Ellis, "Religious Institutions and the Law" (1973) 71 Mich. L. Rev. 1499; A.H. Oosterhoff, "Religious Institutions and the Law in Ontario: An Historical Study of the Law Enabling Religious Organiza-

ered several issues in relation to episcopal corporations since the late nineteenth century.

To determine whether an episcopal corporation has the legal power to guarantee a mortgage, it may be necessary to examine, in addition to post-Confederation legislation, pre-Confederation legislation and the legislative authority of pre-Confederation legislatures to grant such legal powers. Thus, such examination has disclosed that a Roman Catholic episcopal corporation was bound by a guarantee made by a diocesan administrator during a vacancy in the see.[123]

The necessity for strict interpretation of the private legislation incorporating an episcopal corporation sole is demonstrated by *Basil v. Spratt*,[124] which was concerned with the legal right of a bishop to interfere with the discipline and expulsion of a member of a religious order that was also incorporated. The court found that the act incorporating the episcopal corporation did not vest in the bishop any spiritual jurisdiction or ecclesiastical rights over the order, which by its own incorporating act was essentially self-governing. Thus, the episcopal corporation was not liable in relation to a legal action brought by a person compelled by the bishop to leave the religious society. The legal rights and duties of each corporation were to be defined pursuant to their respective private acts and the conduct of the bishop, himself, did not bind the episcopal corporation if *ultra vires*.

The distinction between the bishop himself and the episcopal corporation has been made by the courts in relation to the question of whether a bishop may bind his successors in office by contract where contracting in his private right. Thus, a Roman Catholic bishop who executed a mortgage in the name of his "successors, administrators and executors," did not thereby bind his successors as the corporation sole, because they were not expressly named.[125] Conversely, a lender is not entitled to recover from the successor of a Roman Catholic bishop, incorporated as a corporation sole but with no powers to borrow so as to bind his successor,

---

tions to Hold Land" (1981) 13 Ott. L. Rev. 441; and O.L.R.C., *Report on Mortmain: Charitable Uses and Religious Institutions* (Toronto, 1976).

123 *Sunlife Assurance Co. v. Sisters Adorers of the Precious Blood*, [1943] 1 D.L.R. 596 (Ont. C.A.).

124 (1918), 45 D.L.R. 554 (Ont. C.A.).

125 *Paris v. Bishop of New Westminster* (1897), 5 B.C.R. 450 (S.C.). *Cf. McGuire v. Evans* (1920), 19 O.W.N. 174 (C.A.).

even where the money was borrowed under the corporate seal for church purposes.[126] It may be doubted whether this case, decided in 1870, would be decided the same way today in light of the contemporary understanding of *ultra vires* in relation to corporations.

b) Authority of Clergy

The issue of whether or not a priest may bind the episcopal corporation of his parish by executing legal documents in place of the bishop has been considered in two cases. In *Purdy and Henderson v. Parish of St. Patrick*,[127] the court decided that where a priest had signed an agreement for the purchase of land for the purpose of erecting a church with the knowledge of the bishop, then the contract will be presumed to have been executed with the bishop's authority and bind the ecclesiastical corporation, although the articles of incorporation required that the parish corporation be represented by the bishop, the priest, and two other corporation members. The absence of the corporation's seal was not found to affect the validity of the agreement. Moreover, in *Leonard v. St. Patrick's Parish*,[128] the court found that where a priest had also signed a contract on behalf of a parish corporation to borrow money, the loan was binding on the corporation, even though the bishop subsequently sought to prescribe additional formalities beyond those for which the incorporation provided.

An ecclesiastical corporation may also be bound where its seal alone is affixed to an agreement, although a corporation sole is not required to use a seal in its legal transactions, so that the signature of the appropriate clergyman is also sufficient.[129]

c) Remuneration of Clergy

There would appear to be only one reported decision concerned with legal liability to pay the salary[130] of a non-Anglican minister.[131] In *Stewart v. Martin*,[132] which concerned an action brought by a Presbyterian minis-

---

126 *Ruitz v. Sandwich Roman Catholic Episcopal Corp.* (1870), 30 U.C.Q.B. 269.
127 (1917), 37 D.L.R. 642 (Alta. C.A.).
128 (1922), 66 D.L.R. 304 (Alta. C.A.).
129 *Eastview v. Roman Catholic Episcopal Corp. of Ottawa* (1918), 47 D.L.R. 47 (Ont. C.A.).
130 For the difference, if any, between "salary" and "stipend," see below chapter 9, section C.
131 Above section E(1)(a).
132 (1859), 18 U.C.Q.B. 477 (C.A.).

ter called by a congregation at a stipulated stipend against the individual members of a congregational committee for arrears, the court found that they were not liable unless contractually bound to be personally liable. Rather, since they were not a corporate body, had no corporate funds, and the congregation's constitution imposed no duty on them to pay the stipend, the minister's action failed.

d) Trustees and Officers

The practice of vesting property in ecclesiastical corporations, whether by common law as in England or by private legislation as in Canada, has not been historically as characteristic of non-episcopal Christian polities and non-Christian religious organizations as it has been of episcopal polities in England or Canada. Instead, from the early nineteenth century onward, the predominant practice of congregational and presbyterian polities has been to vest property in trustees, who hold it under a trust deed, and this practice was adopted by non-Christian religious groups coming to Canada from the mid nineteenth century onward. Recently, with the advent of not-for-profit corporation legislation, many religious organizations at the local and national levels have moved away from the trust to the corporation for the purposes of holding property and managing their temporal affairs. This trend is reflected in the predominance of nineteenth and early twentieth-century cases dealing with trusts and trustees.[133]

To act legally so as to bind a congregation, trustees must first be validly elected as such, according to the provisions of the trust deed or any other valid constitutional document of the congregation. In *Levinsky v. Hallett*,[134] the election of trustees by a general meeting of the members of a Jewish synagogue was found to be invalid because the period of notice prior to general meetings as required by the applicable legislation[135] had not been given; the meeting was improperly called and the

---

133 To date there is very little case law on the use of incorporations to hold property; however, there is a small literature on practical issues relating to incorporation. See *Fit To Be Tithed: Risks and Rewards for Charities and Trusts* (Toronto: Law Society of Upper Canada, 1994); *Fit To Be Tithed 2: Reducing Risks for Charities and Not-For-Profits* (Toronto: Law Society of Upper Canada, 1998); and *Fundamental New Developments in the Law of Charities in Canada* (Toronto: Canadian Bar Association – Ontario Continuing Legal Education, 2000).

134 (1904), 5 O.W.R. 1 (H.C.).

135 *Religious Institutions Act*, R.S.O. 1897, c. 307, s. 16.

election invalid. An election of trustees is also invalid where persons who are not qualified to vote are allowed to do so.[136] Where a particular congregation is subject both to a denominational constitution, such as a Methodist Book of Discipline, and a trust deed in relation to the election of trustees, the provisions of the trust deed prevail so that trustees not elected pursuant to the trust deed are invalidly elected and cannot act on behalf of the congregation.[137]

A person whose nomination as a trustee is not in accordance with the trust deed cannot validly be a trustee and will not replace as a trustee a person whose nomination was in accordance with the trust deed. Thus, where the trust deed of the "Coloured Wesleyan Methodist Church" provided that a new trustee be nominated by a "coloured minister," a person not so nominated was held not to be a trustee.[138] A trustee of a congregation who ceases to be a member of that congregation can no longer be a trustee, and may be found guilty of trespass should he or she attempt to exercise the powers of a trustee.[139]

Where a list of church officers elected at a parish meeting must be confirmed by a higher body, such a body is bound to confirm the officers in the absence of evidence of irregularity in the election. Thus, in nineteenth-century New Brunswick, a General Sessions was obliged pursuant to provincial legislation to confirm those elected at a parish meeting.[140]

The duties, rights, and responsibilities of trustees of denominations or congregations that are not incorporated, or that have no trust deed, or whose trust deed does not provide for the duties, rights, and responsibilities of the trustees, are governed by provincial religious institutions legislation.[141] This legislation explicitly provides for the management by trustees of the property of religious institutions and by implication excludes the application of corresponding provisions of general provincial trustee legislation.[142]

Trustees governed by provincial legislation have been granted the corporate attribute of succession and have been described as a "quasi-

---

136 *Tully v. Farrell* (1876), 23 Gr. 49.
137 *Coleman v. Moore* (1879), 44 U.C.Q.B. 328 (C.A.).
138 *Smallwood v. Abbott* (1859), 18 U.C.Q.B. 564 (C.A.).
139 *Everett v. Howell* (1837), 5 O.S. 592 (U.C.C.A.).
140 *Ex parte Robinson* (1873), 14 N.B.R. 321 (S.C.).
141 For a fuller discussion of this legislation, see below section F.
142 *Re Hamilton Lutheran Church* (1915), 24 D.L.R. 879 (Ont. H.C.).

corporation."[143] By virtue of the corporate status bestowed by the legislation, duly appointed trustees are not personally liable upon a mortgage for congregational property although they have signed and sealed it individually.[144] Otherwise trustees who have signed and sealed individually a contract for work to be done on a parsonage may be individually liable to pay for the work done.[145]

Where legal proceedings are commenced against a religious institution governed by provincial religious institutions legislation, the trustees are empowered to act in the name of the corporate body so that individual members are not liable for any liability of the institution; an action is properly brought against the institution, not the individual members as trustees.[146] Where trustees wish to bring an action to set aside a deed,[147] or to maintain an ejectment,[148] or to recover a subscription,[149] they should do so as a corporate body, in the name of "The Trustees of ... ," and there is no need to add individual trustees' names. In order to sue or be sued in the corporate name, trustees must show that they were properly appointed; otherwise, an action in which they purport to act as a validly constituted corporation will fail.[150]

Where a person brings a suit for an injury suffered while working on church property due to the alleged negligence of a church employee, the suit should be brought against the trustees for and on behalf of the congregation, not against the individual trustees in their own names alone.[151]

Where a congregation has a separate fund and appoints members to manage it, these trustees may be sued in the corporate name of the separate fund, and there is no need for the congregation to appoint represen-

---

143 *A.G. Upper Canada v. Jeffrey* (1863), 10 Gr. 273 (Ch.); *Wansley v. Brown* (1891), 21 O.R. 34 (Ch.); and *East Selkirk Greek Catholic Ruthenian Church v. Portage La Prairie Farmers Mutual Fire Insurance Co.* (1917), 31 D.L.R. 33 (Man. C.A.).
144 *Beaty v. Gregory* (1897), 24 O.A.R. 325.
145 *Cullen v. Nickerson* (1861), 10 U.C.C.P. 549 (C.A.).
146 *Kicul v. Bulycz*, [1933] 1 W.W.R. 45 (Sask. K.B.).
147 *Franklin Church Trustees v. Maguire* (1876), 23 Gr. 102 (Ont. H.C.).
148 *Humphreys v. Hunter* (1870), 20 U.C.C.P. 456 (C.A.); and *Ainleyville Wesleyan Methodist Church Trustees v. Grewer* (1874), 23 U.C.C.P. 533 (C.A.).
149 *Berkeley Street Church Trustees v. Stevens* (1875), 37 U.C.Q.B. 9 (C.A.).
150 *Doe d. Galt Presbyterian Church v. Bain* (1847), 3 U.C.Q.B. 198 (C.A.); see also *Calvin Church v. Logan* (1884), Tru. 221 (N.B.S.C.).
151 *Mitchell v. Foster* (1928), 35 O.W.N. 203 (H.C.).

tatives to bring an action on its own behalf.[152] A judgment against a church is only enforceable against exigible assets in the hands of the trustees, not against buildings or lands held on special trust.[153]

Trustees desiring to sell church property are required to comply with any provincial legislative provisions relating to meetings and notices of meetings to procure approval for the sale.[154] Again, where provincial legislation requires trustees to give notices at the end of "public worship," religious services held in a private house are public worship for the purposes of the legislation.[155] Again, where provincial legislation requires an habendum clause on a conveyance, although the legislation still applies, in its absence, trustees and their successors may hold the land conveyed and procure insurance on the buildings.[156]

Persons who have been acting as trustees of a congregation with the congregation's acquiescence may be treated as *de facto* trustees for the purpose of bringing an action on behalf of the congregation for injury done to church property.[157] However, former trustees are not permitted to bring an action for ejectment in the corporate name of the congregation, but rather must do so in their own names only.[158]

When validly elected trustees of a congregation sign a promissory note on behalf of a congregation that is incorporated, and where no provincial religious institutions legislation is in place, the trustees may be personally liable on the note.[159]

Provincial religious institutions legislation typically provides only for the appointment of trustees and not for their removal, and certainly not for the capricious removal of a trustee competent and willing to act; such a removal is, therefore, invalid.[160]

An individual member of a religious corporation who wishes to sue in relation to the illegal diversion of funds that the corporation holds as

152 *Neufeld v. Fehr*, [1929] 4 D.L.R. 1070 (Man. C.A.).

153 *Kicul v. Bulycz*, above note 146.

154 *Cummins v. Congregational Church Trustees* (1885), 4 Man. R. 374 (Q.B.); *Wansley v. Brown*, above note 143; and *Harder v. Lindgren*, [1950] 1 W.W.R. 833 (Alta. T.D.).

155 *Schmunk v. Brook*, [1944] 3 D.L.R. 643 (B.C.C.A.).

156 *East Selkirk Greek Catholic Ruthenian Church*, above note 143.

157 *Everett v. Howell* (1837), 5 O.S. 592 (U.C.C.A.).

158 *Doe d. Methodist Church Trustees v. Carwin* (1837), 1 Ont. Case Law Dig. 965.

159 *McDougall v. McLean* (1893), 1 Terr. L.R. 450 (N.W.T.C.A.).

160 *Lage v. MacKenson* (1877), 40 U.C.Q.B. 388 (C.A.).

trustee, even though he or she has no pecuniary interest in the funds, must sue on behalf of him or herself and all other members of the corporation.[161] On the other hand, a representative action on behalf of the members of a Muslim mosque could not be maintained where there was no membership as such in the mosque, no trustees had ever been appointed, and there was no evidence of same interest as between the two disputing groups.[162]

Finally, the "indoor management" rule would also appear to be applicable vis à vis third parties. Thus, a contract for the purchase of land by an incorporated religious community was not set aside merely because the internal formalities of community approval by resolution and approval by a diocesan official had not occurred.[163] Nor was a mortgage set aside as against a bank, when the church's officers failed to get approval, as required by the church's constitution, by a special resolution at a general meeting in relation to changes on church property.[164]

It would appear that congregational officers have authority within the congregation even over matters of a trivial nature that are not regulated by law. Thus, in *Carleton Place Methodist Church Trustees* v. *Keyes*,[165] the congregational trustees were found to have the power to allot pews and seats for the purpose of preventing disorder during the service, although all seats in the church were free seats.[166]

e) Congregational Meetings

Proper notice is normally required for legally constituted congregational meetings and a court will order a new meeting in accordance with a constitution to reconsider a disputed matter.[167] Where congregational bylaws provided that notice of a general meeting is to be given by the best possible means, a decision to give notice by oral announcement from the pulpit supplemented by written notices on a notice board will be valid in the absence of evidence of improper motives or want of good faith. A resolution made at a general meeting of a synagogue that was sparsely

---

161 *Armstrong* v. *Church Society of the Diocese of Toronto* (1867), 13 Gr. 552 (Ch.).

162 *Judge* v. *Muslim Society of Toronto Inc.* (1973), 2 O.R. 45 (H.C.).

163 *Hôpital du Sacré Coeur* v. *Lefebvre* (1891), 17 Q.L.R. 35 (S.C.).

164 *Bank of Nova Scotia* v. *Ukrainian Greek Orthodox Congregation of Holy Trinity* (1991), 83 D.L.R. (4th) 477 (Alta. Q.B.).

165 (1902), 3 O.L.R. 165 (C.A.).

166 Below chapter 9, section D.

167 *Jeon*, above note 50.

attended and for which the notice requirements were not complied with was invalid, and the trustees were restrained by an injunction from acting on it.[168]

In *Re Canadian Temple Cathedral of the Universal Christian Apostolic Church*,[169] the general meeting enacted a bylaw adding a new ground for loss of membership; however, congregational dissidents who lost their membership by the operation of the bylaw and who waited three years to challenge it were prevented by laches from doing so effectively.

Where the practice of a particular denomination is to permit the majority of the members at a properly convened meeting to select through the trustees such incumbent as they see fit, then provided the candidate has been properly ordained, the election should proceed. But if the candidate has done something uncanonical, that is a matter for the courts of the denomination, not the civil courts.[170]

Where a Sikh society's constitution provided that matters of faith be determined by a majority, a court will make an order to uphold a majority's decision although a minority felt unable by virtue of religious convictions to deal with the majority.[171] Where a congregational meeting is properly convened in accordance with the church's constitution to pass a resolution in relation to a sale of church land and the purchase of other land for rebuilding, a decision by the majority is binding on the minority, but the majority should exercise its power strictly according to the church constitution so as to respect the minority and protect it from hardship.[172]

f) Congregational Records

Congregational records are clearly the property of the congregation and the control of access to them vested in the congregational body, usually the trustees or officers, who are responsible to the congregation for them. Thus, where a congregation ratifies a decision of its board of directors to refuse a member access to congregational records, the civil courts will not interfere with the decision in the absence of bad faith or malice.[173]

---

168 *Kopman v. Simonsky* (1903), 2 O.W.R. 617 (H.C.).
169 (1971), 21 D.L.R. (3d) 193 (B.C.S.C.).
170 *Dwirnichuk v. Zaichuk*, [1926] 3 W.W.R. 508 (Sask. K.B.).
171 *Gill v. Bhandal*, above note 50.
172 *Heine v. Schaffer* (1905), 2 W.L.R. 310 (Man. K.B.).
173 *Wetmon v. Bayne*, [1928] D.L.R. 848 (Alta. C.A.).

In presbyterian polities, responsibility for congregational records normally vests in the clerk of the kirk session, and access disputes arose after 1925 as to such records. Thus, in *Griffiths v. Fraser*,[174] when the clerk of the kirk session of a Presbyterian congregation left to become a member of the United Church of Canada, and refused to give up the records on the ground that they related to two other congregations that joined the United Church, a court ordered that he retain custody of the records but permit the other two congregations to inspect them and obtain copies of entries particularly concerning them.

F. OWNING AND USING PROPERTY

1) Ontario

There are four sources of law relating to the ownership and use of real property by religious institutions: (i) the common law, including the law relating to trusts; (ii) any private or special act of incorporation of a particular religious institution; (iii) provincial religious institutions legislation of general application; and, (iv) federal, and in most provinces, corporations legislation in relation to non-profit corporations.[175] In addition, since religious institutions are also the recipients of both real and personal[176] property, the uses to which such property may be put may be found in the terms on which it is given. It is, therefore, essential to identify the particular law or laws relating to the religious institution at issue, and this must be done on an institution-by-institution and issue-by-issue basis. Frequently, resort must be had to several sources for any particular issue.

In *Re Incorporated Synod of the Diocese of Toronto and H.E.C. Hotels Ltd.*,[177] the question was which legislation applied when the diocese wished to lease property for a ninety-nine-year period, although the applicable provincial religious institutions legislation[178] permitted forty-year leases only. The Ontario Court of Appeal found that where there is

---

174 [1928] 2 D.L.R. 540 (N.S.C.A.).

175 *Societies Act*, R.S.A. 1980, c. S-18; *Society Act*, R.S.B.C. 1979, c. 390; *Corporations Act*, R.S.M. 1987, c. C-225; *Companies Act*, R.S.N.B. 1973, c. C-13; *Corporations Act*, R.S.N. 1990, c. C-36; *Societies Act*, R.S.N.S. 1989, c. 435; *Corporations Act*, R.S.O. 1990, c. C. 38; *Companies Act*, R.S.P.E.I. 1988, c. C-14; *Non-Profit Corporations Act*, S.S. 1995, c. N-42; and *Canada Corporations Act*, R.S.C. 1970, c. C-32.

176 *Re Manning Estate*, [1947] 2 W.W.R. 487 (Man. K.B.).

177 (1987), 44 D.L.R. (4th) 161 (Ont. C.A.).

a conflict between private legislation and public legislation of general application, the private legislation will apply, so that, in that case, the diocese was permitted to enter the longer-term lease because its own act made no provision for restrictions on its powers to lease real property.[179]

Whether the source of law is federal or provincial legislation or the common law, property is held by religious institutions in one of four ways: (i) by trust deed, regulated by the terms of the trust and the common law relating to trusts; (ii) pursuant to provincial legislation of general application, which bestows a "quasi-corporate" status on a religious organization holding property by trust deed; (iii) by letters patent, pursuant to which a religious organization acquires the status of a body corporate; or (iv) pursuant to private legislation that bestows the status of body corporate. Where property is held by trust deed or act of incorporation the terms of its use will be found in the deed or statutes together with any additional constitutional documents such as bylaws or congregational constitutions. Where property is held pursuant to legislation bestowing quasi-corporate status, the terms are found in the legislation further considered in this section.

Provincial religious institutions legislation is the usual source of law for many religious institutions, so this section will briefly restate some of the main elements of that legislative framework — in relation, first, to Ontario, and then to the Western provinces. This legislation is broadly similar across the common law provinces but local legislation must be consulted.[180] While many religious organizations continue to hold property on trust on the basis of public legislation of general application,[181] there is a trend toward private legislation and this must be consulted first in accordance with the direction from the Ontario Court of Appeal.[182]

---

178 *Religious Organizations' Lands Act*, R.S.O. 1980, c. 448, s. 10(1).

179 See also M.H. Ogilvie, "The Legal Status of Ecclesiastical Corporations" (1989) 15 Can. Bus. L.J. 74; *Lakeside Colony of Hutterian Brethren v. Hofer*, [1992] 3 S.C.R. 165; and M.H. Ogilvie, "Ecclesiastical Law - Jurisdiction of Civil Courts - Governing Documents of Religious Organizations - Natural Justice: *Lakeside Colony of Hutterian Brethren v. Hofer*" (1993) 72 Can. Bar Rev. 238.

180 In addition to the provinces discussed below, for the other provinces, the legislation is as set out, above note 8.

181 Above notes 8 and 175.

182 For discussions of the practical aspects in deciding whether to incorporate and how to do so, see the materials, above note 133; especially Terrance S. Carter, "To Be or Not To Be — Incorporation of Autonomous Churches in Ontario" in

The *Religious Organizations' Lands Act (R.O.L.A.)*[183] is the current version of provincial legislation of general application to religious institutions in Ontario, which dates originally to 1828.[184] For the purposes of the Act, a "religious organization" means an association of persons that is charitable according to the law of Ontario; that is, organized for the advancement of religion and for the conduct of religious worship, services, or rites; and that is permanently established both as to its existence and as to its religious beliefs, rituals, and practices, and includes an association of persons organized for the advancement of, and for the conduct of worship, services, and rites of the Buddhist, Christian, Hindu, Islamic, Jewish, Baha'i, Longhouse Indian, Sikh, Unitarian, or Zoroastrian faith or of a subdivision or denomination thereof.[185] The requirement that the organization is to be charitable according to the laws of Ontario is to be interpreted so as to include a religious organization that carries on ancillary charitable purposes,[186] and a religious organization formed out of an existing religious organization, whether voluntary or otherwise.[187]

A religious organization may acquire and hold land for a place of worship, for a residence for its religious leader, for a burial or cremation ground, for a bookstore or a printing or publishing office, for a theological seminary or similar institution of religious instruction, for a religious camp, retreat or training centre, or for any other religious purpose.[188] The land must be held in the name of trustees,[189] individually or by collective designation, and their successors in perpetual succession for the benefit of the religious organization.[190] The appointment and tenure of the trustees is by resolution of a meeting[191] of the religious organization.[192]

Fit To Be Tithed (1994), reprinted (2002) 3 Journal of the Church Law Association 237.

183 R.S.O. 1990, c. R. 23.

184 *An Act for the Relief of the Religious Societies therein mentioned,* (U.C.), 1828, c. 2.

185 Section 1(1) "religious organization."

186 Section 1(2).

187 Section 1(3).

188 Sections 2(a)–(g).

189 Section 1(1) "trustees."

190 Section 2.

191 Section 1(1) "meeting."

192 Section 3(1).

A trustee holds office until he or she dies, resigns, or ceases to be a member,[193] and where there is a vacancy the remaining trustees have all the estate and title and powers originally vested in the whole number.[194] A trustee appointed to fill a vacancy and all other trustees appointed or subsequently appointed and remaining in office have all the estate, title, and powers vested in the original trustees.[195] Where no trustees remain in office, the organization's land vests automatically in trustees subsequently appointed without the necessity of any conveyance.[196] Where there are no provisions for successor trustees, the organization's land is automatically vested in such trustees as are finally appointed without the necessity of any conveyance.[197]

Where it is the custom or practice of a religious organization to vest property in one person, that person is deemed to be a trustee with all the powers and duties of trustees under the Act.[198] Each of two or more religious organizations may appoint joint trustees with all the powers and duties of a trustee under the Act in relation to property vested in them pursuant to the Act.[199]

The trustees of a religious organization may not exercise the powers conferred by the Act until they are authorized to do so by resolution of the organization, which may attach such terms and conditions as it deems expedient.[200] Where there are joint trustees for two or more religious organizations, authorization from each religious organization is required.[201]

The Act expressly permits trustees to enter agreements to purchase land for any of the purposes of the Act;[202] to maintain and defend actions for the protection of the land and the interest of the religious organization therein;[203] to mortgage land for its acquisition or improvement, or

---

193 Section 3(2).
194 Section 3(3).
195 Section 3(4).
196 Section 3(5).
197 Section 3(6).
198 Section 4.
199 Section 5.
200 Section 6(1).
201 Section 6(2).
202 Section 7.
203 Section 8.

for the building, repairing, extending, or improving of any buildings thereon;[204] to lease, for a term of forty years or for more than one term of not more than forty years in all, any land held for the benefit of the organization which is no longer required for any of the purposes set out in the Act, at such rent and upon such terms and conditions as they consider expedient;[205] to approve or grant easements or enter into covenants in respect of land held by them;[206] to sell or exchange land subject to a resolution by the organization;[207] to convey or transfer to the trustees of a separate religious organization such part of the land held by them as is appropriate;[208] to convey or transfer land to a uniting religious organization;[209] and to convey or transfer land to an incorporated board or to trustees of the denomination or a subdivision thereof.[210]

The trustees of a religious organization have a duty to have ready and open for inspection by the members of the organization on the first Monday in June in each year a detailed statement of the rents accrued in the previous year, and of all sums in their hands for the use and benefit of the organization derived from land under their control or management, and also showing the application of any portion of that money expended on behalf of the organization.[211]

A notice of a meeting of a religious organization must specify the purpose of the meeting and be given in accordance with the constitution, practice, or custom of the religious organization. In the absence of such constitution, practice, or custom, at least two weeks' notice must be given personally or by mail, or notice may be given by announcement at an open service at least once in each of the two weeks immediately preceding the week in which the meeting is proposed to be held.[212]

A resolution at a meeting is adopted where approved by a majority of those present at the meeting and entitled to vote.[213] A copy of such a resolution must be signed by the chair and the secretary of the meeting at

---

204 Section 9.
205 Section 10.
206 Section 11.
207 Section 12.
208 Section 13.
209 Section 14.
210 Section 15.
211 Section 16.
212 Section 18(2).
213 Section 17.

which it was adopted, and must be entered in the minute book or other record kept for that purpose.[214] A true copy of a resolution, certified as being a true copy by an officer of the religious institution, is regarded as proof of the matters therein stated in the absence of evidence to the contrary.[215] Failure to comply with the requirement that a resolution be signed by the chair and secretary and entered in the minute book does not invalidate a resolution or anything done under it.[216]

An instrument affecting land made by or to trustees under the Act is to be expressed to be made under the Act, but failure to do so does not render the instrument void.[217] Where letters patent from the Crown, or a grant, conveyance, or devise made before 14 June 1979 is made to persons described as trustees for a religious organization and to their successors, the Act applies to them and to the religious organization in the same manner as if the persons were duly appointed trustees under the Act.[218] Where different names have been used, the organization may by resolution adopt either of one of those names or another name as the name in which the trustees are to hold the land.[219] A change in the name of a religious organization or in the manner in which the trustees are described does not affect the title to land held by the organization or its trustees in the former name.[220]

Where a religious organization has ceased to exist, or where, for a reason other than a dispute among the members of the organization concerning the organization's property, the organization does not adopt a resolution authorizing the trustees to act,[221] the trustees or, upon their failure to do so or where no trustees remain in office, any interested person or the Public Trustee may apply to the Ontario Court (General Division) for directions, and the court may authorize the trustees or may appoint or authorize any other person to exercise the powers conferred by the Act.[222] The court may, upon such an application, direct the sale or

---

214 Section 19(1).
215 Section 19(2).
216 Section 19(3).
217 Section 20.
218 Section 21(1).
219 Section 21(2).
220 Section 22.
221 Section 6.
222 Section 23(1).

distribution of the land or any part thereof, and specify the manner of the distribution of the land or the proceeds of its sale.[223]

Any organization or other body that wishes to have determined whether it is entitled to acquire, hold, and possess land under the Act may apply to the Ontario Court (General Division) for a determination of the matter,[224] as may the Public Trustee.[225] Notice of an application to the court other than by the Public Trustee must be given by the applicant to the Public Trustee,[226] and the court may direct that such notice be given in any proceeding in which the application of the Act is in issue.[227]

The *R.O.L.A.* is subject to any special act applying to a religious organization,[228] and to any trusts or powers of trustees in any deed, conveyance, or other instrument.[229] A religious organization or subsidiary thereof in Ontario may, as an alternative to becoming a religious organization with property vested in trustees in perpetual succession under *R.O.L.A.*, be incorporated pursuant to a private or special act of the legislature or pursuant to the *Corporations Act* as a non-profit corporation.[230] A religious organization incorporated pursuant to one of these acts is subject to that act in relation to its internal laws and practices.[231]

2) Western Provinces

Provincial legislation in all four Western provinces permits a religious society, as defined, to appoint trustees in whom property acquired and held by the society vests. Such trustees hold land in trust for the society in accordance with the provisions of the legislation and the terms of the trust deed.[232] The legislation in each of the four provinces empowers duly

---

223 Section 23(2).

224 Section 24(1).

225 Section 24(2).

226 Section 25(1).

227 Section 25(2).

228 Section 26(1); *Re Incorporated Synod of the Diocese of Toronto*, above note 177.

229 Section 26(2).

230 R.S.O. 1990, c. C. 38.

231 *Re Incorporated Synod of the Diocese of Toronto*, above note 177, per Morden J.A. at 164–5.

232 *Religious Societies' Land Act*, R.S.A. 1980, c. R-14, s. 2; *Trustee (Church Property) Act*, R.S.B.C. 1996, c. 465, s. 1; *Religious Societies' Lands Act*, R.S.M. 1987, c. 270, s. 3(1); and *Religious Societies' Land Act*, R.S.S. 1978, c. R-19, s. 3.

appointed trustees to take and hold land on behalf of that society[233] and to mortgage,[234] lease,[235] and sell such land.[236] A grant of real property to a religious institution must conform to provincial legislation and the property conveyed must be for the purposes set out in the legislation.[237] Acreage limitations are applicable in Alberta and Manitoba,[238] and the acquisition of land for cemetery purposes may require special permission of the municipality in which the land is situated in British Columbia and Manitoba.[239]

In Alberta, a religious society or congregation may appoint trustees to take a conveyance or transfer of land for the site of a church building or burial ground, or for the support of public worship and the propagation of knowledge.[240] The trustees must be appointed in the manner specified in the deed of conveyance or transfer, or by resolution pursuant to the Act.[241] The manner in which trustees are to be chosen pursuant to the Act is by a meeting called according to the constitution or practice of the society or congregation, and by resolution of a majority of those present and entitled to vote at the meeting according to the constitution or practice of the society or congregation.[242] Such a resolution, endorsed on or annexed to the grant, transfer, or agreement under which the land is held for use, and signed by the chair and secretary of the meeting at which it is adopted, governs the manner in which successor trustees are to be appointed.[243] Where such a resolution is passed, the Act automatically applies to the society and its trustees.[244]

Trustees under the *Alberta Religious Societies' Land Act* enjoy perpetual succession, and may take, hold, and possess land and maintain and

---

233 Alberta, s. 2(3); B.C., ss. 6, 8; Manitoba, s. 12(2); and Saskatchewan, s. 2.1.

234 Alberta, ss. 4, 14(2); B.C., ss. 3, 6; Manitoba, s. 15; and Saskatchewan, s. 4.

235 Alberta, s. 15; B.C., s. 4; Manitoba, s. 17; and Saskatchewan, s. 5.

236 Alberta, ss. 7, 14(1); B.C., s. 6; Manitoba, s. 21; and Saskatchewan, s. 8.

237 Alberta, s. 2(1); B.C., s. 1; and Saskatchewan, s. 2.1.

238 Alberta, s. 2(4) (320 acres); and Manitoba, ss. 3(1)(a) (300 acres), (b) (20 acres for cemeteries).

239 B.C., s. 10; and Manitoba, s. 3(2).

240 Alberta, s. 2(1).

241 Section 2(2).

242 Section 9(1).

243 Section 9(2).

244 Section 9(3). See also s. 10 for land held by the Presbyterian Church in Canada.

defend all actions or suits in relation thereto.[245] They may take a mortgage for the building, repairing, or improving of a church building or for the purchase of land for a building, provided they are authorized to do so by a majority resolution of members present and entitled to vote at a meeting called for the purpose of considering such authorization.[246] They may also lease for a term not exceeding twenty-one years land held by them under the Act, at any rent and on any terms they consider reasonable, but they may not lease land necessary for the purpose of erecting a church building or for a burial ground, nor may they lease land for a term exceeding three years without authorization by a majority resolution of the congregation or society.[247] Trustees may also renew a lease for a further term of up to twenty-one years,[248] and may, with the approval of a judge of the Court of Queen's Bench and after giving public notice, sell land when it is unnecessary to retain it and it is considered advantageous to sell it, if the price offered is adequate in the judgment of the trustees.[249]

Trustees who have arranged for the sale or lease of land are required to prepare for inspection by every member of the society a statement showing all rents that have accrued during the preceding year and all moneys derived from land under their control or from the proceeds of sale, and the manner in which such moneys have been expended.[250] Trustees of an incorporated congregation must, when required to do so by the Minister charged with the administration of the *Business Corporations Act*,[251] prepare a written return of the society's property, membership, citizenship, and officers verified by affidavit,[252] and must present the membership list of the congregation for inspection at any properly constituted meeting; add to or take from that list as appropriate; and prepare any return required under the *Religious Societies' Land Act*.[253]

In Alberta, the Act provides that a religious denomination or congregation may be incorporated pursuant to it for the purpose of dealing with

---

245 Section 2(3). See also s. 3.
246 Section 4.
247 Section 5.
248 Section 6.
249 Section 7.
250 Section 8.
251 R.S.A. 1980, c. B-15.
252 Section 21.
253 Section 20.

real or personal property.[254] Such incorporation must be by way of a declaration in the prescribed form passed by the vote of a majority of eligible members at a meeting called for the purpose of considering
incorporation,[255] which declaration must be signed by the chair and secretary of the meeting and verified by affidavit by any officers of the congregation present at the meeting.[256] The certificate of incorporation must
be registered,[257] and the incorporation of the congregation takes effect on
the date mentioned in the certificate.[258]

Subsequent to incorporation, the majority of any properly constituted meeting is deemed to be the majority of the congregation.[259] An incorporated congregation has the power, by resolution passed at a meeting of
its members duly called for that purpose, to amend its constitution and
to make, amend, vary, and rescind bylaws regulating the conduct of its
officers and servants and providing for the management of its affairs.[260]
All such resolutions, bylaws, and amendments must be registered in
order to be of effect.[261]

A congregation incorporated under the Alberta Act may acquire real
and personal property by purchase or gift, or by devise or bequest made
at least six months before the death of the testator, and hold it for the
purposes of the congregation and alienate it at pleasure; may mortgage,
charge, or otherwise encumber land in any manner the congregation
determines;[262] and may change its name by resolution of a majority subject to the approval of the Registrar of Business Corporations.[263] Where a
congregation that vests property in trustees is subsequently incorporated, the trustees may transfer the property to the congregation,[264] and the
transfer must be registered and the land thereupon vested in the incorporated congregation.[265]

---

254 Section 11(1).
255 Section 11(2).
256 Section 11(3).
257 Section 12. See also s. 23.
258 Sections 13(1) and (2).
259 Section 13(3).
260 Section 15(1).
261 Sections 15(2), (3); and s. 16(1).
262 Sections 14(1) and (2). See also ss. 17 and 18.
263 Section 22.
264 Section 19(1).
265 Section 19(2).

An officer of a congregation who fails to present a list of members of the congregation for inspection at a properly constituted meeting or who fails to make any return required by the *Religious Societies' Land Act*, including returns required by the Minister charged with the administration of the *Business Corporations Act*;[266] by the regulations under the *Agricultural and Recreational Land Ownership Act*;[267] and by the federal *Citizenship Act*,[268] is guilty of an offence and liable to a fine of not more than fifty dollars.[269]

In Alberta, non-compliance with the statutory requirement[270] of execution under the corporate seal with attestation by signature of corporate officers and attachment of an affidavit of authorization renders an instrument dealing with the property of an incorporated congregation unenforceable. The requirements apply to the mortgaging of property of the congregation, but not to the mere borrowing of money secured by a promissory note.[271] Finally, the Alberta Act provides for the winding up of an unincorporated congregation pursuant to an order by a judge of the Court of Queen's Bench;[272] for the application of the *Business Corporations Act*[273] to inactive congregations;[274] and for the making of regulations by the Lieutenant Governor in Council.[275]

In British Columbia, successors to trustees who have taken a conveyance of land are to be appointed in the manner specified in the conveyance. Where no manner of appointment is specified, the society may appoint or elect successors at a regular annual congregational meeting or at any special meeting called in accordance with the *Trustee (Church Property) Act*.[276] The trustees so appointed or elected have the same powers, rights, and duties, and are subject to the same trusts, as the original trustees.[277]

---

266 S.A. 1981, c. B-15.

267 R.S.A. 1980, c. A-9.

268 R.S.C. 1985, c. C-29, s. 35.

269 Section 20. See also s. 21.

270 Section 18(1).

271 *Bank of Nova Scotia v. Ukrainian Greek Orthodox Community of Holy Trinity*, [1992] 1 W.W.R. 310 (Alta. Q.B.).

272 Section 24.

273 S.A. 1981, c. B-15.

274 Section 25.

275 Section 26.

276 Above note 232.

277 Section 1.

In Manitoba, a religious society may, at any annual or special meeting, as defined,[278] adopt a resolution appointing from its membership trustees to hold land for any of the purposes set out in the Act.[279] Each of the trustees holds office until he or she dies, resigns, ceases to be a member of the religious society, or is removed from office.[280] A trustee may be removed, and another appointed in his or her stead, by resolution at an annual or special meeting[281] passed by the majority of those persons present who are members of the religious society entitled to vote in respect of the business of the society.[282] Where the trustees have not been incorporated, each trustee so appointed, along with the trustees originally named in the conveyance or transfer, together have all the estate and powers vested in the original trustees.[283] Where a trustee ceases to hold office, the remaining trustees possess all the estate and powers vested in the whole number until the vacancy has been filled.[284] Successors have the same powers as the original trustees.[285]

The legislation in British Columbia and Manitoba requires trustees who sell, mortgage, or lease land to prepare for the first Monday in each July a detailed statement showing all rents that have accrued during the previous year, all sums of money derived from the lands under their management, and the application of any portion of those moneys expended on behalf of the religious society. Such statement is to be open for inspection by the congregation and any minister of it.[286]

In Saskatchewan, a religious society may, at any annual or special meeting, as defined,[287] adopt a resolution appointing trustees for the purpose of holding land in accordance with the provisions of the *Religious Societies Land Act*.[288] A trustee may be removed and another appointed in his or her stead by a majority vote of the members present at an annual or special

---

278 *Religious Societies' Land Act*, R.S.M. 1987, c. 70, s. 1(1).
279 Section 4.
280 Section 8.
281 Section 10(1).
282 Section 2(2).
283 Section 10(2). See also s. 6.
284 Section 9.
285 Sections 9 and 10(2).
286 British Columbia, s. 7; and Manitoba, s. 28.
287 *Religious Societies' Land Act*, R.S.S. 1978, c. R-19, s. 2(a).
288 Section 2.2.

meeting.[289] A trustee so appointed, together with the remaining trustees, possesses all the estate and powers of the original trustees.[290] Trustees who sell or lease land are required to have a statement of accounts ready and available for inspection each January at a meeting of the religious society.[291]

When it is no longer necessary to retain land held by trustees for the use of a religious society and it is considered advantageous to sell it, the trustees may put the land up for sale,[292] subject in Manitoba and Saskatchewan to the consent of the religious society or congregation.[293] In Alberta and Manitoba, the trustees require approval of the court prior to the execution of the agreement.[294] Trustees in each of the four Western provinces are required to provide the congregation or religious society with a statement of the transaction and an accounting of the proceeds of sale.[295]

The legislation in Alberta, Manitoba, and Saskatchewan provides that upon incorporation, property vested in trustees may be transferred to the newly created corporation.[296] With the consent of the corporation property may also be transferred to another society of the same denomination.[297] With congregational consent,[298] trustees may also lease property not otherwise required by the society[299] at any rent and on any terms considered desirable, for a term not exceeding twenty-one years,[300] and may covenant to renew a lease for a further term of up to twenty-one years.[301] Trustees are required to provide the congregation with an annual accounting of the proceeds and the disposition of the rents accrued.[302]

---

289 Section 2.3.
290 Section 2.4.
291 Section 12.
292 Alberta, ss. 7(1), (2); British Columbia, s. 6; Manitoba, s. 21; and Saskatchewan, s. 8.
293 Manitoba, s. 21; and Saskatchewan, s. 10.
294 Alberta, s. 7(3); and Manitoba, s. 22(1).
295 Alberta, s. 8; British Columbia, s. 7; Manitoba, s. 28; and Saskatchewan, s. 12.
296 Alberta, s. 19; Manitoba, s. 24; and Saskatchewan s. 14.
297 Alberta, s. 24; Manitoba, ss. 25, 26(1); and Saskatchewan, ss. 10, 14(1), 15.
298 Alberta, s. 5(2) (b); British Columbia, s. 5; Manitoba, s. 19(1); and Saskatchewan, s. 5(3).
299 Alberta, s. 5(2) (a); British Columbia, s. 5; Manitoba, s. 19(2); and Saskatchewan, s. 5(2).
300 Alberta, s. 5(1); British Columbia, s. 4; Manitoba, s. 17; and Saskatchewan, s. 5.
301 Alberta, s. 6; British Columbia, s. 4; Manitoba, s. 18(1); and Saskatchewan, s. 6.
302 Alberta, s. 8; British Columbia, s. 7; Manitoba, s. 28; and Saskatchewan, s. 12.

The legislation in British Columbia, Manitoba, and Saskatchewan specifically allows trustees, in their own names or by any name by which they hold land, to sue or distrain for rent and to take such means for its recovery as landlords are entitled to take.[303] Where a debt is contracted for the building, repairing, extending, or improving of a church, chapel, meeting house, residence for a minister, bookstore, printing or publishing office, or other building on land held by the trustees for the benefit of any religious society or congregation, or for the purchase of land on which the same has been or is intended to be erected, the trustees, or a majority of them, may secure the debt or any part thereof by a mortgage upon the land.[304]

3) Judicial Interpretation of Religious Institutions Legislation Generally

Once a religious institution has acquired legal personality either by incorporation or by quasi-incorporation pursuant to religious institutions legislation, it is endowed for all legal purposes with the characteristics of a corporate body, including the right to sue as such, without having to prove that it is an incorporated body prior to starting an action.[305] However, the rights of trustees to sue or be sued as a corporation depend on whether they are trustees or merely representatives of a congregation.[306] Where they are suing as trustees, they may do so in their corporate name only, without their individual names.[307] The nineteenth-century cases in which these principles were stated pre-date contemporary legal understandings of corporations and of trustees' duties; however, the underlying principles are clear and can be readily adapted to contemporary legal conceptions.

---

303 Alberta, s. 4; British Columbia, s. 3; and Saskatchewan, s. 4; see also Manitoba s. 16.

304 *Ainleyville Wesleyan Methodist Church Trustees v. Grewer*, above note 148; *Berkley Street Church Trustees v. Stevens*, above note 149; and *Wansley v. Brown*, above note 143.

305 *East Selkirk Greek Catholic Ruthenian Church*, above note 143.

306 *Humphreys v. Hunter*, above note 148; *Berkley Street Church Trustees v. Stevens*, above note 149; *Franklin Church Trustees v. Maguire*, above note 147; and *McGuire v. Evans*, above note 125.

307 *Humphreys v. Hunter*, above note 148; and *Ainleyville Wesleyan Methodist Church Trustees v. Grewer*, above note 148.

An individual member of a religious institution may sue, either in his or her own name alone or on behalf of him or herself and all other members, to prevent a breach of trust by the trustees, such as disposing of property in a manner inconsistent with congregational goals.[308] This action may not succeed, however, where the disposition is approved by a majority in a congregational polity.[309] Again, in a congregational polity, where a congregation is not incorporated and by a majority vote authorizes the execution of a building contract, individual members of the congregation may be personally liable under that contract, provided they voted in favour of it at the meeting.[310]

Trustees and their successors must hold land in trust for a religious institution in accordance with the terms of the trust deed or the provisions of the appropriate governing legislation, whether it be a private act or provincial legislation of general application to religious institutions.[311] Where its constitution so provides, a religious institution or individual congregation may deal with its property as it sees fit, so long as the procedures conform with the constitution, customs, or practices of the institution; in relation, for example, to notice of meetings,[312] voting requirements,[313] and the apportionment of sale proceeds between different parts of the organization.[314]

An exception to this requirement exists in relation to property held by the trustees for the use of a minister, and not for the religious body as a whole, which should be administered according to the terms of its own trust, rather than the provisions of general application to the religious institution itself.[315]

---

308 *Huegli v. Pauli*, above note 75.

309 *Ibid.*

310 *Rohl v. Pfaffenroth* (1915), 31 W.L.R. 197 (Alta. T.D.); and *McQuarrie v. Calnek* (1895), 27 N.S.R. 483 (C.A.).

311 *Brewster v. Hendershot* (1900), 27 O.A.R. 232 (C.A.); and *Huegli v. Pauli*, above note 75.

312 *Kopman v. Simonsky* (1903), 2 O.W.R. 617 (H.C.); and *Levinsky v. Hallett* (1904), 5 O.W.R. 1 (H.C.).

313 *Heine v. Schaffer*, above note 172.

314 *Swayne v. Synod of the Diocese of Ontario* (1920), 18 O.W.N. 390 (H.C.).

315 *Re Methodist Episcopal Church Property in Churchville* (1868), 1 Chy. Chrs. 305 (Ont.); and *Swayne v. Synod of the Diocese of Ontario*, above note 314.

Successor trustees must be appointed in accordance with the provisions for the appointment of trustees in the trust deed[316] or any applicable legislation,[317] and appointments made in accordance with a prior custom or practice are invalid.[318] Other legislation of general application is also ousted where specific religious institutions legislation provides for the method of appointment of trustees.[319] Where there is a trust deed but no provision in it for the appointment of successor trustees, new trustees should be appointed pursuant to provincial religious institutions legislation and subsequently endowed with the powers of the original trustees.[320] Where statutory requirements for the proper election of trustees are either not complied with[321] or, at least, not substantially complied with,[322] trustees may not subsequently be found to act validly.

Normally, trustees are granted discretion in the manner in which they carry out their duties and the courts have upheld their decisions made in good faith. Thus, where a trust deed empowered trustees to vary the disposition of moneys in a trust fund, they were permitted to do so.[323] However, where a trust deed made specific provision for how pews were to be let, the trustees were obliged to comply with those provisions.[324]

Trustees generally do not have authority to represent a religious institution on ecclesiastical matters, except to the extent that they are expressly empowered to do so.[325] Nor can they delegate their powers pursuant to provincial legislation to a congregational committee.[326] Trust property should be administered by trustees who hold the same religious

---

316 *Coleman v. Moore* (1879), 44 U.C.Q.B. 328 (C.A.).

317 *Ex parte Robinson* (1873), 14 N.B.R. 321 (S.C.); and *Leonard v. St. Patrick's Parish*, [1922] 1 W.W.R. 601 (Alta. C.A.).

318 *Ex parte Robinson*, ibid.

319 *Re Hamilton Lutheran Church* (1915), 34 O.L.R. 228 (H.C.).

320 *Ibid.*

321 *Levinsky v. Hallett*, above note 312.

322 *Schmunk v. Brook*, above note 155.

323 *Dobie v. Presbyterian Temporalities Board* (1882), 7 App. Cas. 136 (P.C.); and *Wright v. Incorporated Synod of the Diocese of Huron*, above note 94.

324 *Carleton Place Methodist Church Trustees v. Keyes*, above note 165; and *Gold v. Moldaver* (1912), 6 D.L.R. 333 (Ont. H.C.).

325 *Ukrainian Greek Orthodox Church v. Ukrainian Greek Orthodox Cathedral of St. Mary the Protectress*, above note 55.

326 *Irving v. McLachlan* (1856), 5 Gr. 625 (Ch.).

beliefs and opinions as those for whose benefit the trust was intended;[327] however, in practice they need not all be members of the religious institution. Many denominations permit a minority of adherents, rather than members, to sit on trustee boards.

4) Owning Property

Religious institutions frequently come into ownership of real property as a result of bequests or gifts made by deceased, former, or present members or supporters, as well as by the usual means of purchase. Where property is bequeathed to or purchased by a religious institution, it is to be used for the purpose for which it was given or acquired. Thus, a trust established for the benefit of a named congregation, for example, should be devoted to the interests of that congregation.[328] Where a permit is given to cut timber for the purpose of constructing a church for a particular denomination on government land, it may not subsequently be vested in the ecclesiastical authorities of another denomination for the purpose of constructing a church for that other denomination.[329] Again, where property is purchased by a congregation of a particular denomination, it is a fraud to attempt to convey it to one of their members in trust for a congregation of another denomination.[330]

Where a parish is enlarged and then subsequently divided and renamed, the parish corresponding theoretically to the original parish is entitled to the benefits of a trust established for the original parish.[331]

Provincial religious institutions legislation typically required that land granted to trustees for religious purposes be registered, and it was said in a mid nineteenth-century case that failure to comply with that statutory requirement of registration of a deed resulted in a failure to pass title and that an action for ejectment depending on such putative title failed.[332]

Religious institutions typically use real property for places of worship, for residences for clergy, or for graveyards; some congregations have also historically enjoyed the use of glebes. Land conveyed for such pur-

---

327 *Brewster v. Hendershot,* above note 311.

328 *Re Armstrong* (1969), 7 D.L.R. (3d) 36 (N.S.T.D.) See also *Re Mountain,* [1912] 4 D.L.R. 737 (Ont. C.A.).

329 *Zacklynski v. Polushie,* [1908] A.C. 65 (P.C.).

330 *Ruthenian Greek Catholic Church v. Fetsyk,* [1922] 3 W.W.R. 872 (Man. K.B.).

331 *St. Stephen's Parish v. St. Edward's Parish* (1912), 2 D.L.R. 594 (S.C.C.).

332 *Doe d. Bowman v. Cameron* (1847), 4 U.C.Q.B. 155.

poses is usually understood to belong to the congregation. Where land is conveyed to the trustees of an association for the purpose of establishing a congregation and erecting a building for worship and for other congregational purposes, the congregation rather than the originating association is understood to be the beneficiary of the trust once the building has been erected.[333]

Once land has been conveyed and title has passed to the religious institution, neither the original grantor nor his or her heirs-at-law have any claim as to the subsequent use of that land. Thus, where land was originally conveyed for the sole purpose of building a church or a school and completely divested by the grantor, it can be subsequently sold, and the grantor's heirs-at-law have no claim.[334] Where land is conveyed to the incumbent of a church and his or her successors, rather than to the trustees for the purpose of building a church, an action need not be brought by a successor to compel the original incumbent to reconvey the property, since a conveyance to successors is sufficient.[335]

A bequest providing for a residence for the clergy of a particular congregation may lapse when that congregation ceases to exist because the devise is specific and without a general charitable intention, so that the fund should be divided among the residuary legatees.[336]

Where a testator provides land for a burial ground for a particular denomination on the condition that the land not be subsequently alienated to another denomination, the congregation in which title is vested may not alienate it for use as a burial ground by another denomination. Rather, since the title could not be conferred on another denomination, it reverted to the heirs of the grantor, although those in the congregation continuing in the original denomination are entitled to use the burial ground.[337] Again, property purchased by a congregation of a particular denomination on condition that it be used solely as a burial ground for that denomination is available for use by members of that denomination only, even where the majority of the congregation subsequently unites with another denomination.[338]

---

333 *Melnychuk v. Susko*, [1954] 2 D.L.R. 218 (Ont. C.A.).
334 *Moser v. Barss*, [1947] 4 D.L.R. 313 (N.S.T.D.).
335 *Sanson v. Mitchell* (1858), 6 Gr. 582 (Ch.).
336 *Re McMillan Estate* (1917), 11 O.W.N. 443 (H.C.).
337 *Douglas v. Hawes* (1875), R.E.D. 147 (N.S.T.D.).
338 *Attorney-General v. Christie* (1867), 13 Gr. 495 (Ch.).

Historically, churches thought to be established or actually established have enjoyed glebe lands, which have been the source of some litigation. Where a Crown grant of land was made to trustees "in trust to hold the same to and for a glebe for the use and benefit of the ministers and congregations of the established Church of England in the Town of Chatham," and there were two such congregations, it was held that both were entitled to share equally in the glebe lands and revenues; that the ministers and congregations of each were to be treated as a single entity; and that payment was to be made to the rector and churchwardens with apportionment between minister and congregation to be determined by each congregation. Where there was more than one minister attached to each congregation, the minister's share for that congregation was to be divided equally between or among them.[339] Where land has been granted as a glebe to a church corporation, the rector is the proper person to maintain an action for trespass in respect to it.[340]

5) Selling Property

By most trust deeds and provincial religious institutions legislation, the power of sale of church property is vested in trustees, subject to such congregational or denominational internal constitutional requirements as are in place. Normally, both institutional and trustee approvals are required; thus, where a committee of a congregation purported to sell church lands without the sanction of the trustees, the sale was held to be invalid.[341] Occasionally, land may be held by the trustees for the use of the minister or of some specific body within a religious institution. Where land was so held, by trustees, for the use of the minister of the congregation, and not for the use of the congregation itself, its sale may not be sustained by a court without the authority of the minister.[342]

When a congregation has decided to sell property, its trustees must ensure compliance with the requirements of the applicable provincial legislation, including the requirements for proper public notice by adver-

---

339 *Re Chatham Glebe Trust* (1915), 22 D.L.R. 798 (Ont. H.C.).
340 *St. Stephen's Church v. Tortelot* (1842), 3 N.B.R. 537 (C.A.). See also above section E(1)(a).
341 *Irving v. McLachlan*, above note 326.
342 *Re Methodist Episcopal Church Property in Churchville*, above note 315.

tisement of the sale,[343] fulfilment of the requirements for a private sale,[344] and court sanction.[345] A court may also confirm a sale where eighty percent of a congregation voted to approve the sale of land and this constituted substantial compliance with the applicable provincial legislation.[346] Generally speaking, a court will not intervene in what are regarded essentially as the private affairs of a congregation, where the congregation by majority vote and in accordance with its own constitution and the law of the province approves a sale of church land.[347]

Finally, where the land that is sold was originally part of the clergy reserves and located partly in a town and partly in an adjoining township, the proceeds of the distribution should be divided equally among all the incumbents of congregations in both town and township.[348]

6) Leasing Property

Religious institutions, historically, have leased interests in land that are ecclesiastical in nature such as pews or glebe lands as well as, more recently, excess land or air rights to commercial lessors for largely commercial purposes. An early question posed for courts in those colonies that subsequently formed provinces of Canada in which there was or was asserted to be an Anglican establishment was whether English ecclesiastical legislation relating to the lease of church property that predated the reception date for the jurisdiction in question remained in effect. Thus, in *Bedell v. Christ's Church, Fredericton*,[349] the question of whether the *Ecclesiastical Leases Act, 1571*,[350] was still in force was answered negative-

---

343 *Re Second Congregational Church Property, Toronto* (1868), 1 Chy. Chrs. 349 (Ont. H.C.); *Re Stratford Baptist Church Property* (1869), 2 Chy. Chrs. 388 (Ont. H.C.); *Cummins v. Congregational Church Trustees*, above note 154; and *Levinsky v. Hallett*, above note 312.

344 *Harder v. Lindgren*, [1950] 1 W.W.R. 833 (Alta. T.D.).

345 *Wansley v. Brown*, above note 143; and *Re Methodist Church, Manitou* (1892), 8 Man. R. 136 (Q.B.).

346 *Kowalchuk v. Ukrainian Greek Orthodox Church*, [1946] 3 W.W.R. 538 (Sask. C.A.).

347 *Heine v. Schaffer*, above note 172. See also below section L.

348 *Incorporated Synod of the Diocese of Toronto v. Lewis* (1887), 13 O.R. 738 (H.C.); and *Synod of Huron v. Smith* (1887), 13 O.R. 755n (H.C.).

349 (1856), 8 N.B.R. 217 (S.C.).

350 (Eng.) 13 Eliz. I, c. 10 (1571).

ly because subsequent provincial legislation had expressly overtaken it. Presumably, however, the usual rule of reception of the common law would otherwise apply.

A lease of glebe lands by the rector of an Anglican parish is binding upon that rector only during his or her incumbency; at the end of the incumbency, the freehold reverts to the corporation, in which title had remained, which has a right to bring an action for injury to the reversion.[351] A new rector may dispute a leasehold given by a predecessor, and may recover a judgment in ejectment against the lessees.[352] A rector has no power in making a lease to bind successors to pay for improvements, or to enter into any other arrangements that have the effect of extending the lease beyond its original term.[353]

In *Re Incorporated Synod of the Diocese of Toronto and H.E.C. Hotels Ltd.*,[354] the Ontario Court of Appeal held that an incorporated religious institution with unlimited statutory powers to lease property is not subject to any restrictions on leasing contained in provincial legislation of general application. However, while non-profit religious institutions are generally exempted by provincial human rights legislation from certain statutory prohibitions on the basis of religious or theological reasons, in *Association A.D.G.Q.* v. *Montreal Catholic School Board*,[355] the Quebec Superior Court found that there may be laws of general application limiting, on grounds of discrimination, the powers of religious institutions in leasing property. The court found that a Roman Catholic school board was not entitled to refuse to rent space to a homosexual group because it had never reserved the right to control the nature of discussions in the building, although it is well-known that the Roman Catholic Church teaches that homosexual activity is sinful.

At one time, when churches funded on a voluntary basis raised funds from leasing sittings, disputes about the lease of church pews or sittings occasionally erupted into the courts. In an early case, the New Brunswick Court of Appeal decided that, although it was unclear in law whether a right to a pew is an incorporeal hereditament, an interest in a pew is an

---

351 *St. Paul's Church* v. *Titus* (1849), 6 N.B.R. 278 (C.A.).

352 *Shaw* v. *Phoenix Insurance Co.* (1869), 20 U.C.C.P. 170 (H.C.).

353 *Lyster* v. *Kirkpatrick*, above note 46.

354 Above note 177.

355 (1979), 112 D.L.R. (3d) 230 (Que. S.C.).

usufructuary right for which an action in contract may lie.[356] A right in a pew exists only as long as the building in which the pew is situated exists, so that a pewholder's rights are not revived in nor are they transferable to a new building.[357]

An interest in a pew can only be transmitted to another member of the congregation.[358] Where the bylaws of a congregation provide that seats in the place of worship are to be sold only to members at regular or special congregational meetings called for that purpose, the existing pewholders have no right to restrain such a sale by injunction.[359]

Finally, where trustees have the power to lease pews and seats but do not do so, so that all pews are free, any vacant seat might be occupied by any member of the congregation, although ushers might indicate where members should sit in the interests of an undisrupted service of worship.[360]

7. Borrowing Powers

Most trust deeds and provincial religious institutions legislation of general application grant to trustees the power to borrow against the security of a mortgage on church property, subject to internal approval procedures that differ from institution to institution. Where those church authorities who are legally empowered to do so borrow funds and all the requisite formalities have been satisfied, then the resulting mortgage is valid and enforceable against the body corporate.[361] Conversely, where they are not, the mortgage may be personally enforceable against the church authority that executed it; thus, where a Roman Catholic bishop was not permitted by an incorporating act to charge church property for a loan, although the money was borrowed for church purposes, it was not recoverable from the corporation sole, rather from the bishop personally.[362]

---

356 *St. Andrew's Church Trustees v. Ferguson* (1868), 12 N.B.R. 273 (C.A.). *Cf. Ridout v. Harris* (1866), 17 U.C.C.P. 88 (C.A.).

357 *Brunskill v. Harris* (1854), 1 E. & A. 322 (U.C.C.P.).

358 *Ridout v. Harris*, above note 356.

359 *Gold v. Moldaver* (1912), 6 D.L.R. 333 (Ont. H.C.).

360 *Carleton Place Methodist Church Trustees v. Keyes*, above note 165.

361 *Re St. John's Church*, [1927] 3 D.L.R. 535 (Ont. H.C.).

362 *Ruitz v. Sandwich Roman Catholic Episcopal Corp.*, above note 126.

In *Bank of Nova Scotia* v. *Ukrainian Greek Orthodox Congregation of Holy Trinity*,[363] the church officers did not get the special resolution at a general meeting as required by the incorporation document, nor did they inform the bank of the requirement when they mortgaged church land to raise money. The court gave judgment for the bank by simple application of the indoor management rule;[364] moreover, the court further found that although the applicable provincial religious institutions legislation rendered the mortgage on church land unenforceable, it did not have that same effect on the promissory note, although given in conjunction with a mortgage, and therefore enforced the note. The burden of proof is on those asserting that a special resolution to borrow was not passed by the requisite majority.[365]

The principle that religious institutions may still be liable to repay a loan where internal procedures have not been followed, provided the lender has no actual or constructive knowledge, has been applied in several cases. Thus, one lender was found to have a lien on the church property for money advanced against congregational property even where the mortgage was executed by persons without the authority to do so.[366] Again, where the necessary episcopal approval for borrowing was not obtained, the agreement to repay was found to bind the parish in question.[367] On the other hand, it remains the case that where trustees have acted properly in executing a mortgage on behalf of a congregation, they are not personally liable on it.[368]

Finally, trustees may also be empowered to give chattel mortgages on the personal property of a congregation pursuant either to a trust deed or provincial religious institutions legislation.[369]

---

363 Above note 164.

364 *Royal British Bank* v. *Turquand* (1856), 6 El. & Bl. 327, 119 E.R. 886.

365 *Gill* v. *Khalsa Diwan Society*, unreported decision of 17 May 1999, Doc. Vancouver A991007 (B.C.S.C.), additional reasons of 16 June 1999, Doc. Vancouver A991007 (B.C.S.C.).

366 *Glavasky* v. *Stadnick*, [1937] 1 D.L.R. 473 (Ont. C.A.).

367 *Leonard* v. *St. Patrick's Parish*, above note 128.

368 *Beaty* v. *Gregory*, above note 144. See also for transfer of liability to a third party *Kershner* v. *Convention of Baptist Churches*, [1930] 4 D.L.R. 135 (C.A.).

369 *Brown* v. *Sweet* (1882), 7 O.A.R. 725.

G. CHANGES IN CONSTITUTIONS

Typically, the constitutions of religious institutions provide for procedures whereby they may be changed, either internally or by amendment to private legislation. Only two reported cases deal with such matters and these emphasize the importance of fairness and formality when making constitutional changes. Where the constitution of a religious institution permits alternatives to be made by a designated body of persons, that body must proceed with caution and deliberation as well as with formal correctness, and the original constitution must be upheld where changes cause excessive dissension.[370] Where the Lieutenant Governor in Council has authority to cancel the incorporation of a congregation for cause, then prior to cancellation, due notice and an opportunity to appear should be given, and a fair and impartial inquiry should be held.[371]

H. TAXATION

1) Municipal Taxation

Religious institutions are exempted by legislation in each province from liability to pay property taxes on real property used for religious purposes. Religious purposes extend to property used as a place of worship as well as property used for churchyards, graveyards, schools, colleges, seminaries, or other places where religion is included in teaching, as well as property used for charitable or philanthropic purposes associated with the religious institution asserting the exemption. Property leased by religious institutions to other persons not using that land for religious purposes as well as property leased to a religious institution for non-religious purposes is typically subject to municipal taxation. Provincial legislation in relation to municipal taxation is beyond the scope of the present volume and the provisions relating to religious exemptions are too various; therefore, it is necessary to consult the applicable legislation directly to ascertain how the religious exemption applies from province to

---

370 *Doe d. Methodist Episcopal Church (Kingston) v. Bell* (1837), 5 O.S. 344 (U.C.Q.B.).

371 *Greek Catholic Church of St. Mary's v. McKinnon* (1916), 28 D.L.R. 509 (Alta. T.D.).

province.[372] Nevertheless, judicial interpretation of provincial municipal taxation legislation suggests that certain approaches to and principles for the interpretation of this legislation are apparent in the case law.[373]

The exemption is to be strictly construed so as to apply to buildings and grounds used for the immediate ends and purposes of the religious institution; thus, a manse built on land entirely separate and apparent from the church building for a Presbyterian minister and vested in the congregational trustees was not exempt.[374] Nor is land exempt that is owned by a church but leased to a non-profit corporation that uses it for both charitable and commercial purposes.[375] An exemption from municipal taxation will also be denied where a religious order establishes a separate charitable corporation to hold land for a retirement home where the tenants either paid their own way or were subsidized by the government.[376] The onus of showing that the land in question is statutorily exempt is on the person claiming the exemption,[377] but an exemption

---

372 The main pieces of provincial legislation follow. These are frequently amended, so readers must thoroughly update the relevant legislation for their jurisdictions: *Municipal Taxation Act*, R.S.A. 1980, c. M-31; *Municipal Act*, R.S.B.C. 1996, c. 323; *Vancouver Charter*, S.B.C. 1953, c. 55 (1st Sess.); *Municipal Assessment Act*, S.M. 1989–90, c. 24; *Assessment Act*, R.S.N.B. 1973, c. A-14; *Assessment Act*, R.S.N. 1990, c. A-18; *Assessment Act*, R.S.N.S. 1989, c. 23; *Assessment Act*, R.S.O. 1990, c. A-31; *Provincial Land Tax Act*, R.S.O., c. P. 32; *Municipalities Act*, R.S. P.E.I. 1988, c. M-13; *Northern Municipalities Act*, S.S. 1983, c. N-5.1; *Rural Municipality Act*, S.S. 1989–90 c. R-261; and *Urban Municipality Act*, S.S. 1983–84, c. U-11. See also *I.V.C.F. v. Muskoka Assessment Commissioner* (1979), 23 O.R. (2d) 589 (H.C.).

373 The statements of law that follow must all be understood to be based on the express legislation judicially considered; nevertheless, general principles may be seen.

374 *Re Melville Presbyterian Church*, [1926] 4 D.L.R. 1149 (Ont. H.C.); and *First Place, Hamilton v. City of Hamilton* (1979), 9 M.P.L.R. 119 (Ont. H.C.). See also *City of Victoria v. Trustees of the Church of Our Lord*, [1915] 25 D.L.R. 617 (B.C.S.C.).

375 *First Place, Hamilton v. City of Hamilton*, ibid.

376 *Religious Hospitallers of St. Joseph of Cornwall v. Ontario Regional Assessment Commissioner, Region 1* (1998), 168 D.L.R. (4th) 132 (Ont. C.A.).

377 *Montreal v. Corp. du College Ste-Marie*, [1921] A.C. 288 (P.C.) per Duff J.; *Ruthenian Catholic Mission v. Mundare School District*, [1924] S.C.R. 620; *City of London v. Ursuline Religious of the Diocese of London* (1964), 43 D.L.R. (2d) 220 (Ont. C.A.); and *Singh v. City of Sudbury* (1975), 8 O.R. (2d) 377 (Dist. Ct.).

that is clearly provided for is not to be taken away except by clear words.[378] Thus, where a building that is still suitable for use as a religious institution stands vacant while awaiting sale, it remains a church edifice owned by a religious institution within the legislation, and exempt from taxation.[379] But a building previously used as a church and subsequently purchased for use as a mosque is not exempt where the building is not used as a place of worship and there are no plans to use it as a place of worship.[380] A room set aside for worship within a private home may be a place of worship within municipal tax exemption provisions provided the individual worshippers come from different places and might be personally unknown to one another.[381]

Whether or not property falls within the exemption in relation to buildings used for worship may be dependent on the wording of the provincial legislation being judicially considered. Thus, in an older Ontario case, the exemption was extended to all the parts of buildings owned by a religious order open to the public for worship, such as the chapel, but did not extend to those parts, such as the cloister, which were not open to the public and thereby could not be, in the view of the court, a place of worship.[382] On the other hand, in a more recent Alberta case, the court found that a monastic cloister was exempt from municipal taxation because cloistered cells were places of prayer or spiritual reading. Moreover, the court also found that ancillary facilities, including kitchen and dining facilities, were also exempt where the cloister was a place of retreat for visitors, so that an exemption is not lost simply because part of the building was used for ancillary purposes.[383]

Again, in Ontario, a caretaker's flat, where the caretaker's presence was necessary for the efficient operation of a place of worship, has been found

---

378 *Presbyterian Church Building Corp.* v. *Algoma Assessment Commissioner*, [1973] 3 O.R. 1007 (Dist. Ct.).

379 *Ibid.*

380 *Hussain* v. *Director of Assessment (N.S.)* (1995), 148 N.S.R. (2d) 100, 429 A.P.R. 100 (S.C.).

381 *Singh* v. *City of Sudbury*, above note 377. See also *Church of Jesus Christ of Latter Day Saints* v. *Henning*, [1963] 2 All E.R. 733 (H.L.); and *Ex parte Segerdal*, [1970] 3 All E.R. 886 (C.A.).

382 *Soeurs de la visitation d'Ottawa* v. *City of Ottawa*, [1952] 2 D.L.R. 343 (Ont. H.C.), aff'd [1952] 3 D.L.R. 640 (C.A.).

383 *Carmelite Nuns of Western Canada* v. *Alberta (Assessment Appeal Board)* (1994), 21 Alta. L.R. (3d) 382 (Q.B.).

to be within the exemption,[384] whereas in Alberta, a caretaker's residence was found not to be exempt.[385] But the exemption does not extend to lands appurtenent to a place of worship used as a manse or parsonage.[386]

The use of property that is exempt from liability for municipal taxation for other ancillary uses will not necessarily deprive the property of its religious exemption. In the *Carmelite Nuns*[387] case, the kitchen and dining room facilities ancillary to the cloisters were found to be within the exemption as ancillary to the religious purpose of providing a retreat location. Again, the occasional rental of small portions of a Salvation Army campsite to members and others using it for a spiritual purpose was also found not to defeat the exemption granted on the basis that the property was primarily a non-profit summer church camp.[388] However, where a religious order rents out part of a building otherwise used for the charitable purposes of the order, and there is no evidence that the rented premises are used for charitable purposes, the rented portions are not exempt from taxation.[389] The test would appear to be that so long as the property is *bona fide* used for religious purposes, it does not matter that the whole property is not used or not used constantly for those purposes.[390]

Where a municipality installs improvements along land abutting church lands, the religious institution will be exempt from liability to pay for them unless the legislation clearly imposes an obligation on a religious institution to pay for the improvements.[391]

---

384 *Centenery United Church (Trustees)* v. *Ontario Regional Assessment Commissioner, Region No. 19* (1979), 27 O.R. (2d) 790 (Co. Ct.).

385 *Carmelite Nuns of Western Canada* v. *Alberta (Assessment Appeal Board)*, above note 383.

386 *Re Melville Presbyterian Church*, above note 374; and *St. Mary's Anglican Church* v. *Windsor Assessment Commissioners*, [1942] O.W.N. 102 (C.A.).

387 Above note 383.

388 *Salvation Army, Canada East* v. *Ontario Regional Assessment Commissioner, Region No. 14* (1984), 45 O.R. (2d) 263 (H.C.).

389 *Religious Hospitallers of St. Joseph of Cornwall* v. *Ontario Regional Assessment Commissioner, Region 1* (1998), 168 D.L.R. (4th) 132 (Ont. C.A.). For recovery of interest or overpayments, see at 148.

390 *Salvation Army, Canada East* v. *Ontario Regional Assessment Region No. 22* (1983), 21 M.P.L.R. 99 (Ont. H.C.). See also *National Ballet School* v. *Assessment Commissioner for Region 9* (1979), 25 O.R. (2d) 50 (H.C.).

391 *Baptist Convention of Ontario and Quebec* v. *City of Kanata* (1985), 51 O.R. (2d) 400 (H.C.).

A cemetery associated with a place of worship will enjoy the municipal tax exemption provided it is maintained as a cemetery, although it is no longer actually used for interments.[392] The exemption has also been extended to cemetery land used for ornamental purposes and not intended as the site of interments[393] as well as to cemetery land on which are situated houses for the superintendent or gardeners, greenhouses, hot beds, and cold frames, since these are all necessary for the proper operation of the cemetery.[394] The exemption has been further extended to cemetery land on which was built a funeral home and crematorium since these are incidental to the integrated operation of a cemetery.[395]

The meaning of the phrase a "seminary for learning for religious purposes," which is found in successive *Ontario Assessment Acts*, has yielded a significant volume of cases in which its meaning and application have been considered. The courts have largely concluded that in relation to municipal taxation legislation, "seminary" has no clear and fixed legal meaning, but simply bears its primary meaning of a place of learning.[396] The issue, then, is defining which educational institutions can claim the exemption on the grounds of being a seminary.

"Seminary" for the purpose of exemption from municipal taxation has been found to include the following: lands and buildings owned by a non-profit corporation used only as a summer camp to teach the principles of Orthodox Judaism;[397] a seminary operated by the Roman Catholic Christian Brothers where students received both academic and religious instruction with a view to becoming teachers;[398] a building

---

392 *Roman Catholic Episcopal Corp. of Sault Ste. Marie v. Town of Sault Ste. Marie* (1911), 24 O.L.R. 35 (H.C.); and *Scarborough Township v. Scarborough Lawn Cemetery Co.*, [1945] 4 D.L.R. 577 (Ont. C.A.).

393 *Memory Gardens Ltd. v. Township of Waterloo*, [1955] O.W.N. 424 (H.C.).

394 *Toronto General Burying Grounds v. Scarborough Township*, [1959] O.R. 514 (H.C.).

395 *Burnaby/New Westminster Assessor, Area No. 10 v. SCI Canada Ltd.* (2000), 73 B.C.L.R. 17 (B.C.C.A.).

396 *Worldwide Evangelization Crusade (Canada) v. Village of Beamsville*, [1960] S.C.R. 49. Again, the property need only be substantially dedicated to this purpose; *County of Kings v. International Christian Mission Inc.* (1962), 34 D.L.R. (2d) 428 (N.S.S.C.).

397 *Mizrachi Organization of Canada v. Township of Ennismore*, [1973] 1 O.R. 465 (H.C.). See also *Agudath Israel of Toronto v. Town of Orillia*, [1962] O.R. 305 (C.A.).

398 *Christian Brothers of Ireland in Canada v. Wellington and Dufferin Assessment Commissioners*, [1969] 2 O.R. 374 (H.C.).

owned by a Ukrainian ethnic organization, where university students were housed and taught Ukrainian language, history, and religion;[399] an evangelical missionary training centre;[400] a building where a non-profit Roman Catholic corporation held retreats for Roman Catholic families to teach them how to fulfil a family vocation within the Roman Catholic Church;[401] and a Free Methodist campground, the purpose of which was to combine recreation with religious and spiritual activities and at which lots for camping vehicles were leased.[402] Where a Roman Catholic non-profit corporation owned property, only part of which was used for retreats, it was held that only that part was exempt from assessment.[403]

On the other hand, the following have been found not to be seminaries for the purpose of exemption from municipal taxation: a church-owned residence for university students that had no defined religious purpose;[404] a church-run institution that provided lectures to people with addictions;[405] a church-run college providing courses for which credit was given for a degree from another university;[406] a summer camp run by a non-profit religious organization but not dedicated to religious activities and run in competition with secular summer camps;[407] and two farms from which a religious organization published educational materials and containing a printing-shop and administration building.[408] Where Roman Catholic sisters of a seminary of learning rented some of their rooms to

399 *St. Vladimir Ukrainian Institute v. City of Toronto* (1966), 57 D.L.R. (2d) 97 (Ont. H.C.), aff'd (1966), 58 D.L.R. (2d) 485n (Ont. C.A.).

400 *Worldwide Evangelization Crusade (Canada) v. Village of Beamsville*, above note 396.

401 *Nazareth Catholic Family Life Centre of Combermere v. Renfrew Regional Assessment Commissioner* (1987), 35 M.P.L.R. 77 (Ont. H.C.).

402 *Camp Grounds Association of Canada-Great Lakes Conference of Free Methodist Church v. Township of Zorra* (1988), 38 M.P.L.R. (Ont. Dist. Ct.).

403 *Augustinian Fathers (Ontario) Inc. v. Ontario Regional Assessment Commissioner Region No. 14* (1985), 52 O.R. (2d) 536 (H.C.).

404 *Westminster College v. City of London* (1963), 38 D.L.R. (2d) 397 (Ont. H.C.). Cf. *Ottawa Y.M.C.A. v. City of Ottawa* (1913), 29 O.L.R. 574 (Ont. A.D.).

405 *Emmanuel Convalescent Foundation v. Township of Whitchurch*, [1967] 2 O.R. 487 (H.C.), aff'd [1967] 2 O.R. 676 (C.A.).

406 *City of London v. Ursuline Religious of the Diocese of London*, above note 377.

407 *I.V.C.F. v. Muskoka Assessment Commissioner*, above note 372.

408 *International Bible Students Association of Canada v. Town of Halton Hills* (1986), 32 D.L.R. (4th) 140 (Ont. Div. Ct.).

persons other than students at the seminary, the entire building was held to be subject to municipal taxation even though the income from renting the rooms was applied to the purposes of the seminary.[409]

Finally, the courts have proven willing to expand the concept of "seminary" from a fixed educational site at which instruction is given to electronic education. In *Canadian Sunday School Mission v. Winnipeg (City), Assessor*,[410] religious organization premises where religious educational materials were prepared and then transmitted through the Internet were granted exemption from municipal taxation.

The impact of the *Canadian Charter of Rights and Freedoms* on assessment legislation was considered in *Girgenti v. Ontario Regional Assessment Commissioner for Region 12*,[411] in relation to premises rented by a small Evangelical group and used as a place of worship and for the purpose of conducting religious education classes. The trial judge found that the premises were not primarily used as a seminary but rather as a place of worship, and were therefore not exempt from municipal taxation as a seminary. Since the exemption was only available to places of worship that are owned rather than rented, the plaintiff challenged this statutory distinction as an infringement of section 2(a) and section 15(1) of the *Charter*. Both challenges failed. The court found that the denial of the exemption did not interfere with freedom of belief and practice under section 2(a), while there was no unequal treatment under section 15(1) because the additional burden of having to pay municipal taxes imposed on those who rent rather than own flows from the lease not a statute or the government.

Finally, the exemption from municipal taxes enjoyed by schools might also have a religious dimension when the schools are religious schools. Generally, all schools are exempted by provincial legislation from the payment of municipal taxes. Thus, schools and universities that are denominationally owned or religious in essential nature, may claim exemption from municipal taxation on the alternative ground of being an educational institution.[412] However, where the purpose of the institution is not primarily educational, its religious affiliation will not save it from

---

409 *Sisters of Notre Dame v. City of Ottawa* (1912), 1 D.L.R. 329 (Ont. C.A.); *cf.* *City of Ottawa v. Grey Nuns* (1913), 15 D.L.R. 725 (Ont. C.A.).
410 (1998), 156 D.L.R. (4th) 654 (Man. C.A.).
411 (1993), 100 D.L.R. (4th) 488 (Ont. Gen. Div.).
412 *St. Andrew's College v. York Assessment Commissioner*, [1971] 3 O.R. 91 (H.C.).

assessment, except where it satisfies the statutory requirements for exemption on religious grounds.[413]

2) Income Tax

For a religious institution and its financial supporters to enjoy the tax exemptions set out in the *Income Tax Act*,[414] it is necessary for the religious institution to register as a charity pursuant to the Act.[415] With registration, the institution is exempt from the payment of income tax in Canada,[416] certain of its clergy and other employees may be entitled to tax deductions relating to their terms of employment,[417] and financial supporters may be entitled to tax deductions for some portion of their financial contributions to the religious institution.[418] Once registered, the religious institution is required to fulfil all the requirements of the Act, such as making returns[419] and keeping records,[420] if it is to maintain charitable registration, which may be revoked at any time.[421] The technical details as to the requirements for registration, record-keeping, and claiming are exceptionally complex and beyond the bounds of this volume.[422] The discussion that follows is limited to those provisions that have resulted in litigation and are, therefore, of considerable controversy today.

---

413 *Evangelical Lutheran Synod of Missouri, Ohio* v. *City of Edmonton*, [1934] S.C.R. 280; *Trinity College* v. *City of Toronto*, [1968] 2 O.R. 24 (H.C.); and *City of London* v. *Ursuline Religious of the Diocese of London*, above note 377.

414 For detailed discussions of income tax legislation, textbooks on tax law ought to be consulted.

415 R.S.C. 1985, c. 1 (5th Supp.); ss. 149.1(1) "charitable organization," 248(1) "registered charity." The Act is so frequently amended that it must be consulted annually, so this section will only briefly overview its requirements.

416 Section 149.1 [am. 1994, c. 7, Sched. II, s. 123; c. 21, s. 74].

417 Sections 6(1)(b)(vi) and 8(1)(c).

418 Section 110.

419 Section 149.1(4).

420 Section 230(2) [re-en. 1994, c. 21, s. 105].

421 Sections 149.1 and 168.

422 See various papers in the conference proceedings cited above note 133. For discussions of current policy issues, see Phillips, Chapman, and Stevens, above note 19; and Patrick J. Monahan and Elie S. Roch, *Federal Regulation of Charities: A Critical Assessment of Recent Proposals For Legislation and Regulatory Reform* (Toronto: York University, 2000).

423 See Phillips, above note 19.

The question of what is a charitable organization is very controversial and while some would argue that religious organizations should not be so categorized in law,[423] it is clear that most religious institutions such as churches, synagogues, mosques, and temples and closely related institutions such as schools, colleges, and eleemosynary organizations normally qualify for registration.[424] The exercise of ministerial discretion to deregister charities that promote views said to be religiously based has recently been considered. However, the Minister should not do so simply at the request of a disgruntled member of a religious organization; in *Reed v. R.*[425] a "disfellowshipped" former member of the Jehovah's Witnesses who objected to the secrecy of its internal disciplinary tribunals and who also wished to question its financing dealings, failed in an attempt to use legal proceedings to procure a court order to the Minister to revoke the sect's charitable status, the court regarding this action as wrongly conceived in law.

Deregistration by the Minister on the ground that a charity is substantially involved in political activity[426] has been upheld by appellate courts in two decisions. In neither case did the taxpayer expressly invoke religion in support of its right to charitable status although it was clear that religious beliefs lay behind the charity's work. In *Human Life International in Canada Inc. v. M.N.R.*,[427] the charity's goals were to promote its views about abortion, natural family planning, chastity, Christian family values, and euthanasia. The Federal Court of Appeal upheld the deregistration as a charity. Since "charity" is not defined in the *Income Tax Act*, the court used the definition found in *Commissioners of Income Tax v. Pemsel*;[428] that is, activities to include the relief of poverty, the advancement of education, the advancement of religion, and other purposes beneficial to the community. The group's activities did not advance education because they were neither directed toward formal training of the mind nor improved a useful branch of human knowledge. Nor were the group's activities beneficial to the community because they were devoted to

---

424 Sections 149, 168, and 180.
425 (1989), 41 C.R.R. 371 (Fed. T.D.), aff'd (1990), 2 C.R.R. (2d) 192 (Fed. A.D.), leave to appeal to S.C.C. refused (1990), 4 C.R.R. (2d) 192 (S.C.C.).
426 Sections 149.1(1), (6.2), 168(1)(b).
427 (1998), 98 D.T.C. 6196 (Fed. C.A.), leave to appeal dismissed (1999), 236 N.R. 187 (S.C.C.).
428 [1891] A.C. 531 (H.L.) per Lord Macnaghten at 583.

swaying public opinion on controversial issues and, therefore, political rather than charitable in nature. The court also found that the revocation of charitable registration did not infringe the charity's section 2(b) or section 15 *Charter* rights to freedom of expression and freedom from discrimination since it continues to be allowed to express its views; *Charter* rights are not tied to public funding through tax exemptions for the promotion of opinions no matter how sincerely held. The court did not consider advancement of religion as a possible head of charity.[429]

In *Alliance for Life* v. *M.N.R.*,[430] the Federal Court of Appeal also upheld the revocation of charitable status of an organization whose primary purpose was to promote respect for human life from conception onwards through a variety of activities including education services to various public groups and counselling and referral services to the public in relation to pregnancy and post-abortion trauma. The court found that some of these activities were charitable, such as the counselling and referral services, but the other activities said to be educational were not because the materials were designed to promote the organization's views about abortion and euthanasia not encourage public debate and were therefore political. Nor were these activities beneficial to the community, again because of their advocacy of one view only. Section 2(b) rights of expression were not infringed by deregistration.[431] Again, advancement of religion was not considered. Considerable ambiguity remains in relation to the boundary to be drawn in law between religion and purely political advocacy and it is not clear that the courts have come to grips with establishing criteria for distinguishing these two or even that they are distinguishable.

Once a religious institution is registered as a charity under the *Income Tax Act*, taxpayers who make charitable contributions to religious institutions registered as charities may claim a portion of those contribu-

---

429 Several English cases that also draw the line between advocacy as a political activity and the advancement of religion include: *Keven Kayemeth Le Jisroel*, [1932] A.C. 650 (H.L.); *Commissioners of Inland Revenue* v. *Temperance Council of the Christian Churches of England and Wales* (1926), 42 T.L.R. 618 (Ch.D.); and *Oxford Group* v. *Inland Revenue Commissioners* (1949), 2 All E.R. 537 (C.A.).

430 (1999), 174 D.L.R. (4th) 442 (Fed. C.A.).

431 The court had the benefit of the views of the S.C.C. in *Vancouver Society of Immigrant and Visible Minority Women* v. *M.N.R.* (1999), 169 D.L.R. (4th) 34 (S.C.C.) about the *Pemsel* test but it is unclear how helpful these actually are.

tions as a tax deduction.[432] Where a corporate taxpayer pays money to a religious school, which is registered as a charity and which provides both secular and religious education at a time when one of the taxpayer's shareholders has children at the school for whom no fixed tuition fees are required, the money is properly deductible as a charitable donation because it is a gift to charity, not tuition fees.[433] On the other hand, where a taxpayer admits to being under a religious duty to ensure that his or her children are educated at a religious school, the money paid is not deductible as a charitable donation because of that sense of religious obligation, but rather is considered to be tuition fees.[434]

While financial contributors to religious organizations registered as charities may claim a portion of certain contributions as tax deductions, the *Income Tax Act* also makes provision for expenses as defined by the Act, which a member of the clergy as defined by the Act may claim as a tax deduction, including various expenditures incurred while furthering the goals of the religious institution, a housing deduction, and a transportation deduction. The first category has been considered in several cases relating to members of religious orders and a case relating to an evangelical minister.

Where a taxpayer is a member of a religious order and has taken a vow of perpetual poverty, but lives and works away from the order's house and pays only part of his or her income to the order, the moneys expended on living expenses are not deductible as a charitable contribution, because such a person must pay his or her entire income directly to the order to be able to claim the deduction.[435]

A minister who incurs losses in attempting to establish an independent congregation may deduct those losses from profits earned in a business

---

432 Section 110 1(1)(a) [re-en. 1994, c. 7, Sched. II, s. 79].

433 *Bleeker Stereo and Television Ltd.* v. *Minister of National Revenue* (1984), 84 D.T.C. 1761 (T.C.C.).

434 *McBurney v. Minister of National Revenue* (1985), 62 N.R. 104 (Fed. A.D.), leave to appeal to S.C.C. refused (1986), 65 N.R. 320 (S.C.C.). See the earlier case *R. v. Zandstra* (1974), 74 D.T.C. 6416 (F.C.T.D.); and the following case in relation to a student-aid program from which all students would receive bursaries: *Woolner v A.G. of Canada* (1999), 99 D.T.C. 5722 (F.C.A.).

435 *Aubry v. R.* (1976), D.T.C. 6343 (Fed. T.D.); and *Savard v. R.*, unreported decision of 9 December 1996 (T.C.C.), s. 110(2).

carried on concurrently where he or she had a reasonable expectation that the congregation would be successfully established and profits earned.[436]

The *Income Tax Act* provides that a reasonable allowance for transportation in the performance of his or her duties is to be included in the income of a taxpayer who is a member of the clergy.[437] A member of the clergy may also deduct an amount equal to the value of his or her accommodation in computing taxable income.[438] This clergy residence housing deduction has been so difficult to administer that a large volume of case law has resulted in which the courts have been required to define who may be eligible under the Act for the deduction.[439] Section 8(1)(c) sets out a two-fold test, which must be satisfied if a member of the clergy as defined by the Act is to enjoy the deduction. The status test requires that the taxpayer be: (i) a member of the clergy; (ii) a member of a religious order; or (iii) a regular minister of a religious denomination.

The function test requires that the taxpayer be: (i) in charge of, or ministering to a diocese, parish, or congregation; or (ii) engaged in full-time administrative service by appointment of a religious order or religious denomination. The Act does not define these words[440] and the variety of "ministries" practised today further complicates legal matters.

Taking all the reported cases together, a "member of the clergy" now includes the following: commended workers for the Plymouth Brethren;[441] an (unordained) recognized minister in the Church of Christ;[442] and staff members of Youth for Christ who are "credentialed" by that organization to work with street youth.[443] "Member of a religious order" includes: an overseas missionary sponsored by a Baptist mission board as the religious order;[444] a minister sponsored by a para-church organization that engages

---

436 *Cheshire v. Minister of National Revenue* (1984), 84 D.T.C. 1719 (T.C.C.).

437 Section 6(1)(b)(vi).

438 Section 8(1)(c).

439 See generally M.H. Ogilvie, "Statutory Interpretation - Church and State - Income Tax Act - Clergy Housing Deduction - The Clergy Residence Deduction Cases" (2001) 80 Can. Bar Rev. 990.

440 See also for interpretative difficulties: IT-141 (31 December 1973); Directive T1P 92-02; IT-141R (4 May 2000).

441 *Kraft v. R.* (1999), 99 D.T.C. 693 (T.C.C.).

442 *Fitch v. R.* (1999), 99 D.T.C. 721 (T.C.C.).

443 *Koop v. R.* (1999), 99 D.T.C. 707 (T.C.C.).

444 *McGorman v. R.* (1999), 99 D.T.C. 699 (T.C.C.).

in missionary work among Somalis in Canada;[445] and the employees of Christian Horizons, a non-profit corporation that runs group homes for the mentally disabled and is almost entirely funded by the Ontario government;[446] as well as Youth for Christ staff members.[447] A "regular minister" includes: an unordained, female pastoral care worker in a Roman Catholic parish;[448] a director of music at a Pentecostal congregation;[449] and a commended worker of the Plymouth Brethren employed by a para-church organization to provide various clergy services to a variety of evangelical congregations.[450]

"Ministering to a congregation" includes: serving as a chaplain at a private school;[451] serving as a chaplain at an interdenominational Bible college;[452] an unordained Christian education leader in a United Church of Canada congregation;[453] ministering to several congregations while also an employee of the Canadian Bible Society;[454] being a director of music;[455] engaging in interchurch missionary work;[456] being a hospital administrator as an overseas missionary;[457] serving as minister of several congregations of one denomination;[458] serving as a chaplain at a correctional facility with a religiously heterogeneous inmate population;[459] an employee of a para-church organization providing clergy services to various evangelical congregations;[460] an employee of a para-church organization working with various native communities;[461] a chaplain to various

---

445 *Ibid.*
446 *Alemu v. R.* (1999), 99 D.T.C. 714 (T.C.C.).
447 *Koop*, above note 443.
448 *Noseworthy v. R.* (1999), 99 D.T.C. 541 (T.C.C.).
449 *Austin v. R.* (1999), 99 D.T.C. 710 (T.C.C.); *cf. Côté v. R.*, unreported decision of 2 September 1998 (T.C.C.).
450 *Kraft*, above note 441.
451 *Atwell v. M.N.R.* (1967), 67 D.T.C. 611 (T.A.B.).
452 *Adam v. M.N.R.* (1974), 74 D.T.C. 1220 (T.A.B.).
453 *Kolot v. R.* (1992), 92 D.T.C. 2391 (T.C.C.).
454 *Vibe v. R.* (1998), 98 D.T.C. 1684 (T.C.C.).
455 *Austin*, above note 449.
456 *Kraft*, above note 441.
457 *McGorman*, above note 444.
458 *Kraft*, above note 441.
459 *Ibid.*
460 *Ibid.*
461 *Ibid.*

Christian Horizons group houses;[462] and a Youth for Christ staff member working with street youth in various community-based projects.[463]

"Full-time administrative service" includes: a Baptist overseas missionary;[464] a president of a Bible college whose board is controlled by a religious denomination although the appointment is made by the board;[465] and senior officers of Christian Horizons.[466]

It appears that the following categories of persons still do not satisfy either the status or the function requirements of section 8(1)(c) of the *Income Tax Act*: an ordained minister teaching at a theological college;[467] ordained clergy teaching at an interdenominational seminary;[468] a lay pastoral minister in a Roman Catholic parish whose appointment was not permanent;[469] a lay regional director of an interdenominational missionary organization;[470] and a teacher at a Seventh Day Adventist school.[471] It seems possible on the facts that these situations could also create an entitlement for the deduction should future courts follow recent decisions in expanding the definition of "ministry" beyond the traditional categories of ordained ministers, priests, and religious for which the Act was originally designed.[472]

In *Wipf v. R.*,[473] the taxpayer was a member of a Hutterite colony, which in keeping with the theological beliefs of the Hutterian Brethren, owned property communally through a corporation. The Federal Court

---

462 *Alemu*, above note 446.

463 *Koop*, above note 443.

464 *McGorman*, above note 444.

465 *Fitch*, above note 442.

466 *Alemu*, above note 446.

467 *Zylstra Estate v. M.N.R.* (1989), 89 D.T.C. 657 (T.C.C.); *Small v. M.N.R.* (1989), 89 D.T.C. 663 (T.C.C.); and *Zylstra v. R.* (1994), 94 D.T.C. 6687 (F.C.T.C.), aff'd *sub nom. McRae v. R.* (1997), 97 D.T.C. 5124 (F.C.A.). *Cf. Guthrie v. M.N.R.* (1955), 55 D.T.C. 605 (T.A.B.).

468 *Ibid.*

469 *Hardy v. R.* (1998), 98 D.T.C. 3358 (T.C.C.).

470 *Oligny v. R.* (1996), 2 C.T.C. 2666 (T.C.C.).

471 *Osmond v. R.* (1999), 1 C.T.C. 2550 (T.C.C.).

472 S.C. 1949 (2d Sess.), c. 25, s. 4(2). For the related issue of disclosure of Canada Customs and Revenue Agency files on clergy deduction cases, see *Canadian Council of Christian Charities v. Minister of Finance* (1999), 99 D.T.C. 5337 (F.C.T.D.).

473 (1975), 54 D.L.R. (3d) 118 (Fed. C.A.), aff'd (1976), 64 D.L.R. (3d) 766 (S.C.C.).

held that since the main purpose of the colony as distinct from the church is to farm for profit, a colony does not qualify as a "religious order" within the *Income Tax Act* because its purpose is not exclusively religious. Therefore, an individual member of the colony is taxable on his or her subsistence allowance granted by the colony, but not on an aliquot portion of the total profits derived from the farming operations, which remained as part of the corporation's taxable profits.

A final issue relating to permissible tax deductions was raised in *Bassila v. R.,*[474] where a taxpayer who knowingly participated in a fraudulent scheme practised by a religious order involving receipts for amounts larger than actual donations was found to be rightly reassessed and subject to penalties under the Act.

Several cases have also dealt with issues arising from conflicts with the tax system on conscientious grounds arising from the religious beliefs of a taxpayer.

Where a taxpayer's spouse lives separate and apart from the taxpayer and receives support payments from him but refuses on religious grounds to sign a separation agreement because, as a Roman Catholic, she does not believe in separation or divorce, the support payments are not deductible since there is a statutory requirement that such payments be part of a separation agreement or court order in order to be deductible. Nor, in these circumstances, was there any obvious interference with freedom of religion and no evidence was presented that the statutory requirement constituted such interference.[475]

In *Prior v. Minister of Revenue,*[476] the taxpayer was a Quaker, opposed on religious grounds to expenditures for war or for military purposes, who withheld a percentage of her taxes equivalent to the percentage of the Canadian budget spent for military purposes. Nevertheless, the court held that the taxpayer was required to pay such taxes for the following reasons: the taxes levied were not so closely related to the government's military expenditures as to be an insult to the taxpayer's beliefs; payment of the taxes did not identify the taxpayer with the military functions of the government; the taxpayer did not show how she had been forced to act contrary to her conscience in breach of section 2(a) of the *Charter*

---

474 (2001), 2001 Carswell Net 1878 (T.C.C.).

475 *Hodson v. R.,* [1987] 1 C.T.C. 219 (Fed. T.D.), aff'd [1988] 1 C.T.C. 2 (Fed. A.D.).

476 (1989), 44 C.R.R. 110 (Fed. A.D.), leave to appeal to S.C.C. refused (1990), 44 C.R.R. 110n (S.C.C.).

and section 15(1) was irrelevant to the issue; the *Charter* does not override the provisions of the *Constitution Act, 1867*, including the power to levy taxes; the Federal Court has no jurisdiction either to amend the rate provisions of the *Income Tax Act* or to create a credit scheme exempting a taxpayer from remitting a portion of the tax otherwise payable.

Finally, a taxpayer who withheld a portion of his taxes on religious grounds in protest against the use of public money to finance abortions was ordered to be reassessed so as to pay that money, because, in the view of the court, the *Charter* makes Canada a secular state, not a theocratic or an atheistic one, and such a secular state can neither enforce the imperatives of anyone's religious beliefs nor permit ardent believers to invite their co-religionists to commit illegal or anti-constitutional acts in the name of any religion or in the name of God. The *Charter* guarantee of freedom of religion only goes so far as not to compel the taxpayer to witness or personally participate in an abortion; it does not compel the state to forgive the taxpayer that share of his or her taxes representing the share of government revenues used to fund abortion facilities.[477] Generally speaking, the courts have taken the position that the guarantees of freedom of religion and of expression do not prevent governments from using general tax revenues in ways that offend the beliefs or consciences of taxpayers, provided taxpayers are not compelled to agree with government policy or forbidden from advocating contrary views.[478]

3) Goods and Services Tax

The Goods and Services Tax, introduced from 1 January 1991,[479] applies to religious institutions as to others in Canada. Under the scheme of the legislation, a registrant engaged in a commercial activity that does not produce exempt supplies is entitled to recover an input tax credit for any GST paid on any goods or services acquired for consumption, use, or supply in the course of commercial activities. The question of how closely tied to an output an expense has to be to qualify for an input tax credit was considered in *Midland Hutterian Brethren* v. *Canada*.[480]

The Hutterite colony was organized as a corporation and its members worked without compensation but were provided with shelter, edu-

---

477 *O'Sullivan* v. *Minister of National Revenue*, [1992] 1 F.C. 522 (T.D.).
478 *Petrini* v. *R.* (1994), 94 D.T.C. 6657 (F.C.A.).
479 *Excise Tax Act*, R.S.C. 1985, c. E-15; as am. S.C. 1990, c. 45, s. 12.
480 (2000), 195 D.L.R. (4th) 450 (F.C.A.).

cation, food, and clothing. The colony allotted two types of cloth for clothing to members, for work purposes and for church. The colony's claim for an input tax credit of fifty percent on the GST paid for the cloth made into work clothes was upheld by the Federal Court of Appeal because the cloth was a supply that contributed to the production of articles or the provision of services that are taxable. The cloth could be tied to commercial activities.[481]

In *Galcom International Inc. v. R.*,[482] the question was whether a charity operated for the purposes of advancing religion could claim the one hundred percent GST rebate for property exported abroad for its charitable purposes. The company transmitted religious programs by radio to third-world countries and provided villagers in those countries with free radios, whose components the company purchased and assembled in Canada and for which it claimed the rebate. The rebate was denied on the ground that it was only available under the legislation[483] if the components had been exported; by assembling the parts there was a consumption of the initial supply to create a new product that was different from the original supply of components received by the company.

I. ZONING AND PLANNING

Occasionally, zoning and land use issues have resulted in litigation involving religious institutions and municipalities. In *Town of Deep River v. St. Barnabas Parish*,[484] it was held that where a municipal bylaw restricted the use of land to churches and buildings necessary thereto, the basement of a church cannot be used as a youth hostel. On the other hand, in *Starland No. 47 (Municipal District) v. Hutterian Brethren Church of Starland*,[485] it was held that development permits were required to be issued pursuant to the applicable land use bylaws and that additional

---

481 In his dissenting opinion, Evans J.A. thought the legislation ambiguous because it does not make clear the degree of connection with a commercial activity for the credit. He thought the cloth was used for personal, communal, and religious purposes and not for commercial purposes.

482 (2001), 2001 Carswell Net 692 (T.C.C.).

483 Above note 479

484 [1972] 3 O.R. 90 (Co. Ct.).

485 (1996), 32 M.P.L.R. (2d) 15 (Alta. Q.B.).

restrictions could not be imposed limiting use in ways not stipulated for or limiting uses flowing from religious considerations.

The need to ensure that the use of land by a church is compatible with its surroundings was considered in *Church on the Rock* v. *Town of Collingwood*,[486] in which a new congregation wished to purchase a vacant industrial building, located on land zoned for heavy industrial uses, adjacent to heavy industrial buildings that produced noise and traffic, day and night. An application for a site-project amendment to the applicable municipal zoning bylaw was rejected on the ground of incompatibility and poor land use planning. The established industrial users and the town needed to have their present zoning and these outweighed the church's need for safe surroundings for their family-orientated activities.

Where a municipal bylaw is enacted in bad faith for the purpose of re-zoning a particular piece of property to prevent it from being used as a Zoroastrian temple, by a group that has indicated an intention to purchase it, the re-zoning has been found to be arbitrary, discriminatory, and illegal.[487]

Property owned by or held in trust for a religious organization, such as a congregation, is not exempt from expropriation simply on religious grounds, but rather may be expropriated like any other property within the terms of the applicable expropriation legislation. The calculation of disturbance damages owing to loss of income from dwindling attendance during a period at temporary premises before a new church was built should be based on the model of other local churches over a brief period of years. Disturbance damages should not include a separate sum for personal time spent by clergy on events caused by the expropriation unless extra pastoral help was hired, because this would amount to double recovery.[488]

The issue of freedom of religion under section 2(a) of the *Charter* has arisen in several cases dealing with municipal law issues. In *Watson* v. *City of Burnaby*,[489] a local resident applied to set aside an agreement between the city and an historical society to construct a replica of a 1914 Masonic Lodge on city-owned lands as a "village museum" site. The peti-

---

486 (1994), 30 O.M.B.R. 485.

487 *H.G. Winton Ltd.* v. *Borough of North York* (1978), 20 O.R. (2d) 737 (Div. Ct.).

488 *Pentecostal Assemblies of Canada* v. *British Columbia (Minister of Transportation and Highways)* (1999), 66 L.C.R. 275 (B.C. Exp. Comp. Bd.).

489 (1994), 22 M.P.L.R. (2d) 136 (B.C.S.C.).

tioner's argument that Masonry was a religion so that the resolution was a violation of his freedom of religion was rejected on the grounds that the purpose of the project was to illustrate the city's history and not promote religion; moreover, the resolution in no way prevented or hindered any person from holding or practising his or her religious beliefs. Where a congregation is offered a building site but is refused re-zoning in accordance with zoning bylaws and official plans, this does not amount to discrimination under section 2(a) of the *Charter* because freedom of religion can be limited by the fundamental rights and freedoms of others.[490]

J. PENSION BENEFITS

The extent to which pension legislation may override the traditional practices and understandings of a religious institution with regard to its relationship with its members was considered for the first time in *Salvation Army, Canada East v. Ontario (A.G.)*.[491] The Salvation Army does not regard its officers as employees, and the courts have upheld its position that its relationship with them is not one of a contract of employment.[492] However, in this case, the Ontario General Division held that where provincial pension benefits legislation defines the employer-employee relationship for the purposes of pensioners so widely as to encompass officers of the Salvation Army, their pension plan must be administered in accordance with the legislation. Such legislation is not impugned pursuant to section 2(a) of the *Charter* because individual officers remain free to choose whether to accept the voluntary relationship between themselves and the association, that is, there is no coercion or compulsion in relation to their religious beliefs or practices. Nor will a statutory requirement for the elimination of gender discrimination in such a plan constitute an infringement of freedom of religion, since gender equality between men and women officers has been a tenet of the Salvation Army

---

490 *McCormick v. South Dumfries (Township) Committee of Adjustment* (1995), 32 O.M.B.R. 142 (O.M.B.). See also *Grushman v. Ottawa (City)* (2000), 15 M.P.L.R. (3d) 167 (Ont. Div. Ct.) that freedom of religion issues are sufficiently important in these cases to merit judicial consideration.

491 (1992), 88 D.L.R. (4th) 238 (Ont. Gen. Div.).

492 *Rogers v. Booth*, [1937] 2 All E.R. 751 (C.A.); and *Lewery v. Governing Council of Salvation Army in Canada* (1993), 104 D.L.R. (4th) 449 (N.B.C.A.), leave to appeal to S.C.C. refused 107 D.L.R. (4th) vii (S.C.C.).

from its beginnings. Where the payment of a retirement allowance is of right rather than being a voluntary payment, the effect upon the practice and profession of an officer can only be regarded as a trivial and substantial infringement of section 2(a).[493]

K. WILLS AND TRUSTS

1) Gifts and Restrictions on Gifts Generally

At one time gifts to churches and other religious institutions or agencies were strictly controlled by mortmain legislation originally enacted in England in the thirteenth century. This was designed to ensure that not too much real property came into the possession of the "dead hand" of the church, which was, by the late Middle Ages, the largest land owner in England, controlling about one-third of all land on the eve of the Reformation. The purpose of this legislation was not only to limit the amount of land controlled by the Church but primarily to ensure that a market existed of freely alienable property.[494] Mortmain legislation was later also enacted by most provinces; however, since gifts and testamentary benefactions to churches have declined considerably in both number and economic value, this legislation has been repealed and replaced by legislation dealing with charitable gifts generally, whether given to a religious institution or some other organization involved in charitable, educational, or other public purposes.[495] This legislation typically deals only with the legal aspects of the disposition by the donor to the recipient charitable institution and places no limitations on the amount given by the donor or received by the institution. Difficulties peculiar to religious institutions have generally concerned issues of interpretation of the purposes of particular gifts, to which much of this section is devoted.

When a gift is given to a charitable or religious institution either by a living donor or as a bequest, it is assumed to be held as a charitable purpose trust for either the general or specific purpose for which it was

---

493 For a closer critique of this case, see Ogilvie, above note 61.

494 See O.L.R.C., *Report on Mortmain, Charitable Uses and Religious Institutions* (Toronto: O.L.R.C., 1976) for the history of this legislation in Canada; and see F. Pollock and F.W. Maitland, *The History of English Law* (Cambridge: Cambridge University Press, 1968), vol. 1 at 332–334 for the medieval background.

495 *Charitable Gifts Act*, R.S.O. 1990, c. C. 8.

given.[496] As such, it has several attributes in law: (i) there need not be a beneficiary to enforce the trust other than the Attorney General exercising a *parens patriae* jurisdiction; (ii) the trust will not fail for uncertainty of objects provided the purpose is exclusively charitable; (iii) a court may make *cy-près* orders to ensure that the charitable purpose will not fail; (iv) the trust is exempt from the rule against perpetuities; and (v) the trust is exempt from the rule against perpetual trusts.

Gifts, whether *inter vivos* or bequests, may be made to religious institutions, whether unincorporated, incorporated, or holding their property by trust deed. The terms on which the gifts may be held and managed are those that govern each institution, as well as general legal standards applicable to all property held in trust and for charitable purposes such as the advancement of religion. Gifts may be held as part of the general assets of a religious institution or subject to a separate charitable trust subject to the terms and conditions agreed to between the donor and the religious institution. Where the terms of the gift are silent or incomplete in relation to investment of funds, then the investment powers found typically in a provincial *Trustee Act*[497] will apply.

Whatever the source of the terms and conditions for the management of funds, the trustees are subject to the usual duties of trustees: to comply with any legal donor restrictions; to invest the funds prudently; to protect and conserve the trust property; and to keep accounts and make reports to the religious institution or a public guardian or trustee. Failure to do so may result in personal liability for all losses resulting from breach of trust. Failure to do so also brings the possibility of public scrutiny pursuant to provincial legislation, such as the Ontario *Charities Accounting Act*,[498] which allows a public trustee to require the submission of accounts for approval by a court and to seek a court order to enforce the terms of the gift; and permits members of the public or the organization to ask a court to investigate and correct any breach of trust. In addition, trustees must

---

496 For what follows, see generally the three collections of materials, above note 133. But see especially Terrance S. Carter, "Donor Restricted Charitable Gifts: A Practical Overview Revisited" in *Fundamental New Developments in the Law of Charities in Canada*, above note 133. See also Timothy G. Youdan, "Investment By Charities" in *Fit To Be Tithed 2*, above note 133.

497 R.S.O. 1990, c. T-23.

498 R.S.O. 1990, c. C-10. See also *Ontario (Public Guardian & Trustee) v. Unity Church of Truth*, unreported decision of 24 March 1998 (Ont. Gen. Div.).

also comply with the *Income Tax Act*, the *Criminal Code*,[499] and the common law generally in relation to property given to religious institutions.

Until very recently, it was long settled in law that while gifts made to a charity without restrictions on their use are beneficially owned by the charity for its general charitable purposes, gifts contributed for a specific charitable purpose are to be held by the charity for that purpose and are not owned beneficially by the charity or available for the general purposes of that charity.[500] However, in *Re Christian Brothers of Ireland in Canada*,[501] the Ontario Court of Appeal effectively abolished the distinction between general charitable purposes and specific charitable trusts by finding that specific purpose charitable trusts are not immune from claims in the tort of vicarious liability brought against the general charity.

In that case, the Christian Brothers were found by a Royal Commission in Newfoundland to be liable for approximately $67 million to numerous claimants who had been sexually and physically abused while under their care in various schools and orphanages. Since their general corporate assets amounted to approximately $4 million dollars, the order was wound up in Ontario where the order's head office was and in the winding-up the question arose of the exigibility of various assets held by the order in special purpose charitable trusts; in particular, two schools in British Columbia, whose combined value was approximately $36 million. While the Ontario Court of Appeal found that the B.C. courts had to determine the factual issues relating to ownership of the special purpose charitable trusts, the issue of whether they ought to be available in tort claims could be determined in Ontario. The court decided that there is no doctrine of charitable immunity from tort claims, so that all assets of the charity were available to satisfy the claims. While the court confirmed that property could be held in special purpose trusts, by assimilating the two categories of property the court effectively abolished the purpose of holding property in special purpose charitable trusts. The court seemed unconcerned by the traditional legal understanding that a special purpose charitable trust is a true trust, which merely happens to be held as a trust by a charity.

---

499 R.S.C. 1985, c. C-46, s. 336, which deals with a criminal breach of trust by conversion or misapplication of funds given for a charitable purpose.

500 J. Warburton and D. Morris, *Tudor on Charities*, 8th ed. (London: Sweet & Maxwell, 1995) at 191.

501 (2000), 47 O.R. (3d) 674 (C.A.), application for leave to appeal dismissed 16 November 2000 (S.C.C.).

Conversely, in the companion case, *Rowland v. Vancouver College Ltd.*,[502] the B.C. Court of Appeal, dealing with the factual issue of ownership of the two schools, found that they were held by the incorporated order as the trustee of the shares of each of the two schools for specific purpose charitable trusts of operating the two schools. The issue before the court was limited to ownership and the court did not consider whether property held on special purpose charitable trusts was exigible for tort claims against the owner. The net result is that the decision of the Ontario Court of Appeal remains as the highest authority in Canada for the position that gifts to charitable and religious institutions for specific purposes may well be defeated by tort claims against the institution.

2) Bequests for General Religious Purposes

Testators may leave bequests to religious institutions either for some general purpose associated with that institution or for some specifically defined purpose. In either case, it may be difficult to determine from the wording of the devise the testator's precise intention and courts may be asked to interpret and define that intention. The case law is, then, largely a forest of single instances and the following discussion reflects that fact.

A bequest to a congregation for the establishment of an endowment fund with interest to be applied to certain specified purposes and the remainder to such purposes as the minister and management committee sees fit is a valid bequest as one "for the increase and improvement of Christian knowledge and promoting religion." As such, it is within the class of charitable gifts and for the public good.[503]

A devise of real and personal estate to executors to hold on trust and to pay the interest to a congregation upon certain conditions, and where these fail, to pay the interest to certain specified missionary societies, is a valid gift for religious purposes.[504] Again, a bequest "to be used to further the cause of Our Lord Jesus Christ" was held to be a good charitable gift and not void for indefiniteness where the trustees had been given

---

502 (2001), 205 D.L.R. (4th) 193 (B.C.C.A.), leave to appeal refused 22 May 2002 (S.C.C.). For thoughtful discussions of these two cases, see Carter, above note 496 and David Stevens, "Vicarious Liability in the Charity Sector: A Comment on *Bazley v. Curry* and *Re Chrisitian Brothers of Ireland in Canada*" in *Fundamental New Developments in the Law of Charities in Canada*, above note 133.

503 *Re Cameron Estate* (1906), 7 O.W.R. 416 (H.C.).

504 *Re Barrett Estate* (1905), 10 O.L.R. 337 (H.C.).

the discretion to direct a scheme for its use.[505] Again, a gift to trustees to pay over remaining sums from an estate to "such religious or charitable societies as in their judgment and discretion require it" is a valid charitable gift for religious purposes.[506]

Where a church is mistakenly named in a devise, the gift will not necessarily fail if the court is satisfied that the testator had in mind a particular church; thus, a gift to the "Union Church" was held to be a valid gift to the United Church, which the testator had attended and supported during her lifetime.[507]

A trust for religious purposes is *prima facie* presumed to be charitable, and the onus is on those attacking its validity to establish that it is not charitable.[508] The issue of whether the trust is for religious or general charitable purposes has arisen where the bequest has specified both. While a bequest for a religious purpose is *prima facie* charitable, where a testator apparently distinguishes between "charitable" and "religious," the court should inquire into whether the testator has distinguished these words in either a legal or popular meaning, and where the testator leaves money for "religious and/or charitable work," and uses these in a popular sense, all contemplated purposes will be regarded as charitable in the legal sense and the gift will be good.[509] Where a testator directs the establishment of a trust fund in favour of "educational and religious objects," this is a valid bequest because the phrase is to be read conjunctively rather than disjunctively; the purpose is the advancement of religion.[510]

Where a testator directs that one-half of his estate is to be paid to various charitable institutions, which were to be selected by his rabbi who was a co-executor, then those so chosen should be the donees of that part of his estate.[511]

However, a bequest to an avowedly agnostic society whose objects were the dissemination of ethical principles and the cultivation of a

---

505 *Phelps v. Lord* (1894), 25 O.R. 259 (H.C.).
506 *Anderson v. Dougall* (1867), 13 Gr. 164 (Ch.). *Cf. Re McCauley Estate* (1897), 28 O.R. 610 (H.C.).
507 *Re Meikle Estate*, [1943] 3 D.L.R. 668 (Alta. T.D.).
508 *Re Morton Estate: Yorkshire and Canadian Trust Ltd. v. Atherton*, [1941] 3 W.W.R. 513 (B.C.S.C).
509 *Re Morton Estate: Summerfield and London and Western Trusts Co. v. Phillips*, [1941] 3 W.W.R. 310 (B.C.S.C.).
510 *Yorkshire and Canadian Trust Ltd. v. Atherton*, above note 508.
511 *Metz Estate v. Jewish National Fund of Canada* (1995), 10 E.T.R. (2d) 89 (N.B.Q.B.).

national religious sentiment by holding lectures and musical concerts for the public and by publications and other social activities, has been found not to be for the advancement of religion and charitable as such. "Religion" is concerned with a person's relationship with God, while "ethics" is concerned with relationships between persons; faith in a god and worship of that god were said to be essential attributes of religion. A society whose objectives included the dissemination of ethical principles existed for the advancement of education, not religion.[512]

Where a will directed the executors of an estate to provide sufficient funds each year to produce a religious book for use in the public schools of a particular town, the bequest was found to be a good charitable bequest for the advancement of religion and enforceable regardless of a public general statute in relation to religious instruction in the public schools.[513]

On the other hand, a trust providing for the religious education of the descendants of a named individual was regarded as a private trust, rather that as a public trust for the advancement of religion.[514]

A religious organization wishing to collect charitable donations from the public is obliged to comply with provincial and municipal legislation regulating the collection of funds for charity.[515]

3) Bequests for Specific Religious Purposes

In addition to making bequests either for the advancement of religion generally or to a religious institution for its general purposes, bequests

---

512 *Baralett v. Attorney-General*, [1980] 3 All E.R. 918 (Ch.D.). At one time, it was held that where a testator had directed that the residue of an estate be used, in the executor's discretion, for the promotion of free thought and speech, such a bequest was void on the ground that it was inimical to Christianity: *Kinsey v. Kinsey*, above note 40; see also *Pringle v. Town of Napanee*, above note 39; *R. v. Dickout*, above note 7; and *Re Orr* (1917), 40 O.L.R. 567 (C.A.). But see also *Bowman v. Secular Society*, above note 42, which probably represents the modern Canadian position.

513 *Re Anderson Estate*, [1943] O.W.N. 303 (H.C.), reversed on other grounds [1943] O.W.N. 698 (C.A.). See also *Homan v. City of Toronto* (1918), 45 D.L.R. 147 (Ont. H.C.), which found that a municipal bylaw providing for the payment of municipal funds for the purpose of providing army huts for Roman Catholic soldiers and religious materials to Roman Catholic soldiers overseas was *ultra vires* because it was not for general charitable purposes.

514 *Re Doering Estate*, [1949] 1 D.L.R. 267 (Ont. H.C.).

515 *International Society for Krishna Consciousness (Iskon Canada) v. City of Edmonton* (1978), 94 D.L.R. (3d) 561 (Alta. T.D.).

may also be given for specific religious purposes. Thus, bequests may be designated for a specific congregation or parish and where a gift is given to a parish, *eo nomine*, it is to be treated as a gift for the repair or improvement of the church building where no other specific instructions for its use are given.[516] Again, where a testator provided that the residue of his estate was to be bestowed on "some good church," in the discretion of his executors, "church" was held to mean a local congregation in the context and not a denomination generally.[517]

Gifts for specified purposes to parishes or congregations have been upheld as valid charitable gifts including a gift for the upkeep of a cemetery and church lawn;[518] for the erection of a German-speaking Roman Catholic parish;[519] for the maintenance and repair of the internal and external fabric of a church building;[520] and for the payment of a congregational debt.[521]

Where a testatrix left her house "for the sole and only use of and occupation by the Rector for the time being" of a named congregation, the gift was held to be a devise to successive rectors of the named church.[522] Where a bequest was left to a named minister "for the use of the Reformed Presbyterian Church," it was found to be a valid charitable gift to be expended by the minister in the manner best calculated by him to advance the principles of that church.[523]

Bequests have frequently been made to churches or congregations for "mission work" and have been upheld as valid, although the specific type of work contemplated, if any, has not been explicitly stated. A bequest of a residue for "foreign missions" is a valid charitable gift that may be paid over to the responsible church agency, since such a bequest has primarily a religious purpose, of supporting organizations seeking to convert people in foreign countries to the religion of the particular organiza-

---

516 *Re Grand Estate*, [1946] 1 D.L.R. 204 (Ont. H.C.); *Sills v. Warner* (1896), 27
        O.R. 266 (C.P.D.); and *Re Finkle* (1924), 25 O.W.N. 588 (H.C.).

517 *Re Gilliland Estate*, [1949] 1 D.L.R. 42 (N.S.T.D.).

518 *Re Welton*, [1950] 2 D.L.R. 280 (N.S.T.D.).

519 *Re Schneckenburger* (1931), 40 O.W.N. 210 (H.C.).

520 *Re Boyd Estate* (1924), 55 O.L.R. 627 (C.A.).

521 *Re Campbell Estate* (1910), 1 O.W.N. 865 (H.C.); and *Meighen v. First Presby-
        terian Church of Brandon* (1978), 3 E.T.R. 70 (Man. Q.B.).

522 *Re McDonagh Estate* (1920), 18 O.W.N. 154 (H.C.).

523 *Chambers v. Johnson* (1903), 5 O.L.R. 459 (C.A.).

tion.[524] As a charitable bequest, a bequest for missions is not subject to the rule against perpetuities and may be devoted to a charity forever.[525] Nor will a bequest to be paid ninety years after the testator's death to the missionary society of a certain named church be made void by the rule against perpetuities.[526] A bequest to a specific Women's Missionary Society is a valid charitable gift,[527] as is a bequest to support the mission work of a specific named individual.[528] A gift of the residue of an estate to be distributed in the discretion of the executors "to the support of Christianity, throughout the world, such as Bible tracts, missionary societies, and institutions of learning of the Baptist denomination" has been held to be a valid charitable bequest for missions.[529]

A bequest made in perpetuity for the saying of masses for the repose of the soul of the testator is a valid charitable bequest, and not a gift for superstitious uses, since it is one made for the purposes of a lawful religion; that is, Roman Catholicism.[530] The rule against perpetuities is not applicable to a bequest for requiem masses, since such a bequest is a charitable one.[531]

Where an agreement to make a bequest for specific religious purposes has not begun to be performed prior to the death of the testator, it becomes unenforceable against the estate.[532]

4) Bequests for Generally Beneficial Purposes

Religious institutions frequently sponsor or provide charitable facilities and services on a purely charitable rather than a religious basis only, both to supporters of their own religions as well as to the population generally. Thus, bequests to religious institutions have been upheld as valid charitable bequests where their purpose is primarily the relief of poverty.

---

524 *Re Long* (1930), 37 O.W.N. 351 (H.C.).

525 *Weatherby v. Weatherby* (1927), 53 N.B.R. 403 (K.B.).

526 *Re Short* (1914), 7 O.W.N. 525 (H.C.). See also *Madill v. McConnell* (1908), 17 O.L.R. 209 (C.A.).

527 *Weatherby v. Weatherby*, above note 525.

528 *Toronto General Trusts Co. v. Wilson* (1895), 26 O.R. 671 (H.C.). See also *Re Mellen Estate*, [1933] O.W.N. 246 (C.A.).

529 *Anderson v. Kilborn* (1875), 22 Gr. 385 (H.C.).

530 *Elmsley v. Madden* (1871), 18 Gr. 386 (H.C.).

531 *Re Hallisy*, [1932] 4 D.L.R. 516 (Ont. C.A.). *Cf. Re Zeagman* (1916), 37 O.L.R. 336 (Div. Ct.).

532 *Reinhart v. Burgar Estate* (1918), O.L.R. 120 (H.C.).

Bequests for the establishment by religious organizations of the following charities have been upheld: a hostel for Anglican girls of low income aspiring to be teachers or clerks;[533] Protestant homes or other institutions for children;[534] a home for Protestant old ladies;[535] a trust to pay for the care of aged and infirm men and women in private homes provided they are "Protestants, Hebrews, or the adherents of the Orthodox, Eastern, or Greek churches;[536] a home for the aged poor and indigent Protestants in a specific county;[537] a gift to the oldest and poorest of a certain parish;[538] a gift to the widows and poor of a named congregation;[539] a gift to poor Jewish converts to Christianity;[540] and a gift to a religious order to help a needy family of European origin.[541] Whether such bequests would be sustained today or held invalid on grounds of religious discrimination has yet to be determined by the courts.

In addition to upholding the validity of bequests to religious institutions for the benefit of the poor, the courts have upheld bequests for a wide variety of purposes beneficial to the community as valid and certain charitable gifts, even though not concurrently for the advancement of religion: a bequest for the establishment by a religious organization of a temperance hotel;[542] a bequest for a building to be used for both social and religious purposes within a community provided it is not conveyed to any particular denomination;[543] and a bequest for the purpose of establishing a faith-healing centre.[544]

---

533 *Public Trustee* v. *Synod of the Diocese of Edmonton* (1977), 74 D.L.R. (3d) 545 (Alta. C.A.).

534 *Canada Permanent Trust Co.* v. *MacFarlane* (1972) 27 D.L.R. (3d) 480 (B.C.C.A.). See also *Jewish Home for the Aged of B.C.* v. *Toronto General Trust Corp.*, [1961] S.C.R. 465.

535 *Protestant Old Ladies Home* v. *Provincial Treasury of P.E.I.*, [1941] 2 D.L.R. 534 (P.E.I. S.C.).

536 *Re Land Estate*, [1939] O.W.N. 329 (H.C.).

537 *Re Stewart* (1925), 29 O.W.N. 140 (H.C.).

538 *Re Short* (1914), 7 O.W.N. 525 (H.C.).

539 *Re Kinney* (1903), 6 O.L.R. 459 (C.P.).

540 *Gillies* v. *McConochie* (1882), 3 O.R. 203 (H.C.).

541 *Re Wedge* (1968), 67 D.L.R. (2d) 433 (B.C.C.A.).

542 *Re Doyle Estate* (1914), 5 O.W.N. 911 (H.C.).

543 *Langille* v. *Nass* (1917), 36 D.L.R. 368 (N.S.C.A.). See also *A.G.* v. *Wahr-Hansen*, [2000] 3 All E.R. 642 (P.C.).

544 *Re Le Cren Clarke*, [1996] 1 All E.R. 715 (Ch. D.).

However, the bequest of the residue of an estate to the Jewish National Fund for the purpose of establishing a Jewish homeland in Palestine was held to be invalid because it was not for a purpose beneficial to the community.[545] Nor was a beneficial charitable purpose found to exist on the facts where a bequest was left to a church to provide a home for unemployed girls and young women.[546]

Religious institutions that fail to apply a bequest as stipulated by a testator may lose it; thus, where a testator left a house to a congregation for use as a school and no steps were taken to carry out the testator's wishes, the provincial Attorney General was held to be entitled to institute legal proceedings to have the house transferred to the municipal commissioner of schools to carry out those wishes.[547]

5) Failure for Uncertainty

While courts have been largely able to find certainty in bequests to religious institutions and for religious or other charitable purposes of those institutions, it is also possible for bequests to fail for a variety of reasons, although chiefly because either the beneficiary institution or the purpose is uncertain, that is, not stated with sufficient clarity by the testator.

The general rule is that courts should interpret the language of bequests generously so as to ascertain and give effect to the charitable intention of the testator. Thus, a gift to "St. Andrew and Wesley Church" was interpreted to be to "St. Andrew Wesley Church," and the funds were to be applied to general church purposes as there was, in fact, no endowment fund as stipulated in the bequest.[548] A bequest for "foreign missions" was held to be a valid and certain bequest and applicable to the foreign mission work of the church concerned.[549] Nor was a trust for the religious education of the male descendants of a testator's family found to be void for uncertainty although they may be difficult to trace.[550]

---

545 *Jewish National Fund v. Royal Trust Co.*, [1965] S.C.R. 784.
546 *Begg v. Holmes* (1930), 37 O.W.N. 402 (H.C.).
547 *A.G. Nova Scotia v. Avery* (1877), R.E.D. 253 (N.S.T.D.).
548 *St. Andrew's-Wesley Church v. Toronto General Trusts Corp.*, [1948] S.C.R. 500.
549 *Re Long*, above note 524. For further examples of judicial construction, see *Re McConaghy Estate* (1920), 18 O.W.N. 223 (H.C.); *Re McGregor* (1920), 17 O.W.N. 354 (H.C.); and *Toronto General Trusts Co. v. Wilson*, above note 528.
550 *Re Doering Estate*, above note 514.

Where a surplus exists after distribution in accordance with a will, the executors may distribute that surplus *pro rata* to the named beneficiaries, including any religious institution, to avoid failure for uncertainty as to a beneficiary.[551] Where permitting the executors to use their discretion to designate beneficiaries would avoid the failure of the bequest for uncertainty, then the courts should permit the executors to do so.[552]

Where the description of the designated beneficiary is inaccurate insofar as it may be confused with more than one beneficiary, in order to ensure that a bequest does not fail for uncertainty, a court may rely on extrinsic evidence to determine the testator's intention.[553]

6) Cy-Près Applications

Where a bequest is made to a religious institution for religious or other charitable purposes, which can no longer be carried out or which the religious institution prefers not to carry out, a court will, if necessary, seek out similar fitting objects, so that the intended charity will not be disappointed, and make a cy-près application of the funds to that charitable object. Thus, where a bequest was made to a church for the purpose of carrying out a mission to convert Jews to Christianity, and the church declined to do so, the court decided to administer the bequest cy-près for other mission purposes.[554] Again, a cy-près application will be made where a bequest is made to an institution that does not have the precise name of an institution carrying out the charitable purpose for which the

---

551 *Ray v. Methodist Annual Conference of New Brunswick and Prince Edward Island* (1881), 6 S.C.R. 308.

552 *Doe d. Anderson v. Todd* (1846), 2 U.C.Q.B. 82 (C.A.); *Phelps v. Lord* (1894), 25 O.R. 259 (H.C.); *Manning v. Robinson* (1898), 29 O.R. 483 (H.C.); *Power v. A.G. Nova Scotia* (1903), 35 S.C.R. 182; *Re Huyck Estate* (1905), 10 O.L.R. 480 (Div. Ct.); and *Re McPherson Estate* (1919), 17 O.W.N. 22 (H.C.).

553 For various examples of the application of this principle, see *Sommerville v. Morton* (1861), 5 N.S.R. 60 (C.A.); *Re McLaurin Legacy* (1911), 9 E.L.R. 326 (P.E.I. Ch.); *Re Otto Estate* (1926), 30 O.W.N. 192 (H.C.); *Re Boutet Estate* (1927), 32 O.W.N. 364 (H.C.); *Re Carrick Estate*, [1929] 3 D.L.R. 373 (Ont. H.C.); *Re Brown* (1931), 40 O.W.N. 282 (C.A.); *Re Mellen Estate*, [1933] O.W.N. 246 (C.A.); *Re Merkle*, [1943] 3 D.L.R. 668 (Alta. T.D.); *Re Humfrey Estate*, [1944] 2 D.L.R. 476 (B.C.S.C.); *Re Manuel*, [1958] O.W.N. 194 (H.C.); *Re Samson* (1966), 59 D.L.R. (2d) 132 (N.S.T.D.); *Re Wardle* (1974), 49 D.L.R. (3d) 507 (Ont. H.C.); *Re Finkle* (1977), 82 D.L.R. (3d) 445 (Man. Q.B.); and *Re Dilger* (1978), 2 E.T.R. 187 (B.C.S.C.).

554 *Gillies v. McConochie*, above note 540.

bequest was made.[555] Where a bequest is made to a religious institution which no longer exists, the court will apply the funds to an institution with similar objects.[556]

Where a specific gift fails because the religious or charitable object no longer exists, and there is no general charitable intention expressed, the bequest will fail and the doctrine of cy-près is inapplicable. Thus, where a bequest was made to a congregation provided it continued to exist, with a gift over to a school for the blind, and the congregation united with several others, the bequest was found to go to the school for the blind and not to the new congregation by a cy-près application.[557] Where a bequest was made for an orphanage catering to certain categories of orphans and no such orphanage existed, the bequest was redirected to residual family beneficiaries.[558]

Where there is a continuing possibility that the original application of the bequests designated by the testator may be fulfilled, a court may decline to make a cy-près application of the bequest; thus, where a bequest was left to a congregation to build a new church building, the court declined to make a cy-près application of the funds to the renovation of the old building because the testator's intention of providing for the eventuality of a new church remained neither impossible nor impracticable of performance in the future.[559] Where a bequest was made for a children's home that no longer existed, because the organization that ran the home still existed, the money was directed to it to apply to similar purposes.[560]

Where a testator provided that the executors were to be instructed by his widow as to the scheme of distribution of a bequest, and she declined to instruct, the court made a cy-près distribution of the fund where the

---

555 *Re Dickson Estate* (1923), 24 O.W.N. 161 (H.C.); and *Re Manning Estate*, [1947] 2 W.W.R. 487 (Man. K.B.).

556 *Re Chisholm* (1977), 29 N.S.R. (2d) 173 (T.D.); and *Amey v. Kingston Orphan's Home* (1910), 2 O.W.N. 111 (H.C.).

557 *Re Kelley*, [1934] 3 D.L.R. 379 (N.S.S.C.). For other examples, see *Re Harding Estate* (1904), 4 O.W.R. 316 (H.C.); *Re McMillan Estate* (1917), 11 O.W.N. 443 (H.C.); *Re Schjaastad Estate*, [1920] 50 D.L.R. 445 (Sask. C.A.); *Re Laing*, [1927] 1 W.W.R. 699 (B.C.S.C.); and *Re Wright Estate*, [1938] O.W.N. 136 (C.A.).

558 *Re Chartesworth Estate*, [1996] 5 W.W.R. 578 (Man. Q.B.).

559 *Christ Church v. Canada Permanent Trust Co.* (1984), 18 E.T.R. 150 (N.S.T.D.); and *Re Meikle Estate* (1988), 72 Nfld. & P.E.I.R. 166 (P.E.I. T.D.).

560 *Re Buchanan Estate* (1996), 11 E.T.R. (2d) 8 (B.C.S.C.).

will indicated the types of charities to benefit, including those for religious purposes.[561] Again, where there are surplus funds, they may be applied cy-près to the named beneficiaries of the testator, including those for religious purposes.[562]

7) Discriminatory Bequests

At one time, bequests were frequently made or trusts established that restricted the class or classes of potential beneficiaries to members or supporters of stipulated religious groups, or alternatively, excluded the members or supporters of stipulated religious groups from benefiting. Today, these categories usually offend provisions of human rights legislation intended to eliminate discrimination from Canadian society.

In *Canada Trust Co.* v. *Ontario Human Rights Commission*,[563] a trust established in 1923 to provide scholarships at certain schools and universities required students to be white, of British parentage or nationality, and Protestant. The Ontario Court of Appeal found that the trust was premised on notions of racism and religious superiority and contravened contemporary public policy by which all races and religions are to be accorded equal regard and equal respect. The court further ordered that the racial and religious restrictions be removed from the qualifications for the scholarships and that the doctrine of cy-près be applied so as to render the scholarships available to all those meeting the scholastic requirements.

It appears, however, that some discriminatory bequests will be upheld by the courts. In *University of Victoria* v. *B.C. (Attorney-General)*,[564] bequests to a university to provide bursaries for Roman Catholic students only were upheld on several grounds: (i) there was no public relationship between the university and the bursaries, rather the university was merely a trustee administering the bursaries in a private relationship between the testatrix and the students; but (ii) even if the relationship was public, the discrimination was innocuous, the words establishing the bursaries were not particularly offensive and it is not offensive for a person to establish a charitable trust to benefit the adherents of one's own faith.

---

561 *Re McCormick* (1921), 21 O.W.N. 230 (H.C.).
562 *Re Holmes Estate* (1916), 10 O.W.N. 354 (H.C.).
563 (1990), 69 D.L.R. (4th) 321 (Ont. C.A.).
564 (2000), 185 D.L.R. (4th) 182 (B.C.S.C.).

8) Renunciation of Bequests

Provided a renunciation of a bequest is clear and unequivocal, whether by conduct or deed, a religious institution may disclaim a bequest made to it; thus, where the deceased had not remade his will after being "disfellowshipped" by a congregation of Jehovah's Witnesses for chewing tobacco, a court found that the congregation could effectively disclaim the gift, which became part of the residue of the estate to be distributed to other heirs.[565]

L. CHURCH PROPERTY DISPUTES

Disputes within individual congregations or entire denominations over property have arisen, generally, in three factual situations: when individual congregations change denominational affiliation; when schism occurs within an individual congregation, on either doctrinal or non-doctrinal issues; and when schism occurs within a denomination, with groups either forming new denominations or free-standing congregations or merging with other denominations.

Measured in terms of the number of members and economic wealth at stake, the largest such schism in Canadian church history was that of the Presbyterian Church in Canada in 1925, when the United Church of Canada was formed from Methodists, Congregationalists, and Presbyterians. This schism resulted in a significant volume of reported cases, which will be considered separately in the following section,[566] and are predicated on the legal nature of the church polities involved. This section will describe church property disputes generally, setting out the general legal principles applicable.

While the courts, as stated earlier,[567] will not adjudicate on matters that are narrowly doctrinal or spiritual in nature, and are expressly reluctant to consider issues relating to religious institutions other than where property and civil rights are involved, they do have jurisdiction to inter-

---

565 *Re Moss* (1977), 77 D.L.R. (3d) 314 (B.C.S.C.).

566 Below section M.

567 Above section D. See also M.H. Ogilvie, "Church Property Disputes: Some Organizing Principles" (1992) 42 U.T.L.J. 377; and "Ecclesiastical Law - Jurisdiction of Civil Courts - Governing Documents of Religious Institutions - Natural Justice: *Lakeside Colony of Hutterian Brethren v. Hofer*" (1993) 72 Can. Bar Rev. 238.

vene and do consider matters of doctrine, polity, and liturgy when these are relevant to disputes about property rights, rights under contract, or civil rights.[568] Dealing with such disputes is always a delicate matter but a court must discharge its duty in this regard as well as possible,[569] even to inquire into the fundamental tenets of the religious institution when it is necessary for the resolution of the dispute.[570]

In determining church property disputes, courts rely on two basic legal categories, contract and trust. Religious organizations are treated in law as voluntary associations whose legal basis is the multipartite contractual consent of all members to the doctrine, practices, and discipline of the organization.[571] Thus, as long as members of a religious organization remain as members of it, they are subject to its doctrine, practices, and discipline as a matter of consent or contract. When property disputes arise they are equally subject to the doctrine, practices, and discipline in relation to such disputes, unless they simply leave.

Whether church property is vested in trustees pursuant to a trust deed or in a corporation pursuant either to a private act or public legislation of general application, the courts view their role, when property disputes arise, as that of determining the rules of the contract and the trusts on which the property is held. The trust is that imposed upon the property by the founders of the religious institution, including the doctrinal principles to which the institution subscribes, and may only be changed in accordance with that institution's practices and formal procedures for changes in doctrine, polity, and liturgy. Thus, where property disputes are at issue, a court will determine what the contractual rules are, whether the trusts imposed upon the property are being duly observed[572] and only then intervene so as to ensure that the rules are followed and the trust administered for the purposes for which it was intended.[573]

It is a well-settled principle of law that the property of a religious institution must be held and applied to the original purposes for which that institution was founded, that is, for the original "trust." Such prop-

---

568 *Ibid.*
569 *Dunnet* v. *Forneri*, above note 36; and *McPherson* v. *McKay*, above note 60.
570 *Ibid.*
571 Above note 3.
572 *Stein* v. *Hauser* (1913), 5 W.W.R. 971 (Sask. T.D.).
573 *Brewster* v. *Hendershot* (1900), 27 O.A.R. 232 (C.A.); and *Wodell* v. *Potter*, [1930] 1 D.L.R. 726 (Ont. H.C.), aff'd [1930] 2 D.L.R. 449 (Ont. C.A.).

erty cannot be redirected to other purposes by a mere majority of members, and where a majority decides upon a diversion, the property remains in trust for the dissenting minority (even one person) who adheres to the original trust for which the property was given.[574] The onus of proof that there has been a departure from the original trust purpose for which property was given is on those alleging such a departure.[575]

The trust is created at the time of the purchase of the property by the religious institution and not at the time when the deed of transfer is registered; thus, where the group named on the certificate of title is not the congregation for whose benefit the trust has been created, the certificate is invalid.[576] Where there is a departure from the doctrinal standards at the time the trust was established, the property may revert to the original donor where all the members have departed from those standards.[577]

Regardless of the denomination or the polity, with one exceptional case[578] the courts have consistently required that institutions follow their

---

574 The principle is well-established in the common law: *Craigdallie v. Aikman* (1813), 1 Dow. P.C. 1, 3 E.R. 601 (H.L. Sc.); *Craigdallie v. Aikman (No. 2)* (1820), 2 Bligh P.C. 529, 4 E.R. 435 (H.L. Sc.); *Davis v. Jenkins* (1814), 3 V. & B. 151, 35 E.R. 436; *A.G. v. Pearson* (1817), 3 Mer. 351, 36 E.R. 135; *Foley v. Wontner* (1820), 2 Jac. & W. 245, 37 E.R. 621; *Milligan v. Mitchell* (1837), 3 My. & Cr. 72, 40 E.R. 852; *Brown v. Summers* (1840), 11 Sim. 353, 59 E.R. 909; *Shore v. Wilson* (1842), 9 Cl. & F. 353, 8 E.R. 355; *A.G. v. Munro* (1842), 2 De G. & Sm. 122, 64 E.R. 55; *A.G. v. Murdoch* (1849), 7 Hare 445, 68 E.R. 183; *A.G. v. Gould* (1860), 28 Beav. 485, 54 E.R. 452; *A.G. v. Aust* (1865), 13 L.T. 235; *A.G. v. Bunce* (1867), L.R. 6 Eq. 563; *Westwood v. McKie* (1869), 21 L.T. 165; *A.G. v. Stewart* (1872), L.R. 14 Eq. 17; *A.G. v. St. John's Hospital, Bath* (1876), 2 Ch. 554; *A.G. v. Anderson* (1888), 57 L.J. Ch. 543; and *General Assembly of the Free Church of Scotland v. Lord Overtoun*, above note 34.
575 *Doe. d. Reynolds v. Flint* (1841), Ont. Case Law Dig. 962; *Doe d. Methodist Episcopal Trustees v. Brass* (1842), 6 O.S. 437 (U.C.Q.B.); *Itter v. Howe* (1896), 23 O.A.R. 256 (C.A.); *Vick v. Toivonen* (1913), 4 O.W.N. 1542 (C.A.); and *Brylinski v. Inkol* (1924), 55 O.L.R. 369 (H.C.).
576 *Ruthenian Greek Catholic Church v. Fetsyk*, [1922] 3 W.W.R. 872 (Man. K.B.).
577 *Bliss v. Christ Church, Fredericton*, above note 4.
578 *United Church of Canada v. Anderson* (1991), 2 O.R. (3d) 304 (Gen. Div.). This case is anomalous and clearly wrongly decided. The trial judge neither took into consideration the earlier case law, nor did he even inquire about the original trust on which the property was given. See M.H. Ogilvie, "Church Property Disputes: Some Organizing Principles" (1992) 42 U.T.L.J. 377. See also the following case from Bermuda concerning a property dispute in an overseas Unit-

procedural rules so as to find that even where a congregation by majority decides to change its affiliation from one denomination to another
subscribing to different doctrinal standards, there is a breach of trust, and
the property of the congregation is vested in the minority that continues
to subscribe to the original trust.[579] Again, regardless of denomination or
polity, where a congregation or denomination decides to change its fundamental doctrinal standards from those for which the property was
given, the property is to be held on trust for those members who adhere
to the original standard.[580] Even where the congregation or denomination
decides to change a fundamental purpose of a non-doctrinal nature from
the original practices or customs on which the property was given, the
property is to be held on trust for those members who adhere to the original standards.[581]

---

ed Church of Canada presbytery in Bermuda in which the Bermudan courts
found for the congregations rather than the UCC because the congregations
continued to subscribe to the original doctrine of the UCC about human sexual expression: *Wesleyan Methodist Trustees v. Lightbourne*, unreported decision
of 10 June 1998 (Bermuda S.C.), aff'd in unreported decision of 21 June 2001
(Bermuda C.A.).

579 *Doe d. Methodist Episcopal Church (Kingston) v. Bell* (1837), 5 O.S. 344 (C.A.);
Doe d. Methodist Episcopal Trustees v. Brass, above note 575; *A.G. Upper Canada
v. Jeffrey* (1863), 10 Gr. 273 (Ch.); *A.G. Ontario v. Christie* (1867), 13 Gr. 495
(Ch.); *Douglas v. Hawes* (1875), R.E.D. 147 (N.S.T.D.); *McPherson v. McKay*,
above note 60; *R. v. Kapij* (1905), 1 W.L.R. 130 (Man. C.A.); *East Selkirk Greek
Catholic Ruthenian Church v. Portage La Prairie Farmers Mutual Fire Insurance
Co.* (1917), 31 D.L.R. 33 (Man. C.A.); *Anderson v. Gislason*, [1920] 3 W.W.R.
301 (Man. C.A.); *First German Evangelical Lutheran Zion's Congregation v. Reik-
er*, [1921] 1 W.W.R. 794 (Sask. C.A.); *Forler v. Brenner* (1922), 20 O.W.N. 489
(H.C.); *Hennig v. Trautman*, [1926] 2 D.L.R. 280 (Alta. T.D.); *Balkou v. Gouleff*
(1989), 68 O.R. (2d) 574 (C.A.); *Montreal & Canadian Diocese of the Russian
Orthodox Church outside of Russia Inc.*, above note 50. See also: *Buma v. Sikke-
ma* (1994), 76 O.A.C. 66 (Ont. C.A.).
580 *Doe d. Methodist Episcopal Church (Kingston) v. Bell*, above note 579; *Doe d.
Methodist Episcopal Trustees v. Brass*, above note 575; *A.G. Upper Canada v. Jeffrey*, above note 579; *Jones v. Dorland*, above note 48; *Bliss v. Christ Church,
Fredericton*, above note 4; *Itter v. Howe*, above note 575; *Brewster v. Hendershot*,
above note 573; *Stein v. Hauser*, above note 572; *Brendzij v. Hajdej*, [1927] 1
D.L.R. 1051 (Man. C.A.); *Wodell v. Potter*, above note 573; *Chong v. Lee* (1981),
29 B.C.L.R. 13 (S.C.); and *Re Christ Church of China* (1983), 15 E.T.R. 272
(B.C.S.C.).
581 *Dorland v. Jones*, above note 48; *Brendzij v. Hajdej*, above note 580.

The sole exceptional fact situation in relation to judicial enforcement of the original trust is not a true exception. Where the constitution of a congregation or denomination provides that fundamental changes may be made by a majority vote or by some other procedure and where those procedures have been properly complied with, then a court will not disturb the decision of the religious institution and will order that the property go to the majority or other lawfully mandated group or organ of the religious institution.[582] Where the trustees in actual possession of the property of a religious institution are part of a dissenting or minority group, they will be treated in law as holding the property in trust for those who represent the "true body" of the institution.[583] Where an insured church building is destroyed by five in the course of a property dispute proceeding, the dissenting group is not necessarily entitled to the proceeds in whole or in part; rather, the proceeds should go to the successful party in the litigation.[584]

M. CHURCH UNION

On 10 June 1925, the Methodist Church of Canada, the Congregational Churches of Canada, and approximately forty percent of the members of the Presbyterian Church in Canada[585] united to form the United Church of Canada.[586] Although the Methodists and Congregationalists had decided to vote as corporate bodies on the question of union and therefore entered the union as such once a positive vote of their national govern-

---

582 *Itter v. Howe*, above note 575; *Dorland v. Jones*, above note 48; *Pauli v. Huegli*, above note 64; *Dwirnichuk v. Zaichuk*, [1926] 3 W.W.R. 508 (Sask. K.B.); *Edmonton Korean Baptist Church v. Kim* (1996), 41 Alta. L.R. (3d) 21 (Q.B.); and *United Pentecostal Church v. Chipman Pentecostal Church Inc.*, unreported decision of 30 June 1997 (N.B.Q.B.).

583 *Brewster v. Hendershot*, above note 573.

584 *East Selkirk Greek Catholic Ruthenian Church*, above note 579.

585 In 1925 it was estimated that about 60% of the membership of the Presbyterian Church in Canada had gone into the union; however, membership statistics of the United Church and the continuing Presbyterian Church, as well as the 1931 and 1941 Religion Censuses of Canada, suggest that by 1941 only about 40% had remained with the United Church, while 60% had either always remained or had returned to the Presbyterian Church.

586 See generally N. Keith Clifford, *The Resistance to Church Union in Canada, 1904–1939* (Vancouver: U.B.C. Press, 1985).

ing bodies was achieved, the Presbyterians, out of keeping with presbyterian polity generally, decided to permit each individual congregation to choose to opt out of the union to which the General Assembly had agreed. The result fragmented both the denomination and individual congregations; voting irregularities occurred and close votes resulted in a significant volume of reported disputes over ownership of congregational property, including disputes where donors of property sought to have it redirected or where testamentary bequests proved difficult to transfer to the new denomination by virtue of their trust terms.

To facilitate the union and to avoid litigation over property ownership similar to that in the *Free Church Case*[587] and the subsequent corrective legislation of the British Parliament, the negotiating parties had agreed that federal and provincial legislation should be enacted to constitute the United Church and make provision for the property transfers to that new corporate body. This legislation[588] made provision in each province for provincial property commissions to deal with transfers and disputes; however, the interpretation of the legislation and the rules of the commissions proved problematical and litigation in the civil courts ensued. The reported cases assumed the legality of the union and understood that both federal and provincial legislation was to operate concurrently to resolve disputes.[589]

1) Voting Procedures

Since it lies within the power of a kirk session to keep the communion roll for a congregation, which was also the voting roll for the vote on church union, where a kirk session purges an old roll and establishes a new one in compliance with proper polity procedures, in the absence of evidence to the contrary, the new roll shall be the voting roll and the kirk session shall be regarded as having acted properly.[590] Any person whose name was on the communion roll of a congregation was eligible to vote, and the compilation of a separate voters' roll was simply for conven-

---

587 Above note 34.

588 *United Church of Canada Act*, S.C. 1924, c. 100.

589 *Ferguson v. MacLean*, [1930] S.C.R. 630. See also *Re United Church*, [1927] 2 D.L.R. 1169 (P.E.I. C.A.) for the authority of the provincial property commissions.

590 *Re Burlington Presbyterian Church*, [1926] 4 D.L.R. 380 (Ont. H.C.).

ience.[591] Only those whose names were on a communion roll at the time of the enactment of the union legislation were entitled to vote, as was provided by that legislation.[592] Moreover, individual congregational voters were to comply with the legislation and the law of the church, and individual congregations were not permitted to devise their own voting procedures or guidelines.[593]

Persons who were admitted as members of a congregation according to kirk session records but whose names were inadvertently left off the communion roll were nevertheless entitled to vote, since admission by the kirk session to membership is sufficient to constitute a person a member of a congregation in presbyterian polity.[594] A person whose name last appeared on a communion roll in 1898 and was not listed when the rolls were purged in 1918 and 1921 was held to be effectively removed from the roll and to have no rights to vote, in the absence of evidence that the name was erroneously purged from the roll.[595] Persons whose names inadvertently remained on the communion roll of a congregation after they had joined another denomination, by letter from their former minister, ceased to be members of the former congregation and had no right to vote.[596]

In addition to disputes as to whether or not a person's name should be on the communion roll of a congregation, disputes also arose as to whether or not those whose names were on the appendix to a roll were eligible to vote. Presbyterian practice is to place the names of those who wish to remain as members of a congregation but who cannot attend communion regularly on an appendix to the roll, but to regard these persons as members of the congregation. Thus, persons whose names were on an appendix to a roll were held to have the full right to vote as members since they remained full members.[597] Where disputes arose as to whether

---

591 *Ogle* v. *Clugston* (1926), 30 O.W.N. 98 (H.C.).

592 *Osborne* v. *Milliken* (1921), 28 O.W.N. 40 (H.C.).

593 *Ibid.*

594 *Rodney Case*, [1926] 2 D.L.R. 516 (Ont. Church Property Comm.).

595 *Re Dalhousie Mills Presbyterian Church*, [1926] 4 D.L.R. 383 (Ont. H.C.).

596 *Re Maple Valley Presbyterian Church*, [1926] 4 D.L.R. 378 (Ont. H.C.).

597 *Richmond Hill Case*, [1926] 1 D.L.R. 795 (Ont. Church Property Comm.); *Re Richmond Hill Presbyterian Church*, [1926] 4 D.L.R. 365 (Ont. H.C.); *Re Conn Presbyterian Church*, [1926] 4 D.L.R. 385 (Ont. H.C.); and *Stover* v. *Drysdale*, [1925] 4 D.L.R. 994 (B.C.S.C.). *Cf. Re Wick Case*, [1926] 1 D.L.R. 829 (Ont. Church Property Comm.).

or not a name should be on a communion roll or an appendix to a roll, these should be resolved on a one-by-one basis in church courts and in accordance with church law, with final appeal only to the civil courts.[598]

The union vote was required by the legislation to be by secret ballot of members of congregations only;[599] thus, attempts by individual congregations to import additional formalities into the process were found to be illegal.[600] Where a congregation rejected union on the first vote and then carried out a second vote, which resulted in approval of union, the Privy Council held the first vote to be the operative one since provision was made for only one vote.[601] Again, where a Methodist congregation and a Presbyterian congregation had shared worship for several years prior to the union vote but had remained as separate congregations with separate communion rolls, it was held that each congregation should be regarded as separate and should vote separately for church union.[602]

Finally, it should be noted that procedural matters were also considered by the civil courts in relation to the unification of the various Presbyterian denominations in Canada in 1875 to form the Presbyterian Church in Canada. In these cases, the courts upheld the principle that the law and custom of the uniting churches should be followed both in respect to the call for a congregational vote[603] and the procedure used in a congregational vote.[604]

2) Property Rights

Under the union legislation, a congregation could vote either to join the union church or to stay out of the union, and congregational property was to follow that vote so as to go with the congregation into the union or stay out in its entirety — there was no middle course.[605] Thus, where minority congregational members purported to retain congregational

---

598 *Stover* v. *Drysdale*, above note 597.

599 Above note 588, s. 10(a).

600 *Re Maple Valley Case*, [1926] 1 D.L.R. 808 (Ont. Church Property Comm.); *Ogle* v. *Clugston*, above note 591; and *Rodney Case*, above note 594.

601 *St. Luke's Presbyterian Church, Saltsprings* v. *Cameron*, [1930] A.C. 673 (P.C.).

602 *Conn Case*, [1926] 1 D.L.R. 1122 (Ont. Church Property Comm.).

603 *Deeks* v. *Davidson* (1879), 26 Gr. 488 (Ch.).

604 *Cowan* v. *Wright* (1876), 23 Gr. 616 (Ch.); *Hall* v. *Ritchie* (1876), 23 Gr. 630 (Ch.); and *McRae* v. *McLeod* (1879), 26 Gr. 255 (Ch.).

605 Above note 588, s. 8.

property, the courts refused to permit them to do so.[606] Regardless of the closeness of the union vote in each congregation, the minority was not entitled to a *pro rata* or any other share of congregational property, which followed the decision of the majority.[607]

The purpose of the federal legislation effecting the union was clearly to ensure that the property did not remain in trust for those who continued to subscribe to the original trusts on which it was given. This had happened in the *Free Church Case*[608] in Scotland with the result that a tiny minority, which had not supported the church union at issue in that case, had been given almost the entire assets of a large and wealthy denomination. Legislation had subsequently to be enacted to overcome the effect of the application of the trust doctrine in that case.[609]

Finally, the courts also addressed the issue of the application of property going into the United Church. Where congregational property was encumbered by a trust for certain specific purposes prior to the union, it was held that it should be applied as closely as possible to those original purposes in the United Church.[610] However, where bequests made prior to union to a church or congregation were made for specific purposes that were not accommodated within the United Church, but continued to exist in the continuing Presbyterian Church, then the courts determined that those properties should stay with the continuing congregation or denomination, as the case may be.[611]

Where a trustee refused to concur in the union after a pro-union congregational vote and to execute a deed transferring the property to the new denomination, a court ordered that the property be vested in the new congregation as it was authorized to do implicitly pursuant to the legislation.[612]

---

606 *Ballantyne v. Craig* (1926), 29 O.W.N. 411 (Div. Ct.); and *McLean v. Ballantyne*, [1928] 4 D.L.R. 37 (Ont. H.C.).

607 *Ferguson v. Maclean*, [1930] S.C.R. 630.

608 Above note 34.

609 (U.K.) *Churches (Scotland) Act*, (1905) c. 12.

610 *Aird v. Johnson*, [1929] 4 D.L.R. 664 (Ont. C.A.).

611 *Re Patriquin. Fraser v. McLellan*, [1930] 3 D.L.R. 241 (S.C.C.); *Re Gray. United Church of Canada v. Presbyterian Church of [sic] Canada*, [1935] 1 D.L.R. 1 (S.C.C.); and *Laird v. MacKay*, [1938] 3 D.L.R. 474 (Ont. C.A.).

612 *Smith's Falls Westminster Congregation v. Ferguson* (1924), 27 O.W.N. 52 (H.C.).

Chapter Nine

Discipline in Religious Institutions

A. INTRODUCTION

Historically, most branches of the Christian church have regarded discipline of both clergy and laity as an appropriate means for ensuring uniformity, homogeneity, and order within the community as well as being for the eternal good of the person under discipline. Occasionally, disciplinary procedures have spilled over into the civil courts when ecclesiastical discipline decisions have been appealed from internal dispute resolution tribunals. Civil courts have repeatedly expressed reluctance to intervene in cases of church discipline,[1] and will not consider matters that are narrowly doctrinal or spiritual in nature. Nevertheless, they do intervene, as their constitutional status permits them to do, in relation to church discipline of both clergy and laity and do consider doctrine and polity issues

---

1   *Balkou* v. *Gouleff* (1989), 68 O.R. (2d) 574 (C.A.) at 576. Compare the English position that a civil court should not interfere in clergy discipline because it is essentially an intimate, spiritual, and religious process and does not engage the public interest, as set out in: R. v. *Chief Rabbi of the United Hebrew Congregations of Great Britain, ex parte Wachmann*, [1993] 2 All E.R. 249 (Q.B.). It may be doubted whether this decision properly considered the sovereignty of the state over all within the kingdom.

when these are involved in the dispute.[2] Civil court intervention does not amount to dictating doctrine,[3] but rather means discerning what the doctrine may be and enforcing it through civil remedies.[4]

In recent years, in addition to the traditional role of judicial review of internal disciplinary processes for enforcement or reversal, civil courts have also been obliged to discipline clergy and other employees of religious institutions for criminal and civil wrongs committed by those persons and to impose vicarious liability on their sponsoring religious organizations. The increase in these cases, usually concerned with sexual and physical assaults of children or other weaker persons, has required the courts to begin to explore the relationship, if any, between internal disciplinary processes and punishments and the civil law of Canada. Both internal and external aspects of clergy and laity discipline are considered in this chapter.

B. CIVIL JURISDICTION TO INTERVENE

The delicacy[5] with which courts intervene in ecclesiastical discipline cases is reflected in the types of situations and the extent of their involvement, as set out in the previous chapter:[6] (i) where church tribunals do not follow their own procedural and substantive rules; (ii) where internal tribunals do not comply with the rules of natural justice; in particular, the rights to know the case, to reply to the case, and to have an unbiased tribunal; (iii) where tribunals act in an *ultra vires* fashion, that is, with malice, *mala fides*, bias, or some other vitiating factor; (iv) where disciplinary disputes occur in religious organizations that have been incorporated pursuant to civil legislation, so as to be thereby subject to

---

2   *Ibid.* See also *Gruner v. McCormack*, unreported decision of 10 March 2000 (Ont. S.C.J.).

3   *Bishop of Columbia v. Cridge* (1874), 1 B.C.R. (Pt. 1) 5 (S.C.); and *Dunnet v. Forneri* (1877), 25 Gr. 199 (Ont. H.C.).

4   *Re Christ Church of China* (1983), 15 E.T.R. 272 (B.C.S.C.).

5   *McPherson v. McKay* (1880), 4 O.A.R. 501 (C.A.); and *Ukrainian Greek Orthodox Church v. Ukrainian Greek Orthodox Cathedral of St. Mary the Protectress*, [1940] S.C.R. 586.

6   Above, chapter 8 at section D. See also *Porter v. Clarke* (1829), 2 Sim. 520, 57 E.R. 882; and *Forbes v. Eden* (1867), L.R. 1 Sc. & Div. 568 (H.L.).

7   *Lindenberger v. United Church of Canada* (1985), 17 C.C.E.L. 143 (Ont. Div. Ct.), aff'd (1987), 17 C.C.E.L. 172 (C.A.).

civil court supervision; (v) where discipline is related to a property or a civil right; and (vi) where a civil court is called upon to carry out a punishment determined by an internal tribunal.

Since the role of the civil courts is essentially one of judicial review of the decision of inferior tribunals,[7] the usual range of administrative remedies is available, including certiorari,[8] prohibition,[9] injunction,[10] and damages.[11] The civil courts may also be willing to consider the award of damages for which ecclesiastical law does not provide, including an award of exemplary damages where an internal abuse of process will result in an injustice to a priest.[12]

C. DISCIPLINE OF CLERGY

The first steps in any process to discipline clergy of a religious institution is within that institution and in compliance with the internal dispute resolution mechanisms of that institution. Virtually all religious institutions in Canada provide in their constitutions for disciplinary processes, some of great formality and complexity and others of great informality and simplicity.[13] Appeal to the civil courts typically occurs either when one of the parties is dissatisfied with the decision of the final ecclesiastical tribunal or attempts to circumvent the internal dispute resolution processes by removing the matter to the civil courts.

The civil courts will generally not accept jurisdiction or interfere with an internal disciplinary process providing it is operating in an *intra vires* fashion.[14] In particular instances where the disciplinary process is regulated by civil legislation incorporating the religious organization, an internal tribunal is subject to the control and supervision of a civil court

---

8   *Ex parte Little* (1895), 33 N.B.R. 210 (C.A.); and *Lindenburger* v. *United Church of Canada, ibid.*

9   *Ex parte Currie* (1886), 26 N.B.R. 403 (C.A.).

10 *Holiness Movement Church in Canada* v. *Horner* (1917), 12 O.W.N. 387 (H.C.); *McCharles* v. *Wyllie* (1927), 32 O.W.N. 202 (H.C.); and *Frogley* v. *Ottawa Presbytery of the United Church of Canada* (1995), 16 C.C.E.L. (2d) 249 (Ont. Gen. Div.).

11 *McCaw* v. *United Church of Canada* (1991), 82 D.L.R. (4th) 289 (Ont. C.A.).

12 *Gruner* v. *McCormack*, above note 2.

13 Above chapter 3.

14 *Ash* v. *Methodist Church* (1901), 31 S.C.R. 497; *Pinke* v. *Bornhold* (1904), 8 O.L.R. 575 (H.C.); *McCharles* v. *Wyllie*, above note 10; and *Wetmon* v. *Bayne*, [1928] 1 D.L.R. 848 (Alta. C.A.).

to the same extent as is any other inferior court in the jurisdiction.[15] Civil courts may interfere where a case is of public interest, and, if appropriate, overturn the decision of an internal tribunal.[16] When civil courts become involved, they will enforce church law,[17] and may assist in enforcing the decision of an internal tribunal against the member of the clergy under discipline.[18]

Since the internal tribunal has primary jurisdiction in cases of clergy discipline, the onus of showing a cause of action for removal from the tribunal to the civil courts is on the party wishing to have the case removed, who is usually the member of the clergy under discipline.[19] The civil courts will not entertain an action until the internal procedures and tribunals have been exhausted,[20] except where there is some impropriety in internal procedures.[21] Where the dispute remains unresolved and a matter is ongoing within the internal dispute resolution process, a court will not issue an interlocutory injunction at the request of a minister to restrain the church from barring him from applying for other appointments, except where the minister can establish a strong *prima facie* case that the church lacked jurisdiction under its own church law to proceed as it did. Nor will a court require a church body to restore the minister to employment while the matter is pending where the minister has denied its authority over him.[22]

Most cases involving the discipline of clergy concern the dismissal of clergy for alleged cause, and the courts have consistently required that dismissals be strictly in compliance with the procedural and substantive requirements of the religious organization.[23] Where the practice is to per-

---

15 *Ex parte Currie*, above note 9; and *Lindenburger v. United Church of Canada*, above note 7.

16 *Ex parte Little*, above note 8.

17 *Halliwell v. Synod of Ontario* (1884), 7 O.R. 67 (H.C.).

18 *Bishop of Columbia v. Cridge*, above note 3.

19 *Orr v. Brown*, [1932] 3 D.L.R. 364 (B.C.C.A.).

20 *Pederson v. Fulton* (1994), 111 D.L.R. (4th) 367 (Ont. Gen. Div.); and *Frogley v. Ottawa Presbytery of the United Church of Canada*, above note 10.

21 As set out above at section B.

22 *Wigglesworth v. Phipps* (2001), 7 C.C.E.L. (3d) 37 (Alta. Q.B.).

23 *A.G. v. Pearson* (1817), 3 Mer. 363; 36 E.R. 135; *Porter v. Clarke* (1829), 2 Sim. 520, 57 E.R. 882; *Milligan v. Mitchell* (1833), 1 My. & K. 446, 39 E.R. 750; *Newell v. Aked* (1835), 7 Sim. 321, 58 E.R. 861; *A.G. v. Welsh* (1844), 4 Hare 572, 67 E.R. 775 (V.C.); *A.G. v. Munro* (1848), 2 De G. & Sm. 122, 64 E.R. 55

mit the dismissal of a minister pursuant to a majority vote of a congregation, a civil court will not interfere provided the vote is proper in all
respects.[24]

However, in one respect, the courts will intervene so as to require
that civil law standards are imported into clergy discipline cases before
internal ecclesiastical tribunals. In several clergy dismissal cases involving the United Church of Canada,[25] and in *Lakeside Colony of Hutterian
Brethren v. Hofer*,[26] the Ontario Court of Appeal and the Supreme Court
of Canada respectively have required that internal tribunals comply with
the principles of natural justice, whether or not the procedural rules for
these tribunals make provision for these principles. Thus, in *Lakeside*,
the Court required that parties under discipline be told the case against
them, be given the right to reply, and receive a hearing from an unbiased
tribunal.[27] On the other hand, in *Lindenburger v. United Church of Canada*,
the Ontario Divisional Court found that slight irregularities in following

---

(V.C.); *A.G. v. Murdoch* (1852), 1 De G.M. & G. 86, 42 E.R. 484 (LJJ.); *Perry v.
Shipway* (1859), 4 De G. & J. 353, 45 E.R. 136; *Daugers v. Rivez* (1860), 28
Beav. 233, 54 E.R. 355; *Long v. Bishop of Capetown* (1863), 1 Moo. P.C.C.N.S.
411, 15 E.R. 756; *Forbes v. Eden*, above note 6; *Cooper v. Gordon* (1869), L.R. 8
Eq. 249; and *Dean v. Bennett* (1870), 6 Ch. App. 489.

24 *R. v. Jotham* (1790), 3 Term Rep. 575, 100 E.R. 741; and *United Pentecostal
Church v. Chipman Pentecostal Church Inc.*, [1997] N.B.J. No. 229 (Q.B.). By the
same token, courts also permit congregations to choose their own clergy by
majority vote where there is no other constitutional provision or denominational attachment: *Dwirnichuk v. Zaichuk*, [1926] 3 W.W.R. 508 (Sask. K.B.).

25 *Lindenburger v. United Church of Canada*, above note 7; *McCaw v. United Church
of Canada*, above note 11; and *Davis v. United Church of Canada* (1992), 92
D.L.R. (4th) 678 (Ont. Gen. Div.). See also *Wetmon v. Bayne*, above note 14.

26 (1992), 97 D.L.R. (4th) 17 (S.C.C.). See also the following Scots law cases that
required natural justice: *Dunbar v. Skinner* (1849), 11 D. 945; *MacMillan v.
General Assembly of the Free Church of Scotland* (1859), 22 D. 290, (1861) 23
D. 1314, (1862) 24 D. 1282, (1864) 2 M. 1444; *Lang v. Presbytery of Irvine*
(1864), 2 M. 823; *Forbes v. Eden*, above note 6; *Skerret v. Oliver* (1896), 23 R.
468; *McDonald v. Burns* (1940), S.C. 376; and *Brentall v. Free Presbyterian
Church of Scotland*, unreported decision of 31 January 1986 (Court of Session).

27 See generally M.H. Ogilvie, "Ecclesiastical Law – Jurisdiction of Civil Courts –
Governing Documents of Religious Organizations – Natural Justice: *Lakeside
Colony of Hutterian Brethren v. Hofer*" (1993) 72 Can. Bar Rev. 238.

the procedures of the religious institution would not necessarily vitiate a decision of an internal tribunal.[28]

Where an internal tribunal dismisses a member of the clergy, that decision may not be reversed or reheard by another body within the religious institution that is not authorized by its constitution to participate in its juridical processes; thus, such a decision cannot be challenged by the temporal corporation of a religious organization, where its powers and duties are restricted solely to matters of property and contract.[29] Again, where provincial religious institutions legislation required that trustees call a general meeting of the congregation to determine whether or not to dismiss a minister, their dismissal of the minister without a meeting is wrongful and the minister is entitled to damages.[30]

Clergy discipline cases have been concerned with four basic fact situations: (i) revocation of a licence to preach or to conduct services, either on the grounds of disobedience[31] or alleged incompetence;[32] (ii) removal from a particular pastoral charge, either on grounds of disobedience,[33] alleged incompetence,[34] or immorality (usually adultery) — this did not include removal of a licence to continue to serve in another congregation;[35] (iii) suspension from a congregation on the ground of

---

28   Above note 7. An interesting related issue was raised in *Roberts v. British Columbia (Council of Human Rights)* (1997), 29 C.H.R.R. D/425 (B.C.S.C.), which held that a human rights tribunal is also required to follow the rules of natural justice when dealing with a complaint by a Roman Catholic priest against his diocese.

29   *Ukrainian Greek Orthodox Church, etc.*, above note 5.

30   *Belding v. Calton Baptist Church*, unreported decision of 22 September 1995 (Ont. Small Cl. Ct.).

31   *Bishop of Columbia v. Cridge*, above note 3; and *Halliwell v. Synod of Ontario*, above note 17.

32   *McCaw v. United Church of Canada*, above note 11.

33   *Bishop of Columbia v. Cridge*, above note 3; *McCharles v. Wyllie*, above note 10; and *Ukrainian Greek Orthodox Church, etc.*, above note 5.

34   *Orr v. Brown*, above note 19; *Lindenburger v. United Church of Canada*, above note 7; *Brewer v. Incorporated Synod of the Diocese of Ottawa of the Anglican Church of Canada*, unreported decision of 16 February 1996 (Ont. Gen. Div.).

35   *Ex parte Currie*, above note 9; *Ex parte Little*, above note 8; *Ash v. Methodist Church*, above note 14; and *Davis v. United Church of Canada*, above note 25. See also *Lewery v. Salvation Army* (1993), 104 D.L.R. (4th) 449 (N.B.C.A.), leave to appeal to S.C.C. refused (1994), 1 C.C.E.L. (2d) 160 (S.C.C.).

immorality until a church tribunal had dealt with the matter;[36] and (iv) removal of a bishop from an episcopal see.[37] In six cases, the courts over-turned the decisions of the ecclesiastical tribunals,[38] while in the other cases, the courts either upheld the decision after reviewing the facts,[39] or redirected the litigant to the ecclesiastical forum on the ground that the internal procedural routes had not been exhausted.[40]

As with the church property dispute cases discussed in the previous chapter, contract and trust are the underlying principles for the judicial position that internal tribunals have jurisdiction and that clergy are sub-ject to them. Furthermore, as the cases above show, the civil courts understand their role to be the enforcement of the contract among mem-bers and adherents of the religious institutions on the basis of the under-lying trusts for which property is held, whether in relation to doctrine, polity, or liturgy, of that religious institution.

However, two additional juridical reasons justifying judicial supervi-sion of clergy discipline cases have also been given. As stated above,[41] incorporation of a religious institution has been understood to give authority to the courts to review ecclesiastical affairs, particularly when the religious institution is so large as to have a "sufficient public charac-ter"[42] to be amenable to judicial supervision. A final reason, specifically applicable to clergy, is the nature of the legal relationship between a member of the clergy and church or congregation, as one similar to, if not of, a contract of employment, which the courts may enforce like any other contract of employment.

The precise nature of the legal relationship between a member of the clergy and the religious institution that has either ordained or otherwise

---

36 *Ash v. Methodist Church*, above note 14.

37 *Holiness Movement Church in Canada v. Horner*, above note 10.

38 *Bishop of Columbia v. Cridge*, above note 3; *Halliwell v. Synod of Ontario*, above note 17; *Ex parte Currie*, above note 9; *Ex parte Little*, above note 8; *McCaw v. United Church of Canada*, above note 11; and *Davis v. United Church of Canada*, above note 25.

39 *Ash v. Methodist Church*, above note 14; *Orr v. Brown*, above note 19; *Ukrainian Greek Orthodox Church, etc.*, above note 5; *Lindenburger v. United Church of Canada*, above note 7; and *Brewer*, above note 34.

40 *Holiness Movement Church in Canada v. Horner*, above note 10; and *McCharles v. Wyllie*, above note 10.

41 Above note 15.

42 *Lindenburger v. United Church of Canada*, above note 7 per Rosenberg J. at 193.

accepted him or her as suitable to hold a pastoral office has yet to be determined in the common law. Religious institutions typically wish to characterize the position of a member of the clergy as a spiritual one only, a "vocation," and to regard the remuneration paid as a "stipend" for living expenses, rather than as a salary. In short, the position is said to be one of status rather than contract.

On the other hand, members of the clergy who hold appointments, whether with congregations, national organizations, or schools or colleges, typically work in accordance with written job descriptions and enjoy employee benefit plans, so that their status from the common law perspective looks very similar to that of an employee. "Ordination" may well have a spiritual dimension but from the perspective of the common law it may be associated with a call to the bar or registration as a doctor; that is, it is simply a professional qualification prerequisite to employment.[43]

Whether or not a member of the clergy is considered to be an office-holder or an employee from the perspective of the law seems to be easiest to determine where there is legislation expressly governing the particular situation.[44] The courts have considered the issue in two types of situations governed by legislation: (i) legislation containing a precise statutory definition of employer and/or employee; and (ii) legislation containing a definition of employer or employee requiring the courts to provide legal content to phrases such as "contract of service" or "contract of employment." While the outcome in the first situation would clearly be compliance with the legislation, in the second situation, the outcome is less certain and courts treat the issue as if little legislative guidance is available — that is, as a question at common law, by looking for guidance to the contract as evidenced by the constitution and practices of the religious institution.

In the only case to date where there was express legislation defining an employer as a person from whom a member of a pension plan receives remuneration to which the pension plan is related, the member of the clergy was treated as an employee and subject to the legislation even

---

43 For a further discussion of the policy issues, see M.H. Ogilvie, "Ecclesiastical Law – Jurisdiction of Civil Courts – Status of Clergy: *McCaw v. United Church of Canada*" (1992) 71 Can. Bar Rev. 597 at 610–615.

44 For an expanded discussion of what follows, see M.H. Ogilvie, "Christian Clergy and the Law of Employment: Office-Holders, Employees or Outlaws" (1999) 3 Journal of the Church Law Association 2.

where the constitutional documents of the religious institution equally expressly provided that a member of the clergy is not an employee or in any way subject to a contractual relationship.[45] Such an outcome is not a breach of section 2(a) of the *Charter* because its effect is trivial and insubstantial and a mere administrative convenience.[46]

The second category of cases, where courts are required to give legal content to vague phrases, consists of two groups of cases. In the first group of two cases, both concerned with the Salvation Army, which expressly provides in its constitutional documents that officers are not employed on a basis of contract, courts have found that officers are not employed under contract and therefore have been excluded from claiming workmen's compensation where the legislation required a claimant to be "under a contract of service"[47] and also excluded from claiming damages for wrongful dismissal since there was no contract from which the officer was dismissed.[48]

In the second group of cases where courts have been required to give legal content to ambiguous legislative phrases, the distinctive feature in contrast to the Salvation Army cases is that there is no express exclusion of a contractual relationship in constitutional documents, only an implied one implicit in the historical understandings and practices of the religious institution. These cases were concerned with giving content to legislative phrases such as "contract of service," and the courts' approach has been assimilated to cases solely at common law, especially' clergy dismissal cases where no legislation is at issue.

In three cases dating from the beginning of the twentieth century in which courts were asked to decide whether certain members of the clergy were employees under a "contract of service" for national insurance purposes, three courts found that Methodist ministers and probationer ministers,[49] Church of England curates,[50] and Presbyterian ministers,[51]

---

45 *Salvation Army Canada East v. Ontario (A.G.)* (1992), 88 D.L.R. (4th) 238 (Ont. Gen. Div.).

46 *Ibid.*

47 *Rogers v. Booth*, [1937] 2 All E.R. 751 (C.A.).

48 *Lewery v. Salvation Army*, above note 35.

49 *Re Employment of Ministers of the United Methodist Church* (1912), 107 L.T. 143 (Ch. D.).

50 *Re National Insurance Act, 1911. Re Employment of Church of England Curates*, [1912] 2 Ch. D. 563 (Ch. D.).

51 *Scottish Insurance Commissioners v. Church of Scotland* 1914 S.C. 16 (1st Div.).

were holders of an ecclesiastical office, not employees, and therefore were excluded from a national insurance scheme.

Again, in relation to the Salvation Army, English[52] and Canadian[53] courts have accepted the Army's regulations governing its officers as determinative of their status, so as to find that an officer's position is spiritual and not contractual. In the former case, this meant that an officer injured while working could not claim workmen's compensation, which required a contract of employment, and in the latter case, that an officer who was dismissed after separation from his wife could be dismissed without notice or cause.

Finally, and more recently, in relation to a Methodist minister[54] and a Presbyterian minister[55] dismissed pursuant to internal church disciplinary proceedings, the English Court of Appeal and House of Lords, respectively, looked to those denominations' constitutions and manuals of discipline and found the positions to be characterized as spiritual and not contractual, with the result that the dismissal decisions could not be appealed to an industrial tribunal because they were not employed on a "contract of service" as required by legislation. This same approach has now been taken in England in relation to a Sikh *granthi* (priest)[56] and a Muslim *khateeb* (preacher),[57] who were also denied appeals to an industrial tribunal when they were dismissed from positions characterized by the courts as spiritual rather than contractual.

In these decisions, the courts have adopted a contractual approach since they looked to the constitutional contract of the religious institution, where they found the position of a member of the clergy defined as spiritual rather than contractual. They then enforced that contract by finding that the relationship of a member of the clergy and a denomination is not one of a contract of employment.

By contrast, where the governing documents of religious organizations contain no express provisions defining their legal relationship with

---

52 *Rogers v. Booth*, above note 47.

53 *Lewery v. Salvation Army*, above note 35.

54 *President of the Methodist Conference v. Parfitt*, [1984] Q.B. 368 (C.A.).

55 *Davies v. Presbyterian Church of Wales*, [1986] 1 All E.R. 705 (H.L.). Again, in *Diocese of Southwark v. Coker*, [1996] I.C.R. 913 (E.A.T.), a Church of England curate was not permitted to appeal a dismissal to an industrial tribunal, on the grounds that he was an ecclesiastical office holder not an employee.

56 *Santokh Singh v. Guru Nanak Gurdwara*, [1990] I.C.R. 309 (C.A.).

57 *Birmingham Mosque Trust Ltd. v. Alavi*, [1992] I.C.R. 435 (E.A.T.).

their clergy as spiritual only, Canadian courts have tended to assimilate that relationship with contracts of employment and to require that dismissal be for cause with damages in lieu. In *McCaw v. United Church of Canada*,[58] a minister was found to have been dismissed by unfair procedures lacking natural justice. To determine the appropriate remedy, the Ontario Court of Appeal was asked to address the nature of the legal relationship between the minister and the pastoral charge; however, it avoided precise characterization of that relationship as one of a contract of employment, preferring instead to characterize it as one in which there was a degree of control over the minister's ability to earn his living for which damages should be awarded if that ability is unlawfully taken from him, as it was when the requirements of *The Manual* were not followed. The calculation of the damages awarded was similar to that when damages are awarded for wrongful dismissal. This hesitation to characterize the relationship as a contract of employment may be contrasted with the position taken by the trial judge, Carruthers J., that a minister may be considered as an employee for wrongful dismissal purposes with the governing documents constituting a part of the contract of employment.[59]

The precise legal characterization of the relationship between a member of the clergy and a religious institution as one of a contract of employment remains uncertain and the position in Canada must still be clarified for those religious institutions that either do not expressly provide that clergy enjoy a spiritual status only or that do not, in fact, enter into written contracts of employment with clergy, as some religious institutions actually do.[60]

D. DISCIPLINE OF LAITY

Members of religious organizations are typically subject to the requirements of those organizations in relation to lifestyle, financial, moral, and

---

58 Above note 11. See also *Brewer v. Diocese of Ottawa*, above note 34 where the court concluded that an Anglican priest was also an office-holder, not employee, but for reasons that are bizarre, to say the least. For further discussion, see Ogilvie, above note 44 at 24–25.

59 *McCaw v. United Church of Canada* (1988), 51 D.L.R. (4th) 86 (Ont. H.C.).

60 *David v. Congregation B'Nai Israel* (1999), 99 C.L.L.C. 210–031 (Ont. Gen. Div.), where a rabbi employed on a contract of employment was entitled to damages for dismissal without notice.

other matters, and to the disciplinary procedures of those organizations when in breach of those requirements. From the perspective of the civil law, submission to disciplinary procedures is entirely voluntary since membership in religious organizations is entirely voluntary. Members may simply avoid these by resignation, although they may still be liable in the civil courts, whether criminal or civil, in relation to wrongful or illegal acts or omissions in breach of the civil law done while still members or officers of a religious institution.

The legal relationship of internal ecclesiastical disciplinary tribunals to the civil courts with respect to the discipline of the laity is identical to that with respect to clergy. The civil courts enjoy general supervisory authority over internal disciplinary tribunals from which appeal may be made to the civil courts by the disciplined member. While some religious institutions purport expressly in their constitutions to deprive disciplined members of a right of appeal to the civil courts, it is clear that such prohibitions are of no effect. It is the right of every citizen of Canada to appeal to the civil courts; therefore, no member of a religious organization may be deprived of this right by any doctrine or procedural rule of a religious organization, nor can a member be expelled automatically from membership simply by seeking redress in the civil courts.[61]

When internal disciplinary tribunals purport to interfere with the civil rights of members, the civil courts will exert jurisdiction to protect those civil rights.[62] Moreover, by virtue of the ownership of property by religious organizations, the civil courts also enjoy jurisdiction to adjudicate upon the civil rights of members as members of an organization possessing property.[63] Again, as with clergy discipline cases, the civil courts will tend to restrict their role to the enforcement of the doctrinal standards of the religious institution, particularly where the institution has a settled, commonly held doctrine and restricts membership to those who subscribe to that doctrine.[64]

---

61 *Heinrichs v. Wiens (No. 2)*, [1917] 35 W.L.R. 306 (Sask. T.D.). See also *Tully v. Farrell* (1876), 23 Gr. 49 (Ch.); and *Dunnet v. Forneri* (1877), 25 Gr. 199 (Ch.).

62 *Ukrainian Greek Orthodox Church, etc.*, above note 5.

63 *Patillo v. Cummings* (1915), 24 D.L.R. 775 (N.S.T.D.).

64 *Hofer v. Hofer*, [1970] S.C.R. 958; and *Re Christ Church of China* (1983), 15 E.T.R. 272 (B.C.S.C.). See also *Walter v. A.G. Alberta* (1969), 3 D.L.R. (3d) 1 (S.C.C.) for necessity to comply with civil legislation in property-holding.

The principles of natural justice are required to be followed in all matters of lay discipline, whether or not the constitution or customary practices of the religious institution so provide; thus, lay members under discipline must be told the full case against them, receive the right to reply, and be heard by an unbiased tribunal.[65]

When a decision is made to expel a member, it must be carried out in accordance with the proper procedures of that institution and the civil court will intervene to order that such procedures be followed.[66] Membership rights in a religious institution can be removed only for cause, and where they have been improperly withdrawn, a civil court will intervene in the internal life of the institution to restore them or to order a proper hearing of the issues.[67]

Once a member of a religious institution has been removed from membership, there may still remain legal issues between that person and the religious institution. Where a cause of action exists in the civil law, including in the criminal law, either party may pursue that matter in the civil courts. Moreover, a person who is removed from membership continues to enjoy the civil rights of a member of the public to worship in the congregation from which he or she has been removed, provided proper decorum is maintained and no injunction is in place, and such a person may not be forcibly removed.[68]

Issues of property may also arise. Where contributions of time and money have been made to a religious institution as a gift, expelled members have no claim in damages for compensation for their contributions, since they were voluntary, and property passed to the religious institution.[69] Members expelled from a Hutterite colony are not permitted to take away any property or any *pro rata* share of the colony property, since all colony property is understood theologically to be held in common

---

65   *Cohen* v. *Hazen Avenue Synagogue* (1920), 47 N.B.R. 400 (Ch.); *Zawidoski* v. *Ruthenian Greek Catholic Parish of St. Vladimir and Olga*, [1937] 2 D.L.R. 509 (Man. K.B.); and *Lakeside Colony of Hutterian Brethren* v. *Hofer*, above note 26.

66   *Otis* v. *James* (1922), 22 O.W.N. 325 (H.C.).

67   *Toews* v. *Isaac*, [1931] 2 D.L.R. 819 (Man. C.A.); *Zawidoski* v. *Ruthenian Greek, etc.*, above note 65; and *Christensen* v. *Bodner* (1976), 65 D.L.R. (3d) 549 (Man. Q.B.).

68   *Reid* v. *Inglis* (1862), 12 U.C.C.P. 191.

69   *Zebroski* v. *Jehovah's Witnesses* (1988), 87 A.R. 229 (C.A.), leave to appeal to S.C.C. refused (1989), 94 A.R. 320 (S.C.C.).

and vested in a non-profit corporation to reflect that belief, instead of being owned by individual members.[70]

In the case of some religious communities that are also closely-knit economically, socially, and culturally, expulsion from the community may result in lost business. Where religious leaders and other members of the community boycott the business of an expelled member, who thereby suffers considerable losses, damages for the resulting lost profits may be awarded against those who encourage the boycott.[71] Moreover, the former member may also succeed for slander and in conspiracy.[72] However, where it is not proven that damage was suffered as a result of an alleged wrongful expulsion from a religious organization, neither damages nor an injunction may be awarded.[73]

A member of a religious organization has an action at common law, generally, for unlawful deprivation of a legal right where there has been a conspiracy to cause his or her expulsion from the organization.[74]

Finally, in a somewhat unrelated matter, when an action has been brought on grounds of sexual harassment by laypersons against a member of the clergy for alleged sexual improprieties, a publication ban may be granted on the ground that victims might otherwise feel inhibited from coming forward.[75]

Examination of the lay discipline cases in Canada demonstrate that a wide variety of factual situations have come before the courts. A number of cases have concerned expulsion from membership on grounds including insufficient financial support,[76] non-attendance at worship,[77]

---

70   *Hofer v. Hofer*, above note 64; and *Canada (Attorney General)* v. *Stahl*, unreported decision of 22 April 1999 (Alta. Q.B.).

71   *Heinrichs v. Wiens*, above note 61.

72   *Uditsky v. Ottawa Vaad Hakashres* (1926), 31 O.W.N. 189 (C.A.). Where a religious organization makes complaints to a law society that disbars a former member and lawyer as a result, an action for defamation may be brought by the lawyer against the religious organization: *Mott-Trille v. Steed*, unreported decision of 17 December 1999 (Ont. C.A.).

73   *Cohen v. Hazen Avenue Synagogue*, above note 65; and *Zebrowski v. Jehovah's Witnesses*, above note 69.

74   *Shaw v. Lewis*, [1948] 1 W.W.R. 627 (B.C.C.A.).

75   *Symons v. United Church of Canada* (1993), 16 O.R. (3d) 379 (Div. Ct.).

76   *Dunnet v. Forneri*, above note 61; and *Patillo v. Cummings*, above note 63.

77   *Patillo v. Cummings*, above note 63.

financial irregularities while serving as a trustee,[78] disruption of meetings,[79] "apostasy,"[80] alleged writing of libellous letters about a priest,[81] and for no given reason.[82] Disputes have also concerned such matters as rights of burial in consecrated ground,[83] access to church records,[84] internal elections to congregational offices,[85] refusal to accept punishment,[86] ownership of property in religious groups where such is forbidden,[87] and damages for lost business profits resulting from expulsion from a religious community.[88]

In most lay discipline cases appealed to the civil courts, those courts have overturned internal church tribunal decisions on the grounds of procedural irregularity.[89] In three cases, the courts declined to intervene because there were no procedural irregularities[90] and in one case because internal appeal routes had not been exhausted.[91] In two cases, the courts found that no civil rights had been interfered with and declined to intervene.[92]

---

78 *Pinke* v. *Bornhold* (1904), 8 O.L.R. 575 (H.C.); and *Toews* v. *Isaac*, above note 67.

79 *Cohen* v. *Hazen Avenue Synagogue*, above note 65.

80 *Christensen* v. *Bodner*, above note 67; and *Zebroski* v. *Jehovah's Witnesses*, above note 69.

81 *Zawidoski* v. *Ruthenian Greek, etc.*, above note 65.

82 *Otis* v. *James*, above note 66.

83 *Dame Henriette Brown* v. *Les curés et marguillieres de l'oeuvre et fabrique de Notre Dame de Montréal* (1874), L.R. 6 P.C. 157 (P.C.).

84 *Wetmon* v. *Bayne*, above note 14.

85 *Tully* v. *Farrell*, above note 61.

86 *Lakeside Colony of Hutterian Brethren* v. *Hofer*, above note 26.

87 *Ibid.*

88 *Heinrichs* v. *Wiens*, above note 61; and *Uditsky* v. *Ottawa Vaad Hakashres*, above note 72.

89 *Dame Henriette Brown, etc.*, above note 83; *Tully* v. *Farrell*, above note 61; *Patillo* v. *Cummings*, above note 63; *Heinrichs* v. *Wiens*, above note 61; *Cohen* v. *Hazen Avenue Synagogue*, above note 65; *Otis* v. *James*, above note 66; *Toews* v. *Isaac*, above note 67; *Zawidoski* v. *Ruthenian Greek, etc.*, above note 65; and *Christensen* v. *Bodner*, above note 67.

90 *Wetmon* v. *Bayne*, above note 14; *Zebrowski* v. *Jehovah's Witnesses*, above note 69; and *Lakeside Colony of Hutterian Brethren* v. *Hofer*, above note 26.

91 *Zebroski* v. *Jehovah's Witnesses*, above note 69.

92 *Dunnet* v. *Forneri*, above note 61; and *Pinke* v. *Bornhold*, above note 78.

E. RELIGIOUS ORDERS

Historically, a number of religious orders, mostly Roman Catholic, have operated in Canada from the founding of New France in the seventeenth century. Most of these are based in a foreign jurisdiction and questions have arisen as to jurisdiction to discipline members of these orders resident in Canada. Where a religious order is based in a foreign jurisdiction but has houses in a Canadian jurisdiction, that Canadian jurisdiction may hear a cause of action brought against the superior of the Canadian houses.[93] An action brought against a religious society may be struck out as frivolous or vexatious in the absence of sufficient evidence.[94] Where a Roman Catholic order makes no provision for the discipline of members, the power to expel a member is found in the civil law.[95]

In a case dating from the beginning of the twentieth century, and no doubt reflecting an anti-Catholic bias, it was said that contracts binding members of religious societies must be subject to the usual rules of contract law, so that vows of obedience and chastity are contrary to public policy and void because the former implies slavery and the latter implies restraint of marriage.[96] It seems unlikely that a similar finding would be made today.

Finally, where a member of a religious order ceases to live in the order's house, carries out work in conflict with the purposes of the order and conducts him or herself in a manner that leads to secularization by church authorities, that person ceases to be a member of the order and is not entitled to a share of the order's property.[97]

F. VICARIOUS LIABILITY FOR CLERGY, EMPLOYEES, AND VOLUNTEERS

In addition to internal discipline of members of the clergy and of the laity for breaches of internal standards and codes and occasional appeals of these disputes to the civil courts, in recent years members of the clergy

---

93　*Archer v. Society of the Sacred Heart of Jesus* (1905), 9 O.L.R. 474 (C.A.).

94　*Christensen v. Bodner*, above note 67.

95　*Basil v. Spratt* (1918), 45 D.L.R. 554 (Ont. C.A.).

96　*Archer v. Society of the Sacred Heart of Jesus*, above note 93.

97　*Dodd v. Society of the Love of Jesus* (1975), 53 D.L.R. (3d) 532 (B.C.S.C.).

and lay employees and volunteers of religious institutions, especially the Christian churches, have also been subject to criminal and civil actions for conduct committed in the context of their institutional duties. This conduct has typically taken the form of sexual, physical, and psychological abuse of children and has resulted in criminal prosecutions as well as civil actions for breach of contract, breach of fiduciary duties, negligence, and vicarious liability brought against both individual perpetrators, their sponsoring religious organizations, and governments that either fund or regulate the activities in the context of which the offending behaviour has occurred. Thus, members of the clergy, lay employees, and volunteers have often, but not always, been subject to both internal ecclesiastical discipline normally resulting in loss of status and employment and to civil proceedings resulting in the applicable criminal and civil law penalties.

In recent years, cases have been brought against individual defendants but there have also been clusters of cases involving particular residential situations such as those against the Christian Brothers, a Roman Catholic lay order, and most infamously, the almost eleven thousand claimants who allege various criminal and civil wrongs experienced in the Indian residential schools over the course of the twentieth century.[98] Since the principles of the criminal law and the laws of contract, tort, fiduciary obligation, evidence, and procedure apply in exactly the same way in these cases as in cases involving defendants who are not associated with religious organizations, there will be no consideration given to them here and readers are directed to legal texts about those areas of the law. However, some novel legal issues are emerging from those cases relating to the disciplinary responsibility of religious institutions: (i) identification of the appropriate part of a religious institution to bear potential vicarious liability for the civil wrongs of clergy, employees, and volunteers; and (ii) the nature of vicarious liability as a head of legal liability in a religious institution context.

Identification of the appropriate part of a religious institution to bear vicarious liability requires specific knowledge and understanding of the

---

98 Two extensive scholarly studies have appeared to date on the residential schools: J.R. Miller, *Shinwauk's Vision: A History of Native Residential Schools* (Toronto: University of Toronto Press, 1996); and John S. Milloy, *A National Crime: The Canadian Government and the Residential School System, 1879 to 1986* (Winnipeg: University of Manitoba Press, 1999).

polity of the religious institution in question, so that a court must consult the constitutional documents of the institution and occasionally receive expert advice on the matter. No single rule or set of rules in law will apply to all of the various religious organizations in existence. Rather, a court must identify the duties, rights, and responsibilities of each part of a hierarchy and then decide whether any act or omission of that part contributed to the civil legal wrong that has occurred.

The largest and most complex religious organization in Canada is the Roman Catholic church and most of the cases in recent years for sexual or physical abuse of children have been brought against various parts of that church, including individuals, religious orders, colleges and schools, dioceses, and the "national" unincorporated association itself. It is not clear that the courts understand either the polity or applicable canon law as the internal dynamic relationships within the Roman Catholic church in the decisions relating to the appropriate part to be sued when a priest, brother, sister, or employee is alleged to have engaged in a criminal or civil wrong.

In two appellate decisions,[99] courts have addressed the issue of whether there is a "national" entity, the "Roman Catholic church," which may be sued as the top responsible entity in the hierarchy of that religious institution. In *Jane Doe* v. *Penney*,[100] in the context of an application to set aside a default judgment, the Newfoundland Court of Appeal decided that that issue should be decided at trial when the issue of the liability of the other defendants would be decided. However, in *Re Residential Schools*,[101] the Alberta Court of Appeal decided that the national entity was an unincorporated association and therefore not a legal entity; it could only be sued if it was a natural person or otherwise recognized by legislation. The court rejected the argument that a diocesan corporation could be sued as a representative party for the national entity.[102] By contrast, the courts have permitted various parts of the Roman Catholic church to join actions as an intervener in which the Church *per*

---

99 The matter is unresolved and there are a number of cases in process.

100 (2001), 202 D.L.R. (4th) 91 (Nfld. C.A.).

101 (2001), 204 D.L.R. (4th) 80 (Alta. C.A.).

102 See also the trial decisions in *John Doe* v. *Bennett* (2000), 188 Nfld. & P.E.I.R. 113, 569 A.P.R. 113 (S.C.-T.D.); and *J.R.S.* v. *Glendinning* (2000), 191 D.L.R. (4th) 750 (Ont. S.C.J.).

se is said to have an interest so that the views of the Roman Catholic church may be aired in the courts;[103] one of these entities said to represent the national church as an intervener is the Canadian Conference of Catholic Bishops, a national organization, which is a federally incorporated body. The status, then, of the "national" entity may still be unclear in the common law.

Other Christian churches that have incorporated federally have been recognized as suable entities in this type of litigation where responsibility is found, including the United Church of Canada[104] and the General Synod of the Anglican Church of Canada.[105] However, in relation to the Anglican Church of Canada, the General Synod will not be found to be a suable party where it was not responsible either in Anglican polity or in fact for alleged sexual assaults by a priest over whom only the local diocesan bishop has authority and responsibility.[106]

Where churches have an episcopal form of church government, bishops have been found to be vicariously liable for the civil wrongs perpetrated by priests of the diocese in both the Roman Catholic Church[107] and the Anglican Church of Canada.[108] In episcopal polities, canon law typically requires the bishop to appoint, supervise, and dismiss priests "employed" in the diocese and these responsibilities are understood to be the bishop's alone; no court has yet been asked to extend responsibility to a higher body such as a province, synod, or pope where it may be shown that its acts or omissions left an inappropriate bishop in place. To date,

---

103 *Bazley v. Curry* (1999), 174 D.L.R. (4th) 45 (S.C.C.), involving vicarious liability; *Jacobi v. Griffiths* (1999), 174 D.L.R. (4th) 71 (S.C.C.), involving vicarious liability; *Chamberlain v. Surrey School District No. 36* (2000), 191 D.L.R. (4th) 128 (B.C.C.A.); and *Trinity Western University v. B.C. College of Teachers* (2001), 199 D.L.R. (4th) 1 (S.C.C.).

104 *B.(W.R.) v. Plint* (1998), 161 D.L.R. (4th) 538 (B.C.S.C.).

105 *M.(F.S.) v. Clarke*, [1999] 11 W.W.R. 301 (B.C.S.C.).

106 *M.(B.) v. Mumford* (2000), 2000 B.C.S.C. 1787.

107 *John Doe v. Bennett*, above note 102; *J.R.S. v. Glendinning*, above note 102; and *K.(W.) v. Pornbacher*, [1998] 3 W.W.R. 149 (B.C.S.C.). Cf. *MacDonald v. Mombourquette* (1996), 152 N.S.R. (2d) 109, 442 A.P.R. 109 (C.A.), leave to appeal dismissed (1998), 164 N.S.R.(2d) 235, 491 A.P.R. 235 (S.C.C.); this case is wrongly decided.

108 *M.(F.S.) v. Clarke*, above note 106; *M.(B.) v. Mumford*, above note 106.

there are no reported decisions in relation to vicarious liability within presbyterian polities; nor are there any reported decisions concerned with congregational polities, although there the only entity available is clearly the congregation itself because there are no higher entities available.

Where there is a finding of shared responsibility for an enterprise between a religious institution and a government, a court may find a shared vicarious liability for civil wrongs perpetrated by a member of the clergy or other employee of the religious organization, such as for the sexual or physical abuse of children in the Indian residential schools.[109]

The second novel issue in cases of sexual, physical, or psychological abuse of children in the context of religious institutions is the imposition of and nature of the vicarious liability of the ecclesiastical entity identified to have facilitated the civil wrong by its acts or omissions. Once the part of a religious institution whose acts or omissions created the environment within which abuse could occur has been identified, whether a diocese or a national church body, vicarious liability has been imposed on that entity for the civil wrongs done by a member of the clergy or lay employee.[110] In two cases dealing with sexual assaults on children in the context of non-profit organizations providing services for children, the Supreme Court of Canada has considered the nature of vicarious liability in situations where abuse of position has occurred.

In *Bazley* v. *Curry*,[111] in which a non-profit foundation that operated residential care facilities for emotionally troubled children was found vicariously liable for an employee who sexually abused the children, the Court found that employers are liable where an employee's acts are authorized by the employer or where the acts are unauthorized but are so connected to authorized acts that they may be regarded as an unauthorized mode of doing an authorized act. Vicarious liability does not attach to entirely independent acts and to distinguish such acts from unauthorized modes of doing authorized acts, courts should look first to precedent for guidance and then to policy. Two policy concerns should

---

109 B.(W.R.) v. *Plint*, above note 104; M.(F.S.) v. *Clarke*, above note 106; P.(V.) v. *Canada (A.G.)*, [2001] 1 W.W.R. 541 (Sask. Q.B.); and D.W. v. *Canada (A.G.) and Starr* (1999), 187 Sask. R. 21 (Q.B.).

110 B.(W.R.) v. *Plint*, above note 104; K.(W.) v. *Pornbacher*, above note 108; M.(F.S.) v. *Clarke*, above note 105; P.(V.) v. *Canada (A.G.)*, above note 109; and D.W. v. *Canada (A.G.)*, above note 109.

111 Above note 103.

guide decisions to impose vicarious liability: the provision of a just and practical remedy for the harm done and the deterrence of future harm. It is just to expect the organization that creates the risks to bear the loss when the risk results in harm and to do so may have a deterrent effect. To determine whether there is a sufficient connection between the employer's creation of a risk and the harm done by an employee, various factors should be considered, including, but not limited to, the opportunity afforded to the employee to abuse power, the extent to which the wrongful act may have furthered the employer's interests, the extent to which the wrongful act was related to intimacy inherent in the employer's enterprise, the amount of power conferred on the employee, and the vulnerability of potential victims to an abuse of power by the employee. The Supreme Court expressly rejected the argument that the imposition of vicarious liability on a non-profit organization would be damaging to the greater community's good done by such organizations by stating that where a court has to choose between two innocent parties to bear the loss, it is preferable that the loss be borne by the party that created the risk rather than the innocent victim of the resulting wrongdoing.

In the companion case, *Jacobi* v. *Griffiths*,[112] the Court split four to three with the majority finding that a children's recreational club was not vicariously liable for the sexual assaults of employees because the conduct was completely unauthorized, being carried on away from the club outside working hours and usually at the employee's home. While the minority would have decided the case in the same way as in *Bazley*, because the risk was still created by the non-profit organization, the majority thought the wrongful conduct to be too independent from the club's activities and the degree of intimacy inherent in the activities too low to justify imposing vicarious liability. The test set out in *Bazley* and *Jacobi* has since been adopted by the House of Lords in *Lister* v. *Hesley Hall Ltd.*,[113] and should now be considered the definitive statement of the test for determining when a religious institution may also be vicariously liable for the wrongful acts of members of the clergy, employees, or volunteers.

The argument that a member of the clergy is not an "employee" but rather an office-holder has still to be addressed by the courts in relation

---

112 *Ibid.*
113 [2001] 2 All E.R. 769 (H.L.). See also the earlier case of *Phelps* v. *London Borough of Hillingdon*, [2001] 4 All E.R. 504 (H.L.).

to vicarious liability, which is framed as liability for an employee; however, it seems unlikely that such an argument will succeed because the definitive factor for vicarious liability is the creation of a risk not the status in law of the person who transforms that risk into harm for an innocent party.[114]

---

114 For a fuller discussion of all of the issues in law relating to sexual abuse, see Elizabeth K.P. Grace and Susan M. Vella, *Civil Liability for Sexual Abuse and Violence in Canada* (Toronto: Butterworths, 2000). For an economic justification for imposing vicarious liability on non-profit organizations, see Kevin E. Davis, "Vicarious Liability, Judgment Proofing, and Non-Profits" (2000) 50 U.T.L.J. 407.

Education

A. INTRODUCTION

Throughout the world, education is one of the most contested areas for religious institutions and believers; all religions are only ever one generation away from oblivion and the education of the next generation in the beliefs and habits of faith is necessary to ensure the survival of all faiths. While the family and religious institutions are the primary places for education, schools are also important as places for the reinforcement of religious values. Thus, religious parents and communities expect schools to provide a positive environment for faith even where those schools are state schools and do not teach any particular religion at all.

Almost all aspects of education are contested in law: the right to educate in a religious school; public funding for religious education; religious instruction; religious exercises; standards of conduct for teachers and students; and the right of religious college graduates to public employment. A large number of *Charter* cases have been concerned in various ways with education and these cases have dealt with significant freedom of religion, freedom of expression, and equality rights issues. Since education is almost entirely a provincial matter in Canada, the focus for much of this chapter will be on individual provinces in relation to establishment, funding, and curriculum issues; however, since *Charter* jurisprudence applies throughout the country the text will adopt a national rather than provincial approach where appropriate.

The *Constitution Act, 1867*,[1] confers exclusive power on the provinces in relation to education, subject to four qualifications: (i) no provincial law may prejudicially affect any right or privilege with respect to denominational schools that any class of persons had by law at the time of Confederation; (ii) denominational schools for Protestants and Roman Catholics in Quebec are placed on the same legal footing as denominational schools for Roman Catholics in Ontario; (iii) a Protestant or Roman Catholic "minority" has a right of appeal to the Governor General in Council from any decision affecting any right or privilege in relation to education; and (iv) Parliament may enact remedial legislation to give effect to any such decision of the Governor General in Council.

Section 93 was applicable to the four original provinces of Confederation, was extended to British Columbia and Prince Edward Island when they joined Confederation,[2] and in slightly different versions, was made part of the terms on which Manitoba, Alberta, Saskatchewan, and Newfoundland entered Confederation.[3] Section 93 was amended in 1997 by the addition of section 93A to provide that section 93 no longer applies in Quebec[4] and in 1998 to remove denominational school privileges in Newfoundland by the amendment of Term 17 of the *Newfoundland Act*.[5]

The constitutionally privileged position of denominational schools in the provinces has proven, since Confederation, to be the source of much litigation, although the actual practices of the provinces in exercising their plenary educational powers have differed from province to province. Some do not fund section 93 denominational schools at all, either because they did not exist by law or by custom when the province entered Confederation (Nova Scotia, New Brunswick, British Columbia, Prince Edward Island, and Manitoba) or because section 93 rights have since been abrogated (Quebec). Some continue to fund section 93

---

1   R.S.C. 1985, App. II, No. 5, s. 93. For a more detailed discussion of the s. 93 jurisprudence, see generally the literature listed in chapter 4, note 149.

2   British Columbia Terms of Union (Order in Council, 16 May 1871) and Prince Edward Island Terms of Union (Order in Council, 26 June 1873).

3   *Manitoba Act* (1870), R.S.C. 1985, App. II, No. 8, s. 22; *Alberta Act* (1905), R.S.C. 1985, App. II, No. 20, s. 17; *Saskatchewan Act* (1905), R.S.C. 1985, App. II, No. 21, s. 17; and *Newfoundland Act* (1949), R.S.C. 1985, App. II, No. 32, Sched. Term. 17.

4   Constitution Amendment, 1997 (Quebec), SI/97–141.

5   Constitution Amendment, 1998 (*Newfoundland Act*), SI/98–25.

denominational schools (Ontario, Alberta, and Saskatchewan). One province (Newfoundland) funds significantly reduced denominational school rights, but most provinces also partially fund religious schools generally pursuant to ordinary provincial legislation rather than any constitutionally entrenched right.[6]

In chapter four, the judicial interpretation of section 93 *qua* constitutional provision was discussed; in this chapter, emphasis will be placed on educational matters, on a province by province basis, reflecting the different approaches of the provinces to denominational and other religious school funding. Subsequently, the chapter will address other religion and education issues, most of which flow from the constitutional entrenchment of denominational school rights. The general principles of constitutional interpretation discussed previously are equally applicable here. Thus, the provisions have been interpreted strictly by the courts, as applicable only to such denominational schools and denominational subjects as existed by law or custom at the time of the province's entry into Confederation. Legislation prejudicially affecting such rights has been found to be void, while legislation enhancing such rights has been sustained.[7]

B. ROMAN CATHOLIC AND OTHER DENOMINATIONAL SCHOOLS

1) Constitutional Protection

a) Quebec[8]

The constitutional protection of Roman Catholic schools in Ontario and of Protestant and Roman Catholic schools in Quebec has been said, by the Supreme Court of Canada, to constitute the original compact on the basis of which Confederation was achieved in 1867.[9] It was once thought that the legal rights guaranteed by law by section 93 to Protestant and Roman Catholic schools were the minimum rights protected by law and

---

6 Provincial educational regulations must be consulted on a province by province basis to be determined precisely.

7 Above chapter 4, section D(3)(a).

8 The order of provinces in this section will follow the chronological order in which they became part of Canada.

9 *Reference Re Bill 30, or An Act to Amend the Education Act (Ontario)*, [1987] 1 S.C.R. 1148.

that it was not possible to derogate from or otherwise prejudicially affect those rights. However, the constitutional amendment process introduced into the Canadian Constitution in 1982 has now been used in Quebec, so that in 1997, section 93A was added to the *Constitution Act, 1867*, to state that "section 93 no longer applies to Quebec."[10] The primary and secondary school systems in Quebec are now organized solely on a linguistic basis rather than on linguistic and religious bases. The net effect would appear to be that the jurisprudence built up over the years interpreting section 93 for Quebec is no longer relevant in Quebec. However, it may still have persuasive value in other provinces where section 93 still applies and will for that reason be reviewed here.

Questions at one time arose as to the extent to which the integrity of the Protestant schools *qua* Protestant schools could be protected by denying access to pupils from other religious traditions. In *Hirsch v. Montreal Protestant School Board*,[11] the Privy Council found that where non-Protestant children had attended Protestant schools in 1867, they may continue to do so; however, where they did not, provincial legislation forcing Protestant schools to accept them is *ultra vires* the province as having a prejudicial effect on denominational school rights. The board further found that Jewish students may attend, Jewish teachers may be hired, and Jewish board members may be appointed where the Protestant schools so permitted, but that the legislature could not compel such. The legislature could make provision for separate religious schools for Jews and members of other religious groups.

On the other hand, Jehovah's Witness children have been found to be entitled to attend Protestant schools, on the ground that the distinguishing feature of a "Protestant" is repudiation of the authority of the Pope and Jehovah's Witnesses do so.[12] But where no Protestant school has been established because of insufficient numbers, and although a Jehovah's Witness is considered to be a Protestant for the purposes of the legislation, Jehovah's Witness children may attend the local Roman Catholic school and be exempted from religious instruction and religious education.[13]

---

10 Above note 4. The linguistic basis for schools in Quebec is enacted by *An Act to Amend the Education Act*, etc., S.Q. 1997, c. 47.

11 [1928] 1 D.L.R. 1041 (P.C.).

12 *Perron v. Rouyn School Trustees* (1955), 1 D.L.R. (2d) 414 (Que. Q.B.).

13 *Chabot v. School Commissioners of Lamorandière* (1957), 12 D.L.R. (2d) 796 (Que. C.A.).

The constitutional rights of denominational schools are restricted to those enjoyed by law in 1867. In *Devlin-Allard* v. *Ste-Croix (Commission scolaire)*,[14] which concerned an application for a declaration that provincial legislation permitting non-Catholics to teach in a Roman Catholic school was *ultra vires*, the Quebec Superior Court stated that the protection granted by section 93 was restricted to denominational schools, whether Roman Catholic or Protestant, existing in 1867, and which were within the jurisdiction of Roman Catholic or Protestant school boards at that time. Thus, the province was free to enact legislation for schools that were not under the jurisdiction of any board in 1867, including the legislation impugned by the application, which was *intra vires* the province.

The restriction of Protestant school rights to those enjoyed by law in 1867 was reaffirmed by the Supreme Court of Canada in *Greater Montreal Protestant School Board* v. *Quebec (Attorney-General)*,[15] which was concerned with provincial legislation for a uniform curriculum throughout all elementary and secondary schools in Quebec. The Court found that the legislation and regulations were *intra vires* the province since the section 93 protection was restricted to the denominational aspects of the Protestant schools, while the legislation affected only the non-denominational aspects. Moreover, by giving school boards power to adapt the prescribed curricula to local needs and to create additional curricula, subject to approval, the legislation allowed the boards to exercise the controls they enjoyed in 1867 by law over the non-denominational aspects of the curricula.

The extent to which provincial legislation may change denominational school rights without prejudicially affecting the rights and privileges enjoyed by law in Quebec in 1867 has been considered by the Supreme Court of Canada in relation to raising funds for denominational schools and to changing the language of instruction in them. Thus, the Court has found legislation to be unconstitutional that replaced Protestant schools' pre-Confederation control over raising funds with a scheme for sharing provincial grants that lacked a principle of proportionality in relation to the number of pupils in non-denominational schools — legislation providing for a referendum on taxation for denominational

---

14 [1983] Que. S.C. 508.
15 (1989), 57 D.L.R. (4th) 521 (S.C.C.), application for re-hearing refused, [1989] 2 S.C.R. 167.

school purposes in which non-denominational school supporters are permitted to vote is also unconstitutional.[16]

On the other hand, provincial legislation changing the language of instruction in Protestant schools does not prejudicially affect section 93 denominational school rights, although legislation providing for the replacement of Roman Catholic and Protestant school boards by linguistic boards for francophones and anglophones is *ultra vires*, as prejudicially affecting the rights enjoyed by law in 1867 of denominational schools over the election of trustees, the selection of teaching staff, and the management of schools.[17] Where English-speaking Roman Catholic students were permitted by local school boards to receive secondary education in English at Protestant schools, and English-speaking Roman Catholic parents claimed to be entitled to have their children educated in English in Roman Catholic schools, the Quebec Superior Court decided that it would not order that Roman Catholic students be permitted to attend English-speaking Protestant schools, as *ultra vires* section 93, which was intended only to protect the educational rights of Protestants in Quebec.[18]

Finally, section 93 does not affect and is not affected by the establishment of collective agreements in Roman Catholic schools in Quebec.[19]

b) Ontario

The legal rights and privileges guaranteed by law in 1867 are protected by section 93 to the same extent for Roman Catholic[20] schools in Ontario as for Protestant schools in Quebec, although the precise nature of what is protected by law in each province differs somewhat, reflecting the legal requirements in each province in 1867.[21] Again, the protection afforded by section 93 extends only to matters of religion and not to matters of

---

16   *A.G. Quebec v. Greater Hull School Board*, [1984] 2 S.C.R. 575.

17   *Reference Re Education Act (Quebec)* (1993), 105 D.L.R. (4th) 266 (S.C.C.).

18   *Griffin v. Blainville Deux-Montagnes (Commission scolaire regionale)* (1989), 63 D.L.R. (4th) 37 (Que. S.C.).

19   *Montréal (Commission des écoles catholiques) v. A.G. Quebec*, [1988] R.J.Q. 1853 (S.C.).

20   It should be noted that s. 93 also protects other Dissentient school rights existing in Ontario in 1867; of the six Protestant Dissentient schools at that time, none remain, having been folded into local public school boards over time.

21   *Greater Montreal Protestant School Board v. Quebec (Attorney General)*, above note 15.

race or language.[22] The protection is limited to rights and privileges established by legislation alone in 1867.[23] The province may validly enact legislation to change the language of instruction in a denominational school from the language at the time of Confederation to the other official language, because language of instruction is not protected by section 93.[24]

While section 93 only expressly protects the rights and privileges of denominational schools in existence by law at the time of entry into Confederation, in *Re Bill 30*[25] the Supreme Court of Canada stated that it does not prohibit the creation of new rights and privileges in relation to denominational schools, nor does section 2(a) of the *Canadian Charter of Rights and Freedoms* preclude the legislature from conferring new denominational school rights on Roman Catholics only. Moreover, the Court further opined that section 93 does not preclude the return of rights understood to be possessed by Roman Catholic schools by law at Confederation.[26] Discrimination, in the form of constitutionally entrenched privileges, in favour of Roman Catholic schools in Ontario is permissible under the *Charter* and section 29 of the *Charter* further underlines the provisions of section 93, rendering such rights and privileges immune from *Charter* review.[27]

Legislation that prejudicially affects section 93 denominational rights and privileges is *ultra vires* the provincial legislature; however, beneficial legislation, such as legislation improving the method of electing separate school trustees from that existing at the time of Confederation is *intra vires* provincial powers.[28] On the other hand, legislation that purports to deprive a separate school board of a right to sue or be sued is invalid, since separate school boards had such powers by law prior to Confederation.[29] Legislation that may be characterized as neutral, such as

---

22 *Ottawa Roman Catholic Separate School Board v. Mackell* (1917), 32 D.L.R. 1 (P.C.).

23 *Maher v. Town of Portland* (1874), cited in G.J. Wheeler, *Confederation Law of Canada* (London: Eyre and Spottiswoode, 1896) at 338 (P.C.).

24 *Ottawa Roman Catholic Separate School Board v. Mackell*, above note 22.

25 Above note 9.

26 *Ibid.*

27 *Ibid.*

28 *Belleville Roman Catholic Separate School Board v. Grainger* (1878), 25 Gr. 570 (Ch.).

29 *Windsor Roman Catholic Separate School Board v. Southam Inc.* (1984), 9 D.L.R. (4th) 284 (Ont. H.C.).

the imposition of liabilities by a provincially appointed school commission operating separate schools, is not prejudicial.[30] Again, legislation providing for a system of education development charges on land being developed for residential purposes and that could be levied in an identical way by both public and separate school boards was upheld; no distinction was made between public and separate school systems so that separate school rights were not prejudicially affected.[31] Nor will legislation designed to create a more efficient management system for schools by reducing the number of boards be considered prejudicial providing proportionality with public boards is kept.[32] Finally, legislation that transferred the power to set the rate of property taxes for separate school boards and public boards from the boards to the provincial minister of finance was also found not to be prejudicial so long as the resulting mechanism ensured fair and equitable funding as between both school systems; in fact, the funding model enhanced separate school funding.[33]

The extent to which the provincial legislature may change the rights and roles of separate school trustees and the language of instruction as existing in 1867, was the subject of considerable litigation in the early twentieth century, after the provincial government enacted Regulation 17 to make changes in relation to both separate school trustees and the use of French in the Roman Catholic school system. The Privy Council held that the rights of separate schools to be managed by denominational trustees cannot be removed by provincial legislation, even where the underlying matter in the dispute is the language of instruction rather than denominational education, since that right existed at Confederation.[34] On the other hand, where the trustees persisted in refusing to comply with valid provincial regulation of denominational schools so that legislation was enacted providing for the temporary suspension of denominational trustees should they persist in not respecting the law in

---

30 *Ottawa Roman Catholic Separate School Board v. Quebec Bank* (1920), 50 D.L.R. 189 (P.C.).

31 *Ontario Home Builders' Association v. York Region Board of Education* (1996), 137 D.L.R. (4th) 449 (S.C.C.).

32 *Berthelot v. Ontario (Education Improvement Commission)* (1998), 168 D.L.R. (4th) 201 (Ont. Div. Ct.).

33 *Ontario English Catholic Teachers Association v. Ontario (Attorney-General)* (2001), 196 D.L.R. (4th) 577 (S.C.C.).

34 *Ottawa Roman Catholic Separate School Board v. City of Ottawa* (1917), 32 D.L.R. 10 (P.C.).

relation to non-denominational matters, such legislation has been found not to be prejudicial to denominational school rights.[35] Moreover, provincial legislation that declared expenditures made by commissioners who carried on the separate schools while the trustees were suspended was deemed to have been made for and at the request of the trustees, and was held to be *intra vires*, since it did not prejudicially affect the rights or privileges of the trustees enjoyed by law in 1867, but rather was neutral in character.[36]

Again, legislation providing for the election of minority language trustees to form separate sections within both public and separate school boards does not prejudicially affect the section 93 rights of separate schools.[37]

The secularization of the public school system[38] and the growing religious pluralism in Ontario have been reflected in recent challenges to the legislation providing funding for public and Roman Catholic schools only in Ontario, on the basis of the *Canadian Charter of Rights and Freedoms*. In the earlier *Re Bill 30* case, the Supreme Court of Canada decided that the *Charter* could not be invoked either to strike down funding for denominational schools of one denomination only or to render unconstitutional the rights and privileges guaranteed to denominational schools.

But once it was established that Roman Catholic school rights were constitutionally entrenched and therefore unassailable, other religious groups have relied upon section 2(a) and section 15 of the *Charter* to argue for funding for other religious schools on an equality basis. In *Adler* v. *Ontario*,[39] in which Jewish and Christian Reformed parents argued that their existing privately-funded religious schools should receive public funding on the basis of section 2(a) and section 15, the majority of the Supreme Court of Canada rejected the claim. Section 93 was found to be a "comprehensive code" concerning the provincial education power, pro-

---

35 *Re Ottawa Separate School Board* (1917), 40 D.L.R. 465 (Ont. C.A.).

36 *Ottawa Roman Catholic Separate School Board* v. *Quebec Bank*, above note 30.

37 *Re Bill 30*, above note 9.

38 Below section C.

39 (1996), 140 D.L.R. (4th) 385 (S.C.C.). For an analysis, see M.H. Ogilvie, "*Adler* v. *Ontario*: Preconceptions, Myths (or Prejudices) About Religion in the Supreme Court of Canada" (1997) 9 N.J.C.L. 79. See also an earlier case, which held that Jewish schools could not be incorporated into the public school system: *North York Board of Education* v. *Ministry of Education* (1978), 19 O.R. (2d) 547 (H.C.).

viding explicitly only for Roman Catholic denominational schools and implicitly for public schools since public school funding is the benchmark for the funding for separate schools. Section 93 cannot be enlarged by section 2(a) or section 15; indeed, section 93 is immune from *Charter* review. The province's plenary educational power over education means that it enjoys a discretion but not an obligation to establish and fund other religious schools by ordinary legislation. Two members of the majority[40] further thought that there was no violation of section 15 because the burden of sending children to fee-paying religious schools is derived from the parents' beliefs not state legislation. In any case, the public school system, as a secular school system, does not discriminate on the basis of religion. In the companion case, *Bal* v. *Ontario (A.G.)*,[41] the Ontario Court of Appeal again found no breach of section 2(a) or section 15 because the public school system was secular and neutral, and did not discriminate nor coerce children to change their religious views. Nor was there a breach of section 2(b) because parents and children and teachers were free to express their religious views inside and outside the classroom.[42] The province finally relented in 2001 by enacting legislation to provide a tax deduction to parents to partially offset the fees for attending privately-funded religious schools.[43] But no parity either financially or constitutionally with Roman Catholic schools has yet been offered.

Denominational schools in Ontario are subject to provincial regulation in relation to their non-denominational aspects and to municipal bylaws in relation to such matters as zoning or building codes. Where a municipal bylaw permitted a district to be used for residential purposes only, that bylaw was enforceable against a separate school board that had erected a school; the Privy Council further stated that section 93 does not affect the application of municipal laws relating to the health and convenience of the population to denominational schools.[44] Again, a separate

---

40 Sopinka and Major JJ.

41 (1994), 121 D.L.R. (4th) 96 (Ont. Gen. Div.), aff'd (1997), 101 O.A.C. 219 (C.A.).

42 In 1999, the U.N. Human Rights Committee decided that the failure to fund other religious schools in Ontario put Canada in breach of the International Covenant on Civil and Political Rights: *Waldman's Case*, CCPR/C/67/D/694/1996 (3 Nov. 1999).

43 *Responsible Choices for Growth and Accountability Act*, S.O. 2001, c. 8, s. 40 (Equity in Education Tax Credit).

school board has been found to be subject to municipal legislation in respect to a municipality collecting taxes for the board and there is no infringement of section 93 where the board had voluntarily agreed to the arrangement.[45] Teachers in denominational schools may be required to have received certificates to teach in the public schools prior to commencing to teach in the separate schools.[46]

The legislative power enjoyed by the province to regulate the non-denominational aspects of denominational schools does not extend to the power to abolish them, although in the past it has been held to extend to the power to restrict the duration of denominational education.[47] However, such restrictions have also been subsequently lifted and the right existing by law at Confederation restored,[48] so it seems unlikely that their restriction would ever occur again in the future in light of *Re Bill 30*.

c) New Brunswick

Only one reported case has dealt with constitutional guarantees in relation to denominational schools in New Brunswick. In *ex parte Renaud*,[49] the question arose as to whether provincial legislation that made no provision for denominational schools was *intra vires*, and the New Brunswick Court of Appeal held that legislation providing for non-denominational schools was *intra vires* the province and did not contravene section 93. Thus, where publicly funded denominational schools did not exist at the time of entry into the union, there is no constitutional guarantee of such.[50]

---

44 *City of Toronto* v. *Toronto Roman Catholic Separate School Board*, [1926] A.C. 81 (P.C.).

45 *Windsor Roman Catholic Separate School Board* v. *City of Windsor* (1988), 49 D.L.R. (4th) 576 (Ont. C.A.).

46 *Brothers of Christian Schools* v. *Ontario Minister of Education*, [1907] A.C. 69 (P.C.).

47 *Tiny Roman Catholic Separate School Board* v. *R.*, [1928] 3 D.L.R. 753 (P.C.). The status of this case is ambiguous after *Re Bill 30*.

48 *Re Bill 30*, above note 9.

49 (1873), 14 N.B.R. 273 (C.A.), aff'd *sub nom. Maher* v. *Town of Portland*, above note 23.

50 There would appear to be no reported cases in relation to the fourth original province, Nova Scotia, nor in relation to P.E.I., to which s. 93 was extended when it entered the union in 1873: see Royal Order in Council of 26 June 1873.

d) Manitoba

In 1890, the government of Manitoba attempted to abridge the provisions of an 1871 act,[51] which had created a dual Protestant and Roman Catholic school system pursuant to section 22 of the *Manitoba Act* (in respect to denominational school rights existing by law or practice in Manitoba at the union), by ending denominational schools and creating a single non-sectarian public school system financed by all ratepayers in each municipality.[52] The resulting litigation was of lasting importance for the interpretation of section 93, both in respect to Manitoba and other provinces.[53]

In *City of Winnipeg v. Barrett*,[54] an application was made by a Roman Catholic taxpayer to quash a municipal bylaw providing for a tax on each ratepayer to finance the new public school system. Although the Supreme Court of Canada had held that the legislation was *ultra vires* the province because it prejudicially affected Roman Catholic school rights existing by practice in 1870,[55] the Privy Council upheld the legislation on the assumption that denominational schools existing at the time of the union were private and not constitutionally entrenched. Although it abolished the denominational schools in existence in 1870, it did not affect denominational school rights because each denomination was left free to establish and maintain its own schools and children were free to attend them since the legislation did not compel them to attend the public schools, but rather merely provided for free public schools for any child in the province.[56]

Subsequently, the Roman Catholic minority appealed to the Governor-General in Council pursuant to section 22(2) (sections 93(3) and (4)) of the *Manitoba Act* for remedial legislation pursuant to section 22(3), and the Privy Council found, in *Brophy v. Manitoba (A.G.)*,[57] that it had the right to remedial action because its denominational school rights had been prejudiced. No such exercise of the powers of the Governor General in

---

51 *School Act*, 34 Vict., c. 12 (1871).

52 *Public Schools Act*, S.M. 1890, c. 38.

53 Gordon Bale, "Law, Politics and the Manitoba School Question: Supreme Court and Privy Council" (1985) 63 Can. Bar Rev. 461.

54 [1892] A.C. 445 (P.C.).

55 *Barrett v. Winnipeg (City)* (1891), 19 S.C.R. 374.

56 The companion case questioning the power to tax Anglican ratepayers to support public schools was heard concurrently by the P.C.: *Logan v. City of Winnipeg* (1891), 8 Man. L.R. 3 (Q.B.).

57 [1895] A.C. 202 (P.C.).

Council proved necessary because a political compromise was achieved by the new federal government after the general election of 1896, whereby religious instruction in any Christian faith could be given in the last half hour of the school day in the public schools, which remained secular.

Since the late nineteenth century, in *Manitoba Association for Rights and Liberties* v. *Manitoba*,[58] the provisions of the provincial legislation dealing with these religious exercises have been considered and struck down pursuant to sections 2(a) and 15 of the *Charter* on the ground that they were not constitutionally entrenched but the creation of provincial legislation, and therefore were subject to *Charter* review because they privileged one religion over others. Thus, a completely non-sectarian public system remains by law in Manitoba.

e) Alberta

The only restriction on the exclusive plenary jurisdiction of the province over education for which provision was made in the 1905 *Alberta Act* by section 17,[59] was that imposed by the 1901 Ordinances of the Northwest Territories,[60] which gave Roman Catholic and Protestant minorities in a district the right to establish separate schools and to be liable in their property taxes to support such schools only.[61] The rights of Roman Catholic and Protestant minorities to their own schools is constitutionally entrenched by virtue of section 17 and therefore is immune to *Charter* review pursuant to either section 2(a) or 15.[62] Sections 93(2), (3), and (4) of the *Constitution Act, 1867*, continue to apply in Alberta.

This fundamental right does not, however, preclude the legislature from making some changes to the educational institutions in Alberta, provided these do not prejudicially affect religious minority school rights existing in 1905. Thus, the province may make legislation in relation to private religious schools and to compel children to attend the public schools where a private religious school does not comply with provincial legislation and is, accordingly, closed.[63] Again, provincial legislation

---

58 (1992), 94 D.L.R. (4th) 678 (Man. Q.B.).

59 S.C. 1905, c. 3.

60 S.N.W.T. 1901, c. 29, 30.

61 *St. Walburg Roman Catholic Separate School District No. 25* v. *Turtleford School Division No. 65*, [1987] 2 W.W.R. 698 (Sask. C.A.).

62 *Jacobi* v. *County of Newell No. 4* (1994), 112 D.L.R. (4th) 229 (Alta. Q.B.); and *Schmidt* v. *Calgary Board of Education*, [1976] 6 W.W.R. 717 (Alta. C.A.).

63 *Brooks* v. *Ulmer*, [1922] 1 D.L.R. (2d) 304 (Alta. App. Div.).

authorizing the formation of new school divisions is *intra vires* the province, provided denominational school rights are protected.[64] Legislation increasing the Roman Catholic school share of school taxes paid by corporations is also *intra vires*, since it is beneficial to denominational school rights rather than prejudicial to them.[65]

In *Public School Boards Association of Alberta* v. *Alberta (Attorney General)*,[66] the Supreme Court of Canada considered a number of changes to provincial legislation relating to the status of denominational schools in Alberta, including replacement of local property taxation as a means of support by a centralized school fund from which all schools would be supported but with permission for Roman Catholic schools to opt out and continue to levy taxes provided there was no change in the overall proportionality between the systems. The Court found that municipal institutions did not have reasonable autonomy in relation to education because this would be inconsistent with the province's plenary power over education. The province was free to exercise this power in distributing funds to provincial schools providing it follows a general concept of fairness in the distribution, although fairness does not necessarily mean that funding for Roman Catholic and public schools mirror each other in equality.

In *Mahe* v. *Alberta*,[67] the Supreme Court of Canada determined that pursuant to section 23 of the *Charter*, French-speaking parents have a right to proportional representation on English-speaking Roman Catholic school boards and that this right does not conflict with the rights and privileges of the Roman Catholic schools guaranteed by section 17 of the *Alberta Act* and section 29 of the *Charter* because it does not affect in any way the denominational aspects of education.

Jacobi v. *County of Newell No. 4*[68] was concerned with the question of the formation of new Roman Catholic school districts in Alberta and of

---

64 *Bailey* v. *Lethbridge School District No. 7*, [1940] 1 D.L.R. 761 (Alta. T.D.); *Starland School Division No. 30* v. *Alberta (Minister of Education)* (1988), 53 D.L.R. (4th) 552 (Alta. Q.B.).

65 *Calgary Board of Education* v. *A.G. Alberta* (1981), 122 D.L.R. (3d) 249 (Alta. C.A.), leave to appeal to S.C.C. refused (1981), 30 A.R. 180 (S.C.C.).

66 (2000), 191 D.L.R. (4th) 513 (S.C.C.). See also a case awaiting this decision: *Living Waters Catholic Regional Division No. 42* v. *Whitecourt (Town)* (2000), 2000 Carswell Alta. 1018 (Q.B.).

67 (1990), 68 D.L.R. (4th) 69 (S.C.C.).

68 Above note 62.

the extent to which they are constitutionally protected. The newly creat-ed district had no school, no denominational program, and employed no teachers, but rather arranged to have Roman Catholic students enrolled in a nearby district's public schools, where parents were required to pay fees. Parents successfully challenged the requirement to pay fees in an action in which the court stated that to acquire constitutional protection, a separate school must have some degree of establishment and of denom-inational character, without which a separate school district could not be considered established. However, once voters have decided to establish a separate school district by amalgamation with a regional public school board, neither a public school board nor a public school taxpayer has a constitutional right to an injunction to prevent the amalgamation.[69]

The final constitutional issue, which has arisen in relation to religious schools generally in Alberta, is whether or not the provincial legislative requirement that private religious schools that are not denominational schools be approved by the province infringes section 2(a) of the *Charter*. Operators of such schools have resisted provincial certification on the ground that this is tantamount to acknowledging that the state rather than God has authority of education; however, the courts have consistent-ly held that section 2(a) does not prevail over the plenary provincial authority over education pursuant to section 93 of the *Constitution*.[70]

f) Saskatchewan

Similarly to Alberta, the only restriction on the exclusive plenary jurisdic-tion of Saskatchewan over education for which provision is made in the 1905 *Saskatchewan Act*, section 17,[71] is the right granted to Roman Catholic and Protestant minorities in a district to separate schools as pro-vided for in 1905 at the time of entry into the union by the 1901 Ordi-nances of the Northwest Territories.[72] Section 17 is again modelled on section 93 and sections 92(2), (3), and (4) are applicable in Saskatchewan.

---

69 *Board of Education of Sturgeon School District No. 24* v. *Alberta* (2001), 272 A.R. 190 (Q.B.).

70 *R.* v. *Bienert* (1985), 39 Alta. L.R. (2d) 198 (Prov. Ct.); and *R.* v. *Jones*, [1986] 2 S.C.R. 284, below section D.

71 S.S. 1905, c. 42.

72 Above note 60. For an older analysis of the law, see A.S. Brent, "The Right to Religious Education and the Constitutional Status of Denominational Schools" (1976) 40 Sask. L. Rev. 239.

The right of a Protestant or Roman Catholic minority in a district to form a separate school was upheld by the Privy Council in *City of Regina* v. *McCarthy*,[73] but was also restricted in that case to members of those religious groups only. Members of each of these religious groups are required to be entered as separate school supporters rather than as public school supporters where minority separate schools have been established, and ratepayers who are members of smaller sects or denominations in communion with either of these have also been required to be assessed in relation to the group with which they are in communion.[74] Moreover, where a Roman Catholic minority in a district has established a separate school, individual Roman Catholic students may be refused enrolment in the public schools, although their parents are public school ratepayers, and such refusal does not amount to discrimination pursuant to provincial human rights legislation.[75] However, unless the legislation otherwise provides, a mere declaration of religious affiliation is sufficient and inquisitions into personal beliefs and practices are not permissible to determine the true religious views of a taxpayer.[76]

The province may make changes in the educational structure in Saskatchewan, provided these do not prejudicially affect denominational school rights existing by law in 1905. Thus, provincial legislation providing for the amalgamation of a separate school district with a public school district, which does not preserve the separate existence of the separate school district, is not *ultra vires* where it merely modifies the way in which minority rights are to be exercised.[77] Moreover, where provin-

---

73 [1918] A.C. 911 (P.C.). See also *Regina Public School Board* v. *Gratton Separate School Board* (1914), 18 D.L.R. 571 (Sask. S.C.).

74 *Pander* v. *Town of Melville*, [1922] 3 W.W.R. 53 (Sask. Local Gov't. Bd.).

75 *Bintner* v. *Regina Public School Board District No. 4* (1965), 55 D.L.R. (2d) 646 (Sask. C.A.). See also the following older case in relation to the apportionment of corporation taxes: *Regina Public School Board* v. *Gratton Separate School Board* (1915), 21 D.L.R. 162 (S.C.C.).

76 *Buhs* v. *Leroy No. 339 (Regional Municipality)* (1999), 178 D.L.R. (4th) 322 (Sask. Q.B.).

77 *St. Walburg Roman Catholic Separate School District No. 25* v. *Turtleford School Division No. 65*, [1987] 2 W.W.R. 698 (Sask. C.A.). In making the decision to establish a separate school district, the minister need only comply with the express requirements of the legislation: *Board of Education of Saskatchewan Rivers School Division No. 119* v. *Saskatchewan (Minister of Education)* (2001), 197 Sask. R. 218 (Q.B.).

cial legislation introduces a two-tier collective bargaining arrangement, which includes the removal of the jurisdiction of both separate and public school boards to settle salaries, but which does not otherwise interfere with denominational school rights, there is no prejudicial effect on any right or privilege pursuant to section 93.[78]

The extent to which a public board might provide services to students on a differential basis without breaching section 15 of the *Charter* was considered in *Blais* v. *Battleford School Division No. 58*,[79] in which Roman Catholic parents argued for compensation to bus grade seven students currently enrolled in a public junior high school to a Roman Catholic elementary school in another municipality since the board already provided busing for grade eight and nine students to a Roman Catholic high school. The court doubted the applicability of the *Charter*, but found there to be no inequality because the school policy affected grades differently. Even if there was discrimination under section 15, it was justifiable under section 1 because the decision not to bus grade seven students was made to ensure the maintenance of local standards of education so far as was economic; nor were parents pressured by that policy into sending their children elsewhere at their own expense.

g) British Columbia

Section 93 was extended to British Columbia when it entered Confederation in 1871.[80] However, there were no denominational schools in British Columbia at that time, so there are no reported cases dealing with denominational school rights in the province, where a variety of religious schools receive partial provincial funding pursuant to ordinary legislation. In the sole *Charter* case, a trial court has held that provincial legislation requiring a school board to adopt an annual budget in accordance with provincial directives does not violate either section 2(a) or section 2(b) of the *Charter*.[81]

---

78 *Moose Jaw School District No. 1* v. *A.G. Saskatchewan* (1975), 57 D.L.R. (3d) 315 (Sask. C.A.).

79 [1995] 2 W.W.R. 259 (Sask. Q.B.).

80 Above note 2.

81 *A.G. B.C.* v. *Cowichan School District No. 65* (1985), 19 D.L.R. (4th) 166 (B.C.S.C.).

h) Newfoundland

Until the constitutional amendment in 1998,[82] Term 17 of the *Treaty of Union*,[83] by which Newfoundland joined Confederation, preserved the rights and privileges of eight denominational school systems existing in Newfoundland after 1949. In the sole reported case involving the interpretation of Term 17, the Newfoundland Court of Appeal has held that a Roman Catholic school board could not violate a collective agreement by placing members of the Christian Brothers in a position of priority over other teachers with more seniority, since this would prejudicially affect teachers who enjoyed the same rights and privileges at the time of the union, whether they were members of religious orders or lay persons.[84]

In 1998, following two referenda and an earlier draft guaranteeing the churches access to the new public school system for religious instruction and religious observances, the final draft for a new Term 17 was entrenched and provided that the legislature shall have exclusive authority in relation to education but shall provide for non-denominational courses in religion and religious observances in schools when requested by parents.[85] In extensive litigation relating to the amendment process, the process itself was upheld,[86] as well as the use of referenda to test pop-

---

82   Above note 5:

    17(1) In lieu of section 93 of the Constitution Act, 1867, this section shall apply in respect of the Province of Newfoundland.

    (2) In and for the province of Newfoundland, the Legislature shall have exclusive authority to make laws in relation to education, but shall provide for courses in religion that are not specific to a religious denomination.

    (3) Religious observances shall be permitted in a school where requested by parents.

83   *Newfoundland Act*, above note 3.

84   *Exploits-White Bay Roman Catholic School Board v. N.T.A.* (1983), 42 Nfld. & P.E.I.R. 40, 122 A.P.R. 40 (Nfld. C.A.), leave to appeal refused (1983), 44 Nfld. & P.E.I.R. 14 (S.C.C.).

85   For a history of the amendments, see John P. McEvoy, "Denominational Schools and Minority Rights: *Hogan v. Newfoundland (Attorney General)*" (2001) 12 N.J.C.L. 449.

86   *Hogan v. Newfoundland (School Boards for Ten Districts)* (1997), 154 Nfld. & P.E.I.R. 121, 479 A.P.R. 121 (Nfld. T.D.); (1999), 173 Nfld. & P.E.I.R. 148, 530 A.P.R. 148 (Nfld. T.D.), rev'd (2000), 189 Nfld. & P.E.I.R. 183, 571 A.P.R. 183 (Nfld. C.A.), leave to appeal refused [2000] 2 S.C.R. ix (S.C.C.).

ular opinion about constitutional amendments[87] and the inappropriateness of using an injunction to prevent the Governor General from issuing the proclamation that the bill was in force.[88] Freedom of religion and of expression were not considered to be infringed in the entire process.

2) Formation of Separate Schools

Although section 93 of the *Constitution Act, 1867*, and its counterparts for post-1867 provinces could be interpreted to restrict the rights and privileges enjoyed by law or custom in 1867 to schools and boards actually existing in 1867, it has not been so understood, with the result that provinces have provided for the creation of new denominational schools and school boards after 1867, pursuant to legislation made under the plenary and exclusive legislative powers of the provinces over education. Whether the separate school to be established pursuant to provincial legislation is Roman Catholic or Protestant, the courts have required strict compliance with legislative requirements in establishing the school.

Where ratepayers sought to establish a Roman Catholic school, but failed to convene a meeting for that purpose in strict compliance as to the number of persons qualified to convene the meeting, all subsequent proceedings in relation to the formation of the school were found to be invalid.[89] But where a Roman Catholic school had originated as a rural school but became an urban school by incorporation of a town, and had carried on for years as such without proper organization as an urban school, it was permitted to be an urban school without obtaining the consent of the majority of school supporters to the change as usually required.[90]

Transitional provisions prior to the commencement of operations of a separate school must also be strictly complied with. Thus, when a township bylaw authorized the establishment of a Protestant separate school because the teacher in the public school was a Roman Catholic, it

---

87 *Hogan v. Newfoundland (Attorney General)* (1998), 166 Nfld. & P.E.I.R. 161, 511 A.P.R. 161 (Nfld. T.D.), aff'd (1998), 172 Nfld. & P.E.I.R. 185, 528 A.P.R. 185 (Nfld. C.A.).

88 *Hogan v. Newfoundland (Attorney General)* (1998), 162 Nfld. & P.E.I.R. 132, 500 A.P.R. 132 (Nfld. T.D.).

89 *Arthur Roman Catholic Separate School Section No. 10 v. Township of Arthur* (1891), 21 O.R. 60 (C.A.).

90 *Fortin v. Hearst Roman Catholic Separate School Board*, [1933] 1 D.L.R. 331 (Ont. H.C.).

was held that Protestant separate school supporters remained liable as public school ratepayers until the new school house was begun.[91] Again, a township bylaw extending the boundaries of the township section so as to be within a Protestant separate school section was *ultra vires* because it did not strictly comply with provincial legislation.[92]

3) Taxation

a) Persons Assessable for Separate School Rates

In most provinces,[93] funding for denominational schools comes either from local municipal taxes paid by supporters of those schools and/or from funds from the general revenues of each province. School rates for both public and separate schools are municipal rates imposed under the authority, typically, of the appropriate provincial education acts.[94] As stated earlier,[95] all legislation relating to funding for denominational schools must comply with the constitutional values contained in section 93 as interpreted by the courts, especially in relation to fairness and proportionality between denominational and public school systems. Since the power to levy school rates is auxiliary to the implementation of education legislation, a municipal bylaw levying school rates is validly enacted only on the requisition of the boards authorized so to request pursuant to provincial legislation.[96] Supporters of Roman Catholic or Protestant separate schools who have taken proper steps pursuant to provincial legislation to have their names inserted on an assessment roll as such, are exempt from taxation for public school purposes, and may be enrolled as separate school supporters required to pay taxes in support of the separate schools.[97]

---

91 *Free* v. *McHugh* (1874), 24 U.C.C.P. 13 (Ont. C.A.).

92 *Banks* v. *Township of Anderdon* (1890), 20 O.R. 296 (H.C.).

93 It is necessary to consult provincial and municipal legislation in relation to any taxation issue in relation to denominational schools. This section only purports to alert readers to specific issues dealt with by the courts, in particular, the Ontario courts, which appear to have entertained most of the reported cases since 1867.

94 *Stratford Public School Board* v. *Stratford* (1910), 2 O.W.N. 499 (C.A.).

95 Above section B(1).

96 *Haacke* v. *Marr* (1859), 8 U.C.C.P. 441 (C.A.); *North Plantagent High School Board* v. *North Plantagent* (1906), 7 O.W.R. 17 (H.C.); and *Re Middleton and Goderich*, [1931] O.R. 392 (H.C.).

97 *Re Middleton and Goderich, ibid.*

Provincial education and assessment legislation contains various provisions relating to the establishment and ongoing functions of separate school district boards. The courts have been required to interpret them, particularly in relation to who is assessable as a separate school supporter and when the duty to support separate schools comes into existence.

Assessment issues have arisen in relation to religiously mixed households. Where one spouse is Protestant and another Roman Catholic, the question of whether the household should be assessed as either a public school or a separate school supporter depends on issues of ownership and possession. Where the Roman Catholic spouse is the tenant in possession, the household has been found to be assessable as a separate school supporter.[98] Where the Roman Catholic spouse owned the property and the Protestant spouse also lived there, the household was found to be a separate school supporter.[99] Where a property is held in joint tenancy by Roman Catholic and Protestant spouses and where the legislation so provides, the wife has no right to have part of the rates applied to the school system of her choice; rather, the husband may determine how the household is to be assessed.[100]

A ratepayer who is not a Roman Catholic is required to be assessed as a public school supporter.[101] But a ratepayer who is a member of a denomination in communion with the Roman Catholic church is assessable as a Roman Catholic.[102]

The obligation to pay school rates and to be assessed as either a public or a separate school supporter only arises after the purchase of property is completed and title has passed.[103] A separate school supporter is only liable to pay public school taxes before he became a separate school supporter or before the establishment of a separate school.[104] The right to become a separate school supporter cannot arise where the sites for a

---

98 *London Board of Education* v. *McDonald* (1966), 57 D.L.R. (2d) 390 (Ont. C.A.).

99 *Township of Schreiber* v. *Beno* (1963), 39 D.L.R. (2d) 453 (Ont. C.A.); *Bishay* v. *Metropolitan Separate School Board* (1988), 22 O.M.B.R. 333.

100 *Holmes* v. *Stiver*, [1934] 4 D.L.R. 358 (Ont. C.A.).

101 *City of Regina* v. *McCarthy*, above note 73.

102 *Pander* v. *Town of Melville*, above note 74.

103 *Katrinsky* v. *Esterhazy Protestant Separate School District* (1902), 7 Terr. L.R. 265 (N.W.T. C.A.).

104 *Ellice School Section No. 1* v. *Township of Ellice* (1906), 7 O.W.R. 6 (H.C.); and *Slevar* v. *Township of Crowland* (1959), 20 D.L.R. (2d) 518 (Ont. C.A.).

new separate school have not yet been determined.[105] A separate school supporter only becomes such after assessment on an assessment roll.[106]

While separate school supporters will normally be assessed as supporters of the separate school nearest to them,[107] it is possible to have an assessment changed in favour of another separate school.[108] Where no separate school exists in the municipality in which ratepayers reside, they may be assessed as supporters of a separate school in an adjoining municipality.[109]

A ratepayer who has been wrongfully assessed as a Roman Catholic or Protestant may claim reassessment.[110] A ratepayer who is not an occupant of assessed premises may also require that the assessment roll be changed.[111]

Where provincial legislation permits both public and separate school boards to levy development charges on land undergoing residential development to fund new schools, the legislation will be upheld provided it does not prejudicially affect the right of separate schools to fair and equitable funding.[112]

b) Corporate Assessments

In addition to funding derived from individual taxpayers, separate schools in most provinces receive funding levied for the purpose on corporations.[113] Such legislation typically requires a corporation to remit school rates reflecting the proportion of the total number of shares held by Roman Catholics as compared to the total number of shares issued. The

---

105 *Comrie v. Leroux* (1956), 2 D.L.R. (2d) 749 (Ont. Co. Ct.).

106 *Dillon v. Catelli Food Products Ltd.*, [1937] 1 D.L.R. 353 (Ont. C.A.).

107 For the old three-mile rule, see *Tytgate v. Tofflemire*, [1951] 3 D.L.R. 572 (Ont. C.A.); *Vandekerckhove v. Township of Middleton*, [1962] S.C.R. 75; *Forestell v. Township of Tyendinaga*, [1963] 1 O.R. 632 (Co. Ct.); and *Chittle v. Maidstone Roman Catholic Separate School Board* (1965), 53 D.L.R. (2d) 529 (Ont. C.A.).

108 *Chittle v. Maidstone Roman Catholic Separate School Board*, ibid.

109 *Sandwich East Roman Catholic Separate School Board v. Town of Walkerville* (1905), 10 O.L.R. 214 (C.A.). *Cf. Gagnon v. Studer*, [1948] 4 D.L.R. 379 (Ont. C.A.).

110 *Re Ontario Roman Catholic Separate Schools* (1889), 18 O.R. 606 (C.A.).

111 *London Board of Education v. Gillespie*, [1973] 2 O.R. 584 (Co. Ct.).

112 *Ontario Home Builders' Association v. York Region Board of Education*, above note 31. This matter was actually resolved in *OECTA*, above note 33.

113 Again, it is necessary to consult the applicable provincial and municipal legislation to ascertain the appropriate principles in any specific situation.

interpretation of the word "share" in the legislation is to be a broad interpretation, giving effect to the purpose and spirit of the legislation in ensuring the funding of Roman Catholic schools.[114] Subsidiary corporations are permitted to make the same tax designation as their parent corporation.[115]

The allocation of corporate assessments must be made in strict compliance with the legislation and where there has been a default by a corporation in making the designation, a Roman Catholic school board has no authority to ask for the invalidation of the process; rather, the court should enforce the legislation as written.[116] Where a dispute arises as to the correct apportionment of a corporate assessment as between public and separate schools, courts of revision established by provincial legislation to deal with apportionment issues have jurisdiction to determine such disputes.[117]

A corporation should be assessed as a public school supporter until it has responded to the notice for rating assessment.[118] Corporations are required to inquire to the best of their ability into the number of Roman Catholic shareholders and to apportion their assessments accordingly.[119] The onus of proving the proportion of the assessment that qualifies for exemption from public school support so as to be applied to separate school support is on the corporation, since only the corporation is in a position to ascertain the number of Roman Catholics among its shareholders.[120]

A shareholder may object to assessment by the company or a separate school supporter and re-direct his or her part of the school rates assessment to the public schools.[121] If the notice is given after the assessment roll has been struck for the year, it cannot be revised until the following

---

114 *Metropolitan Toronto School Board v. Metropolitan Separate School Board* (1987), 20 O.A.C. 400 (Div. Ct.).

115 *Metropolitan Toronto School Board v. Foodcorp. Ltd.* (1986), 18 O.M.B.R. 395.

116 *Calgary Roman Catholic Separate School Board District No. 1 v. Calgary Board of Education* (1985), 40 Alta. L.R. 65 (C.A.).

117 *Jones v. City of Edmonton Catholic School District No. 7*, [1977] 2 S.C.R. 872.

118 *Vonda Roman Catholic Separate School Board v. Town of Vonda*, [1921] 65 D.L.R. 762 (Sask. Dist. Ct.).

119 *Dillon v. Catelli Food Products Ltd.*, above note 106.

120 *Ibid.*; *City of Windsor Board of Education v. Ford Motor Co. of Canada*, [1941] A.C. 453 (P.C.); *Dillon v. Toronto Millstock Co.*, [1943] S.C.R. 268; and *Banque provinciale v. Ogilvie*, [1973] S.C.R. 281.

121 *Re J. Simpson and Sons Ltd.* (1931), 40 O.W.N. 595 (Co. Ct.).

year.[122] The provincial legislature cannot permit the separate school boards themselves to send the notice for assessment to a corporation; rather, this must be done by a municipality.[123]

For the purposes of correction of the assessment roll, the date of assessment for the current assessment year is the date of the return of the roll by the assessor to the clerk, and errors and omissions exist also from that date.[124] Where a correction to the roll is requested, the municipal council must give the appropriate notices to the corporations prior to reassessment, which otherwise is void.[125] Since liability as a separate school supporter exists only so long as a person is a separate school supporter,[126] once the taxpayer becomes a public school supporter, the corporation becomes entitled to have the roll corrected.[127]

4) Right to Attend Separate Schools

Roman Catholic separate schools are only obliged to accommodate children whose parents, natural or adoptive, are enrolled as separate school supporters.[128] Since a parent's faith determines the school system the children are permitted by law to attend, there is no violation of human rights legislation to require payment of the requisite fees when parents wish to send their children to the schools of the other system.[129] Where parents do not enroll as separate school supporters, their children automatically are entitled to attend only the public school system.[130]

---

122 *Regina Public School Board* v. *Gratton Separate School Board* , [1918] 1 W.W.R. 16 (Sask. C.A.).

123 *Regina Public School Board* v. *Gratton Separate School Board* , above note 75.

124 *Re Union Stock Yards of Toronto Ltd.*, [1938] 2 D.L.R. 361 at 365 (Ont. C.A.).

125 *City of Windsor Board of Education* v. *Windsor Roman Catholic Separate School Board* (1995), 24 O.R. (3d) 62 (Div. Ct.).

126 *Re Ontario Separate Schools Act* (1901), 1 O.L.R. 584 (C.A.); *McCarty* v. *Hird*, [1947] 4 D.L.R. 821 (C.A.); *London Board of Education* v. *Gillespie*, above note 111; and *Vandekerckhove* v. *Township of Middleton*, above note 107.

127 *Re Bayack*, [1929] 3 D.L.R. 480 (Ont. C.A.).

128 *Primeau* v. *Russell Separate School Section No. 6* (1926), 29 O.W.N. 442 (H.C.); and *Renaud* v. *Township of Tilbury North Roman Catholic Separate School Section No. 11*, [1933] 3 D.L.R. 172 (Ont. C.A.).

129 *Bintner* v. *Regina Public School District No. 4*, above note 75; and *Schmidt* v. *Calgary Board of Education* (1976), 72 D.L.R. (3d) 330 (Alta. C.A.).

130 *Leblanc* v. *Hamilton Board of Education* (1962), 35 D.L.R. (2d) 548 (Ont. H.C.).

The definition of who is a Roman Catholic or a Protestant, as the case may be, is occasionally problematical. In Quebec, "Protestant" has been interpreted to include Jehovah's Witnesses,[131] but not Jews.[132] But where there was no local Protestant school, Jehovah's Witnesses have been permitted to attend the local Roman Catholic school and be exempted from religious education and exercises.[133] In Saskatchewan, a member of a small denomination in communion with the Roman Catholic Church was permitted to send his children to a Roman Catholic separate school.[134] The courts appear to make these decisions informed by historically accepted understandings of theological differentiation among various religious institutions.

5) Controls over Roman Catholic School Teachers

In recent years, the courts have been required to consider how extensive denominational school rights pursuant to section 93 might be. Cases have considered both the extent to which the private lives of teachers in Roman Catholic schools are subject to the discipline and teachings of the Roman Catholic Church and the extent to which "denominational cause" may be used in the appointment, promotion, and dismissal of non-Roman Catholic teachers. Issues explored include marriage, children, the requirement to educate children in Roman Catholic schools, collective bargaining rights, and freedom of expression.

Roman Catholic schools typically hire as teachers Roman Catholics who can present a pastoral certificate from their priests. This is to ensure that a Roman Catholic culture completely suffuses the entire life of the school. The question is whether section 93 denominational school rights extend beyond existence and funding issues to the right to ensure a complete Roman Catholic culture by whatever means the Roman Catholic Church thinks suitable; that is, whether section 93 permits the promotion of a "denominational cause."

In *Caldwell v. Stuart*,[135] the Supreme Court of Canada upheld the right of a Roman Catholic school to dismiss a teacher for denominational cause and thereby confirmed that denominational cause was the standard for section 93 cases about teachers. The teacher was a Roman Catholic, who,

---

131 *Perron v. Rouyn School Trustees*, above note 12.
132 *Hirsch v. Montreal Protestant School Board*, above note 11.
133 *Perron v. Rouyn School Trustees*, above note 12.
134 *Pander v. Town of Melville*, above note 74.
135 *Caldwell v. Stuart*, [1984] 2 S.C.R. 603.

although a competent teacher, had married a divorced member of another Christian denomination; religious conformity to the church's teachings was said to be a *bona fide* occupational requirement in Roman Catholic schools, where teachers are expected to be moral exemplars for pupils.[136]

This right to dismiss for denominational cause is equated with the right to dismiss for just cause in circumstances that fall within the exemptions for which provincial human rights codes provide, and is sustainable pursuant to section 93 as within denominational rights and privileges.[137] This right is also protected by section 29 of the *Canadian Charter of Rights and Freedoms*, which precludes denominational school rights from being overridden by other *Charter* rights, including the guarantee of freedom of conscience and religion in section 2(a).[138]

A Roman Catholic separate school board may dismiss for denominational cause a teacher who has a child out of wedlock, because extramarital and premarital sexual intercourse is forbidden by the Roman Catholic Church; such a dismissal is sustainable under section 93 as within denominational school rights. The requirements of notice of reasons for dismissal and an opportunity to be heard prior to termination should, however, be granted.[139]

A Roman Catholic separate school board may require its Roman Catholic teachers to be separate school supporters and to send their children to separate schools, and may dismiss teachers who fail to comply with these requirements.[140] The right to dismiss in such circumstances does not violate section 2(a) of the *Charter* because there is no interference with freedom of religion, nor does it constitute discrimination pursuant to section 15 of the *Charter* where all teachers employed by the same board as employer are subject to the same requirements.[141]

---

136 See also *Walsh v. Newfoundland* (1988), 71 Nfld. & P.E.I.R. 21 (Nfld. C.A.), leave to appeal to S.C.C. refused (1989), 76 Nfld. & P.E.I.R. 191 (S.C.C.); and *Stack v. St. John's Roman Catholic School Board* (1979), 99 D.L.R. (3d) 278 (Nfld. T.D.).

137 *Caldwell v. Stuart*, above note 135.

138 *Walsh v. Newfoundland*, above note 136.

139 *Casagrande v. Hinton Roman Catholic Separate School District No. 155* (1987), 38 D.L.R. (4th) 382 (Alta. Q.B.). See also the early case *Moose Jaw School District v. Saskatchewan (Attorney General)* (1973), 41 D.L.R. (3d) 732 (Sask. Q.B.).

140 *Black v. Metropolitan Separate School Board* (1988), 52 D.L.R. (4th) 736 (Ont. Div. Ct.). *Cf. Morra v. Metropolitan Separate School Board* (1981), 3 C.H.R.R. D/1034 (Ont. Bd. of Inquiry).

141 *Black v. Metropolitan Separate School Board*, ibid.

However, a Roman Catholic school board may not discipline a teacher in its schools who was critical in a newspaper article of the church's position on the role of women within the church; when a teacher was refused promotion and removed from teaching religion, which she had previously taught, although she suffered no loss of income in the performance of her reassigned duties, it was held that this constituted punishment without just cause.[142]

Provincial legislation that purports to permit the reinstatement of teachers dismissed for denominational cause because they entered a civil marriage is *ultra vires* as an infringement of section 93 denominational school rights.[143] Provincial legislation in relation to collective bargaining rights ought to be interpreted so as not to compel an employee to submit a case for dismissal for denominational reasons to arbitration, since to interpret it otherwise would be to find such legislation *ultra vires* as an infringement of section 93.[144] Although a province may not legislate so as to derogate from section 93 denominational rights, parties to a collective agreement are free to modify such rights by collective agreement.[145] Provincial legislation instituting collective bargaining for all teachers in a province does not derogate from denominational school rights and privileges pursuant to section 93.[146]

Since Roman Catholic schools have been obliged to fulfil their staffing needs by hiring non-Roman Catholic teachers, legal issues relating to giving preference to Roman Catholic teachers over non-Roman Catholic teachers in hiring, promotion, and dismissal under the heading of denominational cause have been considered. In *Daly v. Ontario (Attorney General)*,[147] the Ontario Court of Appeal found that provincial legislation, which stipulated that all teachers employed by a Roman Catholic

---

142 *Metropolitan Separate School Board v. O.E.C.T.A.* (1994), 41 L.A.C. (4th) 353 (Ont.).

143 *Essex Roman Catholic Separate School Board v. Porter* (1978), 89 D.L.R. (3d) 445 (Ont. C.A.).

144 *Essex Roman Catholic Separate School Board v. Tremblay-Webster* (1984), 5 D.L.R. (4th) 665 (Ont. C.A.).

145 *Ibid.*

146 *Stack v. St. John's Roman Catholic School Board*, above note 136. *Cf. Roman Catholic School Board v. Newfoundland Teachers' Association* (1983), 42 Nfld. & P.E.I.R. 40, 122 A.P.R. 40 (Nfld. C.A.).

147 (1999), 172 D.L.R. (4th) 241 (Ont. C.A.).

school board should enjoy equal opportunity in employment and promotion,[148] was an infringement of the section 93 denominational right to ensure a Roman Catholic culture by preferring Roman Catholic over non-Roman Catholic teachers. In the companion case decided on the same day by the Ontario Court of Appeal, *Ontario English Catholic Teachers Association v. Dufferin-Peel Roman Catholic Separate School Board*,[149] the court upheld a school board policy restricting non-Roman Catholic teachers from being promoted to positions of authority within the board, again on the ground that section 93 denominational rights to do so were constitutionally protected. The policy was also protected within section 24 of the Ontario *Human Rights Code*[150] as a *bona fide* occupational requirement in the separate school context.

Finally, the Ontario Court of Appeal has also considered whether provincial legislation disqualifying employees of Roman Catholic school boards and their spouses from being elected as separate school board members constitutes an infringement of their section 15 equality rights under the *Charter* as well as a violation of section 93 denominational school rights to determine who may be qualified to be a separate school board member.[151] The court concluded that the legislation was an infringement of section 15 on the ground of discrimination based on marital status and cannot be saved under section 1 as a reasonable limit because there was no evidence that the stated objective of the legislation to reduce conflicts of interest responded to any pressing or substantial problem. The court further found, however, that the legislation did not prejudicially affect section 93 denominational rights because there was no evidence that conflict of interest issues were denominationally protected in 1867 nor that the conflict guidelines actually interfered with the management and control of denominational schools.

---

148 *Education Act*, R.S.O. 1990, c. E-2, s. 136(2).

149 (1999), 172 D.L.R. (4th) 260 (Ont. C.A.).

150 R.S.O. 1990, c. H-19, s. 24.

151 *Ontario Public School Boards Association v. Ontario (Attorney General)* (1999), 175 D.L.R. (4th) 609 (Ont. C.A.).

C. PUBLIC SCHOOLS

1) Compulsory Attendance

Legislation in all provinces, as in most of the jurisdictions in the Western world, places a legal duty on parents or legal guardians to ensure that children of school age receive education either in the public or denominational schools of each province, or in a private school, or by home schooling approved and certified by provincial education authorities; failure by parents of school-age children to comply with the legislation will justify conviction for violations of such provisions in accordance with provincial legislation.[152] The requirement that children attend school is of critical importance to society and is not, therefore, a violation of the section 7 guarantees of life, liberty, and security of the person pursuant to the *Canadian Charter of Rights and Freedoms.*[153]

Nor is the requirement that children be educated within an environment certified by provincial educational authorities a violation of section 2(a) of the *Charter*, even where that environment is neither a public nor a denominational school.[154] The primary purpose of the statutory requirement is to regulate the standard of education in non-religious subjects and not to deny freedom of religion.[155] It is not a violation of either section 2(a) or section 7 to require parents who wish to engage in home schooling or to send their children to private religious schools to seek provincial certification for their schooling plans.[156] Even if it could be said that the requirement of provincial certification for non-religious subjects is a violation of section 2(a), the majority of the Supreme Court of Canada in *R. v. Jones* regarded the state's interest in education to be sufficiently compelling that the requirement was a reasonable limit on freedom of religion pursuant to section 1 of the *Charter*.

The legal status of the agreements made between Canada and the Mennonite and Hutterite communities on their entry to Canada at various times during the late nineteenth and early twentieth centuries in

---

152 *R. v. Ulmer*, [1923] 1 D.L.R. 304 (Alta. C.A.).

153 *R. v. J.(N.)* (1987), 83 A.R. 149 (Prov. Ct.); and *R. v. Jones*, [1986] 2 S.C.R. 284.

154 *Arbeau v. R.* (1985), 21 C.R.R. 354 (Nfld. C.A.); *R. v. Powell* (1985), 39 Alta. L.R. (2d) 122 (Prov. Ct.); and *R. v. Jones*, above note 153. *Cf. R. v. Kind* (1984), 50 Nfld. & P.E.I.R. 332 (Nfld. Dist. Ct.).

155 *R. v. Jones*, above note 153; and *R. v. J.(N.)*, above note 153.

156 *R. v. Jones*, above note 153.

relation to educational matters — in particular, the desire of those communities to educate their own children free from the compulsion to attend public schools — is somewhat uncertain in law, although compromises have been largely reached in the Western provinces concerned.[157] In *R. v. Hildebrand*,[158] in 1919, it was held that Mennonites in Manitoba could be penalized for failing to send their children to a public school since the order in council of 13 August 1873 was ineffective because the *Manitoba Act* gave Manitoba exclusive jurisdiction over education within the provinces. On the other hand, in *R. v. Wiebe*[159] in 1978, it was held that there was no violation of the Alberta legislation when a Mennonite child was sent to a school uncertified by the provincial educational authorities. Mennonite religious beliefs were said to be so irrevocably linked to education that a parent charged had his or her freedom of religion under provincial human rights legislation abrogated.

These decisions may now be overtaken by the Supreme Court's decision in *R. v. Jones*. Moreover, in an earlier case involving Doukhobors who refused to send their children to public schools, the British Columbia Court of Appeal stated that pursuant to section 93, the provincial legislature could validly enact legislation that indirectly affected religion so that Doukhobor children were required to attend provincially certified schools, although not necessarily public schools.[160]

Finally, where a school board fulfils its duty to provide for the education of all in the public schools by busing to a distant school a pupil who has been exempted from religious instruction at the local school, no religious discrimination stems from the fact of the busing.[161]

2) School Dress for Students

Public schools historically have not placed restrictions on the mode of dress permitted to students while attending school, other than to require

---

157 See William Janzen, *Limits on Liberty: The Experience of Mennonite, Hutterite and Doukhobor Communities in Canada* (Toronto: University of Toronto Press, 1990) ch. 3.

158 [1919] 3 W.W.R. 286 (Man. C.A.).

159 [1978] 2 W.W.R. 36 (Alta Prov. Ct.).

160 *Perepolkin v. B.C. Superintendent of Child Welfare (No. 2)* (1957), 11 D.L.R. (2d) 417 (B.C.C.A.).

161 *Cusson-Lafleur v. Chavigny (Commission scolaire)*, [1986] R.L. 48 (Que. C.A.), leave to appeal to S.C.C. refused (1986), 1 Q.A.C. 157 (S.C.C.).

compliance with minimum standards of decency and cleanliness; nor do public schools typically require students to wear school uniforms, although many denominational schools require compliance with school uniform standards. The question of the extent to which religious dress or religious symbols may be worn to school in addition to compliance with school dress codes has arisen pursuant to provincial human rights codes. Thus, it is discriminatory pursuant to such legislation to forbid a baptized Sikh male to wear a kirpan to school.[162] It has also been found to be discriminatory to forbid a Sikh student to wear a turban to school, unless the school is a private school, in which case it may limit access to certain religious groups only.[163]

3) Religious Instruction

Until recently, such religious instruction and religious exercises as occurred in the public schools was nominally Christian. However, after the *Charter* came into effect, provincial legislation prescribing both religious instruction and religious exercises was challenged successfully pursuant to section 2(a), with the results that the legislation has been amended and the public schools are now largely free of religion other than in the context of comparative religion courses in some provinces. Religious instruction and religious exercises in the denominational schools remains pursuant to section 93.

In *Canadian Civil Liberties Association v. Ontario*,[164] the Ontario Court of Appeal found that regulations providing for two periods per week of religious instruction violated section 2(a) of the *Charter* because the purpose of the regulation was Christian indoctrination, although the regulation itself did not expressly stipulate for Christianity. The regulation was not saved by the fact that children might be exempted from participation since this exemption amounted to a penalty on religious minorities who might feel set apart and stigmatized as nonconformists. It was further stated that section 2(a) does not prohibit education about religion pro-

---

162 *Tuli v. St. Albert Protestant Separate School District No. 6* (1985), 8 C.H.R.R. D/3906 (Alta. Q.B.); and *Pandori v. Peel Board of Education* (1990), 12 C.H.R.R. D/364 (Ont. Bd. Inq.), aff'd (1991), 80 D.L.R. (4th) 475 (Ont. Div. Ct.).

163 *Sehdev v. Bayview Glen Junior Schools Ltd.* (1988), 9 C.H.R.R. D/4881 (Ont. Bd. of Inquiry); see also *Mandla v. Lee*, [1983] 2 A.C. 548 (H.L.).

164 (1990), 65 D.L.R. (4th) 1 (Ont. C.A.).

vided that it is not indoctrination.[165] The court rejected the argument that
the regulation could be saved under section 1 because religious instruction was one valid means to teach children about morality; it thought
there were other ways to do so but did not state what these were. Where
legislation provided for exemption from attending religious instruction
in the public schools on religious grounds, previous cases had guaranteed that right to minority religious groups, including Jews[166] and Jehovah's Witnesses.[167]

For many faiths, religious instruction includes instruction in what
are considered to be the proper uses of human sexuality and recent
attempts to introduce into public school classrooms sex education that
encourages consideration of human sexuality and family issues beyond
the traditional positions of many religions which promote sexual chastity before marriage between a man and a woman and lifelong fidelity within marriage, have been met by resistance on religious grounds, although
the resistance may not necessarily be framed in law as on those grounds.

In the first reported case,[168] paradoxically concerned with the expo-
sure of children at too young an age, in the opinion of their parents, to
sex education materials in a Roman Catholic school developed and
approved by the Roman Catholic Church, the Saskatchewan Queen's
Bench declined to grant an injunction to restrain the school from implementing the program because not only was there no evidence that children would be harmed by the program but the children could be
exempted from any part of the program to which their parents objected.
The court further found that there was no infringement of the parents'
section 2(a) right in the absence of evidence that the course conflicted
with their religious beliefs about human sexuality.

Religious perspectives can be brought to bear on the question of
classroom resource materials used by public school teachers in secular

---

165 See earlier cases *Rogers v. Bathurst School District* (1896), 1 N.B. Eq. 266
    (S.C.); *Shaver v. Cambridge and Russell Union School Section* (1911), 18 O.W.R.
    501 (H.C.); and *Gallagher v. Winnipeg School District No. 1* (1963), 42 D.L.R.
    (2d) 370 (Man. Q.B.).
166 *North York Board of Education v. Ministry of Education*, above note 39.
167 *Chabot v. Lamorandière School Commissioners*, above note 13.
168 *Dansereau v. Board of Education of North West Catholic School Division No. 16*
    (2000), 190 Sask. R. 55 (Q.B.).

subject areas. In *Chamberlain* v. *Surrey School District No. 36*,[169] the British Columbia Court of Appeal decided that the phrase "strictly secular" in provincial legislation,[170] in relation to the criteria for the conduct of public schools, does not preclude religious school board members from participating in deliberations about primary school readers depicting children with same-sex parents because both religious and non-religious views may be found in this "secular" world. The court upheld the school board's refusal to approve books suggested by a gay and lesbian educators group on the ground that issues of sexual orientation were inappropriate in early primary school grades.

4) Religious Exercises

Again, the Ontario Court of Appeal has also first determined that daily religious exercises in the public schools are a violation of section 2(a) of the *Charter*. In *Zylberberg* v. *Sudbury Board of Education*,[171] an Ontario regulation providing for religious exercises including "the reading of the Scriptures or other suitable readings and the repeating of the Lord's Prayer or other suitable prayers" was found to be a breach of section 2(a) because it imposed Christian observances upon non-Christian pupils. The court further stated that the existence of an exemption for religious minorities did not save the legislation because it may be harmful to students to single themselves out and amount to indirect coercion since peer pressure would compel students to conform by attending. Similar conclusions have been drawn by trial courts subsequently in British Columbia[172] and Manitoba,[173] as well as by a human rights commission in Saskatchewan.[174]

---

169 (2000), 191 D.L.R. (4th) 128 (B.C.C.A.), leave to appeal granted 4 October 2001 (S.C.C.).

170 *School Act*, R.S.B.C. 1996, c. 412, s. 76(1).

171 (1988), 52 D.L.R. (4th) 577 (Ont. C.A.).

172 *Russow v. A.G. B.C.* (1989), 62 D.L.R. (4th) 98 (B.C.S.C.).

173 *Manitoba Association for Rights and Liberties v. Manitoba*, above note 58.

174 *Fancy v. Saskatoon School Div. No. 13* (1999), 35 C.H.R.R. D/9 (Sask. Bd. Iq.), where the Lord's Prayer and Bible reading in public schools was a violation of the provincial human rights act. See also for issues relating to the board's jurisdiction in this case *Board of Education of Saskatoon School Division No. 13 v. Human Rights Commission (Sask.)* (1998), 167 Sask. R. 184 (Q.B.). See also Richard W. Bauman and David Schneiderman, "The Constitutional Context of Religious Practices in Saskatchewan Public Schools: God was in the Details" (1996) 60 Sask. L.R. 265.

Where legislation provides for exemption from such exercises on religious grounds, such exemptions are to be granted to students.[175]

In response to the two decisions of the Ontario Court of Appeal in relation to religious instruction and religious exercises in public schools, the Ontario Government issued "Policy Memorandum 112" to permit education about religion. This approach was challenged by a multi-faith parents' coalition in *Bal* v. *Ontario (A.G.)*[176] on the ground that the secular values implicit in this approach imposed a world view inimical to their religious values on their children and constituted an infringement of their section 2(a) freedom of religion. The Ontario Court of Appeal characterized secular as neutral and rejected their argument entirely.

5) Religious Holidays

While the practice in many public school boards has been to permit students to be absent for religious holidays that differ from the statutory holidays for which provincial legislation provides, the possibility that an entire school board might close for the religious holidays of a particular religious group was considered in one case, *Islamic Schools Federation of Ontario* v. *Ottawa Board of Education*.[177] The applicant sought to have the school board close its schools for two Muslim holy days and challenged a provincial regulation setting out school holidays on the ground that it provided only for "Christian" holidays. The Ontario Divisional Court rejected both arguments. It adopted the prior judicial characterization[178] of the provincial school holidays as secular pause days so that they are neutral and non-discriminatory. The court further observed that Muslim students were already accommodated on Muslim holidays by being exempted from attendance as well as being accommodated in respect to the scheduling of tests and other academic requirements. The court sus-

---

175 *Chabot* v. *Lamorandière School Commissioners*, above note 13. On the issue of repeating the Lord's Prayer in public generally: *Freitag* v. *Penetanguishene (Town)* (1999), 179 D.L.R. (4th) 150 (Ont. C.A.); and *Ontario (Speaker of the Legislative Assembly)* v. *Ontario (Human Rights Commission)* (2001), 54 O.R. (3d) 595 (C.A.). See also Michael D. Mysak, "Houses of the Holy? Reconciling Parliamentary Privilege and Freedom of Religion" (2001) 12 N.J.C.L. 353.

176 (1994), 21 O.R. (3d) 682 (Gen. Div.), aff'd (1997), 101 O.A.C. 219 (C.A.).

177 (1997), 145 D.L.R. (4th) 659 (Ont. Div. Ct.).

178 *Chambly Regional Board of Education* v. *Bergevin* (1994), 115 D.L.R. (4th) 609 (S.C.C.).

tained the law and practice of permitting statutory holidays only but accommodating students who required religious holidays in addition.

6) Patriotic Exercises

Participation in patriotic exercises, such as repeating oaths of allegiance, singing national anthems or other patriotic songs, and saluting flags, is regarded as offensive by some religious groups on the ground that they .acknowledge the sovereignty of God alone, and not that of the state, over their lives on earth. While there have been instances where groups such as the Mennonites and Hutterites have been executed by political authorities for refusal to participate in such exercises,[179] there have also been situations in which at least one religious group, the Jehovah's Witnesses, have come into conflict with the law when their children refused to participate in fighting in time of war.

When Jehovah's Witness children refused to salute a flag, and provincial legislation delegated discretion to local school boards to dismiss from school children who had so refused, a local school board may validly exercise its power of dismissal.[180] However, where provincial legislation provided for exemptions from singing the national anthem and saluting the flag, Jehovah's Witness children may claim such exemption and continue to attend school. Where attempts have been made to exclude them, their father may claim damages.[181]

7) Controls over Teachers

The extent to which teachers in the public schools enjoy freedom of religion and of expression has been considered by the courts in two contexts, in relation to what they may wear in the classroom and the extent to which they enjoy freedom of expression in a public school classroom. Teachers are permitted to wear religious garb or religious symbols in the classroom; thus, a member of a Roman Catholic religious order employed to teach in a public school has been permitted to wear religious garb in the classroom[182] and a baptized Sikh teacher has also been permitted to

---

179 Janzen, above note 157 at ch. 4.

180 *Ruman v. Lethbridge School District No. 51*, [1943] 3 W.W.R. 340 (Alta. T.D.).

181 *Donald v. Hamilton (City) Board of Education*, [1945] 3 D.L.R. 424 (Ont. C.A.).

182 *Rogers v. Bathurst School District*, above note 165.

wear a kirpan while on school property and is so protected by provincial human rights legislation.[183]

While public school teachers appear to enjoy some freedom of religious expression in relation to what they may wear in the classroom, paradoxically, they appear to enjoy very little freedom of religious expression or of expression relating to religious matters in and out of the public school classroom. In *Ross v. New Brunswick School District No. 15*,[184] the right of a public school teacher who disseminated anti-Semitic writings outside the classroom to remain in the classroom was raised; the teacher had never expressed his views in the classroom but Jewish parents and students became aware of them and alleged the classroom environment was poisoned as a result. Ross alleged that his views were based on his religious beliefs. The Supreme Court of Canada upheld a lower tribunal's decision to remove the teacher to an administrative position as well as removing the teacher's section 2(a) right to freedom of religion and section 2(b) right to freedom of expression. However, the Court concluded that this was defensible under section 1 to ensure a non-discriminatory classroom environment for children. The Court opined that section 2(a) rights were limited where a religious belief "denigrates and defames" the religious beliefs of others, thereby denying their equality right to equal respect and dignity.[185]

D. PRIVATE SCHOOLS

1) Constitutional Matters

Since the coming into force of the *Canadian Charter of Rights and Freedoms*, the secularization of the public school systems in most provinces has led to a significant increase in the number of religiously-based

---

183 *Pandori v. Peel Board of Education*, above note 162.

184 (1996), 133 D.L.R. (4th) 1 (S.C.C.).

185 Ross alleged that his views were based on his religious beliefs. For the question of whether newspaper cartoons depicting Ross as a Nazi amount to defamation, see *Ross v. New Brunswick Teachers Association* (2001), 201 D.L.R. (4th) 75 (N.B.C.A.). The question of whether a lesbian teacher may be permitted to disclose her sexual orientation is currently under review as a freedom of expression in the classroom issue: *Assiniboine South Teachers' Association of the Manitoba Teachers' Society v. Assiniboine South School Division No. 3* (2000), 184 D.L.R. (4th) 385 (Man. C.A.).

schools operating alongside the public and denominational schools. Some enjoy partial public funding while others receive none whatsoever. Two major constitutional issues have been considered by the courts in relation to these schools pursuant to the *Charter*: the requirement for provincial certification of such schools and the right to public funding, in light of the fact that as taxpayers, parents whose children attend religious schools are already funding both public and denominational schools, as well as the religious schools to which they actually send their children.

As stated earlier,[186] it is now clearly established that private Christian (and presumably other religious) schools are required to procure provincial certification in relation to the non-religious aspects of their curriculum and that this requirement does not constitute a violation of section 2(a) of the *Charter* because the state has a reasonable interest in ensuring proper instruction for its future citizens in secular subjects, and this requirement is a reasonable limitation on religious freedom under section 1 of the *Charter*.[187] The religious aspects of religiously-based private schools' curricula are largely free of state regulation to date in Canada; moreover, provided provincial certification is procured, there are virtually no requirements concerning teacher qualifications, rights to open such schools, funding, and the nature of the religious education in them.

Additionally, in *Adler* v. *Ontario*,[188] the refusal of a provincial government to provide funding for religiously-based schools was found by the Supreme Court of Canada not to be a violation of either section 2(a) or section 15 of the *Charter* because such a refusal is a reasonable limit in light of the legislative objective of providing for a strong, secular, public education system promoting a tolerant, multicultural society; the public funding of Roman Catholic schools is an irrelevant historical anomaly.

Finally, it may be noted that a municipal zoning bylaw prohibiting the use of church property for a private school is not a violation of section 2(a) because the bylaw was passed for zoning purposes and not for

---

186 Above section B(1)(e).

187 *R.* v. *Bienert*, above note 70; *R.* v. *Jones*, above note 153; and *C.R.B. and S.G.B.* v. *Director of Child Welfare (Nfld.)* (1995), 137 Nfld. & P.E.I.R. 1, 428 A.P.R. 1 (Nfld. S.C.).

188 Above note 39. There is no discrimination on the basis of religion when DIAND refuses to pay school fees to support an Indian child at a private Roman Catholic school: *C.H.R.C.* v. *Canada (DIAND)* (1994), 25 C.R.R. (2d) 230 (F.C.-T.D.).

religious purposes, and the school could be build in a suitably zoned part of the municipality.[189]

2) School Dress

Private schools, whether recently established religiously-based schools or independent schools, typically require certain dress standards of their students and, as private schools, are permitted to do so. However, where a private school wishes to exclude members of certain religious groups from attending that school, it should do so directly by express policy and not indirectly and insidiously by refusing, for example, to permit Sikh students from wearing turbans as part of the school uniform.[190]

3) Controls over Teachers

Religiously-based schools regard their teachers as role models for the application of their religious and moral principles to everyday life and therefore expect teachers, as a term of employment, to practise those principles. Thus, a teacher at a Christian school who is living in a common law relationship may be dismissed without discrimination, since it is a *bona fide* occupational qualification, given the religious nature of such a school, that a teacher comply with the school's religious understanding about Christian marriage.[191] Again, a divorced teacher who remarried while her first spouse was still alive in contravention of a church's teaching on remarriage may also be dismissed on religious grounds.[192] It appears that the courts treat religious schools and school teachers in the same way as Roman Catholic schools and school teachers under section 93, insofar as compliance with the religious values of the sponsoring religious institution is enforced.[193]

---

189 *Town of Milton v. Smith* (1986), 32 M.P.L.R. 107 (Ont. H.C.).
190 *Sehdev v. Bayview Glen Junior Schools Ltd.*, above note 163.
191 *Garrod v. Rhema Christian School* (1990), 15 C.H.R.R. D/477 (Ont. Bd. of Inq.).
192 *Kearley v. Pentecostal Assemblies Board of Education* (1993), 19 C.H.R.R. D/473 (Nfld. Bd. of Inq.).
193 Above section B(5).

E. SUNDAY SCHOOLS

It has been said that there is no fiduciary relationship between a Sunday School teacher and his or her pupil,[194] but this might now be doubted in light of the imposition of vicarious liability on religious and other charitable institutions for the security of children in their charge.[195]

F. UNIVERSITIES AND COLLEGES

It is widely thought that post-secondary institutions, such as colleges and universities, are places where the free discussion of and advocacy of any idea, including very unpopular ideas, should be permitted in the interests of discovering "truth." This understanding is said to be facilitated by the concepts of tenure and academic freedom for university professors and some college teachers, so that they may consider unpopular ideas without the fear of being economically or legally sanctioned for doing so either by the university or the public at large. However, the history of post-secondary institutions in Canada shows that these understandings were always relative and frequently contested, and especially so in religiously-based post-secondary institutions.[196]

Since the purpose of such institutions is partly or even wholly to advance the interests of the sponsoring religion, it may be expected that faculty, staff, and students who are members of the college or university will be required to subscribe to and practise the beliefs of the sponsoring religious institution. When these religious beliefs are at variance with public legal standards, the question arises as to whether or not religiously-based colleges and universities may be permitted to insist on those standards when faculty, staff, or students decline to follow them, without legal penalty for the institution or its members and graduates. The general issue of religion at post-secondary institutions has an internal and an external aspect. The internal aspect is whether the institution can stipulate religious requirements for its members as long as they are members. The external aspect is whether it can stipulate religious requirements that

---

194 *Brauchle* v. *Lloyd* (1915), 21 D.L.R. 321 (Alta. C.A.).
195 Above chapter 9, section F.
196 Michiel Horn, *Academic Freedom in Canada: A History* (Toronto: University of Toronto Press, 1999).

are at variance with legally enforced public standards and still expect public recognition.

In *Schroen v. Steinbach Bible College*,[197] a Manitoba board of inquiry upheld the dismissal of a Mormon secretary by a Mennonite college on the ground that in such a tightly-knit community as a Bible college where students and staff closely interact, it was a *bona fide* occupational qualification to be a Mennonite. The specific religious nature of the college was the basis for the decision. Indirect confirmation that religiously-based universities may require all members to comply with religious codes of conduct may also be found in *Trinity Western University v. British Columbia College of Teachers*.[198]

In that case, the Supreme Court of Canada upheld the right of graduates of the teaching degree program at the evangelical Christian university to subscribe to a Christian code of conduct as required by the university without being presumed thereby to be likely to discriminate against gay and lesbian students when teaching in the public schools as the British Columbia College of Teachers had argued. While not conclusive, this case appears to support the position that religiously-based universities can stipulate for and likely enforce religious standards in relation to all their members except those expressly excluded from them by the institution. The Court based its findings on the legislative grant of a degree-giving charter to the university as well as human rights legislation, which contained exemptions from general anti-discriminatory standards for, *inter alia*, religious institutions.[199]

In *Trinity Western University*, the Supreme Court of Canada confirmed that a religiously-based university could also require its members to subscribe to and uphold a code of moral conduct at substantial variance with the standards found in the general law without penalty for its graduates seeking employment in the publicly-funded public schools. The Court sustained the right under section 2(a) of the *Charter* to entertain religious beliefs in private although conduct in public spaces should comply with public standards. Whether this amounts to any measure of real freedom of religion is unclear from the decision.

---

197 (1999), 35 C.H.R.R. D/1 (Man. Bd. Adj.).

198 (2001), 199 D.L.R. (4th) 1 (S.C.C.). See also M.H. Ogilvie, "After the *Charter*: Religious Free Expression and Other Legal Fictions in Canada" (2003) 2 O.U.C.L.J. forthcoming.

199 *Human Rights Code*, R.S.B.C. 1996, c. 210, s. 41.

The issue of whether a religious institution can be required to employ an instructor whose gay lifestyle is at variance with the moral teaching of the sponsoring religious organization was at issue in *Vriend v. Alberta*,[200] but not resolved in that case. The Supreme Court of Canada read into provincial human rights legislation protection for sexual orientation and redirected the case back to a human rights tribunal for adjudication; however, the complainant decided against pursuing the matter further.[201]

Finally, religion has been considered in one case concerned with promotion through the ranks within a public university. In *Jazairi v. Ontario (H.R.C.)*,[202] the Ontario Court of Appeal found that "creed" in the Ontario *Human Rights Code*[203] did not include a particular political belief, which a professor held and which he alleged resulted in a denial of promotion. Nor did it find that the omission of "political opinion" from the Code contravened his section 15 equality rights under the *Charter* or that he was discriminated against. The court declined to define what "creed" might mean, including whether it might require a set or system of beliefs.[204]

---

200 (1998), 156 D.L.R. (4th) 385 (S.C.C.).
201 For discussions of the issues raised by *Vriend*, see Donna Greschner, "The Right to Belong: The Promise of *Vriend*" (1998) 9 N.J.C.L. 417; Bruce Mac-Dougall, "Silence in the Classroom: Limits on Homosexual Expression and Visibility in Education" (1998) 61 Sask. L.R. 41; and Hilary M.G. Paterson, "The Justifiability of Biblically Based Discrimination: Can Private Christian Schools Legally Refuse to Employ Gay Teachers?" (2001) 59 U.T. Fac. L.R. 59.
202 (1999), 175 D.L.R. (4th) 302 (Ont. C.A.). See also Jazairi's failed action for costs at *Jazairi v. Ontario (Human Rights Commission)* (2001), 141 O.A.C. 394 (C.A.) and failed action to deduct his legal expenses from employment income for tax purposes at *Jazairi v. Canada* (2001), 2001 D.T.C. 5163 (F.C.A.).
203 R.S.O. 1990, c. H-19, s. 5(1).
204 For a faculty dismissal case in which the defendant unsuccessfully relied on a religiously-mandated period of mourning to excuse a failure to appear, see *Azim v. University of Calgary Faculty Association* (2001), 266 A.R. 255 (C.A.).

Chapter Eleven

Family Law

A. INTRODUCTION

Relationships between husband and wife and between parent and child are of essential importance in the belief systems of virtually all of the religions in Canada today, for which the family, that is, a man and a woman together with their natural and adopted children, is understood to be the microcosm of the larger faith community. At one time, the common law regulated a wider variety of conduct between the genders and generations than it does today, including breach of promise to marry, fornication, adultery, homosexuality, and divorce, with legal doctrines reflecting the once predominance in Canada of the sole paradigm of the Christian understanding of marriage as an exclusive, life-long union between a man and a woman, whose primary purpose is the procreation and rearing of children. Over the past half-century, the common law has moved away from reflecting Christian teachings on marriage and family life, so that the only areas left in which religion is still a factor to be considered by the courts relate to the religious upbringing of children of divorced parents and also, in a restricted way, in relation to divorce itself for certain religious groups.

At the same time as the varieties of human relationships regulated by the common law have decreased in some areas, some previously prohibited human relationships have come to be regulated for their own legal protection in contemporary society, of which homosexual relationships are the chief example. Whether or not the common law should regard homosexuals as capable in law of forming "marriages," or of having or adopting children to form "families," has been under social and political debate in Canada, with considerable new law emerging as a result.

This chapter will consider these topics in relation to family life but only insofar as issues of religion are explicitly concerned. Religious people of all faiths continue to regard sexual conduct and concepts of "family" to be subject to the teachings of their respective faiths, and some lobby for the restoration of their views to the common law. However, since their regulation remains within religious law but not secular law, this chapter will focus only on the secular law insofar as religion is concerned.

B. DIVORCE

The constitutional power to solemnize marriages is, pursuant to section 92(12) of the *Constitution Act, 1867*,[1] posited in the provinces, and all provinces have enacted legislation governing who may solemnize marriage within the province.[2] Historically, the English common law recognized only those marriages solemnized by clergy of the established Church of England, and this situation prevailed in the early years in the original common law colonies in pre-modern Canada. However, by the early nineteenth century, the right to solemnize legally recognized marriages was extended to other Christian denominations, and since that time has been extended to those persons recognized by their religious communities as qualified to solemnize legally recognized marriages, regardless of the religious institution, as well as to others so licensed by the provinces. Such marriages are to be solemnized according to the rites, customs, and usages of the religious institution in question.

On the other hand, the constitutional power over marriage and divorce is enjoyed exclusively by Parliament, pursuant to section 91(26)

---

1   R.S.C. 1985, App. II, No. 5.

2   *Marriage Act*, R.S.A. 1980, c. M-6; *Marriage Act*, R.S.B.C. 1996, c. 282; *Marriage Act*, R.S.M. 1987, c. M-50; *Marriage Act*, R.S.N.B. 1973, c. M-3; *Solemnization of Marriage Act*, R.S.N. 1990, c. S-19; *Solemnization of Marriage Act*, R.S.N.S. 1989, c. 436; *Marriage Act*, R.S.O. 1990, c. M-3; *Marriage Act*, R.S. P.E.I. 1988, c. M-3; and *Marriage Act*, R.S.S. 1978, c. M-4. It is self-evident that from a civil law perspective, there can be no valid marriage unless the civil law statutory requirements are complied with and a mere religious ceremony is not enough: *Upadyhaha v. Sehgal*, unreported decision of 12 September 2000 (Ont. S.C.J.).

of the *Constitution Act, 1867*. Prior to the enactment of the *Divorce Act*[3] in 1967, Parliament had not exercised its jurisdiction in relation to marriage and divorce, other than within the context of the criminal law, which had regulated, from time to time, such matters as adultery and homosexuality, so that divorces were granted only through the mechanism of private acts of Parliament on a case-by-case basis. The *Divorce Act* is now the complete code of divorce legislation in Canada, stipulating the various grounds for divorce, that is, breakdown of the marriage as indicated by living apart for one year, adultery and cruelty, as well as providing for relevant procedural matters.[4]

Issues of religion have arisen in only a few cases, to date, in relation to divorce.[5] Cruelty, one of the statutory grounds for divorce, has been found to be established where there is evidence that one spouse attempted to apply his or her own religious beliefs to the other spouse without regard to that spouse's feeling and health, and where there was a constant threat that that spouse ought to leave if he or she did not accept the teachings of the first spouse's faith.[6] Cruelty has also been found to exist as a ground for divorce where there is evidence that one spouse not only ridiculed the other spouse's beliefs but also attempted to exorcise him or her.[7]

Where a spouse seeks a divorce on the ground of a permanent breakdown of the marriage, it has been held that section 2(a) of the *Canadian Charter of Rights and Freedoms* is not infringed by granting a divorce where one spouse believes that marriage for life is a requirement for the practice of his or her religion. The *Charter* is meant to protect the individual from the state, not to define what the individual may exact from the state.[8]

Where one spouse obtained an uncontested divorce on the basis of separation for more than one year, and the other spouse subsequently appealed on the ground that her religious beliefs would not permit her to remarry unless the divorce was on the ground of matrimonial misconduct by her husband, the British Columbia Court of Appeal declined to

---

3   R.S.C. 1985, c. 3 (2d Supp.) as amend.
4   *Ibid.*, s. 8.
5   Readers seeking a fuller discussion of the law relating to marriage and divorce
     per se should consult any of the standard family law texts; only cases involving
     religion are cited here.
6   *Humeniuk v. Humeniuk* (1970), 13 D.L.R. (3d) 417 (Ont. H.C.).
7   *Whetstone v. Whetstone* (1979), 9 R.F.L. (2d) 168 (Alta. T.D.).
8   *Baxter v. Baxter* (1983), 6 D.L.R. (4th) 557 (Ont. H.C.).

rehear the matter in order to change the ground to adultery or cruelty. The law gives no preference to one recognized ground for divorce over another; in fact, the wife admitted that the ground for divorce was true since there was no hope of reconciliation, that she did not belong to a religion that imposed barriers to religious remarriage, and that the reasons given were her own personal religious convictions.[9]

Some religious groups require a religious divorce or annulment as well as a civil law divorce before they will either recognize the divorce as valid, or permit remarriage within the faith, as the case may be. In such circumstances, the administration of justice insofar as it relates to divorce should be concerned solely with the civil law — the court will not interfere with matters of religious faith where civil rights are not in question. This reluctance was expressed in *Morris* v. *Morris*,[10] where the parties had married in accordance with Orthodox Jewish law and practice. Subsequently, the wife successfully petitioned for a civil divorce; however, the husband refused to institute proceedings before a rabbinical court for a bill of divorcement (a *get*) as required by Orthodox Jewish law, with the result that the wife's civil remarriage was not recognized as valid by Orthodox Jewish law. The Manitoba Court of Appeal refused to order the husband to initiate the religious proceedings. Subsequently, Parliament enacted legislation to require that where a spouse has requested the other spouse to remove religious barriers to a civil law divorce and the latter has failed to do so, the civil divorce may proceed.[11] Where a Jewish spouse brings an action for divorce but fails to obtain a *get* from a rabbinical court, thereby creating a religious barrier to the parties' religious remarriages, the divorce action will be dismissed. But once the get is subsequently obtained, a civil divorce will be permitted to proceed over the husband's objections.[12]

The question of whether the enforcement of a Muslim husband's promise to pay *Mahr*, an obligatory gift made under Islamic marriage law

---

9   *Ash* v. *Ash* (1994), 8 R.F.L. (4th) 461 (B.C.C.A.).

10   (1973), 42 D.L.R. (3d) 550 (Man. C.A.).

11   R.S.C. 1985, c. 3 (2d Supp.) as amend. S.C. 1990, c. 18, s. 21.1. Provincial legislation also so provides; see for example *Family Law Act*, R.S.O. 1990, c. F-3, ss. 2(4)–(6), 56(5)–(7). For a full discussion, see John Syrtash, *Religion and Culture in Canadian Family Law* (Toronto: Butterworths, 1992) at 114–178.

12   *Tanny* v. *Tanny* (2000), 8 R.F.L. (5th) 427 (Ont. S.C.J.).

13   (1998), 168 D.L.R. (4th) 503 (Ont. Gen. Div.).

from a husband to a wife for her exclusive property, may be made as part of the civil contract of marriage in the event of divorce has been treated in contradictory ways. In *Kaddoura* v. *Hammond*,[13] an Ontario trial court decided that the obligation was a religious obligation only and not justiciable in the civil courts. But in *Amlani* v. *Hirani*,[14] a British Columbia trial court decided that it satisfied the marriage contract requirements in provincial legislation[15] and was enforceable as a civil marriage contractual provision in divorce.

C. CUSTODY AND ACCESS

The fundamental principle of the common law in relation to custody and access cases, including those in which religious factors are involved, is that decisions should be based on the paramount consideration of the best interests of the child.[16] This will determine which parent gets custody as well as the nature of any access allowed to the other parent.[17] At one time, the custodial parent enjoyed the *prima facie* right of determining the nature of the religious upbringing of a child;[18] however, that question must now be determined in accordance with the best interests of the child as assessed by the court.[19] In some cases, provincial legislation may determine that a child of unmarried parents take the religion of its mother in all cases,[20] but in the absence of legislative guidance, it is the best interests of the child that should determine the child's religious upbringing.[21]

In *Young* v. *Young*,[22] the Supreme Court of Canada considered the meaning of the best interests of the child in relation to religion and to the rights of an access parent concerning the religious upbringing of a child.

---

14 (2000), 194 D.L.R. (4th) 543 (B.C.S.C.).

15 *Family Relations Act*, R.S.B.C. 1996, c. 128, s. 61(2).

16 *McKee* v. *McKee*, [1951] A.C. 352 (P.C.). See also *Divorce Act*, ss. 16, 17.

17 *DeLaurier* v. *Jackson*, [1934] 1 D.L.R. 790 (S.C.C.); and *McKee* v. *McKee, ibid.*

18 *DeLaurier* v. *Jackson, ibid.*; *Strum* v. *Strum* (1969), 8 R.F.L. 140 (N.S.W.S.C.); and *Bateman* v. *Bateman* (1964), 47 W.W.R. 641 (Alta. T.D.), aff'd 51 W.W.R. 633 (Alta. C.A.).

19 *Young* v. *Young* (1993), 108 D.L.R. (4th) 193 (S.C.C.); and *P.(D.)* v. *S.(C.)* (1993), 108 D.L.R. (4th) 287 (S.C.C.).

20 *Re LeBlanc* (1970), 13 D.L.R. (3d) 225 (N.S.T.D.).

21 *DeLaurier* v. *Jackson*, above note 17; and *Maestrello* v. *Maestrello* (1975), 20 R.F.L. 285 (Ont. Div. Ct.).

22 Above note 19.

In that case, the trial judge had granted custody to the mother, an Angli-can, and placed restrictions on the Jehovah's Witness father's religious activities with the children, who had complained of feeling stress. The British Columbia Court of Appeal set aside the restrictions on the ground that it was in the childrens' best interests to know their access parent fully, including his deeply held religious beliefs, provided there was no harmful effect on them, and they were not forced to participate unwill-ingly in religious activities. The majority[23] in the Supreme Court of Cana-da affirmed the position of the Court of Appeal.

All of the judges were agreed on the best interests test in access cases, although they disagreed on its application to the facts. The Court thought the test to be the ultimate test and to encompass a wide variety of factors, including religious considerations. Generally speaking, the Court thought that children should be exposed to the religious views of both custody and access parents so that they might know the whole per-son of their respective parents. However, in relation to religion, the best interests of the child encompasses a genuine discussion of religious belief but not indoctrination, enlistment, or harassment, whose aim or effect is to undermine religious choices made by the custodial parent. Nor should access parents be permitted to share their religious beliefs or require par-ticipation where there is evidence this will harm the children or where the children are unwilling to participate. In such circumstances, restric-tions should be placed on either the religious interaction of access parent and child or, if the access parent is unwilling, then on the access itself.[24]

While the custodial parent will, *prima facie*, retain the power to determine primarily the religious upbringing of the child, it seems clear, although not yet conclusively stated by the courts, that since the test for custody is the best interests test, that this statement in *Young* v. *Young* of that test, insofar as religious considerations are involved, is likely to be at least equally applicable to custody parents in their religious interaction with their children as it is to access parents.

In pre-*Young* cases, the courts have considered a variety of factual issues in relation to both custody and access parents when deciding about the religious upbringing of children in divorce. In deciding whether or

---

23 McLachlin, Sopinka, Cory, and Iacobucci JJ.; L'Heureux-Dubé, LaForest, and Gonthier JJ. dissenting on this point.

24 This test was confirmed in *P.(D.)* v. *S.(C.)*, above note 19 in relation to Quebec. See *Hockey* v. *Hockey* (1989), 60 D.L.R. (4th) 765 (Ont. Div. Ct.).

not to grant custody to one parent rather than another, the courts have denied custody when the following assessments have been made: where religious beliefs or practices have resulted in a sense of instability in the child;[25] where a parent's religious beliefs or practices have rendered that parent incapable of making sensible judgments about the child;[26] where a parent was unwilling to refrain from expressing provocative religious views to a child;[27] where placing a child of an interfaith, interracial marriage with the parent whose skin colour and other physical features most closely resembles the child's determines religious upbringing;[28] where a child was forced against his or her wishes to participate in proselytizing with the parent;[29] where the religious views of one spouse would interfere with the other spouse's relationship with the child;[30] and where a child was still too young for religion to be a factor.[31]

In situations where each parent subscribes to a different faith or denomination, or where there is a conflict between a religious and a secular parent, or some other conflict of views between the parents about the nature of the religious upbringing for the child, the courts have stated that they also will not consider whether one religion is better than another for the child, or make inquiry into the relative merits of different religions on a doctrinal basis.[32] On the other hand, courts have assessed religions on the basis of the extent to which they encourage integration of their adherents with both society and the child's family generally. Thus, religious groups that emphasize separation from both the world and from family members who do not share the views of that group, such as fundamentalist Christians or Jehovah's Witnesses, have tended to be assessed negatively, with custody being awarded to the parent who is a member of

25 *Wingrove v. Wingrove* (1984), 40 R.F.L. (2d) 428 (Ont. Co. Ct.).

26 *Schulz v. Schulz* (1987), 12 R.F.L. (3d) 141 (B.C.S.C.).

27 *Moseley v. Moseley* (1989), 20 R.F.L. (3d) 301 (Alta. Prov. Ct.); and *Retzer v. Retzer* (1974), 19 R.F.L. 365 (S.C.C.).

28 *Hayre v. Hayre* (1975), 21 R.F.L. 191 (B.C.C.A.).

29 *Harvey v. Lapointe* (1988), 13 R.F.L. (3d) 134 (Que. S.C.).

30 *Moseley v. Moseley*, above note 27.

31 *White v. White* (1990), 28 R.F.L. (3d) 439 (B.C.S.C.).

32 *Lyons v. Blenkin* (1823), Jacob 245, 37 E.R. 842; *Re McGrath*, [1893] 1 Ch. 143 (C.A.); *Sullivan v. Fox* (1984), 38 R.F.L. (2d) 293 (P.E.I. S.C.); *Harvey v. Lapointe* (1988), 13 R.F.L. (3d) 134 (Que. S.C.); *Moseley v. Moseley*, above note 27; and *Voortman v. Voortman* (1994), 4 R.F.L. (4th) 250 (Ont. C.A.).

a religious group more fully integrated into the mainstream of Canadian society.[33]

Courts may decide not to consider religious beliefs and practices at all in making a custody decision, preferring to assess the child's best interests by reference to other factors entirely.[34] On the other hand, once a court decides to consider religious factors in making a custody order, it should not take account of religious factors that are irrelevant or merely speculative, such as whether, in the event that a blood transfusion should be required in the future, the fact that a parent is a Jehovah's Witness should preclude his or her receiving custody.[35] Whether or not a court is permitted to consider the best interests of a child to the exclusion of considerations of possible religious discrimination against a particular group pursuant to section 2(a) of the *Charter* has yet to be determined.[36]

In cases of access, where the parents of a child are of different religions or practise their mutual religion with different degrees of commitment, and custody is to be awarded to one of them on the basis of the child's best interests taking into consideration religious upbringing, liberal access rights should be awarded to the other parent in the absence of evidence that the child would be adversely affected thereby.[37] Despite the different faiths or degree of religious commitment of the parents, it is in the child's best interests to have a healthy relationship with each of them.[38] Therefore, in such circumstances, where access is granted, the access parent may exercise access rights even where this disrupts the custodial parent's family plans.[39]

Where custody is granted to one parent on the basis of the best interests of the child and on the understanding that the custodial parent will

33 *Sullivan v. Fox, ibid.; Schulz v. Schulz,* above note 26; *Barrett v. Barrett* (1988), 18 R.F.L. (3d) 186 (Nfld. T.D.); *Moseley v. Moseley,* above note 27; and *Voortman v. Voortman, ibid.*

34 *Sullivan v. Fox,* above note 32; *Harvey v. Lapointe,* above note 32; *Moseley v. Moseley,* above note 27; *Brown v. Brown* (1983), 39 R.F.L. (2d) 396 (Sask. C.A.); *McNeil v. McNeil* (1989), 20 R.F.L. (3d) 52 (B.C.S.C.); and *Britton v. Britton* (1991), 37 R.F.L. (3d) 253 (Ont. Gen. Div.).

35 *Tardif v. Tardif* (1975), 24 R.F.L. 283 (Sask. Q.B.); *Barrett v. Barrett,* above note 33.

36 *B.(G.) v. B.(M.)* (1988), 19 R.F.L. (3d) 283 (Que. C.A.).

37 *Elbaz v. Elbaz* (1980), 16 R.F.L. (2d) 336 (Ont. H.C.).

38 *Ryan v. Ryan* (1986), 3 R.F.L. (3d) 141 (Nfld. Fam. Ct.).

39 *Hart v. Twyne* (1988), 17 R.F.L. (3d) 107 (Nfld. T.D.).

determine the religious upbringing of the child, the access parent should refrain from attempting to influence the child in religious matters.[40] A court may order a custodial parent bringing up a child in his or her own religion also to expose the child to the religion of the access parent.[41] Moreover, a custodial parent is also obliged to ensure that religious beliefs do not impair the relationship between the child and the access parent.[42] It is not in the best interests of children for the mother to isolate them from their access father because of her own extreme religious views.[43]

Where a child is staying in the access parent's house, the access parent is required to be reasonable in relation to the imposition of religious rules on the child.[44] The access parent may be permitted to share his or her religious beliefs with the child provided the effect is not harmful or contrary to the child's best interests.[45] Indeed, both parents may be permitted to share their respective religious beliefs with the child.[46]

When a court is determining the issue of which parent is to get custody, it may be a condition of the grant of custody that neither parent denigrate or comment adversely on the religious beliefs or practices of the other parent.[47] Where joint custody is awarded, neither parent may insist on the dominance of his or her religious views in the upbringing of

---

40 *Sudeyko v. Sudeyko* (1974), 18 R.F.L. 273 (B.C.S.C.); *Skubovius v. Skubovius* (1977), 1 R.F.L. (2d) 284 (Man. Q.B.); *Henderson v. Henderson* (1977), 29 R.F.L. 1 (B.C. Co. Ct.); *Gunn v. Gunn* (1975), 24 R.F.L. 182 (P.E.I. S.C.); *Singh v. Singh* (1981), 26 R.F.L. (2d) 75 (Alta. C.A.), leave to appeal to S.C.C. refused (1982), 42 N.R. 90 (S.C.C.); *Ross v. Britton*, unreported decision of 13 January 1998 (Ont. Gen. Div.); *Mummery v. Campbell* (1998), 38 R.F.L. (4th) 301 (B.C.S.C.); and *Bachor v. Lehmann-Bachor* (2001), 14 R.F.L. (5th) 238 (Alta. C.A.).

41 *Pfeifer v. Pfeifer* (1982), 28 R.F.L. (2d) 236 (Sask. Q.B.).

42 *Harvey v. Lapointe*, above note 29; and *Hewitt v. Hewitt*, [1994] B.C. W.L.D. 2644 (S.C.).

43 *Boudreau v. Boudreau* (1994), 143 N.B.R. (2d) 321, 366 A.P.R. 321 (Q.B.); and *Abbey v. Abbey*, unreported decision of 22 October 1999 (B.C.S.C.).

44 *Mikkelsen v. Mikkelsen* (1989), 23 R.F.L. (3d) 428 (Ont. H.C.).

45 *Gallagher v. Gallagher* (1985), 48 R.F.L. (2d) 249 (N.B.Q.B.); *Hockey v. Hockey*, above note 24; *Fougère v. Fougère* (1986), 6 R.F.L. (3d) 314 (N.B.C.A.), leave to appeal to S.C.C. refused 8 R.F.L. (3d) xxv (S.C.C.); *Young v. Young*, above note 19; and *P.(D.) v. S.(C.)*, above note 19.

46 *Hockey v. Hockey*, above note 24; and *Avitan v. Avitan* (1992), 38 R.F.L. (3d) 382 (Ont. Gen. Div.).

47 *Gunn v. Gunn*, above note 40; and *Sullivan v. Fox*, above note 32.

the child, rather both are expected to work out a compromise since it is in the best interests of the child to know each parent.[48]

Whether the issue is one of custody or of access, the courts have made specific orders in relation to the types of religious activities in which either parent may indulge with the child. Thus, courts have ordered that an access parent may not take a child to religious services during the times of access.[49] On the other hand, a court may also expressly permit an access parent to take a child to religious services.[50] A court may order that a custodial parent not take a child to religious activities, other than worship services, such as door-to-door canvassing.[51] Where the harm caused by the participation of the child in religious activities with the custodial parent is less than the trauma of separation from the custodial parent, participation may be permitted.[52] Where a child is given into the custody of a parent who is a Jehovah's Witness, a court may reserve to the access parent any future decisions about blood transfusions.[53]

In several cases in which custody and access have been at issue, the question of whether or not a custody parent may object on religious grounds to a child staying overnight with an access parent who lives in a common law relationship has been raised; however, while the determination has favoured the access parent, it is unclear from those cases whether the courts seriously considered the religious objections of the custody parent.[54]

48　*Langille v. Dossa* (1994), 136 N.S.R. (2d) 180, 388 A.P.R. 180 (Fam. Ct.); *Ducas v. Varkony* (1995), 16 R.F.L. (4th) 91 (Man. Q.B.); and *Wells v. Nation* (2000), Carswell BC 1639.

49　*Benoit v. Benoit* (1973), 10 R.F.L. 282 (Ont. C.A.); *Brown v. Brown* (1983), 39 R.F.L. (2d) 396 (Sask. C.A.); *Moseley v. Moseley*, above note 27; *Borris v. Borris* (1991), 37 R.F.L. (3d) 339, supplemented [1992] W.D.F.L. 305 (Alta. Q.B.); and *Goldberg v. Goldberg* (1996), 26 R.F.L. (4th) 99 (Ont. Gen. Div.).

50　*H.(N.) v. P.(C.)* (1988), 15 R.F.L. (3d) 418 (Que. S.C.); *K.(R.B.) v. R.(N.J.)*, unreported decision of 16 December 1996 (N.S.S.C.); and *Fruitman v. Fruitman* (1998), 37 R.F.L. (4th) 416 (Ont. Gen. Div.).

51　*Harvey v. Lapointe*, above note 29; *B.(L.) v. C.(J.)* (1991), 91 D.L.R. (4th) 27 (Que.), leave to appeal to S.C.C. refused (1993), 105 D.L.R. (4th) vi (S.C.C.); and *S.(L.) v. S.(C.)* (1997), 37 R.F.L. (4th) 344 (S.C.C.).

52　*Struncova v. Guay* (1984), 39 R.F.L. (2d) 298 (Que. S.C.).

53　*Robb v. Robb* (1977), 2 R.F.L. (2d) 172 (N.S.T.D.).

54　*Seaman v. Seaman* (1981), 24 R.F.L. (2d) 433 (Ont. Co. Ct.); *Mattison v. Mattison* (1982), 42 R.F.L. (2d) 215 (Sask. Q.B.); and *Fullerton v. Fullerton* (1983), 37 R.F.L. (2d) 168 (Nfld. T.D.).

Custody and access orders once made can always be changed in the light of subsequent events, and religious considerations constitute a category of event that may justify such changes. Where a child in custody was subjected to physical and mental abuse in a religious cult, that child may be taken away from the custody parent and placed into wardship where the non-custody parent is equally unsuitable to take custody of the child.[55] Where a child whose custodial parent is a Jehovah's Witness requires a blood transfusion, that child may be made a ward of the court for the transfusion and returned to the custodial parent afterward.[56] However, where the child is found by a court to be old enough to make a decision about medical treatment, then the decision of a child to undergo an abortion[57] or to refuse chemotherapy because it entailed a blood transfusion[58] should be sustained by the courts.

Finally, religious considerations have been reviewed by the courts when the issue is removal of the child from the parents to foster parents. A Jewish child in need of protection by a court should be placed in a Jewish home.[59] Where the contest for custody of a child is between a natural grandparent and a parent whose involvement with a cult group suggests instability, custody should be awarded to the grandparent.[60] A child who is comfortably settled into a foster home of a different religious faith from that of his or her own natural parents should be allowed to stay with the foster parents if this is otherwise in his or her best interests.[61]

Finally, the question of whether child support payments may be made to provide for the expenses of attending a private, religious school

---

55 *Re M.(L. and K.)* (1978), 6 R.F.L. (2d) 297 (Alta. Juv. Ct.).

56 *Pentland v. Pentland* (1978), 20 O.R. (2d) 27 (H.C.); *McTavish v. Director, Alberta Child Welfare Act* (1986), 32 D.L.R. (4th) 394 (Alta. Q.B.); *Re L.(C.P.)* (1988), 70 Nfld. & P.E.I.R. 287, 215 A.P.R. 287 (Nfld. U.F.C.); *Kennett v. Health Sciences Centre* (1990), 72 D.L.R. (4th) 155 (Man. Q.B.), aff'd on other grounds (1991), 83 D.L.R. (4th) 744 (Man. C.A.); and *B.(R.) v. Children's Aid Society of Metropolitan Toronto* (1995), 122 D.L.R. (4th) 1 (S.C.C.).

57 *Catholic Children's Aid Society of Metropolitan Toronto v. R.(N.)* (1985), 47 R.F.L. (2d) 361 (Ont. Div. Ct.).

58 *Re L.D.K.* (1985), 48 R.F.L. (2d) 164 (Ont. Fam. Ct.); *Re A.Y.* (1993), 111 Nfld. & P.E.I.R. 91, 348 A.P.R. 91 (Nfld. U.F.C.); and *Walker v. Region No. 2 Hospital Corp.* (1994), 116 D.L.R. (4th) 477 (N.S.C.A.).

59 *Re B.(P.S.)* (1978), 15 R.F.L. (2d) 199 (Ont. Fam. Ct.).

60 *McQuillan v. McQuillan* (1975), 21 R.F.L. 324 (Ont. H.C.).

61 *DeLaurier v. Jackson*, above note 17.

to reinforce the religious upbringing of a child has also been recently considered. In two cases to date, the courts have found that this is a legitimate expenditure to be considered and ordered if it is in the best interests of the child to attend such schools.[62]

Although the paramount interest to be protected in custody and access cases is the best interests of the child, the coming into effect of the *Canadian Charter of Rights and Freedoms* has raised the question of the extent to which parental rights to freedom of religion pursuant to section 2(a) and fundamental liberty pursuant to section 7 must be considered in making a custody or access order.

The impact of section 2(a) was considered first in relation to restrictions on the religious activities of a custodial parent. The constitutionality of the provision of the *Divorce Act*[63] relating to the power to grant custody has been sustained as overriding any parental rights over a child based on religious teachings and justified pursuant to section 2(a) freedom of religion.[64] Moreover, the fundamental right to freedom of religion means that each parent may practise his or her religion freely in the presence of the child, provided such teaching is respectful of the other spouse's religion and that each parent is respectful of the right of the child to choose his or her own religion when old enough to do so.[65]

The best interests of the child remain the paramount consideration. Thus, in relation to an access parent the Supreme Court of Canada in *Young* v. *Young* stated that because religious freedom is not absolute, it does not extend to activities that may harm the child and, therefore, may not be in his or her best interests. The best interests test does not violate section 2(a), (b), or (d), nor in the view of two members of the majority,[66] section 15 either.

The impact of the *Charter* on freedom of religion for Jehovah's Witnesses to refuse blood transfusions has also been considered by the Supreme Court of Canada when wardship of a child is granted to a court

---

62 *Burton* v. *Burton* (1998), 158 D.L.R. (4th) 174 (N.S.S.C.); and *Green* v. *Green* (2000), 187 D.L.R. (4th) 37 (B.C.C.A.).

63 Ss. 16, 17.

64 *Droit de la famille – 955*, [1991] R.J.Q. 599 (C.A.), leave to appeal to S.C.C. denied (1991), 135 N.R. 78 (S.C.C.).

65 *B.(L.)* v. *C.(J.)* (1991), 91 D.L.R. (4th) 27 (Que. C.A.), leave to appeal to S.C.C. refused (1993), 105 D.L.R. (4th) vi (S.C.C.).

66 Cory and Iacobucci JJ.

for the duration of medical treatment. In *B. (R.) v. Children's Aid Society of Metropolitan Toronto*,[67] the issue was whether or not ordering medical treatment entailing blood transfusions to a prematurely born child could be refused by the parents because it infringed the parents' rights pursuant to section 2(a) and section 7. The child had been made a ward of the court and had received the medical attention required and then was returned to the parents.

The Supreme Court divided on the application of section 7. Four justices[68] found that the section 7 liberty interest of parents was infringed by the legislation pursuant to which wardship was granted, but further defined section 7 not to mean unconstrained freedom. While these justices regarded parents as having a privileged position vis à vis the state in relation to the upbringing of their children, they deemed that nevertheless the state may intervene when parental decisions fall below a socially acceptable threshold, on the ground that fundamental justice must be exercised to protect a child's right to life and health over parental liberty. Three justices[69] thought that section 7 does not include a parent's right to deny necessary medical treatment to a child; rather, in accordance with principles of natural justice and by the legitimate exercise of its *parens patriae* jurisdiction, the *Charter* is to be used to protect the most vulnerable members of society.[70]

With regard to section 2(a), five justices[71] thought that the right of parents to rear their children according to their religious beliefs was a fundamental aspect of freedom of religion, but its infringement was justified under section 1 in order to protect children at risk. Four justices[72] thought that section 2(a) does not include the imposition upon a child of religious practices that threaten his or her safety, health, or life. The denial of medical treatment is an infringement upon the child's freedom of conscience, which includes the right to live long enough to make one's own choice about the religion one wishes to follow.

---

67 Above note 56.

68 *Ibid.*, LaForest, L' Heureux-Dubé, Gonthier, and McLachlin JJ.

69 *Ibid.*, Iacobucci, Major, and Cory JJ.

70 *Ibid.*, Lamer C.J.C. largely argued, while Sopinka J. thought s. 7 irrelevant because the threshold requirement of breach of the principles of fundamental justice had not been met.

71 *Ibid.*, LaForest, L' Heureux-Dubé, Sopinka, Gonthier, and McLachlin JJ.

72 *Ibid.*, Lamer C.J.C., Iacobucci, Major, and Cory JJ.

The net effect of these positions is that a court may intervene to order medical treatment for a child whose parents have refused treatment on religious grounds without fear of infringement of *Charter* freedoms pursuant to either section 2(a) or section 7.

D. PERSONAL TAXATION EXEMPTIONS

The issue of whether or not provisions in the *Income Tax Act,*[73] which differentially treat married couples and common law couples, constitutes discrimination on the basis of religion was considered by the Federal Court of Appeal in *Schachtschneider* v. *Canada.*[74] The applicant, who was married, claimed the "equivalent to married" non-refundable tax credit in respect of the couple's dependent child and this was disallowed on the ground that the credit was not available to married couples. Since this meant that married couples paid more tax than common law couples, the applicant argued that section 2(a) and section 15(1) of the *Charter* had been infringed because the couple regarded marriage as required by their religious beliefs. The court decided there was no infringement of section 2(a) because the income tax provisions neither coerce, determine, nor limit religious conduct or practice; in any case, the differential tax provisions were unrelated to issues of religious discrimination. Nor was there found to be unequal treatment of married couples as a group within Canadian society pursuant to section 15(1) because married persons are not a discrete and disadvantaged minority analogous to the enumerated groups within section 15, but rather have generally been socially, politically, and historically advantaged in Canada. Thus, the application failed.

E. HOMOSEXUALITY AND FAMILY LAW

Religious people of many faiths believe homosexual activity to be forbidden and the sacred texts of these faiths, including the largest faith groups in Canada, expressly forbid homosexual activity for believers.[75] Until

---

73 R.S.C. 1985, c. 1 (5th Supp.).

74 (1993), 105 D.L.R. (4th) 162 (Fed. A.D.), leave to appeal to S.C.C. refused 123 D.L.R. (4th) viii (S.C.C.).

75 For Jews, Christians, and Muslims, the following Biblical texts are among others, decisive of the matter: Lev. 18:22, 20:13; Rom. 1:24, 1:26–27; 1 Cor. 6:9–10; and 1 Tim. 1:8–10.

recently, it was widely accepted that the law should reflect this view and that such matters as employment or welfare benefits be restricted only to heterosexuals or heterosexual couples. However, a sea change has occurred in societal attitudes to homosexual activity in the past generation and this is reflected in the law relating to such areas as marriage or same-sex partnerships, adoption, access to social facilities, and same-sex rights to employment and social welfare benefits historically available only to heterosexual married couples. Religious communities continue to enjoy the civil legal right to enforce their moral views about the appropriate uses of human sexuality within their communities,[76] but in the public sphere, the *Charter* value of equality in section 15 as developed first by the courts and subsequently reflected in legislation requires that discrimination on the basis of sexual orientation be replaced by equality in law in all personal and social relationships.

Thus,[77] protection from discrimination under human rights legislation[78] and tax legislation[79] has been matched by judicial decisions equating same-sex and heterosexual couples for the purposes of private pension plans,[80] bereavement leave,[81] death benefits,[82] public health

---

76 *Trinity Western University* v. *British Columbia College of Teachers* (2001), 199 D.L.R. (4th) 1 (S.C.C.).

77 Over the past decade, there have been numerous cases in this area. Only the most significant are listed below. For greater consideration of these issues, see Donna Greschner, "The Right to Belong: The Promise of *Vriend*" (1998) 9 N.J.C.L. 417; Bruce MacDougall, "Case Comment on M. v. H." (1999) 27 Man. L.J. 141; K.A. Lahey, *Are We Persons Yet? Law and Sexuality in Canada* (Toronto: University of Toronto Press, 1999); Bruce MacDougall, "The Celebration of Same Sex Marriage" (2000) 32 Ott. L.R. 235; Bruce MacDougall, *Queer Judgments: Homosexuality, Expression and the Courts in Canada* (Toronto: University of Toronto Press, 2001); Karen L. Kuffner, "Common-Law and Same-Sex Relationships Under the Matrimonial Property Act"(2000) 63 Sask. L. Rev. 237; and Emma Hitchings, "M. v. H. and Same-Sex Spousal Benefits" (2000) 63 M.LR. 595.

78 *Haig* v. *Canada* (1992), 94 D.L.R. (4th) 1 (Ont. C.A.).

79 *Rosenberg* v. *Canada (Attorney General)* (1998), 158 D.L.R. (4th) 664 (Ont. C.A.).

80 *Leshner* v. *Ontario* (1992), 16 C.H.R.R. D/184 (Ont. Bd. Inq.).

81 *Canada (Attorney-General)* v. *Mossop* (1993), 100 D.L.R. (4th) 658 (S.C.C.).

82 *Kane* v. *Ontario (Attorney-General)* (1997), 152 D.L.R. (4th) 738 (Ont. Gen. Div.).

insurance plans,[83] private dental and health plans,[84] access to housing,[85] access to government services,[86] and access to services in the marketplace.[87] In the private context of a same-sex relationship, same-sex partners have also been permitted to adopt children,[88] have access to artificial insemination,[89] and to receive support when the relationship ends,[90] but the question of whether or not they may marry is still before the courts.[91] Federal and provincial legislation is being or has been amended throughout the country to reflect these changes.

It is clear that heterosexual and homosexual persons will, for the foreseeable future, be treated in an almost identical fashion in law in Canada, in relation to family law matters, so that religious groups that continue to subscribe to and enforce historical teachings on human sexuality will be an isolated minority within Canadian society and law.

---

83 *Knodel* v. *British Columbia*, [1991] 6 W.W.R. 728 (B.C.S.C.).

84 *Nielsen* v. *Canada (Employment and Immigration Commission)* (1997), 215 N.R. 208 (Fed. C.A.), leave to appeal refused [1997] S.C.C.A. No. 466 (S.C.C.).

85 *Grace* v. *Mercedes Homes Inc.* (1995), 23 C.H.R.R. D/350 (Ont. Bd. Inq.).

86 *O'Neill* v. *Ontario (Minister of Transportation)* (1994), 27 C.H.R.R. D/405 (Ont. Bd. Inq.).

87 *L.(C.)* v. *Badyal* (1998), 34 C.H.R.R. D/41 (B.C. Trib.), involving access to a bar; *Brillinger* v. *Brockie (No. 3)* (2000), 37 CH.R.R. D/15 (Ont. Bd. Inq.), involving access to printing services; and *Hellquist* v. *Owens* (2001), 40 C.H.R.R. D/197 (Sask. Bd. Inq.), involving freedom from discriminatory advertising.

88 *Re C.* (1999), 74 Alta. L.R. 1 (Q.B.); and *Re A.* (1999), 181 D.L.R. (4th) 300 (Alta. Q.B.).

89 *Korn* v. *Potter* (1996), 134 D.L.R. (4th) 437 (B.C.S.C.).

90 *M.* v. *H.* (1999), 171 D.L.R. (4th) 577 (S.C.C.).

91 *Halpern* v. *Wong* (2000), 51 O.R. (3d) 742 (Div. Ct.); and *Egale* v. *Canada (Attorney General)* (2002), 19 R.F.L. (5th) 59 (B.C.S.C.).

Chapter Twelve

Health

A. INTRODUCTION

The interaction of law and religion in relation to health has largely been concerned with the beginning and end of life in this world and has traditionally been regulated by the criminal law, which historically sought to uphold Christian beliefs about the sanctity of life as a divine gift to be given and taken again by God. The *Criminal Code* continues to make provision for matters relating to suicide, the preservation of life, and the right to die. While the original reason for the criminalization of these matters was theological, in recent years their legal consideration has been largely secularized and constitutionalized after the introduction of the *Canadian Charter of Rights and Freedoms*. Thus, the abortion provisions of the Code have been found to be an infringement of section 7 of the *Charter*[1] and legal issues at the end of life have been said to be protected because they reflect "fundamental values" in Canadian society,[2] without a court stating either what those values are or their ultimate source. The courts no longer frame these issues as issues in moral theology, rather as issues of secular law, so no further discussion is possible in a legal text.

1　See generally for a discussion of these, chapter 5, sections L–O.
2　*Rodriguez* v. *A.G. B.C.*, [1993] 3 S.C.R. 519.

But for religious people of all faiths, they continue to be so considered and practised in daily life.

The common law has recently addressed issues of life and death in relation to the refusal of medical treatments requiring blood transfusions by Jehovah's Witnesses on explicitly religious grounds.[3] In addition, the common law has also considered various legal issues relating to life, death, and the quality of life, which are characterized by religious people as theological in nature but which are considered in purely secular terms by the courts, including human fertilization,[4] wrongful life resulting from medical procedure failure,[5] refusal of consent to medical treatment that would result in a poor quality of life,[6] and withdrawal of treatment for patients in a persistent vegetative state.[7] These cases will not be discussed here because no explicitly religious issues were before the courts when they were adjudicated.

B. REFUSING MEDICAL TREATMENT

A legally competent adult is entitled to reject medical treatment and may succeed in the tort of battery should medical treatment be given for which there was no consent. In *Malette* v. *Shulman*,[8] a severely injured and unconscious woman was given a blood transfusion after admission to a hospital on an emergency basis; the doctor knew that she carried a card identifying her as a Jehovah's Witness and requesting that no transfusions be given. The doctor further ignored the requests of her daughter to discontinue the transfusions. The Ontario Court of Appeal upheld the woman's right to refuse life-preserving medical treatment and awarded damages to her in the tort of battery. While the judgment was framed by the court in tort rather than in terms of freedom of religion, the deci-

---

3　Gen. 9:3–4; Lev. 17:13–16; and Acts 15:28–29.

4　*R.* v. *Human Fertilisation, ex parte Blood*, [1997] 2 All E.R. 687 (C.A.); and *Cameron* v. *Nova Scotia (Attorney General)* (1999), 177 D.L.R. (4th) 611 (N.S.C.A.).

5　*McFarlane* v. *Tayside Health Board*, [1999] 4 All E.R. 961 (H.L.); and *Mickle* v. *Salvation Army Grace Hospital* (1998), 166 D.L.R. (4th) 743 (Ont. Gen. Div.).

6　*Re T.*, [1997] 1 All E.R. 906 (C.A.).

7　*N.H.S. Trust A.* v. *M.*, [2001] 1 All E.R. 801 (Fam. D.).

8　(1990), 67 D.L.R. (4th) 321 (Ont. C.A.). See also *Wijngaarden* v. *Tzalalis* (1992), 11 O.R. (3d) 779 (C.A.).

sion's reaffirmation of the right of adults to decline treatment accords with the desires of some religious groups for the freedom to do so.[9]

The relationship of a refusal of treatment to the consent-to-treatment form normally required for medical procedures was considered in *Hobbs v. Robertson*,[10] where a woman died as a result of excessive blood loss caused by the negligence of the surgeon. The court found that a refusal of blood transfusions did not relieve the surgeon of a duty to take reasonable care; the patient voluntarily assumed the risks of refusing blood but did not voluntarily assume the risk of negligence.

On the other hand, the courts have been more willing to intervene where the intended recipient of the blood transfusion is a young child or a teenager whose maturity to make the life or death decision must be assessed. Recently, the courts have permitted teenaged children to make the decision as to whether or not to receive a blood transfusion when a court is satisfied, sometimes by actually visiting the child, that the child understands the nature of the decision being taken and its potentially fatal consequences. Thus, a twelve-year-old girl who objected to transfusions associated with chemotherapy and refused to co-operate in the treatment was permitted to stay in the protection of her parents rather than being made a ward of the court for the duration of the treatment.[11] Two fifteen-year-old boys, requiring chemotherapy, have also been permitted to decide for themselves not to be transfused, once the courts were convinced that they understood the consequences.[12] Where such a child is subjected to a transfusion against his or her will, the child's rights under section 7 and section 15(1) of the *Charter* have been found to be violated.[13]

However, it is not clearly the case that a mature minor may be permitted to make a decision about medical treatment that is essential for

---

9   See also the following case for an award of costs when an action was brought for an inquest into the death of a Jehovah's Witness woman who refused a blood transfusion after a caesarean section: *Lawson v. B.C. (Solicitor-General)* (1992), 88 D.L.R. (4th) 533 (B.C.C.A.), leave to appeal to S.C.C. refused (1992), 70 B.C.L.R. (2d) xxxiii (S.C.C.).

10   (2001), 85 B.C.L.R. (3d) 114 (S.C.).

11   *Children's Aid Society of Metropolitan Toronto v. K.* (1985), 48 R.F.L. (2d) 164 (Ont. Fam. Div.).

12   *Re A.Y.* (1993), 111 Nfld. & P.E.I.R. 91, 348 A.P.R. 91 (Nfld. U.F.C.); and *Walker v. Region 2 Hospital Corp.* (1994), 116 D.L.R. (4th) 477 (N.B.C.A.).

13   *Children's Aid Society of Metropolitan Toronto v. K.*, above note 11.

life. In two cases, involving a thirteen-year-old girl[14] and a sixteen-year-old girl[15] respectively, courts have agreed that freedom of religion is infringed under section 2(a) and section 15 where treatment is ordered but decided that such infringement was justified under section 1. Moreover, the precise statutory provisions in each province relating to the terms on which a child may be placed in care for the duration of the treatment may also be at issue in the decision about permitting mature minors to make medical decisions for themselves on religious grounds.[16]

In *Re Dueck*,[17] a thirteen-year-old boy who refused treatment for bone cancer because he believed his authoritarian father's view that God had cured him, was found not to be sufficiently mature to make a medical treatment decision. The court stated that the factors to be considered in deciding whether a child was a mature minor include age and maturity, the complexity of the treatment, and the nature and extent of dependency on parents or guardians. Any court's decision is a complex and difficult one.

Where a young child requires blood transfusions, the courts have taken a different view, placing the child in protection for the duration of the treatment and returning him or her to the parents on completion of the treatment. In *Re L.(C.P.)*,[18] the Newfoundland Court of Appeal held that there was no infringement of the parents' section 2(a) *Charter* rights because these were subservient to the right to life and well-being of the child. To accede to the parents' wishes that no blood transfusions be used would also constitute an infringement of the child's section 7 rights to liberty and security of the person. This position was upheld by the Supreme Court of Canada in *B.(R.)* v. *Children's Aid Society of Metropolitan Toronto*,[19] on the grounds that the parents' freedom of belief is secondary to the child's rights to safety, health, and life, as well as to live long

---

14   *H.(T.)* v. *Children's Aid Society of Metropolitan Toronto* (1996), 138 D.L.R. (4th) 144 (Ont. Gen. Div.).

15   *Undland* v. *Alberta (Director of Child Welfare)*, [2001] 3 W.W.R. 575 (Alta. Q.B.).

16   *Ibid.* per Clarke J. at 583–587.

17   (1999), 171 D.L.R. (4th) 761 (Sask. Q.B.). See also Caroline Bridge, "Religious Beliefs and Teenage Refusal of Medical Treatment" (1999) 62 M.L.R. 585.

18   (1988), 70 Nfld. & P.E.I.R. 287, 215 A.P.R. 287 (Nfld. U.F.C.), aff'd (1993), 112 Nfld. & P.E.I.R. 148 (Nfld. C.A.). See also *McTavish* v. *Director, Alberta Child Welfare Act* (1986), 32 D.L.R. (4th) 394 (Alta. Q.B.).

19   (1995), 122 D.L.R. (4th) 1 (S.C.C.). See also *H.(L.)* v. *Vigeart* (1996), 39 Alta. L.R. (3d) 381 (Q.B.).

enough to make his or her own reasoned choices about the religion he or she wishes to follow.[20] Again, in health matters, as in all others, freedom of religion is a right subject to restriction when a court regards other interests as meriting greater protection by the civil law.[21]

C. ACCESS TO HEALTH CARE

Recent restructuring of provincial health care in many provinces has raised legal issues about access to health care involving religion. Most provinces have long histories of hospitals and clinics being provided by religious institutions as well as state-funded health-care facilities. One aspect of restructuring has been decisions by provincially mandated restructuring commissions to close hospitals, including both those governed by religious organizations or by a provincial government. For many years, all hospitals have received full or partial state support but some have retained religious governance structures.

Where a decision is made for a small town to close the public hospital but retain the hospital operated by the Roman Catholic Church, *Charter* infringement issues may arise in relation to matters such as abortion, birth control, and health care for those with HIV/AIDS, should these not be provided, although publicly funded, in the Roman Catholic hospital for theological reasons. The presence of theological symbols on hospital properties, such as a crucifix, may also raise issues of freedom of religion.

In *Pembroke Civic Hospital v. Ontario (Health Services Restructuring Commission)*,[22] the court agreed such issues might arise engaging section 2(a), section 7, and section 15 of the *Charter*, but found there to be no evidence in the case either of the unavailability of medical services relating to sexuality or of any attempt at religious indoctrination; the mere presence of a religious symbol alone was not enough to infringe any section 2(a) rights. Again, in *Wellesley Central Hospital v. Ontario (Health*

---

20 See above chapter 11, section E for a further discussion of the decision.

21 An attempt by the Jehovah's Witnesses to test the constitutionality of provincial child welfare laws permitting children to be made temporary wards has so far failed; see *Kennett v. Health Sciences Centre* (1990), 72 D.L.R. (4th) 155 (Man. Q.B.), aff'd (1991), 83 D.L.R. (4th) 744 (Man. C.A.); and *Kennett Estate v. Manitoba (Attorney-General)*, [1998] 9 W.W.R. 161 (Man. Q.B.), aff'd, [1999] 1 W.W.R. 639 (Man. C.A.).

22 (1997), 36 O.R. (3d) 41 (Gen. Div.).

Services Restructuring Commission),[23] the court found where a public hospital was ordered to close leaving a Roman Catholic hospital to offer medical services, there was no evidence of a withdrawal of services to gay men with HIV/AIDS or abortion facilities for women sufficient to constitute a breach of section 2(a), section 7, or section 15 because these were available at other hospitals within the same hospital catchment area.

Conversely, when the decision is to close a hospital operated by a Roman Catholic religious order in favour of the public hospital, there is no violation of section 2(a) of the *Charter* because freedom of religion does not guarantee public funding for denominational hospitals so that any decision to withdraw public funding is not unconstitutional.[24] Nor is a provincial measure enacting billing restrictions designed to direct new doctors trained outside the province to practise in rural areas an infringement of the section 2(a) guarantee for an individual doctor who will have no access to a religious institution of his or her choice in that area.[25]

---

23   (1997), 151 D.L.R. (4th) 706 (Ont. Div. Ct.).

24   *Hotel Dieu of Kingston v. Ontario (Health Services Restructuring Commission)* (1999), 175 D.L.R. (4th) 185 (Ont.C.A.).

25   *Waldman v. British Columbia (Medical Services Commission)* (1997), 150 D.L.R. (4th) 405 (B.C.S.C.).

Chapter Thirteen

Sabbath Observance and Employment Accommodations

A. INTRODUCTION

Historically, the most significant religious issue in the workplace in Canada, if measured by the volume of reported cases, has been that of Sunday observance; that is, of ensuring by law that Sunday is maintained as a day of rest, free from work or other distractions, so that Christian observances of that day may proceed. Recently, however, with the rise of religious pluralism in Canada, other religious groups, both Christian and non-Christian, have looked to the law to protect not only the observance of their respective holy days but also to ensure other workplace accommodations required for the practice of their beliefs. This chapter will consider these issues.

Sunday observance legislation in Canada has been considered by the courts primarily in the contexts of constitutional law[1] and criminal law.[2] Such legislation has been held to fall within the federal power over criminal law pursuant to section 91(27) of the *Constitution Act, 1867*,[3] but provincial legislation regulating Sunday activities, whether work or play, has been sustained by the courts by virtue of the opting out provisions of

---

1 See the fuller discussion, above chapter 4, section D(2).
2 See the fuller discussion, above chapter 5, section B.
3 R.S.C. 1985, App. II, No. 5.

the federal legislation from time to time and of the provincial exclusive jurisdiction over property and civil rights within each province pursuant to section 92(13).

While post-*Charter* cases have found that legislation, whether federal or provincial, which attempts to regulate Sunday activities on religious grounds is invalid, jurisdiction over Sunday observance remains, theoretically at least, with Parliament. On the other hand, provincial legislation making Sunday a secular common pause day has been upheld as within provincial jurisdiction over property and civil rights and as demonstrably justifiable under section 1 of the *Canadian Charter of Rights and Freedoms*. There is a large volume of case law on both federal and provincial Lord's Day protection, which seems now to have been superseded by the invalidation of the legislation on which it was based, and this case law will not, therefore, be discussed here.

However, two topics in relation to Sunday activities have survived the impact of the *Charter* on Sunday observance legislation — the validity of provincial common pause-day legislation, which designates Sunday as the common pause day, and the right of employees who are strict Sunday observers to resist working on Sunday. Since the legal tests for the latter issue are similar to those for the larger contemporary issue of workplace religious accommodation generally, it will be discussed in that context below,[4] while the former issue will be discussed independently.

B. PROVINCIAL COMMON PAUSE-DAY RETAIL LEGISLATION[5]

Where provincial retail holidays legislation prescribes that retail stores be closed on Sunday, any store open on Sunday may be convicted for violation of the legislation regardless of whether the breach was accidental or

---

4   Below section C.

5   Only post-*Charter* cases will be considered in this part, which assumes the previous sections of the text as referred to above, notes 1 and 2. Sunday shopping issues have also generated a large secondary literature see H. Barron, "Sunday in North America" (1965) 79 Harv. L. Rev. 42; W. Betts, "Never on a Sunday" (1971) 36 Bus. Quar. 107; Mike Brundrett, "Demythologizing Sunday Shopping: Sunday Retail Restrictions and the Charter" (1992) 50 U.T. Fac. L. Rev. 1; T.J. Christian and K.D. Ewing, "Sunday Trading in Canada" [1987] 46 Camb. L.J. 4; G.D. Creighton, "*Edwards Books* and Section 1: Cutting Down

occurred under circumstances not wholly attributable to the fault of the defendant.[6] An order to close a store may be made where there have been persistent and deliberate breaches of provincial Sunday closing legislation and there is a clear intention on the part of the retailer to continue in such breaches.[7]

Where provincial Sunday retail store closing legislation makes provision for stores to be open provided certain statutory conditions are satisfied, then the courts will strictly enforce such legislation.[8] In such cases, the onus of proof is on the accused to establish that it falls within the statutory exemption and is open for business legally on Sunday.[9] Where provincial legislation[10] or municipal bylaws[11] pursuant to provincial legislation are not clearly drafted, then charges of being open illegally on Sundays against an accused may not be sustained. If invalid, parts of municipal bylaws may be severed, and the remaining parts enforced.[12]

An injunction may be granted to enforce Sunday retail store closing where there are persistent violations.[13] A business that persistently vio-

---

Oakes?" (1987) 55 Crim. Rep. (3d) 269; Robert Curtis, "Sunday Observance Legislation" (1974) 12 Alta. L.R. 236; Bora Laskin, "Freedom of Religion and the *Lord's Day Act*: The *Canadian Bill of Rights* and the *Sunday Bowling Case*" (1964) 42 Can. Bar Rev. 147; and Scott G. Requadt, "Worlds Apart or Words Apart: Re-examining the Doctrine of Shifting Purpose in Statutory Interpretation" (1993) 51 U.T. Fac. L.R. 330. See also Ontario Law Reform Commission, *Report on Sunday Observance Legislation*, 1970; and Law Reform Commission of Canada, *Report on Sunday Observance*, 1976.

6   *A.G. Ontario v. Paul Magder Furs Ltd.* (1989), 65 D.L.R. (4th) 263 (Ont. H.C.).

7   *R. v. TDM Drugs Ltd.* (1988), 53 Man. R. (2d) 295 (Q.B.).

8   *A.G. Quebec v. Centre horticole de la Pinière Inc.*, [1989] R.J.Q. 1541 (S.C.).

9   *R. v. Kern-Hill Co-operation Ltd.* (1988), 56 Man. R. (2d) 12 (Q.B.).

10 *R. v. King* (1982), 65 C.C.C. (2d) 567 (B.C.C.A.); *R. v. Magder* (1983), 4 C.C.C. (3d) 327 (Ont. C.A.); *R. v. Edwards Books and Art Ltd.*, [1986] 2 S.C.R. 713; *Hub Raceway Inc. v. Dieppe* (1986), 76 N.B.R. (2d) 87 (Q.B.); and *London Drugs Ltd. v. City of Red Deer*, [1988] 6 W.W.R. 173 (Alta. C.A.), leave to appeal to S.C.C. denied [1988] 6 W.W.R. 1xix (S.C.C.).

11 *London Drugs Ltd. v. City of Red Deer*, ibid.; *Metropolitan Toronto v. Paul Magder Furs Ltd.* (1990), 72 O.R. (2d) 155 (C.A.); and *City of Yorkton v. Markborough Properties Investments Inc.* (1991), 98 Sask. R. 247 (Q.B.).

12 *City of Yorkton v. Markborough Properties Investments Inc.*, ibid.; and *Canada Safeway Ltd. v. City of Quesnel* (1990), 70 D.L.R. (4th) 742 (B.C.C.A.).

13 *Assn. des détaillants en alimentation du Québec v. Ferme Carnaval Inc.*, [1986] R.J.Q. 2513 (S.C.).

lates such legislation may be found to be in contempt of court and be obliged to purge the contempt by paying the fines before a court will hear another case relating to the issue.[14]

The constitutionality of Sunday closing legislation has been under constant attack in the courts since the coming into effect of the *Charter* in 1982. Generally, legislation regulating Sunday activities on expressly religious grounds has been struck down, while legislation regulating Sunday as a secular holiday has been upheld. Thus, in the leading case, *R. v. Big M Drug Mart Ltd.*,[15] the federal *Lord's Day Act*[16] was declared to be invalid as a violation of section 2(a) of the *Charter*, which could not be demonstrably justified under section 1 since it purported to require some form of Sunday observance of all members of Canadian society regardless of their religious views.[17] It is irrelevant whether it is the purpose or the effect of the legislation to infringe freedom of religion, since it may be struck down on either ground.[18]

On the other hand, provincial common pause-day legislation, which provides that Sunday be the common pause day, has been held not to violate section 2(a), since its purpose is not to enforce Sunday observance as a matter of religion but rather to provide for a secular day of rest for retail workers, pursuant to section 92(13) of the *Constitution Act, 1867*.[19] However, in *R. v. Edwards Books & Art Ltd.*,[20] the Supreme Court of Canada held common pause-day legislation to violate section 2(a), but to be saved by section 1 as it was an infringement of freedom of religion for some groups only in society, which was not disproportionate to the legislation's common pause-day objective. Moreover, a Sunday closing bylaw that does

---

14 *A.G. Ontario v. Paul Magder Furs Ltd.* (1991), 85 D.L.R. (4th) 694 (Ont. C.A.), leave to appeal to S.C.C. refused (1992), 91 D.L.R. (4th) viii (S.C.C.).

15 [1985] 1 S.C.R. 295. *Cf. R. v. W.H. Smith Ltd.*, [1983] 5 W.W.R. 235 (Alta. Prov. Ct.); and *London Drugs Ltd. v. City of Red Deer*, above note 10.

16 S.C. 1906, c. 27.

17 *R. v. Big M Drug Mart Ltd.*, above note 15.

18 *Ibid.*

19 *R. v. Sobey Stores Ltd.* (1986), 73 N.B.R. (2d) 234 (C.A.); *Assn. des détaillants en alimentation du Québec v. Ferme Carnaval Inc.*, above note 13; and *Peel v. Great Atlantic and Pacific Co. of Canada* (1991), 78 D.L.R. (4th) 333 (Ont. C.A.).

20 [1986] 2 S.C.R. 713. *Cf. R. v. Westfair Foods Ltd.* (1989), 65 D.L.R. (4th) 56 (Sask. C.A.).

not provide for exemptions for Saturday observers may be struck down as a violation of section 2(a) and cannot be saved by section 1.[21]

Whether or not other activities on a Sunday must also be struck down as an infringement of section 2(a) has been considered in several other cases. Thus, provincial regulations banning hunting on Sunday have been held not to be a violation of section 2(a) because the purpose of such regulations is safety, not the regulation of freedom of religion.[22] On the other hand, provincial regulations banning the setting or hauling of lobster traps on Sunday have been held to be a violation of section 2(a) and not saved by section 1.[23] The distinction between these two cases appears to be the court's finding in the former that the regulations were motivated by safety considerations, whereas in the latter, the motivation was religious, the preservation of Sunday.

In addition to section 2(a), other provisions of the *Charter* relating to freedom of religion have also been considered by the courts. Thus, in *Coles Book Stores Ltd.* v. *Ontario (Attorney General)*,[24] it was held that provincial legislation, which provides that Sunday be a common pause day, is not a violation of section 2(b) in relation to retail book stores, since its purpose is to regulate the hours of work of employees, not the free circulation of ideas. Nor is section 7 infringed, because a requirement to close at certain times is not a "deprivation," and because section 7 pertains to physical or mental integrity and control over these rather than to the right to work when this is desired.[25]

Finally, the section 15 equality provisions have also been considered. Provided all retail stores similar to the complainant's are required to close on Sunday, there is no violation of section 15 of the *Charter*.[26] Moreover, if Sunday closing legislation contains exemptions for certain types of stores, there is no violation of section 15 if the purposes behind legislative non-uniform treatment are reasonable, such as to accommodate certain reli-

---

21 *Canada Safeway Ltd.* v. *R.*, [1988] 5 W.W.R. 122 (B.C.C.A.); and *Super Sam Red Deer Ltd.* v. *City of Lethbridge* (1990), 75 Alta. L.R. (2d) 99 (Q.B.).

22 *R.* v. *Peddle* (1989), 75 Nfld. & P.E.I.R. 181 (Nfld. C.A.), leave to appeal to S.C.C. refused (1989), 78 Nfld. & P.E.I.R. 180 (S.C.C.).

23 *R.* v. *Quinlan* (1983), 9 C.C.C. (3d) 281 (N.S. Co. Ct.).

24 (1991), 89 D.L.R. (4th) 312 (Ont. Gen. Div.).

25 *R.* v. *Edwards Books & Art Ltd.*, above note 10; and *Assn. des détaillants en alimentation du Québec* v. *Ferme Carnaval Inc.*, above note 13.

26 *Canada Safeway Ltd.* v. *R.*, above note 21.

gious groups or certain distinctive shopping areas.[27] In short, the general position taken by the courts in relation to Sunday closing legislation after the *Charter* is to sustain it, provided there is no hint of a religious purpose or effect, as a permissible legislative attempt to regulate the retail market so as to ensure that retail workers enjoy at least one day's rest in seven.[28]

Procedural issues have also been considered, in particular, pursuant to section 11 of the *Charter*. A thirty-month delay from the date of the charges to the hearing has been found to be an unreasonable period within section 11(b) of the *Charter* and a charge of violating Sunday retail store closing legislation has been dismissed by reason of such a delay.[29] Section 11(d) of the *Charter* has also been considered in relation to Sunday closing insofar as a municipal bylaw prohibiting stores from opening on Sunday may be upheld on a balance of probability without infringement of section 11(d), since the municipality has the right to be presumed innocent until proven guilty.[30]

C. EMPLOYMENT ACCOMMODATIONS

1) Accommodation of Religious Holy Days

Accommodations of religious difference in Canadian society have, from a legal perspective, focused first on the accommodation of religious holy days in addition to the original Christian holy day of Sunday, and secondly on the accommodation of religious practices and lifestyles that differ from those traditionally associated with Christianity. The courts have taken an accommodating approach; indeed, there would appear to be very few reported cases in which they have not supported the minority litigant seeking some religious accommodation.

In a series of cases including *Ontario Human Rights Commission* v. *Simpson-Sears Ltd.*,[31] *Central Alberta Dairy Pool* v. *Alberta Human Rights Commission*,[32] and *Central Okanagan School District No. 23* v. *Renaud*,[33] the

---

27 *A.G. Ontario* v. *Paul Magder Furs Ltd.*, above note 14.

28 *R.* v. *Hy and Zel's Supermarket Drug Store* (2000), 194 D.L.R. (4th) 375 (Ont. S.C.J.).

29 *Oliver* v. *Hudson's Bay Co.*, [1990] 6 W.W.R. 441 (Sask. Q.B.).

30 *City of Saskatoon* v. *Hudson's Bay Co.* (1988), 71 Sask. R. 254 (C.A.).

31 (1985), 23 D.L.R. (4th) 321 (S.C.C.).

32 (1990), 72 D.L.R. (4th) 417 (S.C.C.).

33 (1992), 95 D.L.R. (4th) 577 (S.C.C.).

Supreme Court of Canada has largely defined the legal duty on the employer to accommodate the holy days of members of religious minorities. The duty in law is to take reasonable measures short of undue hardship to accommodate the religious beliefs and practices of employees. Some hardship is required in accommodation and the assessment of what is undue in the circumstances is essentially a factual assessment, which should take into consideration such matters as financial cost, disruption of a collective agreement, morale among other employees, interchangeability of workforce, and facilities.[34] This duty to accommodate is shared by the union and the employee insofar as all three parties must act in good faith to seek a reasonable accommodation, otherwise discrimination pursuant to human rights codes and the values of the *Charter* will likely occur.[35]

Most of the cases to date have concerned Seventh Day Adventists who have sought accommodation of either their sabbath, which is observed from sundown on Friday through Saturday, or of their other holy days, which are during the normal work week; in the reported cases, the rights of Seventh Day Adventists to observe their holy days have generally been upheld by the courts,[36] or by human rights boards of inquiry,[37] except where there was a significant degree of undue hardship for the

---

34 *Central Alberta Dairy Pool*, above note 32 per Wilson J. at 439.

35 Since the trilogy of cases cited relating to religious accommodations, the Supreme Court of Canada has considered workplace accommodation again in the context of women qualifying as firefighters: *British Columbia (Public Service Employee Relations Commission)* v. *British Columbia Government and Service Employees Union* (1999), 35 C.H.R.R. D/257 (S.C.C.). In this case, McLachlin J. at D/275 reformulated the test for accommodation by placing an onus on the employer to show: (i) the adopted standard is rationally connected to the job; (ii) this standard was adopted with honesty and in good faith; and (iii) the standard is reasonably necessary to the accomplishment of a legitimate work-related purpose. The Court stated the general requirement of reasonable accommodation to be the chosen standard. It is not yet clear how this might apply to religious accommodations although it would appear to pose no barrier to such.

36 *Osborne* v. *Inco Ltd.* (1984), 15 D.L.R. (4th) 723 (Man. C.A.), where there was no duty in the circumstances; *Merilees* v. *Sears Canada Inc.* (1988), 49 D.L.R. (4th) 453 (B.C.C.A.); *Ontario Human Rights Commission* v. *Simpsons-Sears Ltd.*, above note 31; *Central Alberta Dairy Pool* v. *Alberta Human Rights Commission*, above note 32; *Central Okanagan School District No. 23* v. *Renaud*, above note 33; *Office and Professional Employees International Union Local 267* v. *Domtar Inc.* (1992), 89 D.L.R. (4th) 305 (Ont. Div. Ct.); and *Quebec* v. *Autobus Legault Inc.*, [1994] R.J.Q. 3027 (T.D.P.Q.).

employer.[38] There have also been cases in which the holy days of other religious minorities have been required to be accommodated within the workplace, including Jews,[39] Evangelicals,[40] and Free Presbyterians.[41] In addition to holy day accommodation, accommodation has also been permitted for occasional religious practices requiring release from employment, such as days of mourning on religious grounds.[42]

While most cases of holy day accommodation are framed as minority religious accommodation in relation to "majority Christian" practice, with the secularization of Sunday in law now a legal fact in Canada, it would appear that Christians who are Sunday observers should also be permitted accommodation should they wish not to work on Sunday. That is, where the majoritarian practice is now a secular Sunday, Christians seeking Sunday release from employment are also, in effect, members of a religious minority. In *Shepherd v. Pines Motel*,[43] an Ontario Board of Inquiry found that a devout Roman Catholic who was fired because he refused to work on Sundays was discriminated against and awarded damages, including exemplary damages.

---

37 *Chrysler Canada Ltd. v. United Automobile Workers, Local 444* (1986), 23 L.A.C. (3d) 366 (Ont.); *Corlis v. Canada Employment and Immigration Commission* (1987), 87 C.L.L.C. 17,0020 (Can. H.R.T.); *Pederson v. Canadian Armed Forces* (1989), 10 C.H.R.R. D/5976 (Can. H.R.T.); and *Drager v. I.A.M. Automotive Lodge 1857* (1994), 20 C.H.R.R. D/119 (B.C.H.R. Council).

38 *Re Canadian Forest Products Ltd. and I.W.A.-Canada* (1995), 50 L.A.C. (4th) 164 (B.C.).

39 *Rand v. Sealy Eastern Ltd.* (1982), 3 C.H.R.R. D/938 (Ont. Bd. Inq.); *Chambly Regional Board of Education v. Bergevin* (1994), 115 D.L.R. (4th) 609 (S.C.C.); *Richmond v. Canada (Attorney General)* (1997), 145 D.L.R. (4th) 622 (Fed. C.A.); *Shapiro v. Peel (Regional Municipality) (No. 2)* (1997), 30 C.H.R.R. D/172 (Ont. Bd. Inq.); and *Billinkoff v. Winnipeg School Division No. 1* (1999), 170 D.L.R. (4th) 50 (Man. C.A.). *Cf. Strauss v. Ontario (Liquor Licence Board)* (1994), 22 C.H.R.R. D/169 (Ont. Bd. Inq.).

40 *Gaalen v. Fabricland Distributors Ltd.* (1988), 10 C.H.R.R. D/5666 (B.C.H.R. Council); and *Ryder v. Cooper Market Ltd.* (1990), 13 C.H.R.R. D/38 (B.C.H.R. Council).

41 *Janssen v. Ontario Milk Marketing Board* (1990), 13 C.H.R.R. D/397 (Ont. Bd. Inq.).

42 *Re Metropolitan Toronto (Municipality) and C.U.P.E., Loc. 79* (1996), 54 L.A.C. (4th) 240 (Ont.).

43 (1993), 22 C.H.R.R. D/343 (Ont. Bd. Inq.). See also *Jones v. C.H.E. Pharmacy Inc.* (2001), 39 C.H.R.R. D/93 (B.C.H.R.T.) in which a Jehovah's Witness was wrongly dismissed for refusing to put up Christmas decorations because his faith does not celebrate Christmas.

The only religious minority for which accommodation of holy days has proven virtually impossible are members of the Worldwide Church of God, who not only observe a Saturday sabbath but approximately fourteen other holy days annually as well. Tribunals have typically found the number of days to be accommodated to constitute undue hardship for employers and other employees alike.[44]

Unemployed persons cannot be denied unemployment insurance benefits because they are not available to work on Sunday.[45] Moreover, agencies that are not strictly speaking "employers," such as milk marketing boards, are also under the same duty to accommodate religious persons dealing with them as "employees."[46] And unions are also under the same duty, so that they may be joined as a co-defendant with an employer in any case involving religious discrimination.[47]

2) Other Accommodations on Religious Grounds

In addition to considering the question of accommodating religious holy days, the courts have also considered a variety of other types of religious accommodations in the workplace. There would appear to be no pattern to the results in these cases to date, since they are largely single factual instances, other than to state that the courts have generally attempted to accommodate religious difference in the workplace, particularly where the complainant is from a non-Christian religious minority.

Thus, it has been found to be discriminatory to require a Sikh employee to shave his beard or to remove his turban,[48] or to require him

44 *Re Varta Batteries and C.A.W., Loc. 2168* (1987), 26 L.A.C. (3d) 397 (Ont.);
    Pederson v. Canada (Canadian Armed Forces) (1989), 10 C.H.R.R. D/5976
    (C.H.R.T.); *MacEachern v. St. Francis Xavier University* (1994), 24 C.H.R.R.
    D/226 (N.S. Bd. Inq.); *Roosma v. Ford Motor Co. of Canada (No. 4)* (1995), 24
    C.H.R.R. D/89 (Ont. Bd. Inq.); and *Ontario v. Grievance Settlement Board*
    (2000), 191 D.L.R. (4th) 489 (Ont. C.A.).
45 *Corlis v. Canada Employment and Immigration Commission*, above note 37.
46 *Gaalen v. Fabricland Distributors Ltd.*, above note 40; *Ryder v. Cooper Market
    Ltd.*, above note 40; and *Janssen v. Ontario Milk Marketing Board*, above note 41.
47 *Roosma v. Ford Motor Co. of Canada* (1987), 19 C.C.E.L. 243 (Ont. Bd. Inq.);
    Central Okanagan School District No. 23 v. Renaud, above note 32; and
    O.P.E.I.U. Local 267 v. Domtar Inc., above note 36.
48 *Khalsa v. Co-op Cabs* (1980), 1 C.H.R.R. D/167 (Ont. Bd. Inq.); *Grewal v.
    Checker Cabs Ltd.* (1988), 9 C.H.R.R. D/4855 (Alta. Bd. Inq.); *Grant v. Canada
    (Attorney General)* (1994), 94 C.L.L.C. 12, 205 (Fed. T.D.), aff'd (1995), 125
    D.L.R. (4th) 556 (Fed. C.A.).

to wear a safety helmet,[49] since a male Sikh is under a religious obligation to remain unshaven and to wear a turban. Again, it is also discriminatory to require a Sikh to remove his kirpan (the dagger or sword worn by Sikhs as a symbol of their religion), even when in hospital undergoing medical treatment[50] or in a school,[51] although kirpans may not be worn in court.[52] No Canadian court has yet found sufficient factual evidence of derogatory remarks about a religious group (in all reported cases, Sikhs) in the workplace as to justify a finding of discrimination; however, the cases suggest little doubt that in appropriate circumstances this might be found.[53]

Moreover, permission to Sikhs to wear turbans as part of a uniform has been found not to constitute violation of the freedom of religion of non-Sikhs. In *Grant* v. *Canada (Attorney General)*,[54] the court found that Sikhs wearing turbans as part of the RCMP uniform did not violate the section 2(a) or section 7 rights of members of the public who were not Sikhs. There was neither a compulsion or coercion in religious expression, nor a deprivation of life, liberty, or security for persons interacting with Sikh officers.

A second group of cases has concerned the extent to which Evangelical Christian institutions may require their employees to conform their lives, especially sexual, to religious codes in order to be employed or to

---

49   *Toor* v. *Finlay Forest Industries Ltd.* (1984), 6 C.H.R.R. D/2873 (B.C. Bd. Inq.); and *Dhillion* v. *B.C. (Ministry of Transportation and Highway)* (1999), 35 C.H.R.R. D/293 (B.C. Trib.). *Cf. Bhinder* v. *C.N.R.*, [1985] 2 S.C.R. 561.

50   *Singh* v. *W.C.B. Hospital and Rehabilitation Centre* (1981), 2 C.H.R.R. D/459 (Ont. Bd. Inq.); and *W.C.B.* v. *B.C. Council of Human Rights* (1990), 70 D.L.R. (4th) 720 (B.C.C.A.).

51   *Tuli* v. *St. Albert Protestant Separate School District No. 6* (1985), 8 C.H.R.R. D/3906 (Alta. Q.B.); and *Ontario Human Rights Commission* v. *Peel Board of Education* (1991), 80 D.L.R. (4th) 475 (Ont. Div. Ct.).

52   *Hothi* v. *Mitchell*, [1985] 3 W.W.R. 671 (Man. C.A.). For the jurisdiction of a judge over his court, see generally *Taylor* v. *Canada (Attorney General)* (1997), 155 D.L.R. (4th) 740 (F.C.T.D.); and *R.* v. *Laws* (1998), 165 D.L.R. (4th) 301 (Ont. C.A.).

53   *Sidhu* v. *Fraser Pulp Chips Ltd.* (1985), 6 C.H.R.R. D/2772 (B.C.H.R. Comm.); and *Makkar* v. *Sabir* (1989), 11 C.H.R.R. D/250 (B.C.H.R. Council). See also *Hadzic* v. *Pizza Hut Canada* (1999), 37 C.H.R.R. D/252 (B.C.H.R.T.), where discrimination was found in relation to comments about a Bosnian Serb, but it is not clear whether it is religion or ethnic origin that is at issue here.

54   Above note 48.

retain employment. The few cases to date are contradictory but the emerging principle seems to be that Evangelical institutions may only require their employees to refrain from common law relationships when this is an express condition of employment.[55] Nor will the courts necessarily imply such a term into the contract for employment, although the relationship would appear to assume it.[56] A religious institution may also require that membership in its sponsoring denomination be an employment condition.[57]

Thirdly, the extent to which employees may express their religious beliefs in the way in which they perform their employment duties has also been considered by the courts and human rights tribunals. Thus, religious discrimination was found when a Pentecostal employee was suspended for two days from his employment as an accounts clerk for refusal to sell tickets for a social event at which alcohol was to be available,[58] and religious discrimination was also found when a Roman Catholic social worker was dismissed from her employment because she had declined to authorize medical coverage to a client for an abortion.[59] In the latter instance, the human rights tribunal further reinstated the complainant and required the employer to accommodate her religious beliefs in its placement of her.

Finally, a fourth group of cases has considered the extent to which employees may be exempt from trade union involvement in unionized workplaces. Most labour legislation in Canada today contains an exemption permitting members with religious objections to unions to opt not to join, or to divert their dues to a mutually agreed-upon charity and the courts are therefore obliged to enforce this provision. This legislation applies only to actual employees who wish not to join or to pay dues, and

---

55 *Garrod* v. *Rhema Christian School* (1991), 92 C.L.L.C. 16,022 (Ont. Bd. Inq.). See also *Kearley* v. *Pentecostal Assemblies Board of Education* (1993), 19 C.H.R.R. D/473 (Nfld. Bd. of Inq.).

56 *Parks* v. *Christian Horizons* (1991), 92 C.L.L.C. 17,008 (Ont. Bd. Inq.). See also *Lothian* v. *Catholic Children's Aid Society of Metropolitan Toronto* (1986), 8 C.H.R.R. D/3969 (Ont. Bd. Inq.).

57 *Schroen* v. *Steinbach Bible College* (1999), 35 C.H.R.R. D/1 (Man. Bd. Adj.).

58 *Warford* v. *Carbonear General Hospital* (1989), 9 C.H.R.R. D/4947 (Nfld. Comm. Inq.)

59 *Moore* v. *B.C. Ministry of Social Services* (1992), 17 C.H.R.R. D/426 (B.C.H.R. Council).

not to applicants for employment who wish to procure an advance ruling that they need not join a union or pay dues.[60] However, even if the church of which the employee is a member is not registered for religious reasons as a charitable organization, an employer is still required to acknowledge the exemption of an employee from payment of dues, and failure to do so constitutes discrimination against the employee.[61] The test for permitting an employee to claim the exemption is simply *prima facie* evidence of a genuine religious belief in the employee about the impermissibility of trade union activity.[62] Once a religious exemption has been gained by an employee, the union cannot validly grieve the promotion of the employee who has greater experience over a union member with lesser experience, otherwise the religious exemption would amount to discrimination against the religious employee.[63]

Where religious discrimination by an employer has been found, in addition to an award of damages and of reinstatement where appropriate, remedies may also include a letter of apology and the posting of a notice of resolve to abide by the applicable human rights legislation.[64]

---

60   *Re Barber* (1993), 91 di 138 (Can. L.R.B.).

61   *Kurvits v. Canada (Treasury Board)* (1991), 14 C.H.R.R. D/469 (Can. H.R.T.).

62   *Enns v. S.U.N.* (1993), 20 C.L.R.B.R. (2d) 286 (Sask. L.R.B.); and *Peters v. C.E.P.*, [1997] Alta. L.R.B.R. 293.

63   *Yorkton Union Hospital v. Chernipeski* (1993), 16 Admin. L.R. (2d) 272 (Sask. C.A.).

64   *Khalsa v. Co-op Cabs*, above note 48.

Table of Cases

Index

441